83358

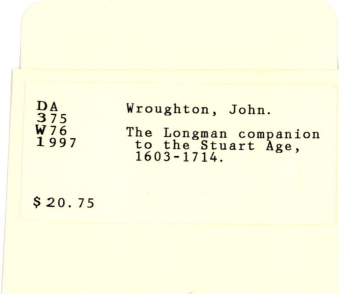

The Longman Companion to

The Stuart Age, 1603–1714

John Wroughton

Longman
London and New York

Addison Wesley Longman Limited
Edinburgh Gate
Harlow, Essex CM20 2JE, United Kingdom
and Associated Companies throughout the world

*Published in the United States of America
by Addison Wesley Longman Inc., New York*

© Addison Wesley Longman Limited 1997

First published 1997

ISBN 0 582 25776 X CSD
ISBN 0 582 25775 1 PPR

British Library Cataloguing-in-Publication Data

A catalogue record for this book is available from the British Library

Library of Congress Cataloging-in-Publication Data

Wroughton, John,
    The Longman companion to the Stuart age, 1603–1714 / John
Wroughton.
        p.   cm. — (Longman companions to history)
    Includes bibliographical references and index.
    ISBN 0-582-25776-X (CSD). — ISBN 0-582-25775-1 (PPR)
    1. Great Britain—History—Stuarts, 1603–1714—Chronology.
2. Great Britain—History—Stuarts, 1603–1714—Registers. 3. Great
Britain—History—Stuarts, 1603–1714—Bibliography. 4. Great
Britain—History—Stuarts, 1603–1714—Biography. I. Title.
II. Series.
    DA375W76 1997
    941.06—dc20   96-43672
                                                                     CIP

Set by 7 in 9½/12pt New Baskerville
Produced by Longman Singapore Publishers (Pte) Ltd.
Printed in Singapore

Contents

Preface

Needless to say, I have consulted a large number of books and other source material in the compilation of this volume. The following have been particularly valuable: E.B. Fryde, D.E. Greenway, Stephen Porter and Ian Roy, eds, *Handbook of British Chronology*, 3rd edn (London, 1986); *Dictionary of National Biography* (Oxford, 1975 edn); Edwin Riddell, ed., *Lives of the Stuart Age, 1603–1714* (London, 1976); C.P. Hill, *Who's Who in Stuart Britain* (London, 1988); Clive Parry and Charity Hopkins, *An Index of British Treaties, 1101–1968*, 3 vols (London, 1970); G.P. Gooch, *Annals of Politics and Culture, 1492–1899* (London, 1901); Godfrey Davies and Mary Freer Keeler, *Bibliography of British History: Stuart Period, 1603–1714* (Oxford, 1970 edn); J.S. Morrill, *Critical Bibliographies in Modern Europe: Seventeenth-Century Britain, 1603–1714* (Folkestone, 1980); J.E. Doherty and D.J. Hickey, *A Chronology of Irish History since 1500* (Dublin, 1989); and Keith M. Brown, *Kingdom or Province? Scotland and the Regal Union, 1603–1715* (London, 1992).

The dates given for days and months are based on the Old Style (or Julian) calendar, which was used in England at the time. This was ten days behind the New Style (or Gregorian) calendar, which was followed in most continental countries. However, although the year in England began officially on 25th March, I have taken the year to begin on 1st January (as was then common on the continent) for the purposes of this book. Hence the execution of Charles I is dated 30th January 1649 (as opposed to the contemporary English style of 30th January 1648 or the continental style of 9th February 1649).

John Wroughton

SECTION ONE

Chronologies: domestic affairs

1   Chronology of political events

1603

Mar. Queen Elizabeth I died; succeeded by James VI of Scotland as James I of England. Irish Rebellion ended after surrender of Earl of Tyrone.

Apr. 'Millenary Petition' presented to James by puritan clergy on his journey from Scotland.

May Robert Cecil granted peerage (Lord Cecil of Essendon).

June Discovery of the Bye Plot to dethrone the king.

July Sir Walter Raleigh imprisoned in Tower for alleged involvement in the Main Plot to install James's cousin, Arabella Stuart, on the throne.

Nov. Raleigh found guilty of treason, sentenced to death, but later reprieved.

1604

Jan. Hampton Court Conference met.

Mar. First session of James I's first parliament (Mar.–July); debates on free trade and the union of England and Scotland; dispute over Buckinghamshire election and the Commons' right to resolve such disputes (the case of *Goodwin* v. *Fortescue*); 'Form of Apology and Satisfaction' drafted by a group of MPs, outlining their anxieties. Conference between Lords and Commons to discuss wardship and purveyance ended in stalemate.

Oct. James I proclaimed 'King of Great Britain'.

1605

Apr. Robert Cecil created Earl of Salisbury.

Nov. Second session of James I's first parliament (Nov.–May 1606). Gunpowder Plot to assassinate king and his ministers. Start of Great Farm of customs duties (i.e. the leasing out of the collection).

1606

Feb. Execution of Gunpowder Plot conspirators.

Apr. Royal proclamation to establish a new Union flag. Three subsidies granted by parliament.

Nov. Third session of James I's first parliament (Nov.–July 1607); debates on the union with Scotland.

Dec. Bate's Case; by imprisoning John Bate for refusing to pay the imposition on currants, the judges confirmed the king's right to levy duties without parliament's consent.

1607

May Rising in the Midlands against enclosures.

Sept. Flight of the Earl of Tyrone and others from Ireland with subsequent confiscation of lands in Ulster and plantation by English and Scots. Robert Carr, the king's favourite, knighted; Francis Bacon appointed Solicitor-General.

1608

May Robert Cecil, Earl of Salisbury, succeeded Thomas Sackville as Lord Treasurer; commenced survey of crown lands.

July Salisbury extended impositions to most imports (except food, munitions and ships' stores) in a new Book of Rates, thereby increasing crown revenue.

Nov. King agreed to reduce number of gifts of crown land. Commissioners appointed to supervise the plantation of Ulster. Calvin's Case (*post nati*) – Scots born after James I's accession were to be classed as English subjects also.

1609

Feb. Chief Justice Coke in dispute with king over the dividing line between ecclesiastical and common law jurisdiction.

May Agreement by James not to dispose of further crown lands.

1610

Feb. Fourth session of James I's first parliament (Feb.–July).

June Prince Henry created Prince of Wales.

July Commons petitioned the king against impositions in a Petition of Grievances (but these continued until 1641). Lady Arabella Stuart, a pretender to the throne, imprisoned for marrying the Earl of Hertford, another claimant.

Oct. Fifth session of James I's first parliament (Oct.–Dec.).

Nov. Negotiations broke down with parliament over 'The Great Contract', designed by Salisbury to grant the king regular taxation in return for his surrender of impositions and feudal rights.

1611

Feb. Dissolution of James I's first parliament.

Mar. Robert Carr created Viscount Rochester.

May Baronetcies first created for sale. Negotiations commenced for marriage between Princess Elizabeth and Frederick, Elector Palatine (a Protestant); and between Prince Henry and the Spanish Infanta Anne (a Roman Catholic).

1612

May Earl of Salisbury died; treasurership put temporarily into commission.

Nov. Prince Henry died. King renewed policy of granting monopolies.

1613

Feb. Marriage of Princess Elizabeth and Frederick, Elector Palatine.

May Don Diego Sarmiento (later Count of Gondomar) reached London as Spanish ambassador.

Sept. Lady Francis Howard and the Earl of Essex divorced with the king's support. Sir Thomas Overby, who had been imprisoned for opposing the divorce, died in the Tower.

Nov. Robert Carr created Earl of Somerset.

Dec. Marriage of Somerset to Lady Howard. Appointments – Sir Edward Coke as Chief Justice of the King's Bench; Sir Francis Bacon as Attorney-General.

1614

Mar. Ralph Winwood, an opponent of Spain, appointed Secretary of State.

Apr. The Addled Parliament met (Apr.–June) – debates over impositions.

July Appointments – Thomas Howard, Lord Suffolk, as Lord Treasurer; Earl of Somerset as Lord Chamberlain.

Dec. Suspension of the Merchant Adventurers' charter and cloth trade monopoly. The Cockayne Project commenced, prohibiting the export of undyed cloth. Possibility of a Spanish marriage for Prince Charles first discussed.

1615

Apr. George Villiers, the king's new favourite, appointed as Gentleman of the Bedchamber.

Sept. Lady Arabella Stuart died in the Tower.

Oct. Somerset and his wife arrested on suspicion of murdering Overbury. Appointment of Lionel Cranfield as Surveyor-General of Customs.

1616

Mar. Sir Walter Raleigh released from the Tower to mount a voyage to Guiana.

May Earl and Countess of Somerset found guilty of Overbury's murder.

Aug. George Villiers created Baron Whaddon and Viscount Villiers.

Nov. Prince Charles created Prince of Wales. Sir Edward Coke replaced as Lord Chief Justice of the King's Bench by Sir Henry Montague, Viscount Brackley.

1617

Jan. George Villiers created Earl of Buckingham.

Mar. Sir Francis Bacon created Keeper of the Great Seal. Death of Lord Chancellor Ellesmere.

May James I visited Scotland.

June Sir Walter Raleigh set sail for Guiana.

Oct. Death of Sir Walter Winwood, Secretary of State. The Cockayne Project terminated; the Merchant Adventurers' Company regained their charter.

1618

Jan. Sir Francis Bacon appointed Lord Chancellor and Sir Robert Norton Secretary of State.

Feb. Buckingham created a marquess.

May Publication by James I of *The Book of Sports.*

July Dismissal of Lord Chancellor Suffolk for corruption.

Oct. Sir Walter Raleigh executed after his return from Guiana.

Lionel Cranfield commenced a programme of financial economies and reform.

1619

Jan. Buckingham appointed Lord High Admiral; Cranfield Master of the Court of Wards.

Feb. Sir Thomas Lake, Secretary of State, dismissed.

Mar. Death of Queen Anne.

1621

Jan. First session of James I's third parliament (Jan.–June). Two subsidies granted. Debate on monopolies; impeachment of monopolists Mitchell and Mompesson; attack on Sir Francis Bacon's involvement in the granting of patents.

May Lionel Cranfield appointed Lord Treasurer and created Earl of Middlesex. Lord Chancellor Bacon fined, imprisoned and dismissed from office over his sanction of monopolies.

Nov. Second session of James I's third parliament (Nov.–Dec.)
Dec. The Commons' Protestation.

1622
Feb. James I's third parliament dissolved.

1623
Feb. Prince Charles and Buckingham visited Madrid to finalise marriage with the Spanish Infanta.
May Buckingham created a duke.
Oct. Prince Charles and Buckingham returned from Madrid offended by Spanish behaviour and intent on war.

1624
Feb. James I's fourth parliament (Feb.– May). Three subsidies and three fifteenths and tenths granted conditionally. Monopolies Act limited the king's right to grant monopolies to new inventions. Lord Treasurer Cranfield impeached.
May Cranfield dismissed.
Nov. Treaty with the French agreed to marriage of Prince Charles and Princess Henrietta Maria and the suspension of the recusancy laws in England.

1625
Mar. Death of James I and dissolution of his fourth parliament; accession of Charles I.
May Marriage of Charles I and Henrietta Maria.
June First session of Charles I's first parliament (June–July); granted two subsidies and tonnage and poundage for one year only. John Pym launched attack on arminian influence.
Aug. Second session of Charles I's first parliament. Members attacked the Duke of Buckingham's policies. Parliament dissolved.
Oct. Attempt by Charles in the Act of Revocation to reclaim all former crown and church land granted in Scotland after 1540.
Nov. Buckingham's Cadiz expedition returned home in disgrace.

1626
Feb. Failure of the York House Conference on Arminianism. Charles I's second parliament met (Feb.–June); failed to grant supply; complained about the unauthorised collection of tonnage and poundage; attempted the impeachment of Buckingham.
June William Laud appointed Bishop of Bath and Wells. Charles I's second parliament dissolved.

July Privy Council stated that tonnage and poundage was an established part of the monarch's revenue, which was not subject to parliament's approval.

Sept. A forced loan imposed to raise money for the war against Spain; judges refused to sanction its legality.

1627

Apr. William Laud appointed to Privy Council.

Aug. Suspension of Archbishop Abbot.

Nov. In the Five Knights' Case (Darnel's Case), Lord Chief Justice Hyde ruled that the king had the right to imprison without trial those who refused to pay the forced loan.

1628

Mar. First session of Charles I's third parliament (Mar.–June); granted five subsidies, but continued its criticism of Arminianism.

June The Commons passed a remonstrance that the unauthorised collection of tonnage and poundage was a breach of fundamental liberties. The Petition of Right was accepted by Charles.

July William Laud appointed Bishop of London; Richard Weston Lord Treasurer.

Aug. Duke of Buckingham assassinated by John Felton.

Dec. Thomas Wentworth created a viscount and appointed President of the Council of the North. Commission for Defective Titles appointed to fine crown tenants who lacked an effective title and those guilty of illegal enclosures of wastes or encroachment on royal forests.

1629

Jan. Second session of Charles I's third parliament (Jan.– Mar.).

Mar. The Three Resolutions passed against innovations in religion and unauthorised taxes with Speaker Finch held down in the Chair. Parliament dissolved, thus commencing the period of the king's personal rule without parliament. Imprisonment of Sir John Eliot in the Tower for his involvement in the above episode.

Nov. Thomas Wentworth appointed to the Privy Council.

1630

Jan. Commission appointed to impose fines on those freeholders worth £40 per annum who had failed to take up knighthood at the king's coronation (i.e. 'forced knighthood').

Apr. William Laud appointed Chancellor of Oxford University.

May Birth of Prince Charles.

Aug. King's right to fine knighthood defaulters confirmed by judges. Attempted trade boycott by London merchants in protest against king's collection of tonnage and poundage.

1631
Jan. Following a series of bad harvests and food riots, a Book of Orders published to ensure that poor relief was fairly distributed in the localities.

1632
Jan. Thomas Wentworth appointed Lord Deputy of Ireland.
Nov. Death of Sir John Eliot in prison.

1633
Feb. Imprisonment of William Prynne in the Tower for his *Histromastix*, which attacked the immorality of stage plays. Lord Treasurer Richard Weston created Lord Portland.
June Charles I crowned in Scotland; decision to introduce the English Prayer Book there.
Aug. Death of Archbishop Abbot; William Laud appointed Archbishop of Canterbury.
Oct. Birth of Prince James. Reissue of the 1618 *Book of Sports*.

1634
May William Prynne sentenced to the loss of his ears for his attacks on stage plays.
Sept. Dismissal of Sir Robert Heath, Chief Justice of the Common Pleas, for his opposition to William Laud's policies; replaced by Sir John Finch. Death of Sir Edward Coke.
Oct. Ship money writs issued to coastal districts for protection against pirates and enemy shipping.

1635
Mar. Death of Lord Treasurer Richard Weston; treasury put in commission. Inquiry into the state of royal finances instigated by the treasury commissioners. Francis Cottington appointed Master of the Court of Wards.
May Commission of Depopulation appointed to grant licences on payment of fine to validate land which had been illegally enclosed.
June Renewal of policy to impose fines for encroachment of royal forests.
Aug. Second ship money writ extended the tax to inland counties – then levied for six succeeding years.
Dec. The legality of ship money collection supported by judges.

1636

Mar. Bishop of London, William Juxon, appointed Lord Treasurer.
Oct. Third writ of ship money issued.

1637

Feb. The king requested common law judges to rule on the legality of ship money. John Lilburne, charged in Star Chamber with printing unlicensed literature, was sentenced to be fined, whipped, pilloried and imprisoned for refusing to take the oath.
Apr. Lilburne whipped and pilloried.
June Puritans Bastwick, Burton and Prynne sentenced to imprisonment, loss of ears and branding for publishing pamphlets which attacked the bishops.
July English Prayer Book imposed on Scotland, resulting in riots in St Giles' Cathedral, Edinburgh.
Nov. Trial of John Hampden commenced over his refusal to pay ship money.

1638

Feb. Royal proclamation making protests against the Scottish Prayer Book an act of treason. The National Covenant drawn up in Scotland to oppose the new Prayer Book and defend traditional Scottish rights.
June In Hampden's case, judges found by 7 votes to 5 in favour of the king's right to impose ship money. The Marquess of Hamilton appointed royal commissioner to negotiate with the Scots.
Sept. A General Assembly and Scottish parliament held with the king's permission.
Nov. Scottish General Assembly abolished bishops in Scotland. Charles vowed to crush these rebels by force.

1639

Apr. Charles summoned the peers to York to provide financial assistance for the war against the Scots. The First Bishops' War commenced with troops raised, but no military engagement.
June Truce of Berwick ended the First Bishops' War.
Sept. Thomas Wentworth, on his return from Ireland, urged the king to recall parliament for finance with which to crush the Scots. Growing resistance to ship money with only £43,417 paid out of £214,000 assessed.

1640

Jan. Thomas Wentworth created Earl of Strafford and Lord Lieutenant of Ireland.

Feb. Sir John Finch appointed Lord Keeper on death of Sir Thomas Coventry.

Apr. Charles I's fourth parliament – the Short Parliament.

May The Short Parliament dissolved without supplies being granted.

June New church canons of 1640 published which codified Laud's innovations and included the controversial 'et cetera clause'.

July The Scots invaded Northumberland.

Aug. Second Bishops' War: Newcastle-on-Tyne occupied by Scottish troops.

Oct. Truce of Ripon, after defeat of English forces; Scots to be paid a subsidy of £850 per day until peace was made.

Nov. Charles I's fifth parliament – the Long Parliament (Nov. 1640–Apr. 1653 in one long session): expelled monopolist members, condemned the new church canons and attacked judges in the Hampden case. The Earl of Strafford impeached for treason and imprisoned.

Dec. The Root and Branch Petition for the complete abolition of episcopacy presented to parliament by the citizens of London. Impeachment of Archbishop William Laud for treason.

1641

Feb. Triennial Act passed. Root and Branch Bill to abolish bishops debated in Commons.

Mar. Laud imprisoned in Tower: his trial commenced in Lords.

May The Commons' Protestation revived the Elizabethan Oath of Association to support the true reformed protestant religion in its struggle against popery. Act against dissolving the Long Parliament without its own consent. Execution of the Earl of Strafford.

June Tonnage and Poundage Act granted the king these duties for two months. Demand that royal ministers should only be appointed with parliamentary approval. Parliament agreed the Ten Propositions as a settlement plan for the king's consideration.

July Abolition of the Courts of Star Chamber and High Commission.

Aug. Act passed to abolish ship money. Charles visited Scotland to seek support.

Oct. Rebellion of Irish Catholics.

Nov. Commons passed by 159 votes to 148 the Grand Remonstrance in unity against popery and in opposition to the oppressions of bishops.

Dec. Parliament demanded the control of the militia in the Militia Bill. London City elections gave control to the king's parliamentary opponents.

1642

Jan. Charles I attempted to arrest 'the Five Members'. He subsequently left London.

Feb. Act passed to exclude bishops from parliament. Queen Henrietta Maria visited the continent in search of military support.

Mar. Militia Ordinance passed to raise troops in the counties. Appointment of county committees to collect the £400,000 subsidy granted by parliament for the payment of the debt in Scotland and the war in Ireland.

Apr. Sir John Hotham denied the king entry to Hull and possession of its arsenal.

June Parliamentary Ordinance to raise money and horses by voluntary contributions. Commissions of Array issued by Charles to raise troops on his behalf in counter to the Militia Ordinance. The Nineteen Propositions put forward by parliament as the basis for a settlement.

July The navy declared for parliament.

Aug. The king raised his standard at Nottingham Castle.

Sept. Theatres closed by order of parliament.

Oct. The first major battle of the Civil War fought at Edgehill.

1643

Jan. Parliamentary Ordinance to empower county committees to tax those who had not contributed freely to parliament – or to seize goods to the value of one-twentieth of their estates.

Feb. Parliamentary Ordinance established the Weekly Assessment to support the war effort. The Oxford 'Treaty' Negotiations commenced between the king and parliament. Queen Henrietta Maria arrived back in England with men and supplies.

Mar. Parliamentary Ordinance established local committees to confiscate and manage estates of known royalists.

Apr. The Oxford Negotiations ended in failure.

May Parliamentary Ordinance to sanction compulsory loans.

June Establishment of the Westminster Assembly to work out a religious settlement.

July Parliamentary excise Ordinance authorised a 'new impost' on a wide range of home-produced and imported items.

Aug. Parliamentary impressment Ordinance issued to legalise conscription.

Sept. Parliament signed the Solemn League and Covenant with the Scots. Charles signed the Cessation Treaty with the Irish.

Nov. The Scots agreed to supply an army to support parliament.

Dec. John Pym died.

1644

Jan. Excise duty extended to other items, including food. The king summoned a 'royalist' parliament in Oxford. A Scottish army crossed the border in support of parliament. Growing disagreements in Westminster Assembly between Presbyterians and Independents.

Feb. The Committee of Both Kingdoms established by parliament to control the war.

July Further extension of the excise duty.

Sept. The Goldsmiths' Hall Committee began compounding with royalists for their estates.

Nov. Clash in parliament between the Earl of Manchester and Oliver Cromwell over the conduct of the war.

Dec. The Self-Denying Ordinance proposed in parliament to exclude all members from also holding military command.

1645

Jan. The Committee of Both Kingdoms recommended the establishment of a permanent army of 22,000 – the New Model Army. The Uxbridge Negotiations between the king and parliament commenced. Parliament approved the Directory of Worship, advocated by the Westminster Assembly as a replacement for the Book of Common Prayer. Execution of Archbishop William Laud.

Feb. Parliament replaced the Weekly Assessment with the Monthly Assessment. The Uxbridge Negotiations ended in failure.

Apr. Parliament passed the Self-Denying Ordinance. The New Model Army officially formed under Sir Thomas Fairfax.

Aug. Parliamentary Ordinance, aimed at establishing the presbyterian church in England, regulated the election of elders for setting up the system at parish level.

1646

Feb. Parliamentary Ordinance ended wardship and the Court of Wards.

Mar. Prince of Wales set sail for the Scilly Isles.

May Charles surrendered to the Scots at Newark.

June The royalist garrison of Oxford surrendered as a final act in the Civil War.

July Parliament agreed to put forward the Propositions of Newcastle to the king as a basis for settlement. Mutinies occurred in the army over pay and indemnity.

Sept. The Earl of Essex died.

Oct. Parliamentary Ordinances abolished the offices of archbishop and bishop and authorised the sale of bishops' lands.

1647

Jan. Anti-excise riots. Charles handed over to parliament by the Scots – confined in Holmby House, Northants.

Feb. Ordinance to justify continuation of excise tax until army disbanded.

May Commons agreed to disband the army with settlement of pay arrears limited to eight weeks. The army mutinied and staged a rendezvous at Newmarket.

June Excise on meat and salt abolished. The king seized from Holmby House by soldiers of the New Model Army – confined at Newmarket. *A Solemn Engagement* and a *Declaration of the Army* set out the army's demands, including the impeachment of 11 MPs.

July Leveller-inspired 'agitators' appointed to represent the ordinary soldiers in policy debates within the army.

Aug. The army marched on London and published its *Heads of Proposals* as a basis for a settlement with the king.

Oct. The Levellers gained in influence within the army and published their first *Agreement of the People* and *The Case of the Army Truly Stated*. The Putney Debates of the army's General Council commenced to discuss constitutional problems.

Nov. Charles escaped from the army's confinement to Carisbroke Castle, Isle of Wight. An army mutiny, inspired by Leveller factions, crushed at Ware.

Dec. The king signed the Engagement with the Scots, refusing peace propositions submitted by parliament.

1648

Jan. Parliament passed the Vote of No Addresses.

Apr. Second Civil War began. Rebellion in south Wales.

July Scottish forces, under the Duke of Hamilton, invaded England in support of the king.

Aug. Defeat of the Scots at Preston ended the Second Civil War.

Sept. The 'Newport Treaty' reopened negotiations between parliament and the king, much to the army's anger. The Humble Petition was sent to parliament from the citizens of London.

Nov. The army presented its *Remonstrance of the Army* to parliament, who rejected it.

Dec. The Levellers published their second *Agreement of the People*. The army entered London, resulting in 'Pride's Purge' of parliament.

1649

Jan. The 'Rump' of the Commons passed an Ordinance for the trial of the king. The trial and execution of Charles I.

Mar. The monarchy and the House of Lords abolished.

Apr. The Diggers set up self-sufficient communities on wasteland in Surrey.

May England declared a Commonwealth or Republic by Act of Parliament. Leveller mutiny in army crushed at Burford.
June Ordinance issued for the sale of the lands of deans and chapters.
July Act passed for the sale of crown assets.
Aug. Cromwell set out with the New Model Army to suppress the Irish rebellion.
Dec. Excise on salt re-established.

1650

Jan. All adult males required to swear the Engagement Oath to the new Commonwealth.
Feb. Act passed for the propagation of the gospel in Wales.
Mar. Act passed ordering capital punishment for adultery.
June Charles II landed in Scotland. Oliver Cromwell appointed Lord General of all parliament's forces.
July Cromwell crossed with an army into Scotland against Charles II and his Scottish allies.
Aug. The Blasphemy Act passed to counter nonconformity in general and the Ranters in particular.
Sept. Laws demanding compulsory church attendance repealed.

1651

Jan. Charles II crowned king in Scotland.
July Charles II's army entered England.
Sept. Charles II's army defeated at Worcester.
Oct. Charles II fled into exile on the continent. The Navigation Act passed. Rate of interest on loans cut from 8 per cent to 6 per cent.

1652

Jan. Hale Commission established to reform the law.
May Commencement of the First Anglo-Dutch War.
Aug. Act to settle Ireland began policy of land confiscation.

1653

Apr. The Rump Parliament expelled by Cromwell.
July Barebone's Parliament met (July–Dec.).
Sept. Parliament abolished the Court of Chancery, legalised civil marriages and ordered the registration of births, marriages and deaths.
Oct. Parliament abolished the lay patronage of clerical livings.
Dec. Parliament failed in its attempt to abolish tithes; and resigned its jurisdiction to the army. The Protectorate was established with Cromwell installed as Lord Protector under the terms of the Instrument of

Government – granted £200,000 per annum to cover military and administrative costs.

1654

Mar. Commission of Triers established. Excise duty extended to most merchandise.

Apr. Ordinance for the Union of England and Scotland. End of the First Anglo-Dutch War.

May Gerard's Plot to assassinate Cromwell.

Aug. Ordinance issued for the reform of Chancery. Commissions of local Ejectors issued.

Sept. First Protectorate Parliament met (Sept. 1654–Jan. 1655).

1655

Jan. First Protectorate Parliament dissolved by Cromwell.

Mar. Penruddock's royalist rising crushed.

May End of rebellion in Scotland.

Aug. Establishment of the system of Major-Generals, backed by a cavalry-militia to be funded by a decimation tax (10 per cent) on royalist estates.

Oct. The Major-Generals commenced their duties, including the tightening of 'moral order'.

Dec. Jews readmitted into England.

1656

Sept. First session of the Second Protectorate Parliament met (Sept. 1656–June 1657); 100 MPs excluded by order of the Council.

Oct. Quaker James Nayler entered Bristol and was arrested for blasphemy.

1657

Jan. The Major-Generals abolished. Cromwell discarded the Instrument of Government.

May Cromwell accepted the Humble Petition and Advice, including the right to nominate his successor; but refused to accept the crown. A 'Second Chamber' established in parliament.

June Cromwell reappointed Lord Protector; granted £1.3 million per annum, including £1 million for the armed forces.

Aug. Admiral Blake died.

Nov. Appointment of Henry Cromwell as Lord President of Ireland.

1658

Jan. Second session of Second Protectorate Parliament met (Jan–Feb.) amid bitter controversy.

Feb. Second Protectorate Parliament dissolved.

Sept. Death of Oliver Cromwell. Richard Cromwell appointed Lord Protector.

1659

Jan. Third Protectorate Parliament met (Jan.–Apr.).

Apr. Third Protectorate Parliament dissolved.

May Resignation of Richard Cromwell. End of Protectorate. Rump Parliament recalled.

June Booth's royalist rising in Cheshire crushed.

Oct. The Rump Parliament expelled by the army. Committee of Safety appointed under Charles Fleetwood.

Dec. The Rump Parliament again recalled.

1660

Jan. General Monck marched south from Scotland in support of the Rump.

Feb. Monck entered London; ordered the reinstatement of those MPs excluded by Pride's Purge in 1648.

Mar. The Long Parliament dissolved itself and called for new elections.

Apr. Declaration of Breda by Charles II. The first session of the Convention Parliament met (Apr.–Sept.) – declared in favour of rule by King, Lords and Commons. Abolition of purveyance and feudal dues; the excise tax retained; the poll tax introduced (2 per cent on income).

May Charles II restored as king; entered London.

June Act confirming Judicial Proceedings passed.

Sept. Ejected ministers restored to their livings; the Navigation Act passed. Earl of Southampton appointed Lord Treasurer with Lord Hyde (later the Earl of Clarendon) continuing as Lord Chancellor.

Aug. Act of Indemnity and Oblivion passed.

Oct. Charles II's Worcester House Declaration on ecclesiastical affairs.

Nov. The second session of the Convention Parliament met (Nov.–Dec.)

Dec. Convention Parliament dissolved.

1661

Jan. Thomas Venner's Rising of Fifth Monarchists. General election for the new parliament. New Model Army disbanded – Charles II's own army recruited. Bodies of Cromwell, Bradshaw and Ireton exhumed.

Apr. Savoy House Conference met to debate religious settlement (Apr.–July).

May First session of the Cavalier Parliament (May 1661–May 1662). Bishops regained their seats in the Lords. Act passed against tumultuous petitioning.

July Milita Act passed, giving the king control of the forces.

Sept. Bishops restored to the Scottish parliament and church.

Nov. Charles II granted total revenue of £1.2 million for government and peace-time military expenses.

Dec. Corporation Act passed.

1662

Jan. The Quaker Act passed.

Mar. New Prayer Book accepted by parliament.

Apr. Act of land settlement in Ireland passed.

May Hearth tax of 2 shillings per hearth introduced. Act of Uniformity passed to impose the new Prayer Book.

Aug. Nearly 1,000 clergy ejected from their livings on St Bartholomew's Day.

Oct. Sale of Dunkirk to France. Sir Henry Bennet (later Lord Arlington) appointed first Secretary of State.

Dec. Charles II's first Declaration of Indulgence.

1663

Feb. Second session of the Cavalier Parliament met (Feb.–July); Commons rejected Charles II's request for a royal dispensing power in ecclesiastical matters. The Staple Act extended the 'Navigation' system.

Apr. Declaration of Indulgence withdrawn.

June Death of William Juxon, Archbishop of Canterbury; succeeded by Gilbert Sheldon.

Aug. Failure of republican conspiracies in the north of England.

1664

Mar. Third session of the Cavalier Parliament met (Mar.–May).

Apr. Triennial Act passed, revising the terms of the 1641 Act. The Conventicle Act passed.

Nov. Fourth session of the Cavalier Parliament met (Nov. 1664–Mar. 1665); voted the king an additional £2.5 million in taxes for war against the United Provinces. Sheldon surrendered the clergy's right to tax themselves.

1665

Mar. Second Anglo-Dutch War began.

Apr. The Great Plague began in London.

Oct. Fifth session of the Cavalier Parliament met. The Thames blockaded by Dutch fleet. The Supply Act, granting an additional £1.25 million for the war effort, ordered a register to be kept in the Exchequer of receipts and disbursements. The Five Mile Act passed against ejected and unlicensed preachers.

1666
Sept. The Great Fire of London. Sixth session of the Cavalier Parliament met (Sept. 1666–Feb. 1667).
Oct. The Supply Act 'appropriated' £380,000 for seamen's wages out of the total additional war grant of over £1.25 million.

1667
Jan. Commission appointed for three years to inspect public accounts.
May Death of the Lord Treasurer, the Earl of Southampton; succeeded by a Treasury Commission.
July The Second Anglo-Dutch War ended by the Peace of Breda.
Oct. Seventh session of the Cavalier Parliament met (Oct. 1667–May 1668). Clarendon dismissed. Succeeded in influence by the Cabal (Clifford, Arlington, Buckingham, Ashley Cooper and Lauderdale).
Nov. Clarendon fled to France to avoid impeachment.
Dec. Accounts Commission established to probe government war expenditure.

1668
May Parliament prorogued until Oct. 1669. Conventicle Act lapsed.

1669
Jan. Duke of York converted to Roman Catholicism.
Oct. Eighth session of the Cavalier Parliament met (Oct.–Dec.). Act of Supremacy passed placing the Scottish Kirk under the jurisdiction of the crown.

1670
Feb. Ninth session of the Cavalier Parliament met (Feb. 1670–Apr. 1671). Additional revenue granted to the king for eight years. Second Conventicle Act passed.
May Secret Treaty of Dover with France signed by Charles II promising war against Holland and toleration for Roman Catholics.
Dec. Official Treaty of Dover signed, omitting the catholic clauses.

1671
Feb. Auxiliary Excise Bill agreed by Commons to augment crown revenue.
Mar. Charles II's proclamation against Jesuit priests.
Oct. Direct collection of customs duties revived under the control of commissioners, thus replacing the system of farming out.

1672

Jan. Stop of the Exchequer: payments to royal creditors suspended for one year in the face of a financial crisis.

Mar. Publication of the second Declaration of Indulgence. The Third Anglo-Dutch War began.

May Henry Coventry appointed Secretary of State.

Nov. Anthony Ashley Cooper created Earl of Shaftesbury and appointed Lord Chancellor; Thomas Clifford (Lord Clifford of Chudleigh) appointed Lord Treasurer.

1673

Feb. Tenth session of Cavalier Parliament met (Feb.–Mar.); granted the king £1,126,000 for the war effort, but lodged religious grievances. Bill for the Ease of Protestant Dissention passed.

Mar. Declaration of Indulgence withdrawn by the king. Test Act passed.

June Resignation of the Duke of York and Lord Clifford as a result of the Test Act. Sir Thomas Osborne (Earl of Danby) appointed Lord Treasurer.

Sept. Duke of York married Mary of Modena, a Roman Catholic.

Oct. Eleventh session of the Cavalier Parliament met (Oct.–Nov.). Protests in Commons about Duke of York's marriage and the growing catholic influence.

Nov. Shaftesbury dismissed as Lord Chancellor.

1674

Jan. Twelfth session of the Cavalier Parliament met (Jan.–Feb.). Buckingham dismissed.

Feb. Third Anglo-Dutch War ended (Treaty of Westminster).

Sept. Arlington retired; Danby emerged as the most prominent politician.

1675

Jan. Danby launched new policies against Catholics and dissenters.

Apr. Thirteenth session of Cavalier Parliament met (Apr.–June); Danby and Lauderdale survived attacks on their policies.

Aug. Louis XIV granted Charles II a subsidy in a secret treaty.

Oct. Fourteenth session of the Cavalier Parliament met (Oct.–Nov.), but only granted £300,000 in supply.

1676

Jan. Danby launched a national ecclesiastical census organised by Bishop Compton.

Feb. Second secret treaty between Charles II and Louis XIV promising subsidies.

1677
Feb. Fifteenth session of the Cavalier Parliament met (Feb. 1677–July 1678). Shaftesbury, Salisbury, Buckingham and Wharton imprisoned. Generous supply voted.
May Failure of Danby's Bill to limit the power of any catholic monarch in religious matters.
Nov. Princess Mary married William of Orange.
Dec. William Sancroft appointed Archbishop of Canterbury.

1678
Feb. Commons granted £1 million supply for war purposes.
May Further secret treaty between Charles II and Louis XIV concerning subsidies.
June Commons granted £206,462 for disbandment of the Flanders army and 'to no other intent' (i.e. appropriation).
Aug. Allegations of a Popish Plot to assassinate the king put forward by Titus Oates and Israel Tonge.
Oct. Sixteenth session of the Cavalier Parliament met (Oct.–Dec.). Murder of Sir Edmund Berry Godfrey further excited anti-catholic feeling.
Nov. Second Test Act passed. Edward Coleman, former secretary of the Duke of York, executed for treason. Further executions commenced of those involved in the Popish Plot.
Dec. Impeachment proceedings commenced against Danby.

1679
Jan. The Cavalier Parliament dissolved.
Feb. Danby's party heavily defeated in the General Election. Earl of Sunderland appointed Secretary of State.
Mar. First Exclusion Parliament met (Mar.–May). Danby impeached for involvement in secret negotiations with France over subsidies. The Duke of York went abroad into temporary exile.
Apr. Shaftesbury appointed President of the Council and Finch First Lord of the Admiralty. Danby committed to Tower. First Exclusion Bill passed the Commons.
May Habeas Corpus Amendment Act passed.
Aug. Charles II became seriously ill; the Duke of York returned to England. The General Election resulted in a big Exclusionist majority, but parliament prorogued until Oct. 1680.

Oct. Shaftesbury dismissed. The Meal Tub Plot was 'revealed' by Roman Catholics. The Duke of York sent to Scotland as a commissioner.

Nov. Pope-burning demonstrations in London. Laurence Hyde (later Earl of Rochester) appointed First Lord of the Treasury.

Dec. The 'Whigs' commenced a petitioning campaign in support of calling parliament.

1680

Jan. Monster petition presented to Charles II in support of the meeting of parliament.

Apr. Counter-campaign by 'Tories' abhorring the 'Whig' petitions.

Aug. The Duke of Monmouth's 'Western Progress' to boost his claim to the protestant succession.

Oct. Second Exclusion Parliament met (Oct. 1680–Jan. 1681). The Duke of York returned to exile abroad. Second Exclusion Bill defeated in Lords.

Dec. Execution of Lord Stafford in connection with the Popish Plot.

1681

Feb. Earl of Conway appointed Secretary of State to replace Sunderland.

Mar. Third Exclusion Parliament met briefly in Oxford. The Third Exclusion Bill passed both Commons and Lords.

June Shaftesbury imprisoned for treason (but later acquitted).

July Tory campaign commenced to replace Whigs on commissions of peace.

1682

Jan. Tory *quo warranto* campaign commenced to remove Whigs from town corporations.

Apr. Duke of York returned to England.

May Sir George Jeffreys appointed Lord Chief Justice.

Sept. Duke of Monmouth staged another 'progress' to raise support in north-west England.

Nov. Shaftesbury fled to Holland, fearing arrest for treason.

1683

Jan. Death of Shaftesbury. *Quo warranto* proceedings against London corporation. Sunderland again appointed Secretary of State.

June Details revealed of the Rye House Plot to assassinate Charles II and the Duke of York.

July Death of two Rye House Plotters – Lord Russell executed and the Earl of Essex committed suicide in prison.

Dec. Algernon Sydney executed for involvement in the Rye House Plot.

1684
Feb. Danby released from imprisonment.
Mar. Charles II, in contravention of the Triennial Act, failed to summon a new parliament.
June Trial of Titus Oates.
Aug. Rochester appointed Lord Lieutenant of Ireland and Godolphin First Lord of the Treasury.

1685
Feb. Death of Charles II: accession of James II of England and James VII of Scotland. Marquess of Halifax appointed Lord President of the Council.
Mar. Earl of Rochester appointed Lord Treasurer and Earl of Clarendon Lord Privy Seal.
Apr. The Whigs heavily defeated in the General Election.
May First session of James II's first parliament met (May–July) – supply granted. Failure of the Earl of Argyle's rebellion in Scotland. Sir George Jeffreys created Baron Jeffreys of Wem. Earl of Danby released from the Tower. King pledged to the Commons to defend the Church of England.
June Monmouth landed at Lyme to launch rebellion. Parliament granted James increased customs duties.
July Monmouth defeated at Sedgemoor and executed.
Aug. The Bloody Assizes of Judge Jeffreys commenced.
Sept. Clarendon appointed Lord Lieutenant of Ireland and Lord Jeffreys Lord Chancellor.
Oct. Halifax dismissed as Lord President of the Council.
Nov. Second session of James II's first parliament met briefly, opposing the king's request to appoint catholic officers in the army.

1686
Mar. James II issued his Direction to Preachers in an attempt to silence anti-catholic sermons.
May Anti-catholic sermons preached by John Sharp, rector of St Giles' in London.
June Judges, in the case of *Godden* v. *Hales*, ruled in favour of the king's dispensing power. James proceeded to appoint Catholics to offices.
Aug. Court of Ecclesiastical Commission established (illegally) by James II to tighten control over the Church; chaired by Lord Jeffreys.
Sept. Bishop Compton suspended by the Court of Ecclesiastical Commission for refusing to suspend the rector of St Giles'.

Nov. Licensing Office established to sell dispensation certificates to dissenters.

Dec. Rochester dismissed as Lord Treasurer.

1687

Jan. Lord Belasyse (a Roman Catholic) appointed First Lord of the Treasury. Clarendon dismissed as Lord Lieutenant of Ireland.

Mar. Lord Arundel (a Roman Catholic) appointed Lord Privy Seal.

Apr. James II issued his first Declaration of Indulgence; and attempted to compel Magdalen College, Oxford, to comply with his wish for a Roman Catholic president.

July Parliament was dissolved. D'Adda was received in public as the papal nuncio. James began a purge of anglican office-holders, replacing them by Catholics and nonconformists.

Oct. James II ordered the 'Three Questions' to be put to JPs and Lords Lieutenants concerning the repeal of the Test and Corporation Acts.

Nov. Establishment of a Board of Regulators to reshape corporations.

1688

Apr. James II's second Declaration of Indulgence.

May Archbishop Sancroft and six bishops petitioned to be excused from publishing the Declaration of Indulgence in their churches, as ordered by the king.

June Birth of a son, Prince James Edward, to James II and Mary. The Seven Bishops acquitted of seditious libel. Seven opposition leaders sent an invitation to William of Orange to invade England.

Aug. James II refused offer by Louis XIV of help against an invasion.

Sept. William of Orange published his Declaration.

Oct. James II offered concessions on religion and other issues.

Nov. William of Orange landed at Torbay: James retreated back to London from Salisbury.

Dec. James II fled to France. A Convention Parliament called.

1689

Jan. General Election returned a Whig majority. The first session of the Convention Parliament met (Jan.–Aug.) and declared the throne vacant. Rebellion of Irish Catholics.

Feb. Declaration of Rights read to William and Mary, who accepted the offer of joint sovereignty put by the Convention.

Mar. James II landed at Kinsale in Ireland. Mutiny Act was passed. Over 400 non–juror clergy refused the oaths of allegiance and supremacy. Earl of Nottingham appointed Secretary of State.

Apr. Scottish Convention passed Articles of Grievance, but offered the crown to William and Mary. Scottish Jacobites rose under Graham of Claverhouse to fight for James II. Coronation of William and Mary.

May Toleration Act passed. William and Mary accepted the Scottish crown.

Aug. William III dispatched an army to Ireland against James II. Jacobite rebels in Scotland defeated at Dunkeld.

Oct. Second session of the Convention Parliament met (Oct 1689–Jan. 1690) – granted £2 million for the war effort.

Dec. Bill of Rights passed, prohibiting a Roman Catholic from succeeding to the throne.

1690

Feb. Convention Parliament dissolved. The 400 non-juror clergy, including Archbishop Sancroft and five bishops, deprived of their livings. Halifax resigned as Lord Privy Seal.

Mar. First session of William III's first parliament met (Mar.–May); granted William and Mary excise for life and customs for four years. Act of Recognition passed, confirming the legality of the acts of the Convention Parliament.

Apr. John Tillotson appointed Archbishop of Canterbury.

May Act of Grace passed, indemnifying supporters of James II.

June William III departed for Ireland, leaving a Council of Nine to advise Mary. Shrewsbury resigned as Secretary of State.

July James II defeated in the Battle of the Boyne.

Oct. Second session of William III's first parliament met (Oct. 1690–Jan. 1691); granted £2.3 million for an army of 69,000.

Nov. Godolphin appointed First Lord of the Treasury.

Dec. Commission of Public Accounts established. Lord Sidney appointed Secretary of State.

1691

July Catholic forces in Ireland defeated at the Battle of Aughrim.

Oct. Third session of William III's first parliament met (Oct. 1691–Feb. 1692). End of Irish war (Treaty of Limerick).

1692

Jan. Earl of Marlborough, under suspicion of intriguing with James II, dismissed from his command.

Feb. Massacre of Glencoe.

Mar. Earl of Pembroke appointed Lord Privy Seal; and the Earl of Nottingham sole Secretary of State.

Nov. Fourth session of Willam III's first parliament met (Nov.

1692–Mar. 1693) – granted over £4 million for the war effort and revenue from a new land tax.

1693

Jan. Bill passed to establish a permanent land tax. The Loan Act passed, making possible the establishment of a National Debt.

Mar. Lord Somers (leader of the Whig 'Junto') appointed Lord Keeper of the Great Seal.

Nov. Fifth session of William III's first parliament met (Nov. 1693–Apr. 1694). Earl of Nottingham dismissed as Secretary of State. William III vetoed Triennial Bill and Place Bill.

1694

Mar. Shrewsbury (of the Whig Junto) appointed Secretary of State and Edward Russell Lord High Admiral.

Apr. Establishment by charter of the Bank of England to raise a loan of £1.2 million for the war effort.

May William III reshaped his ministry, giving effective power to the Whig Junto (Somers, Shrewsbury, Wharton, Russell and Montagu).

July A Jacobite conspiracy in the north (the Lancashire Plot) failed.

Nov. Sixth session of William III's first parliament met (Nov. 1694–May 1695). The Triennial Act passed. Death of Archbishop Tillotson. Appointment of Thomas Tenison as his successor.

Dec. Death of Queen Mary. The Triennial Act, requiring a new parliament to be elected every three years, gained royal assent.

1695

May Sir William Trumbull appointed Secretary of State. The Licensing Act expired, effectively bringing to an end press censorship. The Duke of Leeds (formerly Danby) ordered to absent himself from the Council after impeachment proceedings against him lapsed.

Oct. William III dissolved parliament.

Nov. First session of William III's second parliament met (Nov. 1695–Apr. 1696) with a large Whig majority.

Dec. The Recoinage Bill passed to halt the practice of clipping.

1696

Jan. Trial of Treasons Act passed, requiring more than one prosecution witness to gain conviction.

Feb. Uncovering of plot by Sir John Fenwick and Jacobites to assassinate the king. Adoption by both Commons and Lords of the 'Oath of Association' to defend William and the protestant succession (though 90 Tory MPs refused to swear).

May Sir Stephen Fox succeeded Godolphin as First Lord of the Treasury.

Oct. Second session of William III's second parliament met (Oct. 1696–Apr. 1697).

Nov. Royal Board of Trade established.

1697

Jan. Execution of Sir John Fenwick.

Apr. Somers appointed Lord Chancellor; Sunderland Lord Chamberlain; and Montagu First Lord of the Treasury. Bank of England's powers extended in the renewal of its charter.

Sept. End of the War of the League of Augsburg (Treaty of Ryswick).

Dec. Third session of William III's second parliament met (Dec. 1697–July 1698). Sunderland resigned. Parliament agreed to disband all forces raised since 1680.

1698

Jan. Supply granted for only 10,000 troops in peace-time.

June Civil List Act passed, granting William III £700,000 per annum for life for the maintenance of his personal household and expenses of government.

July Parliament dissolved.

Oct. William III signed the First Partition Treaty with Holland and France without consultation with his ministers.

Dec. First session of William III's third parliament met (Dec. 1698–May 1699). Shrewsbury resigned as Secretary of State. Commons voted for the further reduction of the standing army to 7,000.

1699

Jan. Disbandment Bill was passed.

Mar. Disbandment of the king's Dutch Guards forced on William III.

Oct. Earl of Tankervill succeeded Montagu as First Lord of the Treasury.

Nov. Second session of William III's third parliament met (Nov. 1699–Apr. 1700).

Dec. Naval peace-time establishment reduced to 7,000.

1700

Mar. Second Partition Treaty with Holland and France signed.

Apr. Somers dismissed as Lord Chancellor.

July Death of the Duke of Gloucester, the son of Princess Anne and heir to the throne.

Nov. Sir Charles Hedges appointed Secretary of State.

Dec. Godolphin appointed First Lord of the Treasury; and Rochester Lord Lieutenant of Ireland. Parliament dissolved.

1701

Feb. William III's fourth parliament met (Feb.– June). Sir Robert Harley elected Speaker by Tory majority.

Apr. Impeachment of Portland, Somers, Halifax and Orford over the Partition Treaties.

May Act of Settlement passed, establishing a protestant succession through the Hanoverian line.

Sept. Death of James II; his son, James Edward, recognised by Louis XIV as the lawful king.

Nov. Parliament dissolved. Resignation of Somers.

Dec. William III's fifth parliament met (Dec. 1701–May 1702).

1702

Jan. Rochester dismissed as Lord Lieutenant of Ireland.

Feb. Act of Abjuration of Pretender passed, requiring compulsory oath of loyalty to William and repudiation of the Pretender.

Mar. Death of William III; accession of Queen Anne. Godolphin appointed Lord Treasurer; Marlborough Captain-General of Armed Forces.

Apr. Tories Rochester, Nottingham and Seymour also appointed to Anne's ministry. Coronation of Anne.

May War declared on France and Spain.

July Queen Anne proclaimed by Scottish parliament, which also appointed commissioners to discuss Union with England. General Election returned Tories with a large majority.

Oct. First session of Anne's first parliament met (Oct. 1702–Feb. 1703).

Nov. Official discussions took place in London concerning the Union of England and Scotland.

1703

Jan. Occasional Conformity Bill passed in Commons, but defeated in Lords.

Feb. Rochester resigned as Lord Lieutenant of Ireland.

May New Scottish parliament met.

Aug. Act of Security passed by Scottish parliament, claiming right to name its own protestant successor to Queen Anne; refused royal assent.

Nov. Second session of Anne's first parliament met (Nov. 1703–Apr. 1704).

Dec. Second Occasional Conformity Bill again defeated in Lords.

1704

Apr. Establishment of Queen Anne's Bounty to relieve poor clergy. Henry St John appointed Secretary of War.

May Harley appointed Secretary of State to replace Nottingham.

Aug. Marlborough's allied army won the Battle of Blenheim. Amended Scottish Act of Security given royal assent.

Oct. Third session of Anne's first parliament met (Oct. 1704–Mar. 1705).

Dec. Occasional Conformity Bill again defeated in the Lords.

1705

Mar. Aliens Act passed to pressurise the Scottish parliament over the matter of Union.

Apr. Anne's first parliament dissolved.

Sept. Scottish parliament agreed to allow the Queen to select its commissioners on the matter of Union.

Oct. First session of Anne's second parliament met (Oct. 1705–May 1706).

1706

Mar. Regency Act passed.

Apr. Scottish and English commissioners met at Westminster.

July Scottish and English commissioners signed Treaty of Union.

Dec. Earl of Sunderland appointed Secretary of State. Second session of Anne's second parliament met (Dec. 1706–Apr. 1707).

1707

Jan. Treaty of Union ratified by Scottish parliament.

Mar. Act of Union between England and Scotland (to be named Great Britain) passed.

Apr. Final dissolution of Scottish parliament.

Oct. Third session of Anne's second parliament met – the first of Great Britain (Oct. 1707– Apr. 1708).

1708

Feb. Walpole replaced St John as Secretary at War. Henry Boyle replaced Harley as Secretary of State.

Apr. The old Pretender (James Edward) landed in Scotland, but his attempt at invasion failed. Anne's second parliament dissolved.

May General Election returned a Whig majority.

Oct. Death of Prince George, Anne's husband.

Nov. First session of Anne's third parliament met (Nov. 1708–Apr. 1709). Somers and Wharton returned to the ministry.

1709

Feb. Bank of England's charter renewed for 21 years.

Mar. Treasons Act passed. Naturalisation of Foreign Protestants Act passed to settle protestant refugees from abroad.

Oct. Copyright Act passed.

Nov. Dr Henry Sacheverell condemned the toleration of non-conformists in a sermon preached in St Paul's. Second session of Anne's third parliament met (Nov. 1709–Apr. 1710). Orford appointed First Lord of the Admiralty.

Dec. Impeachment by the Commons of Sacheverell for libel.

1710

Feb. Trial of Sacheverell.

Mar. London riots in favour of Sacheverell, who was found guilty and suspended from preaching for three years.

Apr. Shrewsbury appointed Lord Chamberlain.

June Sunderland dismissed as Secretary of State and replaced by the Earl of Dartmouth.

Aug. Whig ministry dismissed, including Godolphin (Lord Treasurer); replaced by Tories under Harley (Chancellor of the Exchequer), St John (Secretary of State) and Rochester (Lord Admiral).

Sept. Dissolution of parliament.

Nov. First session of Anne's fourth parliament met with a large Tory majority (Nov. 1710–June 1711). Harcourt appointed Lord Keeper.

1711

Feb. Act passed setting property qualification values for MPs.

Mar. Harley appointed Lord Treasurer.

May Harley created Earl of Oxford. South Sea Company founded.

Dec. Marlborough dismissed as Commander-in-Chief and replaced by the Duke of Ormond. Second session of Anne's fourth parliament met (Dec. 1711–June 1712). Fourth Occasional Conformity Bill passed.

1712

Jan. Creation of 12 new peers to ensure the passage of peace proposals in the Lords. Repeal of the Naturalisation of Foreign Protestants Act. Walpole sent to the Tower on charges of corruption.

Feb. Toleration Act passed for Scottish Episcopalians.

July St John created Viscount Bolingbroke.

1713

Apr. Third session of Anne's fourth parliament met (Apr.–July). Treaty of Utrecht signed.

Aug. Parliament dissolved. William Bromley appointed Secretary of State.

Sept. General Election returned large Tory majority.

1714

Feb. First session of Anne's fifth parliament met (Feb.–July). Bolingbroke opened negotiations with the Pretender.

Apr. Cabinet split between Oxford and Bolingbroke.

June Death of heir to the throne, Sophia; succeeded by her son, George. Reward offered for capture of the Pretender. Schism Act passed, stipulating that only Anglicans were permitted to maintain schools.

July Oxford, on Bolingbroke's advice, dismissed as Lord Treasurer and replaced by Shrewsbury. Bolingbroke attempted to promote Jacobite sympathisers in the cabinet.

Aug. Second session of Anne's fifth parliament; death of Queen Anne; accession of George I. Bolingbroke dismissed.

Sept. Whig ministry appointed under Lord Stanhope.

Oct. Coronation of George I.

2 Chronology of religious change

1603   Millenary Petition presented to James by puritan clergy on his journey from Scotland. James confirmed the continuation of recusancy fines. The Bye Plot discovered, organised by a Roman Catholic priest (William Watson), in protest at the continuation of recusancy fines.

1604   Hampton Court Conference met to debate differences between the bishops and the Puritans. Archbishop Whitgift died – succeeded by Richard Bancroft as Archbishop of Canterbury. Parliament re-enacted the penal laws against Roman Catholics and prohibited bishops from alienating their lands. New church canons issued and a proclamation ordering conformity to them by November. The 1559 Prayer Book reissued with minor changes which failed to satisfy the Puritans. Bancroft launched a campaign to force clergy to subscribe to the new canons by threatening nonconformists with loss of livings (over 80 subsequently deprived). Proclamation to banish Jesuit priests.

1605   James launched a new campaign against recusants (i.e. Roman Catholics who refused to conform). Petitions, in support of nonconformist ministers, protested at their loss of livings. The Gunpowder Plot, a plan to blow up the king and parliament as a prelude to a catholic rising, discovered – many Roman Catholics arrested on slim evidence in consequence.

1606   Guy Fawkes, Henry Garnet (the Jesuit superior) and six others executed for their alleged involvement in the Gunpowder Plot. The Penal Laws passed, requiring Roman Catholics to take the Oath of Allegiance (which renounced the belief that the Pope could depose kings) and the anglican communion once a year.

1607   Archpriest Blackwell, superior of the secular catholic clergy in England, was deposed for his approval of the Oath of Allegiance. The Pope reissued the Papal Brief of 1602, forbidding the Archpriest from dealing with the Jesuits on matters concerning English Catholics. The 'prohibitions' dispute between Lord Chief Justice Coke and Archbishop Bancroft ended with Coke insisting on the power of common law courts to decide which cases should be heard in ecclesiastical courts.

1610   Bancroft urged James I to halt the Bill to abolish pluralities, fearing that many churches would be left without a minister. The Commons' Petition on Religion denied the king's power to change laws relating to religion without parliament's consent, objected to the deprivations of clergy for nonconformity and demanded the more strict enforcement of the recusancy laws against Roman Catholics. Death of Archbishop Bancroft.

1611   George Abbot appointed Archbishop of Canterbury. Publication of the Authorised Version of the Bible. Following attempts to challenge its authority in common law courts, James I issued new letters patent for the Court of High Commission, defining its powers and areas of jurisdiction. James I defended the calvinist doctrine in a theological dispute with Conrad Vorstius, the Dutch Arminian.

1612   Two English Anabaptists burnt at the stake for heresy – the last such burnings in England.

1616   During negotiations for the marriage of Prince Charles to the Spanish Infanta Maria, Spanish theologians demanded toleration for English Catholics as a basic condition.

1618   *The Book of Sports*, issued by James I as a counter to growing restrictions on the sabbath imposed by Puritans, listed games and recreations to be permitted on Sundays; but, after fierce opposition from Puritans, did not insist on its publication from pulpits throughout England. The Synod of Dort opened in the United Provinces to discuss differences between the Arminians and the Calvinists with James I's representative, eventually (in 1619) speaking in favour of the latter.

1620   The Pilgrim Fathers set up a colony at Plymouth in New England.

1621   A Bill for the stricter observance of the sabbath debated by parliament as a counter to *The Book of Sports*. The Commons Protestation re-affirmed its right to debate any matter, including religion, where the security of the realm was at stake. A petition presented to James I by the Commons, expressed dislike of the encouragement given to catholic recusants by the Spanish marriage negotiations.

1622   James I, in response to the growth of sermons critical of the government's foreign policy, issued instructions to bishops to exercise more care in licensing preachers and authorising the subject matter of sermons.

1623   The Pope appointed William Bishop as Bishop of Chalcedon with responsibility for the secular clergy in England and Wales.

1624   Treaty agreed between England and France, agreeing to the marriage of Prince Charles and Princess Henrietta Maria, the suspension of the recusancy laws against English Catholics and the provision of English military assistance against the protestant Huguenots in La Rochelle.

1625   Charles I issued the Instructions on Papists, ordering a search for papists and their suppression. Richard Montague, who had published a clear statement on Arminianism in *Appello Caesarum*, was protected from action by the Commons by virtue of his appointment as a royal chaplain. Twelve puritan clergy and laity set up a scheme as feoffees to buy vacant lay impropriations, to fill the related benefices with puritan clergy and to establish lectureships with any surplus funds. John Pym led attacks on Arminianism in parliament.

1626   Failure of a conference at York House to silence the controversy on religious doctrine, with the Duke of Buckingham speaking in favour of Arminianism. The Declaration against Controversy was subsequently issued by Charles I as a further attempt to silence the debate. William Laud, Bishop of St. David's, appointed Bishop of Bath and Wells. The French priests in Henrietta Maria's court expelled from England by Charles I.

1627   Archbishop Abbot, who refused to license a sermon by Dr Robert Sibthorpe affirming the king's supremacy in both church and state and defending the forced loan, was suspended from office.

1628   The Commons impeached Dr Roger Mainwaring for two sermons which emphasised the duty of subjects to obey the king's orders irrespective of their apparent illegality. Richard Montague appointed Bishop of Chichester; and William Laud Bishop of London. The Commons, in a remonstrance, demanded the suppression of arminian teaching and the firm enforcement of the laws against Roman Catholics. A new edition of the Thirty-Nine Articles was prefaced by Charles I with a further Declaration against Controversy, emphasising that the articles were not to be debated.

1629   The Commons' committee on religion reported in favour of strict enforcement of laws against papists and the imposition of firm punishment on those holding arminian beliefs. In their Three Resolutions, the Commons denounced as traitors any who brought innovations in religion with the aim of furthering papacy or Arminianism. William Laud issued his Instructions to Bishops, which forbade the alienation of episcopal property, imposed serious restrictions on lecturers and ordered bishops to reside permanently in their dioceses.

1630   Alexander Leighton was arrested and sentenced in Star Chamber for his fierce attack on the bishops in his *Appeal to Parliament* (published in 1628).

1633   On the death of Archbishop Abbot, William Laud was appointed Archbishop of Canterbury. Laud disbanded the feoffees for impropriations, because of their success in spreading puritan teaching from the pulpit. *The Book of Sports* was reissued. In his instructions to bishops, Laud forbade the ordination of clergy who were without livings and ordered the drawing up of an inventory of church property.

1637   Puritans John Bastwick, Robert Burton and William Prynne were tried by Star Chamber for attacking arminian bishops in their pamphlets – fined, imprisoned for life and sentenced to the loss of their ears. A new Prayer Book, based on the English version, was imposed on Scotland; protest riots in St Giles' Cathedral, Edinburgh.

1638   The National Covenant drawn up by the Scottish National Assembly, which also abolished the Prayer Book and the office of bishop.

1639   The First Bishops' War ended with the Treaty of Berwick.

1640   The Second Bishops' War ended with the Treaty of Ripon. The Canons of 1640 were issued by Convocation, summarising Laud's recent innovations and including the controversial 'et cetera oath'. The Commons declared these canons illegal and non-binding, because they had not been ratified by parliament. The Root and Branch Petition in favour of the abolition of episcopacy was presented to the Commons by London citizens. The Commons impeached and imprisoned Archbishop Laud. Parliament established the Committee for Scandalous Ministers to investigate the opinions of clergy.

1641   Petitions presented to parliament included one against bishops by the county of Kent and several in support of bishops, including *Remonstrance against Presbytery* by Sir Thomas Aston. The Root and Branch Bill was debated amid fierce disagreement, but not passed. The Protestation Oath was agreed by parliament as a revival of the Elizabethan Oath of Association to unite the nation against popery. The Court of High Commission was abolished. Laudian innovations were suppressed by a resolution of the Commons, which also ordered the proper observation of the sabbath. The Grand Remonstrance was passed by the Commons, insisting that bishops should lose their temporal powers. Twelve bishops were impeached by the Commons after they had not only protested against the mob that had obstructed their entry into parliament, but had also demanded that decisions taken in their absence were nullified.

1642   The Clerical Disabilities Bill was passed, depriving bishops of temporal jurisdiction and, therefore, their seats in the House of Lords. The Nineteen Propositions put forward to Charles I by parliament included the proposal that the king should accept the reformation of the Church by a synod. The Committee for Plundered Ministers was established to relieve those oppressed by royalists and to deal with matters of scandal or popery in relation to malignant clergy.

1643   Parliament ordered the sequestration of delinqents' estates, including those of royalist clergy. In the Solemn League and Covenant with the Scots, parliament agreed to establish a presbyterian system of religion in England in return for military help. Parliament established the Assembly of Learned and Godly Divines at Westminster to discuss plans for the settlement of the Church along presbyterian lines.

1644   Disagreements in the Westminster Assembly between the presbyterian majority and the independent minority were illustrated by *An Apologeticall Narration*, an independent publication. The Westminster Assembly approved the new Directory of Worship and made provisions for the ordination of ministers by specified presbyters. The Uxbridge Peace Propositions, put forward to the king by parliament, included the abolition of bishops and the reform of religion on presbyterian lines. Parliament passed the first of several Acts and Ordinances ordering the payment of tithes to parochial clergy; also an Ordinance stipulating that Christmas be celebrated as a fast.

1645   Parliament passed Ordinances authorising the new Directory of Worship, prohibiting the use of the Prayer Book, regulating the election of elders for the establishment of the presbyterian system in the localities and banning all but ordained clergy from preaching. Archbishop Laud was executed. The first of several Ordinances was passed to exclude from the sacrament people who had committed specified offences.

1646   Parliament passed an Ordinance for the abolition of archbishops and bishops, the closure of their courts and the sale of their lands for the purposes of the Commonwealth and the maintenance of the clergy; also an Ordinance for the ordination of ministers by classical presbyteries. An Act was passed to exclude all papists from the cities of London and Westminster. Thomas Edwards published a fierce attack on the spread of extremist doctrine through the growth of religious sects in his *Gangraena.*

1647   Parliament's Heads of Proposals, put forward to the king as a basis for settlement, included provisions for the repeal of Acts enforcing the use of the Prayer Book and the granting of toleration to all but Roman Catholics. Acts of Parliament were passed to confirm the rights of possession of clergy intruded into livings from which delinquent clergy had been ejected; and to abolish festivals. Protests against Presbyterianism were staged on Christmas Day in Canterbury.

1648   Further Ordinances were passed to finalise the arrangements for fully establishing the presbyterian system of church government throughout the country. The Commons ordered that presbyterian classes should be empowered to institute ministers; and passed an Ordinance for the punishment of blasphemies and heresies.

1649   Act passed for the abolition of deans and chapters of cathedrals, also abolishing archidiaconal courts and authorising the sale of their lands. Trustees for the maintenance of ministers were appointed to administer the income from the lands of bishops, deans and chapters and to provide salaries for ministers.

1650   Acts were passed for the propagation of the gospel in Wales; for encouraging the discovery of priests and Jesuits; for the prevention of profane swearing and cursing; and for the punishment of adultery by death. The Blasphemy Act was passed against the spread of 'atheistical, blasphemous and execrable opinions', mainly as an attempt to silence the Ranters. All statutes requiring compulsory attendance at church were repealed.

1651   The start of the Fifth Monarchy movement in England. An Act passed to discover, convict and repress papist recusants.

1653   The Barebone's Parliament passed an Act to legalise civil marriages; narrowly failed in a vote to abolish tithes; and saw a vote in favour of the abolition of lay patronage of church livings thwarted by the dissolution of parliament. The Instrument of Government proposed toleration in religion, except to papists and those who 'practise licentiousness'. Cromwell's Council of State assumed responsibility for dealing with scandalous ministers when the Committee for Plundered Ministers was ended.

1654   Commissioners for the approbation of public preachers (the 'Triers') were appointed with powers to examine the worthiness of ministers prior to their appointment to livings. Commissioners were also appointed in each county for ejecting, after trial, all scandalous, ignorant and insufficient ministers and school-masters (the 'Ejectors').

1655   Cromwell authorised the readmission of Jews to England.

1656   Attempt by the Second Protectorate Parliament to restrict religious toleration. The Quaker, James Nayler, was arrested on charges of blasphemy after his entry into Bristol in a manner similar to Christ's entry into Jerusalem.

1657   The Humble Petition and Advice, which was presented to Cromwell, included a proposal for the drawing up of a confession of faith.

1659   The Committee for Plundered Ministers was revived by the restored Rump Parliament.

1660   An Act passed to bring about the speedy execution of laws against Jesuits and priests. In the Declaration of Breda, Charles II promised to support any Bill in favour of religious toleration. An Act was passed to restore ejected ministers to their livings, resulting in the ejection of 695 formerly intruded clergy. At the Worcester House conference on religious affairs, Charles II issued a declaration in favour of restoring the Church of England with its episcopacy; the review of the Prayer Book by a commission of divines; and dispensation for individual clergy who objected to specific ceremonies and ritual. This was rejected by the Convention Parliament.

1661   Rising in London by Thomas Venner's Fifth Monarchy Men failed, but prejudiced the cause of nonconformity. Bishops were restored to the House of Lords and all church courts revived, except the Court of High Commission. Bishops were also readmitted to the Scottish Parliament and Church. The Savoy Conference, a meeting of Anglicans and Presbyterians to discuss a religious settlement, ended in deadlock. The Corporation Act included in its clauses the exclusion from borough corporations of those who failed to receive the anglican communion or to renounce the Solemn League and Covenant.

1662   The Quaker Act was passed against those who refused to swear an oath or who met with five or more other Quakers. A new Prayer Book, which had been revised by Convocation and largely ignored the demands of Puritans, was accepted by parliament. Its use was authorised by the Act of Uniformity and made compulsory for all services in the Church of England; the Act also required all clergy to be episcopally ordained and to declare their assent to the Prayer Book. Nine hundred clergy were ejected for non-compliance. Charles II failed in his attempts to suspend the implementation of the Act of Uniformity for three months; and to exercise a dispensing power in favour of individual presbyterian ministers. The king issued his first Declaration of Indulgence in support of exercising a royal dispensing power on behalf of dissenters, subject to the agreement of parliament.

1663   The Commons rejected the king's claim to a dispensing power to relieve dissenters. Charles II withdrew his Declaration of Indulgence. Gilbert Sheldon succeeded as Archbishop of Canterbury on the death of Archishop Juxon.

1664   The Conventicles Act made it illegal for any person to attend a meeting of more than five people for worship without use of the anglican Prayer Book. Sheldon persuaded convocation to end the clergy's right to tax themselves.

1665   The Five Mile Act passed, banning ministers ejected under the terms of the Uniformity Act and any other unlicensed preachers from coming within five miles of their former parish or of any town or city.

1670   In a secret clause in the Treaty of Dover, Charles II agreed to grant toleration to English Catholics. The Second Conventicles Act was passed with increased fines for offenders.

1672   The second Declaration of Indulgence issued by Charles II suspended all penal laws against nonconformists and recusants, required the licensing of nonconformist ministers and meeting houses and allowed Roman Catholics to worship in private.

1673   Charles II was forced by parliament to withdraw the Declaration of Indulgence. The First Test Act was passed, requiring all holding civil office or commissions in the forces to take the oaths of supremacy and allegiance, to receive the anglican communion (i.e. if dissenters, they were required to practise 'occasional conformity') and to sign a repudiation of the doctrine of transubstantiation.

1675   The Privy Council ordered the strict enforcement of all laws against dissenters to safeguard the monopoly of the anglican church.

1676   Bishop Compton undertook a religious census of the country on behalf of Archbishop Sheldon.

1677   William Sancroft appointed to succeed Sheldon as Archbishop of Canterbury

1678   Titus Oates and Israel Tonge revealed the Popish Plot to assassinate Charles II and impose Catholicism on the country. The murder of Sir Edmund Berry Godfrey, the magistrate who had taken evidence from Oates, created anti-catholic hysteria. Thirty-nine people eventually executed for complicity. The Second Test Act was passed excluding all Roman Catholics from parliament, although an amendment made a special exception of the Duke of York.

1679   The First Exclusion Bill to exclude the Duke of York from the succession passed both Houses, but was halted by the proroguement of parliament. The new parliament with a large exclusionist majority was prevented from meeting by repeated proroguement. Pope-burning processions took place in London.

1680   The Second Exclusion Bill passed the Commons when parliament at last met, but was defeated in the Lords.

1681   The Third Exclusion Bill passed both Commons and Lords, but was halted by the dissolution of parliament.

1683   A Whig conspiracy (the Rye House Plot) was uncovered to murder both Charles II and the Duke of York and to install the Duke of Monmouth on the throne as the defender of the protestant cause. This resulted in the renewed persecution of nonconformists ('the Great Persecution').

1685   James II decided to appoint catholic army officers, thus dispensing them from the terms of the Test Act; Halifax, the Lord Privy Seal, was dismissed for his opposition to this; the king prorogued parliament when it voiced its protest. The Pope divided England into four districts (northern, midland, western,

London), each under the control of a papal vicar with powers similar to that exercised by the ordinary (i.e. bishop). John Leyburne, Bishop of Andrumetum, was appointed to supervise the catholic secular clergy in England.

1686 James II began the policy of admitting Roman Catholics into the commissions of the peace and lieutenancies, after granting dispensations from the Test Act. In Ireland, the Marshal of the army, Tyrconnell, began a purge of its protestant members. In Scotland, James II granted freedom of worship in private to Catholics and Quakers through use of his prerogative. He also established the Court of Ecclesiastical Commission (contrary to law) to maintain control over the Church of England with Lord Chancellor Jeffreys as its chairman. James II issued his Directions to Preachers to silence the growth of anti-catholic sermons; John Sharp, Rector of St Giles' in London, defied this ruling in a series of outspoken sermons; Bishop Compton of London refused to suspend Sharp and was himself suspended in consequence by the Court of Ecclesiastical Commission. In the case of *Godden* v. *Hales* the judges ruled in favour of the use of the king's dispensing power in relation to the Test Act. In Oxford a Roman Catholic, John Massey, was elected Dean of Christ Church.

1687 James II appointed Roman Catholics to offices of state, including Lord Belasyse as First Lord of the Treasury and Lord Arundel as Lord Privy Seal. A Declaration of Indulgence for Scotland was issued, granting toleration and the right to public office for Roman Catholics. The Declaration of Indulgence for England suspended the operation of all penal ecclesiastical laws, granting freedom of worship either in private or in churches to Catholics and nonconformists alike. James II continued his attempt to break the anglican control of Oxford by seeking to impose a catholic president on Magdalen College.

1688 James II issued his second Declaration of Indulgence, confirming the terms of the first one; this was followed by an Order-in-Council requiring the Declaration to be read in all churches; seven bishops (including Archbishop Sancroft) petitioned the king, requesting to be excused from this order in view of the illegality of the suspending power; they were subsequently charged with seditious libel, but later acquitted. Faced with the invasion by William of Orange, James II made belated concessions by accepting some of the 10 propositions for the reform of the Church of England submitted by Archbishop Sancroft and five bishops.

1689   The Bill of Rights passed and included the sovereign under the terms of the Test Act. Four hundred English clergy and nine bishops refused to swear the oath of allegiance to William III, believing that James II was still king *de jure*; these non-jurors were subsequently deprived of their livings. William III gave recognition to the presbyterian church as the official church in Scotland and abolished episcopacy there. The Toleration Act was passed, granting all dissenters (with the exception of Catholics and Unitarians) who had sworn the oath and had made a declaration against transubstantiation the right of worship in their own registered meeting houses. The Comprehension Bill, which aimed at attracting dissenters back into the Church of England by allowing limited subscription to its doctrines, failed through opposition by Convocation.

1690   John Tillotson appointed Archbishop of Canterbury in succession to Archbishop Sancroft, who was deprived for refusing the oath to William III.

1694   Death of Archbishop Tillotson and appointment of Thomas Tenison as Archbishop of Canterbury. Publication of Quaker George Fox's *Journal*.

1695   An Act to prevent the growth of popery was passed, which banned priests from practising and prohibited Roman Catholics from purchasing or inheriting land or sending their children abroad, unless they renounced their religion.

1696   Publication of Francis Atterbury's *A Letter to a Convocation Man*, which commenced a lengthy anglican campaign for the recall of Convocation; and John Toland's work *Christianity not Mysterious*, which established the Deist movement in England – burnt by the public hangman.

1697   Concern grew in London about the number of nonconformists holding office as magistrates or common councillors through 'occasional conformity', especially with the appointment of Sir Humphrey Edwin, an ardent Presbyterian, as Lord Mayor.

1701   The Act of Settlement was passed establishing a protestant succession for the English throne and requiring future monarchs to be in communion with the Church of England. Convocation was recalled for the first time since 1689.

1702   First Bill to prevent 'occasional conformity' passed the Commons, but was defeated in the Lords in 1703. Daniel Defoe's *The Shortest Way with the Dissenters* was published, satirising High Church extremists; he was later pilloried in consequence.

1703   Second Occasional Conformity Bill was narrowly defeated in the Lords.

1704   Failure of the third Occasional Conformity Bill, which the Tories attempted to 'tack' on to the Land Bill.

1706   The Kirk Act to secure the protestant religion and presbyterian church government was passed by the Scottish parliament.

1707   The Church of England Security Act was passed as a prelude to the Act of Union.

1709   Dr Henry Sacheverell preached in St Paul's against the toleration of dissenters; he was impeached for libel by the Commons.

1710   Riots broke out in London in support of Sacheverell, who, though found guilty at his trial, escaped with a light sentence.

1711   An Act was passed to build 50 new churches in London, financed by £350,000 of state revenue, as a move to counter the growth of dissent in the capital. The fourth Occasional Conformity Bill, which was less severe than the previous ones, was passed unopposed. Convocation was prorogued.

1712   An Act of toleration for Scottish Episcopalians was passed.

1714   The Schism Act was passed to close down the schools and academies of dissenters by forbidding nonconformists to teach.

3   Chronology of military events in England

The English Civil Wars

1642

Jan. Charles I failed in his attempt to arrest the Five Members in the Commons (4th); London citizens armed themselves and locked the gates (6th); the king moved from London to Hampton Court (10th); parliament appointed Maj.-Gen. Philip Skippon to command the London Trained Bands (10th), which were increased in size (19th); Sir John Hotham was instructed by parliament to seize Hull, a vital northern port (31st).

Feb. The king sent Queen Henrietta Maria to the continent to raise support (23rd).

Mar. The king and Prince Charles departed for York (2nd); the Militia Ordinance was issued by parliament, giving the lords lieutenants control over the county militias (5th).

Apr. Sir John Hotham refused the king entry into Hull (23rd); Hotham was declared a traitor (24th).

May Skippon reviewed the London Trained Bands (10th); the king formed his own life guard, commanded by Sir Thomas Byron (24th).

June The Nineteen Propositions were passed by parliament for the king's consideration (1st); an Ordinance was issued by parliament to raise money and weapons 'for the defence of the king and both Houses of Parliament' (10th); commissions of array were issued by the king to raise the trained bands in his name (11th); the king attempted to establish control over the navy (28th).

July The Earl of Warwick was appointed High Admiral by parliament (1st) and the navy came out in support of their cause (2nd); the king appointed the Earl of Lindsey as General of his army with Sir Jacob Astley as Maj.-Gen. of Foot and Prince Rupert as General of Horse (3rd); the king granted the Marquess of Hertford a commission to command his western forces (12th); parliament appointed the Earl of Essex as commander of all their forces (15th); county committees were appointed by parliament to recruit men and money on their behalf (20th); Hertford arrived in Somerset to raise local forces on the king's behalf (25th).

Aug. George Goring, Governor of Portsmouth, declared for the king (2nd); a muster was held at Chewton Mendip in Somerset of 12,000 supporters of parliament's local committee (5th); Hertford came under fire in Wells and fled to Sherborne Castle (6th); Sir William Waller besieged Portsmouth on behalf of parliament (6th); parliamentary forces seized Dover Castle (21st); the king was joined by his nephews, Prince Rupert and Prince Maurice, from the continent (21st); the king raised his standard at Nottingham Castle (22nd).

Sept. Sherborne Castle was besieged by the Earl of Bedford (2nd); Portsmouth was captured for parliament by Sir William Waller (7th); a skirmish took place at Babylon Hill, near Yeovil, with Sir Ralph Hopton forced back into Sherborne (7th); the Earl of Essex arrived in Northampton with 20,000 troops (10th); Sherborne was abandoned by Hertford (19th); the king based himself in Shrewsbury to facilitate his recruitment in Wales (20th); parliament appointed Lord Fairfax as commander of their northern forces (20th); Prince Rupert defeated parliamentary forces under Colonel John Brown at Powick Bridge (23rd); Hertford and Hopton withdrew from Somerset (23rd); Essex took Worcester (24th).

Oct. Essex moved out of Worcester to intercept the king's march on London (9th); the king began an advance on London from Shrewsbury (12th); the indecisive Battle of Edgehill was fought between the king and Essex (23rd); Essex moved back to Warwick (25th); the king captured Banbury (27th); Rupert captured Broughton Castle for the king (28th); royalist troops entered Oxford (29th).

Nov. The king left Oxford (3rd) and advanced to Reading (4th); Essex's forces re-entered London (8th); Rupert stormed Brentford (12th); Essex blocked the royalist advance at Turnham Green, where he was reinforced by the London Trained Bands under Skippon (13th); the king withdrew to Oxford, where he set up his new headquarters (29th); the king appointed the Earl of Newcastle as commander of his northern forces (30th).

Dec. Newcastle advanced towards York with an army of 8,000 (1st); Waller captured Farnham Castle for parliament (1st); Marlborough was seized for the king by Henry Wilmot (5th); Newcastle took the parliamentary garrison of Tadcaster, forcing Fairfax to retreat to Selby (6th); Waller captured Winchester for parliament (13th); a Midland Association of central counties was organised for parliament under Lord Grey of Groby (15th); a similar Eastern Association was organised for parliament under Lord Grey of Wark (20th); the king reviewed his defences at Oxford (21st); Chichester fell to Waller (27th).

1643

Jan. The Cornish royalists invited Sir Ralph Hopton to become commander of their newly raised army (17th); Hopton and Sir Bevil Grenvile defeated parliamentary forces under Ruthin at Braddock Down (19th); Leeds, Wakefield and Pontefract were taken by parliamentary forces under Sir Thomas Fairfax (23rd); Hopton commenced his siege of Plymouth (25th).

Feb. Prince Rupert took Cirencester by storm (2nd); a Western Association was established by parliament to co-ordinate the war effort in the West (11th); the queen returned from the Netherlands with supplies, landing at Bridlington before advancing to York (22nd).

Mar. The king ordered Maurice to safeguard Gloucestershire in the face of Waller's campaign to control the Severn Valley (2nd); Waller set up his headquarters in Bristol (15th); parliamentary forces under Sir William Brereton and Sir John Gell were defeated at Hopton Heath by the Earl of Northampton (19th); royalist Charles Cavendish took Grantham by storm (23rd); the king's newly raised Welsh forces under Lord Herbert were defeated outside Gloucester at Highnam by Waller (24th); Malmesbury in Wiltshire fell to Waller after a short siege (26th); Lord Goring defeated parliamentary forces under Sir Thomas Fairfax at Seacroft Moor (30th).

Apr. Birmingham was taken by Rupert (3rd); Monmouth was seized by Waller (4th); Chepstow was captured by Waller (6th); Cavendish defeated Lord Willoughby's parliamentarians at Ancaster Heath (11th); Tewkesbury was captured by Edward Massey, parliamentary Governor of Gloucester (12th); Waller was defeated by Maurice at Ripple Field, near Tewkesbury (13th); Essex besieged Reading (15th); Rupert captured Lichfield (21st); James Chudleigh's parliamentary forces were defeated by Hopton at Launceston in Cornwall (23rd); a royalist relief force advancing to Reading was defeated at Caversham Bridge (25th); Hopton suffered a setback at Sourton Down, near Okehampton, when ambushed by Chudleigh (25th); Waller seized Hereford (25th); Reading was captured by Waller, thus threatening the security of Oxford (27th).

May Sir Edward Hungerford captured Wardour Castle, a royalist stronghold (8th); Cavendish was defeated at Grantham by Oliver Cromwell's cavalry (13th); Hopton won an important victory at Stratton in Devon over the Earl of Stamford (16th); Maurice and Hertford set out with reinforcements from Oxford to assist Hopton's Cornish army in its advance (19th); Sir Thomas Fairfax took Wakefield by storm (21st).

June The queen, with 4,500 men, advanced from York to reinforce the king (4th); Maurice and Hertford arrived at Chard in Somerset, where they joined forces with Hopton (4th); Waller staged a rendezvous of his western forces around Bath (8th); a skirmish took place near Chewton Mendip between Hopton's forces and a reconnaissance party under Alexander Popham (10th); parliament appointed Sir Thomas Middleton

Maj.-Gen. of the six counties in North Wales (12th); parliamentarians were defeated by Rupert at Chalgrove Field, where John Hampden was mortally wounded (18th); the Fairfaxes retreated to Hull after suffering a heavy defeat at the hands of Newcastle at Adwalton Moor, near Bradford (29th).

July Cavendish took Burton-on-Trent by storm (2nd); Hopton and Waller fought an indecisive battle at Lansdown outside Bath, in which Grenvile was mortally wounded (5th); Maurice and Wilmot defeated Waller at Roundway Down, near Devizes (13th); the queen arrived in Oxford to rejoin the king (13th); Rupert left Oxford to assist the king's western army (15th); a parliamentary delegation left for Edinburgh to discuss the possibility of Scottish military help (19th); Gainsborough was seized by Willoughby, but immediately besieged by Cavendish (20th); Lord Fairfax was appointed Governor of Hull (22nd); Nathaniel Fiennes surrendered Bristol to Rupert and Maurice after a short siege (26th); Cromwell defeated Cavendish and relieved Gainsborough (28th).

Aug. Newcastle captured Gainsborough for the king after a siege (1st); Maurice gained control of Dorset by seizing Dorchester (4th); the king besieged Massey at Gloucester (10th); Essex advanced from London with the Trained Bands in an attempt to relieve Gloucester (24th); Waller was confirmed by parliament as commander of a new army (26th).

Sept. Newcastle laid siege to Hull (2nd); Maurice captured Barnstaple (2nd) and Exeter (4th); the king broke up the siege of Gloucester as Essex drew nearer (5th); Essex relieved Gloucester (8th); a 'cessation' was arranged on behalf of the king by the Marquess of Ormond with the Catholic Confederates in Ireland based on the hope of bringing back forces to fight in England (15th); the Earl of Manchester, commander of the Eastern Association, captured Lynn (16th); Rupert temporarily halted Essex's return to London at Aldbourne Chase, near Swindon (18th); the king returned to Oxford after his defeat at the first Battle of Newbury and his failure to prevent Essex regaining the capital (20th); parliament gained the promise of military support from Scotland after signing the Solemn League and Covenant (25th).

Oct. Maurice commenced the siege of Plymouth (1st) and seized Dartmouth (6th); Manchester, Cromwell and Fairfax defeated royalist forces at Winceby (11th); Newcastle broke up his siege of Hull (11th).

Nov. Waller was appointed as commander of the newly formed South-Eastern Association (4th); Lincoln was captured for parliament by Sir Thomas Gell (20th); parliament was promised a Scottish army of 20,000 (23rd).

Dec. Hopton took Arundel Castle (9th); Waller stormed Alton (13th); Lord Byron laid siege to Nantwich (13th).

1644

Jan. Arundel Castle was recaptured by Waller (6th); Lord Leven advanced into England with the Scottish army (19th); Sir Thomas Fairfax defeated Byron and relieved Nantwich (25th).

Feb. Rupert set up new headquarters and a recruiting base at Shrewsbury (6th); parliament established the Committee of Both Kingdoms to organise the war effort (16th).

Mar. Rupert defeated Sir John Meldrum and thus relieved Newark from siege (21st); Hopton was defeated by Waller at Cheriton, near Alresford (29th).

Apr. Fairfax took Selby by storm, thus threatening the security of York (11th); the queen left Oxford for Exeter (17th); Newcastle, having abandoned Durham in the face of the Scottish advance, based his army in York (18th); Fairfax and Leven joined forces outside York to begin the siege (22nd).

May The queen arrived at Exeter (1st); Lincoln was stormed by Manchester (6th); royalist forces were thwarted in their attempt to storm Lyme (6th); Rupert left Shrewsbury with a force of 8,000 to relieve York (16th); Reading was abandoned by the royalists (18th); Lyme, under siege by Maurice, was relieved by sea through the ships of Warwick's fleet (23rd); Malmesbury fell to Massey (24th); Rupert stormed Stockport (25th); Abingdon fell to Essex, thus threatening the king's position in Oxford (26th); Rupert stormed Bolton (27th); Goring and Lucas joined forces with Rupert, adding a further 6,000 men (30th).

June The king slipped out of Oxford with a force of 7,500, pursued by Essex and Waller (3rd); Manchester arrived to help in the siege of York (3rd); the king entered Worcester with Waller in pursuit, Essex having decided instead to relieve Lyme (6th); Sudeley Castle fell to Waller (10th); Liverpool was taken by Rupert (11th); Maurice broke up the siege of Lyme as Essex drew near (14th); the queen gave birth to a daughter at Exeter (16th); Waller was beaten by the king at Cropredy Bridge, outside Banbury (29th).

July Rupert entered York, thus ending the siege and relieving Newcastle (1st); the battle of Marston Moor, outside York, ended in victory for the combined armies of Manchester, Fairfax and Leven over the royalist forces of Newcastle and Rupert (2nd); the king's ally in Scotland, the Marquess of Montrose, was reinforced by the arrival from Ireland of Alasdair MacDonald with 1,600 men (2nd); Blake captured Taunton for parliament (8th); the king began a march to the south-west with the aim of protecting the queen in Exeter (12th); parliamentary forces captured York (16th); Essex, en route to relieve Plymouth, took Tavistock (23rd); Waller went back to London with demands for the setting up of a professional army (26th); Essex arrived in Cornwall as the king arrived in Exeter (26th).

Aug. Essex was defeated by the king at Beacon Hill outside Lostwithiel (21st); Essex, encircled by the king's forces at Castle Dore outside Fowey and again defeated, managed to escape personally by sea (31st).

Sept. Lord Elgin's covenanter army was defeated by Montrose at Tippermuir (1st); Skippon surrendered to the king at Lostwithiel 6,000 infantry from Essex's army (2nd); the garrison at Plymouth defied the king's summons (11th); Lord Balfour's covenanter army was defeated by Montrose at Aberdeen (13th).

Oct. The king arrived at Sherborne as Manchester entered Reading (2nd); the king entered Salisbury (15th); Manchester reached Basingstoke (17th); Newcastle fell to Leven's Scottish army (20th); the king outwitted the combined forces of Manchester, Waller and Cromwell, after the Second Battle of Newbury, to escape under the cover of darkness from encirclement near Donnington Castle (27th).

Nov. The king re-entered Oxford (1st); Meldrum and Brereton's parliamentary forces recaptured Liverpool (1st); Rupert was appointed Lieutenant–General of all the king's forces instead of the Earl of Forth (6th); Donnington Castle was relieved by Rupert (9th); Basing House was relieved by Colonel Gage's royalist forces (19th); the king set up his winter quarters in Oxford (23rd).

Dec. The Commons passed Zouch Tate's proposal for the Self-Denying Ordinance, which excluded all Members of Parliament from holding military commissions (19th).

1645

Jan. Sir John Hotham, former Governor of Hull, was executed for conspiring to hand over Hull to the royalists (1st); the establishment of a permanent force of 22,000 men (the New Model Army) was recommended by the Committee of Both Kingdoms (6th); Rupert failed in his bid to recapture Abingdon (11th); the Self-Denying Ordinance was defeated in the Lords (13th).

Feb. The Marquess of Argyle and the Campbells were defeated by Montrose and the MacDonalds at Inverlochy (2nd); Chester, under siege by Brereton, was relieved by Maurice (19th); Colonel Thomas Mytton took Shrewsbury by storm from the royalists (22nd).

Mar. Pontefract was relieved by Langdale's royalist forces (1st); the Prince of Wales left Oxford to set up court in Bristol (4th); Waller defeated royalist forces near Trowbridge and advanced towards Bristol (12th).

Apr. Fairfax submitted his list of New Model Army officers to the Lords

(1st); an amended Self-Denying Ordinance was passed by the Commons and the Lords (3rd); Sir Thomas Fairfax was appointed commander of the New Model Army, with Essex, Waller and Manchester resigning their commissions (4th); Dundee was taken by Montrose (4th); Rupert defeated Massey at Ledbury (22nd); Northampton was defeated at Islip by Cromwell, who went on to capture Bletchingdon House (24th); Cromwell failed in his attempt to capture Faringdon Castle (29th); Fairfax and the New Model Army set out for Somerset to relieve Taunton (30th).

May A rendezvous of royalist forces at Stow-on-the-Wold resulted in decisions to send Goring into the south-west to halt Fairfax and the king to the north to counter the Scots (8th); Sir John Urry's covenanter forces were defeated by Montrose at Auldearn (9th); Fairfax, in a change of plan, moved north to besiege Oxford with the New Model Army, while Weldon advanced to the relief of Taunton (9th); Weldon relieved Taunton (11th); the king arrived at Market Drayton with his army (19th); Massey took Evesham by storm (26th); Rupert stormed Leicester (31st).

June The king moved south in the hope of relieving Oxford (4th); Fairfax moved north from Oxford to Newport Pagnell (5th); Cromwell was appointed Lieutenant-General of Horse in the New Model Army (10th); Fairfax and the New Model Army gained a convincing victory over the king at the Battle of Naseby (14th); Fairfax retook Leicester (18th); Fairfax set out from Marlborough to relieve Blake's garrison in Taunton (28th).

July Baillie's covenanter forces were defeated by Montrose at Alford (2nd); Goring broke up the siege of Taunton as the New Model Army approached (6th); Fairfax defeated Goring at Langport (10th); Bridgwater fell to Fairfax (23rd); a reconnaissance party of the New Model Army under Colonels Rich and Okey captured Bath (30th).

Aug. Royalist Sir Edward Stradling was defeated at Colby Moor in Wales by a combination of Major-General Langharne's troops and Admiral Batten's ships (1st); the king, planning to link up with Montrose, advanced northwards from Wales (5th); the New Model Army captured Sherborne Castle (14th); Baillie was defeated by Montrose at Kilsyth (15th); the king, having arrived at Doncaster, retreated to Huntingdon in the face of Leslie's advancing Scottish force (18th).

Sept. The king reached Hereford (4th); Rupert surrendered Bristol to the New Model Army (10th); Montrose was defeated by Leslie at Philiphaugh (13th); the king again advanced nothwards from Raglan with the aim of joining forces with Montrose (18th); Cromwell captured Devizes Castle (23rd); Langdale was defeated at Rowton Heath by

Colonel-General Poyntz, thus threatening Byron's garrison at Chester with the king also in residence – the king immediately retreated to Newark (24th); Cromwell began the siege of Winchester (27th).

Oct. Winchester fell to Cromwell (5th); Cromwell stormed Basing House (14th); Digby, commander of the king's northern forces, was defeated at Sherburn-in-Elmet and fled northwards to Scotland (20th).

Nov. The king left Newark and returned to Oxford (3rd); Bolton Castle surrendered to parliament after a siege (5th)

1646

Jan. Lord Wentworth was defeated by Cromwell at Bovey Tracey in Devon (9th); Hopton was appointed to command the royalist forces in the west (15th); Fairfax took Dartmouth by storm (19th).

Feb. Byron surrendered Chester (3rd); Hopton was defeated by Fairfax at Torrington (16th).

Mar. The Prince of Wales and his court fled to the Scilly Isles (2nd); Hopton surrendered to Fairfax at Falmouth (12th); the remaining royalist field force under Lord Astley surrendered at Stow-in-the-Wold (21st).

Apr. Sir John Berkeley surrendered Exeter to parliamentary forces (9th); the king escaped from Oxford in disguise and headed for Newark (27th).

May The king surrendered himself into the hands of the Scots at Southwell in Nottinghamshire (5th); the king ordered Lord John Belasyse to surrender Newark (8th).

June Oxford was surrendered to parliamentary forces by Colonel-General Sir John Glemhan (24th).

Aug. Lord Arundel surrendered Pendennis Castle (16th); the Marquess of Worcester surrendered Raglan Castle (19th).

1647

Jan. The Scots handed over the king to parliament, who secured him at Holmby House in Northamptonshire (30th).

Mar. The last royalist garrison, Harlech Castle, surrendered (16th).

May Parliament ordered the disbandment of the New Model Army without payment of its pay arrears (27th); Cornet Joyce was ordered by Cromwell to secure the Oxford artillery train and then to secure the king under army control at Holmby House (31st).

June Cornet Joyce escorted the king to the army at Newmarket (4th); the Declaration of the Army outlined the army's case against disbandment in opposition to parliament (14th).

Aug. The army marched into London (6th).

Oct. The army's General Council held the Putney Debates to discuss the constitutional difficulties (28th).

Nov. The king escaped from the army's custody at Hampton Court and fled to Carisbroke Castle on the Isle of Wight (11th).

Dec. The king signed the Engagement with the Scots (26th).

1648

Mar. The Governor of Pembroke Castle declared for the king to signify the start of the Second Civil War (23rd).

Apr. Berwick was captured for the king by Sir Marmaduke Langdale (28th); Carlisle was captured for the king by Sir Philip Musgrave (29th).

May The revolt spread into Kent, as royalists took control of Rochester (21st); Chepstow Castle was stormed by parliamentary forces under Colonel Ewer (25th); royalists captured Dartford and Deptford (26th); the fleet mutinied in the Downs (27th).

June Maidstone was captured from the Earl of Norwich by Fairfax (1st); Skippon halted the advance of Norwich on London, after his capture of Bow Bridge, by closing the city gates against him (3rd); Colonel Henry Farr led a royalist rising in Colchester (4th); Sir Charles Lucas thwarted Fairfax's attempt to take Colchester by storm (13th); Fairfax commenced the siege of Colchester (14th).

July A Scottish army of 9,000 under the Duke of Hamilton advanced into England in support of the king (8th); Pembroke Castle surrendered to Cromwell (11th).

Aug. Cromwell and Lambert joined forces at Wetherby to challenge the Scottish advance (12th); the Scots were defeated by Cromwell at the Battle of Preston (17th–19th); Colchester surrendered (28th).

Nov. The New Model Army transferred the king to Hurst Castle (30th).

Dec. The army instructed Colonel Pride to exclude from parliament by force those members who were in favour of continuing negotiations with the king (6th).

1649

Jan. A High Court of Justice was established by the army to try the king (6th); Charles I was executed (30th).

Penruddock's Rising, 1655

Feb. A group of royalist conspirators ('The Sealed Knot') – Colonel Edward Villiers, Sir John Compton, Lord Belasyse, Colonel John Russell, Sir Richard Willys and Lord Loughborough – planned a rising in

England to restore Charles II to the throne. John Thurloe's government spies unearthed the plot, resulting in a series of arrests and the strengthening of garrisons in towns.

Mar. The Earl of Rochester was sent by Charles to lead the rising; but only six incidents were reported on the chosen day (8th); further arrests followed; Rochester fled. Sir Joseph Wagstaffe, Hugh Grove and John Penruddock planned another attempt in the West and seized Salisbury, taking High Sheriff Dove as a hostage (12th); proceeded with a force of 400 to Blandford, where Charles II was proclaimed King (12th); entered Yeovil (13th); reached South Molton in search of recruits (14th). Major-General Desborough, sent by Cromwell to put down the rising, reached Wincanton with his regiment (14th). Capt. Unton Crooke, with a cavalry troop from Exeter, tracked down the rebels to South Molton and defeated them, taking 50 prisoners. Wagstaffe escaped to the continent (14th). Desborough commenced interrogation and a mopping-up exercise (17th).

Apr. Trials of prisoners at Exeter, Salisbury and Chard; 39 condemned to death, though some later transported.

May Executions of rebels took place, including Grove and Penruddock.

The Duke of Monmouth's Rebellion, 1685

June James, Duke of Monmouth, anchored off the port of Lyme Regis with three ships and 150 men (10th); landed at Lyme (11th); enlisted local recruits (12th); unsuccessfully attacked Bridport (14th); occupied Axminster with a force of 3,000 men (15th); camped at Chard (16th), Ilminster (17th) and Taunton (18th–20th), where Monmouth was proclaimed King and further recruitment took place; reached Bridgwater (21st), Glastonbury (22nd), Shepton Mallet (23rd), Pensford (24th) and Keynsham (25th), where plans to attack Bristol were abandoned on news of the approach of the king's main army; withdrew to Norton St Philip (26th), where a skirmish was fought against the king's army (27th); marched to Frome (28th), where he became despondent about the lack of recruits; and moved on to Shepton Mallet (30th).

July Monmouth entered Wells (1st); reached Bridgwater, where expected reinforcements failed to materialise (2nd); decided on a night attack on the king's army at Sedgemoor (5th), where he was heavily defeated (6th); fled in disguise towards the New Forest, but was eventually captured in a ditch near Ringwood (7th); imprisoned in the Tower (13th); and executed (15th).

Sept. Judge George Jeffreys, in his 'Bloody Assizes' at Salisbury, Dorchester, Exeter, Taunton, Wells and Bristol, sentenced some 300 of

Monmouth's supporters to death and another 800 or so to transportation as slaves in the West Indies.

The Glorious Revolution, 1688

June 30th William of Orange was invited by leading politicians (including Danby, Russell, Devonshire, Shrewsbury, Compton, Lumley and Sidney) to invade England for the protection of the subjects' liberties.

Sept. 30th William accepted the invitation to invade and issued a declaration condemning arbitrary government and advocating a 'free and lawful parliament'.

Oct. 19th William's Dutch fleet of nearly 500 ships set sail from Helvoetslys, near the Hague, but was driven back by storms.

Nov. 1st William's invasion force of 15,400 troops again set sail for England, accompanied by his chaplain, Bishop Burnet.

5th The fleet entered Torbay, his troops landing at Brixham.

7th His army marched out towards Exeter.

8th He reached Newton Abbot, where his Declaration was read publicly for the first time.

9th He made a ceremonial entrance to Exeter in front of cheering crowds.

11th Bishop Burnet preached in Exeter Cathedral.

11th/25th Chester, Manchester, Derby, York, Nottingham, Newcastle, Norwich, Hull, Bristol, Worcester, Ludlow and Oxford were all secured for William.

17th James II left Whitehall.

19th James joined his army at Salisbury.

21st William left Exeter for Salisbury with over 15,000 troops, 21 pieces of heavy cannon, 180 smaller pieces, a mobile smithy and a printing press.

24th James called a council of war, ordering his army to retreat to Reading. John Churchill, Commander-in-Chief of the king's army, deserted to William's camp at Crewkerne together with the Duke of Grafton, the Earl of Berkeley and Admiral Byng of the king's navy. Lord Cornbury also defected with three regiments. Leading rebels in the North and Midlands issued 'A Declaration of the Nobility, Gentry and Commonalty' at Nottingham, listing their grievances and urging all protestant subjects to support William.

25th James left Salisbury for London with the Duke of Ormond and Lord Drumlanrig, both of whom defected during the night.

26th In London, James discovered that his daughter, Princess

Anne, Sarah Churchill, the Bishop of London and the Earl of Dorset had all left to join the midland rebels.

27th James summoned a Great Council and agreed to major concessions (including the dismissal of Roman Catholics from office, the granting of a general pardon and the calling of a new parliament).

29th James gave instructions for his son to depart for France.

30th James appointed Halifax, Godolphin and Nottingham to treat with William on his behalf.

Dec. 6th William entered Hungerford, as did the king's commissioners.

8th The two delegations met and agreed terms based on the concessions granted by James on 27th November. Both armies were to remain 30 miles away from Westminster.

10th The queen and the Prince of Wales fled to France. James ordered the disbandment of his troops; and fled, discarding the Great Seal in the Thames.

11th A meeting of peers and bishops in London issued the Guildhall Declaration for the establishment of a free parliament. William reached Wallingford en route for London.

12th James was intercepted at Sheerness. Lord Dartmouth pledged control of the fleet to William. A provisional government under Lord Halifax was established. William reached Henley.

13th William received a delegation of bishops, peers and aldermen of London at Henley; ordered the control of James II's disbanded army.

14th William reached Windsor.

16th William ordered the fleet to proceed to Nore. James, on William's instructions, returned to London.

17th William called a meeting of peers at Windsor to debate the problem of the king. James refused to take up temporary residence at Ham, near Richmond.

18th James left for Rochester unguarded. William entered London.

19th William held court at St James's Palace.

21st William met 70 peers to gain advice on how to proceed.

23rd James left for France. William summoned all Members of Parliament who had sat during Charles II's reign, and a delegation from London's city council to meet and advise him.

29th Members of both Commons and Lords finally agreed that the throne was vacant; and requested William both to take control of the government and to call a Convention Parliament. William accepted.

4 Chronology of cultural developments

Landmarks in literature, drama, art, music, architecture, science, education, censorship and the press.

1603   An Act passed to prevent anyone from keeping a school or becoming a schoolmaster, except in a public or free grammar school, or in the house of a non-recusant; a licence was also required from the archbishop or bishop; failure to conform resulted in a fine of 40 shillings a day. By this date, the licensing of all printing had been introduced (1553), with a licence from a bishop or university chancellor necessary (1559); control of printing and the discovery of seditious libel had been placed in the hands of the Stationers' Company (1557) with the right to search workshops (1566); and all printing activity had been limited to London, Oxford and Cambridge with a set number of authorised printers (1586). Publication of James I's *True Lawes of Free Monarchies*.

1604   By order of the English church canons, teachers were required to subscribe to the article of the king's supremacy and accept the Church of England as a true and apostolic church. Orlando Gibbons (1583–1625) was appointed organist of the Chapel Royal. Publication of James I's *Counterblast to Tobacco;* and *Hamlet* by William Shakespeare (1564–1616). First performance of *Othello* by William Shakespeare.

1605   Publication of *The Advancement of Learning* by Francis Bacon (1561–1626).

1606   First performance of *Volpone* by Ben Jonson (1572–1637).

1607   Publication of Dr John Cowell's *Dictionary*, which was suppressed by royal proclamation because some of its definitions related to the royal prerogative.

1608   Publication of *King Lear* and *Coriolanus* by William Shakespeare;

and *A Mad World, My Masters* by Thomas Middleton (1570?–1627). First performance of *The White Devil* by John Webster (1580?–1625?).

1609   Publication of *Pericles* and *Troilus and Cressida* by William Shakespeare.

1610   Inigo Jones (1573–1652) was appointed Surveyor of the Works to Henry, Prince of Wales. First performance of *The Alchemist* by Ben Jonson. Publication of John Speed's collection of maps, *Theatrum.*

1611   Publication of *Pseudo-Martyr* by John Donne (1571/2–1631); and the *Authorised Version* of the Bible. *The Tempest* written by William Shakespeare.

1612   Foundation of Wadham College, Oxford. Publication of *Madrigals and Motets of Five Parts* by Orlando Gibbons; and the second edition of *Essays: Counsels Civil and Moral* by Francis Bacon.

1613   James I instructed the Court of High Commission to enforce the previous ban on the printing of unlicensed books; George Withers (1588–1667) was imprisoned for his satire *Abuses Stript and Whipt.* First performance of *Henry VIII* by William Shakespeare.

1614   Publication of *History of the World* by Sir Walter Raleigh (1552–1618), which was suppressed 'for being too saucy to princes'; and *Bartholomew Fair* by Ben Jonson. John Napier (1550–1617) invented logarithms and published his *Mirifici Logarithmorum Canoris Descriptio.*

1615   Appointment of Inigo Jones as Surveyor of the King's Works.

1616   Inigo Jones commenced his work on the Queen's House at Greenwich (completed 1635). Publication of *The Devil is an Ass* and *Collected Works* by Ben Jonson. Death of William Shakespeare.

1617   Publication of *Rabdologia* by John Napier, explaining the use of 'Napier's bones' in multiplication and division. New logarithm tables, calculated to a base of 10, were constructed by Henry Briggs (1561–1630). A charter was granted to the Society of Apothecaries, giving it control over the examination of apprentices, the supervision of apothecaries and the distribution of medicines.

1618   Inigo Jones assisted in the design of Lincoln's Inn Fields. Publication of *Pharmacopoeia Londinensis* by the College of Physicians, which celebrated its centenary.

1619   A new Banqueting Hall in Whitehall to replace that destroyed by fire was designed by Inigo Jones (completed 1622). Henry Briggs was appointed Professor of Astronomy at Oxford. He and John Napier began to use the decimal notation for fractions. Sir William Harvey (1578–1657) explained his discovery of the circulation of the blood in lectures at St Bartholomew's Hospital.

1620   Francis Bacon published his *Novum Organum* as a contribution to the improvement of science, and put forward the view that heat may be a movement. English newsbooks were first printed in the Netherlands, carrying reports of continental battles.

1621   Anthony van Dyck (1599–1641) visited England for the first time. *The Anatomy of Melancholy* published by Robert Burton (1576–1640).

1622   Thomas Archer and Nicholas Bourne, two London stationers, were given authority to publish weekly journals (usually called 'corantos') containing foreign news only. *The History of the Reign of King Henry the Seventh* published by Francis Bacon.

1623   Inigo Jones commenced work on the Queen's Chapel in St James's Palace (completed 1627). Publication of the first collected edition of the plays of William Shakespeare; and of *The Duchess of Malfi* and *The Devil's Law Case* by John Webster.

1624   Performances of *A Game of Chess*, a play by Thomas Middleton, were banned by the Privy Council because it dealt with the breakdown of Prince Charles's marriage negotiations in Spain. The printing or import of any book dealing with religion or state affairs without prior approval was banned by royal proclamation. Publication of *Arithmetica Logarithmica* by Henry Briggs, which extended further the work of John Napier.

1625   Daniel Mytens (1590?–1645?) was appointed Court Painter to Charles I. Publication of the third edition of *Essays: Counsels Civil and Moral* by Francis Bacon.

1626   Writing on matters of religious controversy was banned by royal proclamation in an attempt to stifle puritan opinion. Publication of *The Maid's Revenge* and *The Wedding* by James Shirley (1596–1666).

1628   Publication of *De Motu Cordis et Sanguinis* by Sir William Harvey, based on years of experiments in dissecting animals.

1629   Sir Peter Rubens (1577–1640) visited England and was commissioned to paint for Charles I.

1630   William Laud appointed Chancellor of Oxford University.

1631   Publication of *Clavis Mathematicae Denuo Limata* by William Oughtred, an arithmetic and algebra textbook; and of *Match Me in London* by Thomas Dekker (1570?–1632).

1632   The printing of all newsbooks was banned by the Star Chamber. Anthony van Dyck, a pupil of Rubens, was appointed Court Painter to Charles I and settled in England. William Harvey was appointed Physician to Charles I.

1633   Henry Lawes (1596–1662) was appointed Musician in Ordinary to Charles I. Publication of *Trigonometria Britannica* by Henry Briggs, a book of tables for the logarithms of sines, tangents and secants. Publication of *A Tale of a Tub* by Ben Jonson; *Histriomastix* by William Prynne (1600–69); *Poems*, an anthology by John Donne; *New Way to Pay Old Debts* by Philip Massinger (1583–1640); and *Poems* by George Herbert (1593–1633).

1634   The trial took place of William Prynne before the Star Chamber for writing *Histriomastix*, an attack on immorality in the theatre. Publication of the masque *Comus* by John Milton (1608–74), with music by Henry Lawes for its performance at Ludlow Castle.

1636   Anthony van Dyck painted *Charles I on Horseback*. Publication of
            The Wonder of a Kingdom by Thomas Dekker; and *The Platonic
            Lovers* by Sir William D'Avenant (1606–68).

1637   Trial and punishment by the Star Chamber of John Bastwick
            (for his attack on archbishops in *The Litany of John Bastwick*), Dr
            Henry Burton (for his attack on Archbishop Laud in *For God and
            King*) and William Prynne (for his attack on Bishop Wren in
            News from Ipswich). Ordinances issued by the Star Chamber
            increased penalties for printing unlicensed books; stipulated
            who had the power to license specific types of books; and
            ordered that no English books were to be printed abroad or
            foreign books sold without permission of the Church. John
            Lilburne was tried and punished by the Star Chamber for
            printing English books at Rotterdam for importation.

1638   The Star Chamber granted to Nicholas Bourne and Nathaniel
            Butter the exclusive right to print journals containing foreign
            news. Jeremiah Horrocks (1617?–1641) applied the elliptical
            theory to the moon. Publication of *Lycidas* by John Milton.

1639   The transit of Venus was first observed by Jeremiah Horrocks.

1640   Publication of *Eighty Sermons* by John Donne.

1641   Parliament abolished the Star Chamber, which effectively
            brought an end to the licensing laws and made possible the
            growth of political pamphlets and newsbooks reporting
            domestic affairs. The Commons ordered an investigation into
            the state of all free schools in England and Wales; and resolved
            that the lands of Deans and Chapters should be used for the
            advancement of learning. William Dobson (1610–1646) was
            appointed Court Painter to Charles I. Publication of *The
            Antipathy of English Lordly Prelacy* by William Prynne.

1642   The closing of all theatres was ordered by the Long Parliament.
            Publication of *Religio Medici* by Sir Thomas Browne (1605–82).

1643   Ordinances stipulated that money previously used for edu-
            cational purposes from crown revenues or sequestered royalist
            estates was to be safeguarded. The Commons granted power to
            the Committee for Plundered Ministers to investigate malignant

schoolmasters. Censorship was revived by the Long Parliament with the appointment of Henry Whalley, Clerk to the Stationers' Company, as Licenser; offenders were to be tried at the Old Bailey, which replaced the Star Chamber for this purpose. Weekly newsbooks began to appear, reporting on domestic issues and the progress of the Civil War. The first to appear was *A Perfect Diurnall* (1643–49), edited by Samuel Pecke and impartial. This was followed by *Mercurius Aulicus* (1643–45), edited by John Berkenhead in Oxford and royalist; *Mercurius Britanicus* (1643–46), edited by Thomas Audley and parliamentarian; *Mercuricus Civicus* (1643–46), edited by Richard Collings, illustrated and presbyterian; *The Kingdomes Weekly Intelligencer* (1643–49), edited by Richard Collings and presbyterian; *The Parliament Scout* (1643–45), edited by John Dillingham, presbyterian and royalist; and *The Weekly Account* (1643–47), edited by Daniel Border. Publication commenced of *Jehovah Jireh, or England's Parliamentarie Chronicle*.

1644   John Rushworth was appointed Licenser. John Milton protested against censorship in his *Areopagitica, A Speech for the Liberty of Unlicensed Printing*. All organs were ordered by parliament to be removed from churches and destroyed. Publication of *A Breviate of the Life of William Laud* by William Prynne; and *The Bloudy Tenent of Persecution* by Roger Williams (1604–83).

1645   The monopoly of the Stationers' Company to control the press was confirmed by parliamentary Ordinance. John Lilburne was imprisoned for unlicensed publications. Robert Boyle, Robert Hooke, William Petty, John Wallis, Seth Ward, John Wilkins and others commenced weekly meetings at Gresham College to discuss scientific and mathematical topics. Publication commenced of the weekly newsbooks, *Perfect Occurences* (1645–49), edited by Henry Walker and impartial; and *The Moderate Intelligencer* (1645–49), edited by John Dillingham, presbyterian and royalist.

1646   The Ordinance abolishing government of the church by bishops and archbishops ended the need for teachers to secure a licence from the bishop. Publication of *Gangraena* by Thomas Edwards, which attacked the religious extremism of the sects; and *Canterbury's Doom* by William Prynne. Edward Hyde (later Earl of Clarendon) commenced work on his *History of the Rebellion and the Civil Wars in England* (published 1702–4).

1647   An Ordinance for the financial support of Fairfax's army excluded the colleges of Winchester, Eton and Westminster and all free schools from payment of the rate. All actors were branded as rogues by a parliamentary Ordinance, which heralded a spate of raids on theatres with seats destroyed and spectators fined five shillings for attendance. Publication commenced of the weekly newsbook *Mercurius Pragmaticus* (1647–50), edited by Marchamont Nedham, Samuel Shepherd and John Cleveland, and royalist in sympathy.

1648   Publication of *Choice Psalms put into Musick for Three Voices* by Henry and William Lawes. Wadham College, Oxford, appointed John Wilkins (1614–72) as Warden, who was joined in the university by many of the distinguished scientists from Gresham College. Publication commenced of the weekly newsbook *The Moderate* (1648–49), edited by Gilbert Mabbot and Leveller in sympathy.

1649   An annual sum of £20,000 was set aside by Act of Parliament for educational purposes, including the payment of schoolmasters. The Commons resolved that the schoolmasters of Eton, Winchester and Westminster be required to take an engagement of loyalty to the Commonwealth 'without a King or a House of Lords'. The suppression of many newsbooks resulted from the Rump Parliament's Press Act, which imposed heavy penalties on those who wrote, printed, published or bought unauthorised books. Richard Hatter was appointed Licenser. Charles I's fine collection of paintings was sold by order of parliament and dispersed world-wide. Publication of *Eikonoklastes* and *Tenure of Kings and Magistrates* by John Milton; and *New Law of Righteousness* by Gerrard Winstanley (1609?–60?). Publication commenced of the weekly newsbooks *A Brief Relation* (1649–50), edited by Walter Frost and official; and *Several (or Perfect) Proceedings* (1649–55), edited by Henry Walker and official.

1650   Commissioners were appointed by the Act for the Propagation of the Gospel in Wales with powers to eject unsuitable schoolmasters, to appoint 'fit' schoolmasters and to establish new schools (over 60 were established in consequence). Similarly, the Act for the Better Propagating of the Gospel in the Four Northern Counties resulted in the establishment of several new schools in the north. Publication of *The English Dancing Master* by England's first full-time music publisher, John Playford (1623–86?). Samuel Cooper (1609–72) began to paint his famous miniatures. Publication of *Saints' Everlasting Rest* by Richard Baxter (1615–91); and 'Horatian Ode Upon Cromwell's Return from Ireland' by Andrew Marvell (1621–78). Publication commenced of the weekly newsbook *Mercurius Politicus* (1650–60), edited by Marchamont Nedham (later John Canne) and official.

1651   All school primers used under kingship were suppressed by order of parliament. Publication of *De Generatione Animalium* by Sir William Harvey, a textbook of embryology; and of *Leviathan, or the Matter, Forme and Power of a Commonwealth Ecclesiastical and Civil* by Thomas Hobbes (1588–1679).

1652   Publication of *The English Physician* by Nicholas Culpeper (1616–54); and of *The Law of Freedom in a Platform* by Gerrard Winstanley.

1653   Appointment of Gilbert Mabbott as Licenser. Peter Lely (1618–80) painted the portrait of Oliver Cromwell. Publication of *The Compleat Angler* by Izaak Walton (1593–1683).

1654   Ordinances were passed to appoint commissioners to examine schoolmasters and eject those who were ignorant, scandalous, insufficient or negligent; and to appoint other commissioners to visit Oxford, Cambridge, Eton, Winchester, Westminster and Merchant Taylors' and to assess what legislation would be needed to promote 'piety, learning and good nurture'. Robert Boyle (1627–91) copied Guericke's vacuum pump to show that air pressure is equal in all directions. Publication by John Playford of *A Brief Introduction to the Skill of Musick.*

1655   Those who had been ejected from a benefice or school for delinquency or scandal were banned by an Order of Council from keeping any school in future on pain of imprisonment. The Long Parliament's Printing and Printers' Ordinance resulted in the further suppression of newsbooks. Only the 'official' journals survived, including two edited by Marchamont Nedham – *Mercurius Politicus* and *The Publicke Intelligencer* (1655–60). Publication of *Church History of Britain* by Thomas Fuller (1608–61); *De Corpore* by Thomas Hobbes; and *Annals of the Reign of King Charles I* by Hamon L'Estrange (1605–60).

1656   William D'Avenant composed the first English opera, *The Siege of Rhodes*, with music by Henry Lawes. This was performed at the Cockpit Theatre, Drury Lane. Publication of *Commonwealth of Oceana* by James Harrington (1611–77).

1657   Appointment of Christopher Wren (1632–1723) as Professor of Astronomy at Gresham College, London.

1658   Performance of *The Cruelty of the Spaniards in Peru*, an opera by Sir William D'Avenant. Publication of *The Prerogative of Popular Government* by James Harrington; and *De Homine* by Thomas Hobbes.

1659   After a brief revival of licensed newsbooks under the restored Rump Parliament, these were again suppressed, leaving only four 'official' journals for circulation. Publication of *Holy Commonwealth* by Richard Baxter; and the first part of *Historical Collections of Private Passages of State, 1618–1649* by John Rushworth (1612–90) (completed in 1701).

1660   General search warrants were issued by the Long Parliament in an attempt to stamp out unlicensed pamphlets. After the Restoration, Sir John Birkenhead was appointed Licenser and the Stationers' Company ordered to seize anti-monarchical literature. London theatres were permitted to reopen, including The King's, The Duke's and The Royal. A 'college' founded at Gresham College, London, by John Wilkins and others for 'physico-mathematical experimental learning'. Publication of *The Spring and Weight of the Air* by Robert Boyle; and *Flora of Cambridge*, a catalogue by John Ray (1627–1705). Hooke's law on springs was established by Robert Hooke (1635–1703). Samuel Pepys (1633–1703) commenced his *Diary*.

1661   A setting of *Zadok the Priest* was composed by Henry Lawes for the coronation of Charles II. Appointment of Peter Lely as Court Painter to Charles II. Appointment of Christopher Wren as Professor of Astronomy at Oxford. Publication by Robert Boyle of Boyle's Law (the Law of Compressibilty) and his book, *The Sceptical Chemist*, which dealt with the composition of matter and the nature of chemical compounds.

1662   Schoolmasters were required by the Act of Uniformity to conform to the Prayer Book, renounce the Solemn League and Covenant, declare against armed resistance to the king and obtain a licence from the archbishop or bishop. The number of master printers in the Stationers' Company was limited to 20 by the Licensing Act, which also stipulated that no book was to be published without a licence from a censor, that presses were to be limited to the cities of Oxford, Cambridge and London and that searches for libellous material were permissible. The Royal Society of London for Improving Natural Knowledge was founded by Robert Boyle, Christopher Wren, John Wilkins and others with Charles II as its president. Publication of *The History of the Worthies of England* by Thomas Fuller.

1663   Appointment of Sir Roger L'Estrange as Surveyor of the Imprimery and Printing Presses. Appointment of Samuel Cooper as His Majesty's Lymer to Charles II. Discovery of the Binomial Theorem by Isaac Newton (1642–1727). Publication of *Flagellum* by James Heath (1629–64); and *Hudibras* by Samuel Butler (1612–80).

1664   John Twyn was hung, drawn and quartered for printing a seditious pamphlet. The Sheldonian Theatre, Oxford, was designed by Christopher Wren. Publication of *Anatome Cerebri* by Thomas Willis (1621–75), an investigation of the brain.

1665   Dissenters were banned from teaching in any public or private school by the Five Mile Act. Bishops were required by Archbishop Seldon to compile lists of all schoolmasters in each diocese with a note on their church attendance and their attitude to both the government and the doctrine of the Church of England. Robert Boyle proved that a candle could not burn nor an animal breathe without air. Publication of *Philosophical Transactions* by the Royal Society; and *Micrographia* by Robert Hooke, a study of observations made through a microscope. Publication of *The Holy City, or The New Jerusalem* by John Bunyan (1628–88).

1666   Establishment of *The London Gazette*, edited by Henry Muddiman, with almost a complete monopoly of news. Appointment of Robert Hooke as City Surveyor after the Fire of London. A museum was established by the Royal Society. Isaac Newton discovered gravitation, discovered the dispersion of light and measured the moon's orbit. Publication of *Grace Abounding to the Chief of Sinners* by John Bunyan.

1667 Publication of *Paradise Lost* by John Milton.

1668 Appointment of Christopher Wren as Surveyor-General for the rebuilding of London; he personally designed 51 churches and 36 companies' halls. Isaac Newton produced the first successful reflecting telescope.

1669 Appointment of John Blow (1649–1708) as Musician of the Virginals to Charles II. Appointment of Isaac Newton as Professor of Mathematics at Cambridge.

1670 In Bates's Case, judgement was given in favour of William Bates, enabling an unlicensed schoolmaster to teach, if appointed by the founder or lay patron of the school. This led to the growth of dissenting academies, founded by nonconformists. Publication of the *Catalogue of Plants* by John Ray.

1671 Publication of *Paradise Regain'd* and *Samson Agonistes* by John Milton; and *The Gentleman Dancing-Master* by William Wycherley (1640–1716).

1672 The first-ever series of public concerts in Europe was organised from his home in Whitefriars by John Banister, former Master of the King's Band. Isaac Newton outlined the laws of refraction to the Royal Society.

1673 Christopher Wren commenced work on the rebuilding of St Paul's Cathedral.

1674 Appointment of John Blow as Gentleman of the Chapel Royal and Master of the Children.

1675 Appointment of John Flamsteed (1646–1719) as Astronomer Royal in the newly-established Royal Observatory at Greenwich. Publication of *Satire against Mankind* by Lord Rochester (1648–80).

1676 Publication of *Ornithology* by Francis Willoughby, edited by John Ray.

1677   Appointment of Henry Purcell (1659–95) as Composer in Ordinary to Charles II. Election of Robert Hooke as Secretary of the Royal Society. Publication of *Account of the Growth of Popery and Arbitrary Government in England* by Andrew Marvell.

1678   Commencement of a series of weekly concerts in a warehouse loft in Clerkenwell, organised by Thomas Britton, a coal merchant. Publication of *The Pilgrim's Progress* by John Bunyan. Narcissus Luttrell (1657–1732) commenced work on *A Brief Historical Relation of State Affairs, 1678–1714.*

1679   The Licensing Act lapsed, resulting in a sudden growth of political pamphlets. Publication of *Catalogus Stellarum Australium* by Edmund Halley (1656–1742), who was elected a Fellow of the Royal Society. Publication of *Behemoth: The History of the Causes of the Civil Wars of England* by Thomas Hobbes.

1680   Lord Chief Justice Scroggs, in finding Henry Carr guilty of publishing a newsbook without authority, ruled that in common law even inoffensive journals were illegal if unauthorised. Appointment of Geoffrey Kneller (1646–1723) as Court Painter to Charles II.

1681   Appointment of Sir Christopher Wren as President of the Royal Society. Publication of *Absalom and Achitapel,* a satire on the Duke of Monmouth, by John Dryden (1631–1700).

1682   Appointment of Henry Purcell as organist in the Chapel Royal. Sir Christopher Wren commenced his work on Chelsea Hospital. Publication of two important books in the study of botany – *Methodus Plantarum Nova* by John Ray, putting forward a system for the classification of plants; and *The Anatomy of Plants* by Nehemiah Grew (1614–1712), illustrating the use of microscopes. Publication of *The Holy War* by John Bunyan; *An Impartial Collection of the Great Affairs of State* by John Nalson (1638?–86); and *Memorials of the English Affairs* by Bulstrode Whitelock (1605–75).

1683   Appointment of Henry Purcell as Keeper of the King's Instruments; and the composition of his first chamber music, *Sonatas of III Parts.*

1685   The Licensing Act was revived. Composition by John Blow of an anthem for the coronation of James II, *God Spake Sometime in Visions*; and a masque, *Venus and Adonis*. Circulation of *Character of a Trimmer* by George Savile, Viscount Halifax (1633–95).

1686   Publication of *Historia Plantarum Generalia,* vol. I, by John Ray, a study of theoretical botany.

1687   Publication of *Principia* by Isaac Newton, a major study of mechanics and dynamics. Publication of *A Letter to a Dissenter* by Viscount Halifax.

1688   Composition of *Lilliburlero* by Thomas Wharton (1648–1715), an anti-Jacobite song, with music by Henry Purcell.

1689   John Locke (1632–1704) published two *Treatises on Civil Government,* justifying the 1688 Revolution; and his *First Letter on Toleration.*

1690   *The Athenian Gazette,* published by John Dunton, was a forerunner of *The Spectator.* John Locke published his *Essay on Understanding;* and his *Second Letter Concerning Toleration.*

1691   Antony Wood (1632–95) published *Athenae Oxonienses.* Death of Richard Baxter, Robert Boyle and George Fox (1624–91).

1692   Sir William Temple (1628–99) published *Of Ancient and Modern Learning. The Fairy Queen* by Henry Purcell was performed in London. Richard Bentley (1662–1742) gave the first Boyle Lecture, 'proving the Christian religion'.

1693   Publication of *Life of Bishop Williams* by John Hacket (1592–1670); *Short and Easy Method with the Deists* by Charles Leslie; and *Some Thoughts Concerning Education* by John Locke, stressing the importance of individuality, character and methods of thought. In *Synopsis Animalium* John Ray attempted a new classification. Edmund Halley explained a method of ascertaining the distance of the sun.

1694   Publication of George Fox's *Journal;* and *A Serious Proposal to Ladies* by Mary Astell (1668–1731), supporting the idea of an all-female institute of learning. Henry Purcell published his *Te Deum and Jubilate.*

1695   Publication of *The Reasonableness of Christianity* by John Locke; and *Love for Love* by William Congreve (1670–1729). The 1662 Licensing Act was allowed to lapse. Death of Henry Purcell.

1696   Publication of *Christianity not Mysterious* by John Toland (1670–1722), founding the Deist movement; and Richard Baxter's *Autobiography*.

1697   Publication of *Alexander's Feast* by John Dryden.

1698   Publication of *Short View of the Immorality and Profaneness of the English Stage* by Jeremy Collier (1650–1726); *Life of Milton* and *Anglia Libera* by John Toland; and *Essay on Projects* by Daniel Defoe (1660?– 1731), which recommended income tax and the higher education of women. Thomas Savery (1650–1715) patented a pumping engine for clearing water from mines.

1699   Publication of *The Letters of Phalaris* by Richard Bentley (1662–1742).

1700   *The Way of the World* by William Congreve first performed. Death of John Dryden.

1701   Publication of *The True-born Englishman* by Daniel Defoe, defending King William.

1702   Publication of *The Shortest Way with the Dissenters* by Daniel Defoe; and the first part of *History of the Rebellion and the Civil War* by the Earl of Clarendon (1609–74). *The Daily Courant*, the first daily newspaper, was founded.

1703   Death of Samuel Pepys.

1704   Publication of *Tale of a Tub*, satirising the sectarian spirit, and *Battle of the Books* by Jonathan Swift (1667–1745); *Letters to Serena*, discussing belief in immortality, by John Toland; and the first volume of *Foedera*, a collection of public records and treaties, by Thomas Rymer (1641–1713). Daniel Defoe commenced publication of *The Review*, a political journal. In *Optics*, Isaac Newton explained the emission theory of light, rejecting the wave theory. Death of John Locke.

1705   Thomas Newcomen (1663–1724) improved the steam engine by forming a vacuum under the piston. Sir John Vanbrugh

(1664–1726) designed Blenheim Palace for the Duke of Marlborough. The Haymarket Theatre opened.

1707   *The Beaux Strategem* by George Farquhar (1678–1707) was first performed.

1709   Publication of *Pastorals* by Alexander Pope (1688–1744). *The Tatler*, a literary periodical by Richard Steele (1672–1729), began publication three times a week. George Berkeley's (1685–1753) *New Theory of Vision* argued that the eye conveyed only a sensation of colour. The first Copyright Act was passed.

1710   Publication of *Principles of Human Knowledge* by George Berkeley; and the first part of *Journal to Stella* by Jonathan Swift. Jonathan Swift and others began to edit *The Examiner*, a Tory publication. George Friedrich Handel arrived in London and produced his opera *Rinaldo* in 1711.

1711   Publication of *Essay on Criticism* by Alexander Pope; *Conduct of the Allies and the Late Ministry* by Jonathan Swift, attacking the war; and *History of the Exchequer* by Thomas Madox (1666–1727). Richard Steele and Joseph Addison (1672–1719) began to edit *The Spectator*.

1712   Publication of *Rape of the Lock*, a mock heroic by Alexander Pope; and *John Bull*, a political satire by John Arbuthnot (1667–1733). A Newspaper Stamp Act was passed.

1713   *History of My Own Time* by Gilbert Burnet (1643–1715) was completed.

SECTION TWO

Chronologies: foreign and colonial affairs

1 Chronology of foreign policy (including treaties, alliances, expeditions and foreign wars)

1603   A royal proclamation by James I announced the ending of the war with Spain (23rd June). A treaty was signed with France for the defence of the United Provinces (19th July).

1604   The Treaty of London, signed with Spain and Burgundy, brought an official end to the war and proposed the marriage of Prince Henry, heir to James I, and the Spanish Infanta Anne, daughter of Philip III (18th Aug.).

1606   The Treaty of Paris was signed with France, establishing security and freedom of commerce (24th Feb.).

1608   The Treaty of The Hague was signed with the United Provinces, concerning debts, privileges and mutual defence (26th June).

1609   An agreement was made with France and the United Provinces to guarantee the 12-year truce signed between Spain and the United Provinces in March (17th June).

1610   The Treaty of London was signed with France concerning confederacy and alliance (29th Aug.).

1613   Princess Elizabeth, daughter of James I, married Frederick, Elector Palatine (Feb.). Don Diego Sarmiento de Acuna (later Count of Gondomar) was appointed Spanish ambassador in London (May).

1614   Negotiations commenced between Sarmiento and James to arrange a Spanish marriage for Prince Charles.

1615   Sarmiento put forward to James the conditions for a Spanish marriage for Charles, including the possibility of a catholic succession to the throne.

1616   Marriage negotiations continued with Spain, in spite of stipulations over religion. Sarmiento lodged a protest concerning Sir Walter Raleigh's expedition to Guiana.

1617   Spain insisted on toleration for English Catholics as a prerequisite for a marriage treaty concerning Prince Charles.

1618   Start of the Thirty Years War with the revolt of Bohemia against the Emperor (Aug.). Negotiations for the marriage of Prince Charles to the Spanish Infanta were halted.

1619   The Emperor invaded Bohemia following the election as king of Frederick, the protestant Elector Palatine, who was James I's son-in-law (Aug.)

1620   After defeat at the Battle of the White Mountain (Oct.), Frederick was driven out of his new kingdom of Bohemia. The Palatinate was invaded by the Emperor's forces.

1622   Spanish marriage negotiations were revived with the visit of John Digby, Earl of Bristol, to Madrid.

1623   Prince Charles and the Duke of Buckingham visited Madrid to further the marriage negotiations (Mar.), but returned insulted and in favour of war (Oct.). Elector Frederick was expelled from the Palatinate (June). The Treaty of Westminster was signed with Russia for the encouragement of trade (16th June).

1624   The Treaty of London was signed with the United Provinces to continue the defensive league (5th June). Ernst Mansfeld's expedition with 12,000 men, sent by James I to help recover the Palatinate for his son-in-law, broke up in failure through illness and shortage of supplies. The Treaty of Paris, which was signed with France to ratify the marriage of Prince Charles and Princess Henrietta Maria, also agreed to the suspension of the recusancy laws in England and the provision of English military help against the Huguenots at La Rochelle (20th Nov.).

1625   Following the death of James I (27th Mar.), Charles I commenced a naval war against Spain, but Buckingham's Cadiz expedition ended in humiliating failure (Sept.–Nov.). A marriage contract, by proxy, was signed in Paris between Charles I and

Henrietta Maria (3rd May). A treaty of alliance was signed at The Hague with Denmark and the United Provinces (9th Dec.).

1626   A dispute over shipping hastened the outbreak of war with France (Apr.).

1627   War was declared on France. Buckingham's expedition with 7,000 men to capture the Isle of Ré (as a base from which to assist the Huguenots in La Rochelle) ended in humiliating failure (Oct.).

1628   Failure of further expeditions to assist the Huguenots in La Rochelle, which finally fell to French government forces (Oct.).

1629   The Peace Treaty of Susa was signed to end the war with France (24th Apr.).

1630   The Peace Treaty of Madrid was signed to end the war with Spain (15th Nov.).

1632   The Treaty of St. Germain-en-Laye was signed with France for the re-establishment of commerce (29th Mar.).

1639   The Treaty of Gluckstat was signed with Denmark to renew the 1625 treaty (6th Apr.).

1642   The Treaty of London was signed with Portugal, providing for peace (29th Jan.).

1651   Breakdown of negotiations at The Hague for an alliance between England and the United Provinces. The Navigation Act was passed, undermining the Dutch carrying trade (9th Oct.).

1652   Outbreak of the First Anglo-Dutch War (May), following England's insistence on the right of salute in the English Channel. The Battle of the Dunes, off Dover, between Admiral Robert Blake and Admiral Martin Tromp resulted in a Dutch retreat (19th May). In the Battle of the Kentish Knock, Blake's 68 ships won a victory over Tromp's 57 vessels (28th Sept.). The Battle of Dungeness, with Blake outnumbered by 85 ships to 42, resulted in a Dutch victory (30th Nov.).

1653   In the Three Days' Battle off Portland, Tromp failed in his attempt to provide safe passage for a convoy of 150 merchant ships, losing 11 warships and 50 merchant ships in a running engagement (18th–20th Feb.). The Battle of Gabbard Bank, an English victory, resulted in the loss of 20 Dutch ships (2nd–3rd June). The Battle of Scheveningen, fought off the river Texel over 12 hours with 130 ships on each side, resulted in a major English victory, the death of Tromp and the loss of 30 Dutch ships (31st July).

1654   In the Treaty of Westminster with the United Provinces, which ended the First Anglo-Dutch War, the Dutch agreed to respect the Navigation Act and the right of salute in the Channel (5th Apr.). The Treaty of Upsala was signed with Sweden (11th Apr.) and the Treaty of Westminster with Portugal (10th July), each providing for peace and commerce. The Treaty of Westminster was signed with Denmark (15th Sept.), providing for peace and alliance. The 'Western Design' expedition of 38 ships and 6,000 men set sail for the West Indies to attack Spain in the colonies (Dec.).

1655   The expeditionary force failed to capture San Domingo in Hispaniola (Apr.), but captured Jamaica (May). The Treaty of Westminster was signed with France, a defensive agreement which also excluded the exiled Stuarts from French territory (3rd Nov.).

1656   Spain declared war on England (Feb.). Although Admiral Blake failed to capture a treasure fleet on its voyage from the New World (Mar.), Captain Stayner's squadron later captured part of a treasure fleet off Cadiz (Sept.).

1657   England signed a defensive alliance with France against Spain, agreeing to provide 6,000 men and a fleet to join 20,000 French troops for a campaign in Flanders (23rd Mar.) Blake won a major naval victory at the Battle of Santa Cruz in the Canaries, destroying 11 Spanish ships (20th Apr.). Mardyck was captured from the Spanish (Sept.).

1658   The alliance with France was extended by a further treaty (28th Mar.). In the Battle of the Dunes, an Anglo-French army defeated the Spanish (14th June), who subsequently surrendered Dunkirk to the English.

1659   The Treaty of the Pyrenees brought peace between France and Spain (7th Nov.). Various treaties were signed with France (3rd Feb.), the United Provinces (24th July) and France and the United Provinces jointly (21st May, 4th Aug.) to bring about peace between Sweden and Denmark.

1660   A treaty of alliance was signed with Portugal (28th Apr.).

1661   The Treaty of London was signed with Denmark, concerning peace and commerce (13th Feb.). The Treaty of London was signed with Portugal, concerning the marriage of Charles II and Princess Catherine of Braganza (23rd June). The Treaty of London was signed with Sweden, concerning peace and commerce (21st Oct.).

1662   A treaty of peace and alliance was signed with the United Provinces at Whitehall to settle outstanding disputes (4th Sept.). The Treaty of London was signed to sell Dunkirk to the French (27th Oct.).

1664   English merchants listed their grievances against the Dutch in the Commons (Apr.). The Dutch colony of New Amsterdam (later granted to the Duke of York and renamed New York) was seized by Sir Robert Holmes (Aug.). Dutch bases on the West African coast were attacked by a force under Prince Rupert (Sept.). Dutch troops under De Ruyter reoccupied the West African bases, but failed to recapture New York (Dec.).

1665   The Second Anglo-Dutch War commenced with war declarations by the Dutch (Feb.) and the English (4th Mar.). The Treaty of Stockholm, a defensive alliance, was signed with Sweden (1st Mar.). A treaty of commerce was signed with Denmark (29th Apr.). In the naval Battle of Lowestoft, the Dutch fleet of 100 ships lost 17 to the English, who were blockading the Texel (3rd June). A treaty of alliance was signed in London with the Bishop of Münster (13th June). Sir Thomas Tedding's 30 ships attacked Dutch merchant ships in the neutral port of Bergen, but eventually withdrew (1st Aug.). A plan by Louis XIV to mediate in the Anglo-Dutch dispute failed (Aug.). The Dutch blockaded the Thames for three weeks (Oct.). The Treaty of Madrid, concerning peace and commerce, was signed with Spain (17th Dec.).

1666   France (Jan.) and Denmark (Feb.) entered the war on the side of the Dutch. England's ally, the Bishop of Münster, defected (Apr.). England lost its West Indian islands of St Kitts (Apr.) and Antigua (Nov.) to French attacks. A treaty of commerce was signed at Stockholm with Sweden (16th Feb.). A treaty of peace was signed at Tangier with Morocco (12th Apr.). In the Four Days' Battle at sea, Albemarle with 56 ships was outnumbered by De Ruyter with 84 and forced to withdraw (1st–4th June). Rupert and Albemarle scored a decisive victory at North Foreland when 20 Dutch ships were destroyed or captured (25th July). Sir Robert Holmes destroyed 250 Dutch merchant ships in the Zuyder Zee – 'Holmes's Bonfire' (Aug.).

1667   The Treaty of Madrid, concerning peace and friendship, was signed with Spain (23rd May). The Dutch won a major naval victory in the Medway when De Ruyter, in a surprise attack with 80 ships, burnt English battleships laid up in the river (June). Admiral Sir John Harman protected English possessions in the West Indies from annexation by defeating the French off Martinique (20th June). The Peace of Breda ended the Second Anglo-Dutch War with concessions being made to the Dutch, who in turn ratified English colonies in North America; France gained Acadia and the Dutch Surinam (31st July).

1668   A Triple Alliance was formed between England, the United Provinces and Sweden to counter French aggressions in the Netherlands (23rd Jan. – amended 25th Apr.). The Treaty of The Hague, concerning commerce, was signed with the United Provinces (17th Feb.). Charles Albert de Croissy, appointed French ambassador in London, set out proposals for an alliance with England (Aug.–Dec.).

1669   Secret negotiations took place for an Anglo-French alliance (Jan.). A convention was signed at The Hague with Sweden and the United Provinces guaranteeing Spanish territory (7th May). Commercial treaties were signed at Florence with Savoy (6th Sept.) and at Westminster with Denmark (29th Nov.). The first draft of a secret treaty with France was prepared (18th Dec.).

1670   A secret meeting took place at Dover between Charles II and the Duchess of Orléans regarding treaty negotiations with France (16th May). The Secret Treaty of Dover was signed between England and France with Charles promising his reconciliation with Rome and military support against the United Provinces in return for large subsidies (22nd May). The Public Treaty of Dover, an offensive alliance against the Dutch with the clauses relating to Catholicism deleted, was signed later (21st Dec.).

1672   England declared war on the United Provinces, thus commencing the Third Anglo-Dutch War (17th Mar.). In the Battle of Solebay, the Anglo-French fleet was attacked by De Ruyter, forcing it to withdraw for a refit (28th May). The allied fleet was broken up by a storm off the river Texel (July).

1673   The Dutch made an unsuccessful attempt to block access to the Thames (2nd May). The allied fleet unsuccessfully attacked Dutch ships at anchor in the Battle of Schoonveldt Channel (28th May); was forced to withdraw to the Nore when counter-attacked by De Ruyter (4th June); and failed to prevent De Ruyter's escort of a convoy of merchant ships from the East Indies in the Battle of the Texel (11th Aug.). Spain, the Emperor and Lorraine made alliances with the Dutch against France (Aug.). All these setbacks undermined Anglo-French plans for a descent on Holland.

1674   In the Treaty of Westminster between England and the United Provinces, which ended the Third Anglo-Dutch War, captured territories were restored on both sides; and the Dutch not only conceded the right of salute but also paid an indemnity (19th Feb.).

1675   Louis XIV agreed to grant a subsidy to Charles II on condition that the latter maintained his proroguement of an anti-catholic parliament (Aug.). Charles II suggested to Louis XIV the notion of a new secret treaty (Dec.).

1676   A new secret treaty was signed between Charles II and Louis XIV, involving the payment of further French subsidies (Feb.).

1677   The Treaty of St Germain-en-Laye, a commercial alliance, was signed between England and France (24th Feb.). The Commons demanded the adoption of an anti-French foreign policy (Mar.) – combined with a firm Dutch alliance (May). A further

French subsidy to Charles II was provided in return for the continued proroguement of parliament to April 1678 (Aug.). The marriage of Princess Mary to William of Orange took place (Nov.).

1678   A defensive treaty between England and the United Provinces (concluded Dec. 1677) was ratified at Westminster, with agreement on both sides to defend the other's territory if attacked (3rd Mar.). Demands were made in the Commons for a war on France (Mar.). A new secret treaty between Charles II and Louis XIV was signed (May). The Franco-Dutch War was ended by the Treaty of Nijmegen (31st July).

1681   Louis XIV's subsidy to Charles II was renewed (Mar.). Louis XIV launched his policy of encroachment on Empire territory (*Reunions*) by occupying Strasbourg (Sept.).

1682   A treaty of peace and commerce was signed with Algiers (10th Apr.).

1683   The marriage of Princess Anne and the Lutheran Prince George of Denmark was arranged (27th July).

1684   Louis XIV's gains in Germany through his policy of *Reunions* were ratified by the Truce of Ratisbon (Aug.).

1685   A treaty renewing the alliance with the United Provinces was signed (17th Aug.). Louis XIV issued the Revocation of the Edict of Nantes (Oct.) and commenced a policy of *dragonnades* against the Huguenots, causing up to 70,000 refugees to flee into England.

1686   Treaties of peace and commerce were signed with Algiers (5th Apr.) and Tunis (2nd Oct.). The defensive League of Augsburg was established to safeguard German states from further French aggression. A treaty of peace was signed between England and France to secure the neutrality of both parties in America (16th Nov.).

1688   James II declined Louis XIV's offer to strengthen his navy by moving French ships into the Channel (Aug.). William of Orange organised the German states into the League of

Augsburg, an anti-French coalition. Louis XIV invaded the Palatinate (25th Sept.).

1689   The United Provinces declared war on France (Feb.). The Treaty of Whitehall was signed with the United Provinces regarding the fitting out of a fleet (29th Apr.). England declared war on France with the full support of parliament (5th May). A French fleet defeated Admiral Arthur Herbert's fleet at Bantry Bay (May). An alliance was signed between the Empire and the United Provinces to oppose French designs (Treaty of Vienna, 12th May) with the later accession of England (9th Dec.), Spain, Savoy, Brandenburg, Saxony, Hanover and Bavaria forming the Grand Alliance. A treaty was signed with Denmark in Copenhagen (15th Aug.); and a treaty of friendship and alliance with the United Provinces at Whitehall (24th Aug.). A French army was defeated by Prince George Frederick of Waldeck and Marlborough at the Battle of Walcourt (25th Aug.).

1690   A treaty of alliance was signed with the Elector of Brandenburg at Westminster (16th May). Admiral de Tourville's French fleet defeated Admiral Viscount Torrington's Anglo-Dutch fleet off Beachy Head, giving France control of the Channel (June). French forces under the Duc de Luxembourg inflicted a serious defeat on the allied army at the Battle of Fleurus in the Netherlands (1st July). A French army gained a further victory at the Battle of Staffarda over the Duke of Savoy's forces (Aug). A treaty was signed with the protestant cantons of Switzerland at Arau (23rd Aug). The French fleet under de Tourville returned to port in Brest, easing anxieties over a possible invasion (Aug.). A treaty was signed with the United Provinces and Savoy at The Hague with a secret article concerning the Vaudois (20th Oct.). A defensive alliance was signed with Denmark and the United Provinces at Copenhagen (3rd Nov.).

1691   William III returned to the Netherlands to lead an enlarged English army (Jan.). French forces succeeded in capturing Mons (8th Apr.). The French defeated Waldeck at the Battle of Leuze (20th Sept.).

1692   A French fleet was equipped in readiness for invasion (Apr.). The French fleet under de Tourville was outnumbered and defeated by the Anglo-Dutch fleet under Admirals Rooke and Russell at the Battle of La Hogue (29th May–3rd June). French forces captured the stronghold of Namur in the Netherlands (June). William III's army, attempting to regain Namur, was driven back by Luxembourg at the Battle of Steenkerke (3rd Aug.). A convention was signed at The Hague with Spain and the United Provinces concerning the fleet in the Mediterranean (31st Oct.). A subsidy treaty with the Elector of Hanover was signed by England and the United Provinces at The Hague (22nd Dec.).

1693   A subsidy treaty with the Elector of Saxony was signed at Dresden (20th Feb.). An Anglo-Dutch Smyrna convoy, escorted by Rooke, was attacked by de Tourville's Mediterranean fleet in the Battle of Lagos, losing a considerable amount of cargo and 100 ships (27th–28th June). William III's army of 50,000 men was heavily defeated by Luxembourg at the Battle of Neerwinden, suffering an estimated 16,000 casualties (29th July). French forces captured Charleroi (11th Oct.).

1694   A subsidy treaty was signed with Saxony at Dresden by England and the United Provinces (23rd May). An allied fleet under Russell was based in the Mediterranean in response to the earlier losses sustained off Lagos (June); it was later ordered to winter at Cadiz (Oct.).

1695   The Duc de Villeroi succeeded as French army commander on the death of Luxembourg (Jan.). An alliance was signed with the Emperor, the United Provinces and the Bishop of Münster at The Hague (18th Mar.). William III's army recaptured Namur (1st Sept.).

1696   Plans were made, on a secret visit to England by the Duke of Berwick, for a French invasion force to coincide with a Jacobite rising (Feb.). The French halted plans for invasion after the execution of leading Jacobites (Mar.). An alliance was signed at The Hague with the United Provinces and the Duke of Schleswig-Holstein-Gottorp (14th May). An allied naval assault on Brest ended in failure (8th June). The Emperor began to withdraw his forces from Italy, conceding defeat (Oct.). An alliance was signed at The Hague with Denmark and the United Provinces with secret articles (3rd Dec.).

1697   The Treaty of Ryswick was signed by France, England, the
          United Provinces and Spain (20th Sept.) with the later accession
          of the Empire (10th Oct.); this brought temporary peace at the
          end of the War of the League of Augsburg with the French
          recognising William III as king and restoring all conquests
          gained since 1688 (except Strasbourg).

1698   A defensive triple league formed by England, Sweden and the
          United Provinces at The Hague (20th July). William III visited
          Holland to commence secret negotiations for the partition of
          the Spanish Empire on the death of Carlos II (20th July). The
          First Partition Treaty was signed by England, France and the
          United Provinces at Loo (11th Oct.) agreeing to the settlement
          of the Spanish succession on Joseph Ferdinand, Electoral Prince
          of Bavaria – with Naples, Sicily, Guipuscoa, etc., being granted
          the Dauphin.

1699   Death of Joseph Ferdinand, Electoral Prince of Bavaria (Jan.).

1700   The Treaty of London was signed with Sweden (16th Jan.). An
          alliance was signed with Sweden and the United Provinces at
          The Hague (23rd Jan.). The Second Partition Treaty was signed
          in London by England, France and the United Provinces
          agreeing that the Dauphin should receive Naples, Sicily,
          Tuscany, Lorraine and other Italian territories; that the
          Archduke Charles should receive Spain and the remainder of
          the inheritance; and that the two branches of the House of
          Habsburg should always remain separated (3rd Mar.). Carlos II
          of Spain signed a will leaving the whole empire to the Duke of
          Anjou, grandson to Louis XIV (Sept.). Carlos II died (21st
          Oct.), whereupon Louis XIV accepted the will in support of the
          Duke of Anjou (as Philip V).

1701   French forces took Dutch 'barrier fortresses' in the Spanish
          Netherlands and other strategic centres (Jan.). Marlborough
          was sent to The Hague to negotiate a new alliance against the
          French (Jan.). A treaty establishing the Second Grand Alliance
          was signed at The Hague between England, the Empire and the
          United Provinces (7th Sept.), with the later accessions of Prussia
          (18th Feb. 1701), the Bishop of Münster (18th Mar. 1703) and
          Savoy (4th Aug. 1704). On the death of the former king,
          James II (5th Sept.), France recognised his son, James Edward,

as James III. A treaty of perpetual alliance for security and defence was signed with the United Provinces at The Hague (11th Nov.). A subsidy treaty with Prussia was signed by England and the United Provinces at The Hague (30th Dec.).

1702 Death of William III and accession of Anne (8th Mar.). England, the Empire and the United Provinces declared war on France and Spain, thus commencing the War of Spanish Succession (15th May). An alliance was signed with the United Provinces and the Elector of Treves at The Hague (17th May); and with Brunswick Luneburg at The Hague (21st June). Marlborough's forces entered the Spanish Netherlands, but the States-General opposed plans to engage the French in action (June–Aug.). Bavaria allied with France and Spain (Sept.). Marlborough laid siege to the barrier fortresses, securing Liège, Venlo and Roermond (Sept.–Oct.). An allied expedition under Rooke with 50 ships and 15,000 men failed to capture Cadiz (Sept.), but won the Battle of Vigo Bay (Oct.), destroying the Spanish treasure fleet and capturing a large amount of booty (12th Oct.).

1703 An alliance was signed with the United Provinces and the Bishop of Münster at The Hague (13th Mar.); and another with the United Provinces and Holstein at The Hague (15th Mar.). A treaty was signed at The Hague with the Empire and the United Provinces for the prohibition of commerce and letters of exchange with France (11th Apr.). A defensive alliance (the First Methuen Treaty) was signed in Lisbon between England, the Empire, the United Provinces and Portugal (16th May) – Portugal committed itself to the war, on condition that the Archduke Charles came to Lisbon as the focus for the war in the Peninsula and that it was compensated with Spanish barrier fortresses. The Electorate of Cologne was invaded by Marlborough's forces, who captured Bonn (May), but his scheme to attack the 'Lines of Brabant' in Flanders was thwarted by lack of Dutch support (Aug.). Savoy joined the Grand Alliance (4th Aug.). A French and Bavarian army defeated the Emperor's forces at Hochstadt, later seizing Augsburg, Altbreisach and Landen (Sept.). A treaty of commerce was signed with Portugal at Lisbon (27th Dec.), granting free entry of English cloth into Portugal and preferential rates for the export of Portuguese wine into England.

1704   Archduke Charles was landed at Lisbon by Admiral Rooke with 2,000 allied troops (Feb.). Marlborough led an allied army of 35,000 men from Flanders towards the Danube in an attempt to relieve the enemy threat on Vienna and expel the French from Germany (May). The allied force defeated French and Bavarian troops under Marshal Marsin at Schellenberg (June). Marlborough's army took Donauworth, pushing the French forces to the south (2nd July). The French armies of Marshal Marsin and Marshal Tallard joined forces at Augsburg (3rd July). Rooke captured Gibraltar (4th July). Marlborough's army united with that of Prince Eugene, commander of the Emperor's forces (6th Aug.). Marlborough and Eugene (with 52,000 men) scored a decisive victory over the French and Bavarians (with 54,000 men) in the Battle of Blenheim (13th Aug.). Rooke defeated the Count of Toulouse's French fleet in the Battle of Malaga (24th Aug,), the French retreating to Toulon. Eugene's forces occupied Bavaria, which effectively withdrew from the war (Sept.). The French army was pushed across the Rhine westwards (Sept.). Marlborough captured Trier and other fortresses (Oct.).

1705   The siege of Gibraltar by Admiral de Pointis was lifted when Admiral Sir John Leake won the Battle of Marbella (10th Mar.). Lord Peterborough and Admiral Sir Cloudesley Shovell staged an allied landing in Catalonia (June). Marlborough halted his plan to invade France along the line of the Moselle (June); his army, having broken through the Lines of Brabant at Tirlemont (18th July), was again thwarted by lack of Dutch enthusiasm. Peterborough's army in the Peninsula captured Barcelona (3rd Oct.), which was immediately besieged by the French. Catalonia declared for the Archduke Charles (Oct.). An alliance was signed in Hanover with the Elector of Hanover (8th Dec.).

1706   Lord Henry Galway's Anglo-French army advanced from Portugal into Spain, causing the French to lift the siege of Barcelona (30th Apr.). Marlborough's army inflicted a decisive defeat on Villeroi's forces at the Battle of Ramillies (30th Apr.). An alliance was signed with the United Provinces and the Elector Palatine at The Hague (26th May). Marlborough systematically freed the Spanish Netherlands from French occupation, capturing Dunkirk, Antwerp, Ath, Menin and Dendermonde (June–Oct.). Galway's forces captured Madrid

(26th June), but Peterborough and the Archduke Charles later retreated from there to Valencia (July–Oct.). Leake's English fleet captured Alicante, Cartagena, Ibiza and Mallorca (June–Sept.). A commercial treaty was signed with Danzig (22nd Oct.).

1707   In the Battle of Almanza, a French army under the Duke of Berwick decisively beat the allied army under Galway, who was attempting an advance on Madrid (25th Aug.). Austrian troops under Eugene failed in an attempt to besiege Toulon with the backing of Shovell's allied fleet, although 50 French ships had been scuttled as a precautionary measure (July–Aug.). There was stalemate on the Flanders front.

1708   A French army counter-attacked in the Netherlands, capturing Ghent and Bruges after a minor insurrection (4th–5th July). Marborough gained a crushing victory over Vendôme (who had succeeded Villeroi as the French commander) at the Battle of Oudenarde (11th July). After Eugene had opposed Marlborough's plan to advance on Paris, the allies instead besieged Lille (Aug.), which finally fell (22nd Oct.). Leake's naval expedition captured Sardinia (Aug.). General James Stanhope captured Minorca with its important naval base of Mahon (Sept.).

1709   Allied forces retook Ghent and Bruges (Jan.); captured Tournai (29th July); and besieged Mons. French forces unders Villars advanced to defend Mons, digging in at Malplaquet. Marlborough and Eugene won a pyrrhic victory at the Battle of Malplaquet with over 20,000 allied casualities (11th Sept.), causing the Dutch to press for peace. Mons surrendered (26th Oct.). In the Barrier Treaty between England and the United Provinces, signed at The Hague, the United Provinces were promised the right of garrisoning nine fortresses in the Spanish Netherlands in return for promising England armed assistance, if needed, to secure their protestant succession (29th Oct.).

1710   Peace negotiations broke down (Mar.). In Spain, Stanhope was driven back in his advance on Madrid by Vendôme's French army (May); won the Battle of Almenara (July); but was defeated and captured at Bihuega (10th Dec.). Marlborough captured Douai (10th June) and Béthune (30th Aug.).

1711   On the death of Joseph I, Archduke Charles succeeded as Emperor (Apr.). Preliminary peace negotiations commenced with France (Sept.). Marlborough broke through the French *ne plus ultra* lines (Aug.). Marlborough was dismissed as military commander (31st Dec.).

1712   A Peace Congress was convened at Utrecht (Jan.). The government ordered the Duke of Ormond, who had succeeded Marlborough as commander, to refrain from future action (May). Villars defeated Dutch forces at Denain (24th July).

1713   In the Second Barrier Treaty which was signed at Utrecht between England and the United Provinces, the United Provinces guaranteed to protect the protestant succession against attack from the Pretender with 6,000 troops in return for barrier fortresses in the Spanish Netherlands (29th Jan.). In a treaty of peace and friendship with France signed at Utrecht (11th Apr.), France recognised the protestant succession to the British throne; promised to withhold support from the Stuarts; renounced any prospect of the union of the French and Spanish crowns; agreed to the demolition of the Dunkirk fortifications; ceded to Britain St Kitts, Newfoundland, Nova Scotia and Hudson Bay territory; and promised Britain's allies just and reasonable satisfaction. In a separate commercial treaty, both parties agreed to favourable trading arrangements for each other (11th April). In a treaty of peace and friendship signed with Spain at Utrecht (13th July), Spain recognised the Hanoverian succession in Britain; renounced Philip V's claim to the French throne; ceded Gibraltar and Minorca to Britain; and agreed to the Asiento contract for the supply of black slaves to the West Indies for 30 years and the despatch of an annual ship to central America. A further treaty of navigation and commerce was signed with Spain at Utrecht (9th Dec.).

2 Chronology of trade and colonies

1604   Sir Henry Middleton set sail for the Indies. James I granted Sir Edward Michelborne a licence to trade in China and elsewhere in the East.

1606   An expedition set sail to establish a colony in Virginia, backed by the London Company and the Plymouth Company of investors. An expedition set sail to investigate the North-West Passage, led by John Knight.

1607   A colony was successfully established in Virginia at Jamestown. Henry Hudson set sail for Greenland and Spitzbergen. A factory was established at Surat, north of Bombay, by William Hawkins for the East India Company (established in 1600) with the agreement of the Great Mogul.

1609   The Virginia Company received a royal charter, creating a joint-stock company with Sir Thomas Smith as treasurer. The Hudson river was discovered by Sir Henry Hudson. Sir Thomas Somers was shipwrecked on islands in the Bermudas. James I confirmed the exclusive privilege of the East India Company to trade in the East.

1610   Hudson's Bay was discovered by Sir Henry Hudson. Lord Delaware was appointed Governor of Virginia. Sir Thomas Roe sailed up the Amazon in search of gold in Guiana. Colonisation of Newfoundland commenced with small fishing settlements under the terms of a charter granted to John Guy.

1611   Hudson's crew mutinied on his expedition to explore the North-West Passage. English cloth traders were readmitted to Hamburg after their expulsion in 1577.

1612   The Virginia settlers established a colony in the Bermudas (the Somers Islands), which was added to their charter. John Smith published his *Map of Virginia*. The North-West Passage Company received its charter. The western shore of Hudson's Bay was discovered by Sir Thomas Button.

1613   Tobacco imports to England commenced from Virginia.

1614   The Cockayne Project, forbidding the export of unfinished cloth, was launched. Suspension of the charter of the Merchant Adventurers' Company and its cloth trade monopoly. William Gibbon set out on an expedition to Labrador. Start of a three-year trade crisis.

1615   Control of Bermuda was granted to the Somers Islands Company. An English fleet under Nicholas Dowton secured British interests in Surat by defeating the Portuguese at Swally Roads. An Order in Council stipulated that goods from the Mediterranean should only be carried in English ships.

1616   Sir Walter Raleigh began preparations for a voyage to Guiana after his release from prison. William Baffin's expedition explored Baffin Bay.

1617   The Cockayne Project was terminated. The charter of the Merchant Adventurers' Company was restored. Raleigh departed for Guiana, but failed in his attempt to discover gold mines.

1619   The inaugural meeting took place of the colonial parliament at Jamestown, Virginia. The Amazon Company was established under Capt. Roger North. England and Holland signed a treaty concerning trade in the Spice Islands.

1620   The Pilgrim Fathers set sail in *The Mayflower* and established a colony at Plymouth, New England, from where they exported furs, maize and timber. Scottish colonisation of Nova Scotia commenced. Start of a depression in trade (1620–24).

1621   The English government ordered the Virginia Company to export its tobacco solely to England. William Bradford succeeded John Carver as Governor of the Plymouth colony, serving for 33 years in that office.

1622   An Order in Council stipulated that goods from the Baltic should only be carried in English ships. An Indian rising took place in Virginia.

1623   The Dutch murdered officials of the East India Company in the Massacre of Amboyna.

1624   Government of the colony of Virginia became a crown responsibility (along with Bermuda and New England), following the forfeiture of the Virginia Company's charter after bankruptcy. Sir Thomas Warner established a colony at St Kitts.

1625   Capt. John Powell established crown rights to Barbados.

1626   Harvard College was founded in New England.

1627   A start was made to the colonisation of Barbados under the direction of Sir William Courteen, to produce cotton and tobacco. The Guiana Company was established.

1628   John Endicott explored Salem in Massachusetts. The island of St Kitts was divided with France. The colonies of Montserrat, Nevis and Antigua were established in the Leeward Islands. The puritan New England Company was established under John Venn and Hugh Peter – at first supplied an older settlement at Salem, but later merged into the Massachusetts Bay Company.

1629   A serious trade depression commenced (1629–31). The Massachusetts Bay Company was established by royal charter. The colony of New Hampshire was established. Peace with France brought about the abandonment of the Scottish settlement in Nova Scotia (became Acadia under the French).

1630   The Guinea Company was established. John Winthrop established a colony in Massachusetts to begin a great puritan migration. The Providence Island Company was set up under Lords Warwick, Brooke and Saye and Sele to establish puritan settlements in the West Indian islands of Providence and Association.

1632   A start was made to the colonisation of Montserrat and Antigua.

1633   The colony of Connecticut was established with land purchased from the Mohican Indians.

1634   A start was made to the colonisation of Maryland (named after Queen Henrietta Maria) at St Mary's for Catholics with Lord Baltimore as proprietor and tobacco as the staple product. The first standing committee of the Privy Council for foreign plantations was appointed to regulate affairs in the New World colonies.

1635   The right to trade through ports on the west coast of India was granted to English merchants by the Portuguese in the Convention of Goa. The Courteen's Association (or Assada Merchants) was established by royal charter to trade in those parts of the east not already controlled by the East India Company.

1636   Roger Williams commenced the colonisation of Rhode Island at Providence with land bought from the Indians.

1637   The colonisation of Maine commenced.

1638   The colony of New Haven was established by Theophilus Eaton and John Davenport.

1639   The inaugural meeting of the Barbados Assembly took place. The port of Madras in India was acquired, protected by the newly constructed Fort St George.

1640   The boundaries of the Plymouth and Massachusetts Bay colonies were firmly established to eliminate disputes. Sugar plantations were established in Barbados. Start of a two-year trade crisis.

1641   Settlements were gradually made in Bengal, culminating in the establishment of a factory at Hughli. The settlers in Providence and Association were driven out by the Spanish.

1642   A treaty between England and Portugal agreed to peaceful trading between their nationals in India.

1643   The New England Confederacy (of Plymouth, Massachusetts, Connecticut and New Haven) was formed for mutual protection against the Indians. The settlements in Rhode Island were united by Roger Williams following the grant of a charter.

1646   Colonisation of parts of the Bahamas commenced with the production of salt and cotton.

1649   The East India Company and Courteen's Association amalgamated. The government set up a commission for the plantations. The colonies of Antigua, Barbados, Bermuda, Maryland and Virginia rebelled against control by the Commonwealth and pledged loyalty to Charles II.

1650   The Navigation Act prohibited trade with English colonies in foreign ships. A parliamentary Ordinance appointed Sir Henry Vane and 14 other commissioners to advise on and regulate trade and colonies.

1651   In an attempt by parliament to gain control over pro-royalist colonies, Sir George Ayescue's fleet sailed for the West Indies, gaining the submission of Barbados, Virginia and Maryland (1652). The Navigation Act was passed forbidding the import of European goods, except in English ships or ships of the country of origin; and the import of goods from Asia, Africa and America, except in English, Irish or colonial ships with the majority of their crews English, Irish or colonial. A start was made to the colonisation of Surinam.

1652   Formal recognition of parliament's authority was given by the American colonies to end the rebellion.

1654   A military expedition set out for the West Indies against Spanish colonies in the New World (Cromwell's 'Western Design'). Acadia (Nova Scotia) was captured from the French. A treaty with Portugal secured freedom of trade with all Portuguese lands beyond the sea.

1655   Jamaica was captured from Spain by the expeditionary force, after their failure to seize Hispaniola. The colony of the Cayman Islands was established.

1657   Cromwell formed the East India Company and the old Courteen's Association into one joint-stock company, granting them a monopoly of all trade in the east.

1660   The Navigation Act was passed to amend the 1651 Act and stipulate that listed colonial goods (sugar, tobacco, cotton wool, indigo, ginger and dyestuffs) could be directly shipped only to England, Ireland or other English colonies. The Spanish finally abandoned their attempt to retain Jamaica with the departure of their Governor, de Ysassi.

1661   Bombay was ceded by Portugal to Charles II as part of the dowry of Catherine of Braganza.

1662   'The Royal Adventurers trading to Africa Company' (or Africa Company) was granted a charter with a monopoly to sell slaves to settlements in the New World. The colony of Connecticut was granted a royal charter.

1663   Charles II founded North Carolina largely for royalists ruined by the Civil War. The colony of Rhode Island was granted a royal charter. The Staple Act was passed stipulating that colonies must buy all their European manufactured goods in England – thus establishing an important ingredient of the 'Old Colonial System'.

1664   Charles II laid claim to the Dutch settlements at the mouths of the Hudson and Delaware rivers, appointing James, Duke of York, as proprietor; an expedition under Colonel Richard Nicholls captured New Amsterdam from the Dutch, renaming it New York. The inaugural colonial assembly was held in Jamaica. Port James was established in the Gambia as a slave-trading centre. Thomas Mun's book advocating mercantilism, *England's Treasure by Foreign Trade*, was published (but probably written pre-1630).

1665   Outbreak of the Second Anglo-Dutch War (1665–67). New Jersey was captured from the Dutch. The Dutch fleet under De Ruyter was repulsed from Barbados chiefly by English buccaneers. Henry Morgan's buccaneers began a series of raids (1665–71) on the Spanish towns of Granada, Porto Bello and Panama.

1666   The colony of the Virgin Islands was established. The French seized Antigua, St Kitts and Montserrat; the Dutch captured Surinam.

1667   English forces retook Surinam from the Dutch and both Antigua and Montserrat from the French. The Treaty of Breda confirmed New York, New Jersey and part of St Kitts as English, but Surinam was restored to the Dutch and Acadia (Nova Scotia) to the French.

1668   The East India Company acquired Bombay from Charles II. Sir Henry Morgan sacked Porto Bello.

1669   Morgan sacked Maracaibo and Gibraltar on the Spanish Main.

1670   A more systematic settlement of South Carolina commenced. The Treaty of Madrid with Spain ratified England's sovereignty over Jamaica and other West Indian colonies. The Hudson's Bay Company was granted a royal charter on a joint-stock basis, granting Prince Rupert the right to trade in that area and to search for the North-West Passage.

1671   Administration of the Leeward Islands was separated from that of Barbados.

1672   The Royal Africa Company was granted a royal charter to trade in slaves (thus succeeding the bankrupt Africa Company) – set up six forts on the Gold Coast and one on the Slave Coast. The Third Anglo-Dutch War commenced (1672–74).

1673   The Plantation Duty Act imposed a duty on colonial goods destined for other English colonies (i.e. rather than for England). The Dutch seized New York.

1674   The Treaty of Westminster, which ended the Third Anglo-Dutch War, restored New York to England.

1675   A serious rebellion by Indians was suppressed in New England.

1676   An Indian rising was suppressed in Virginia.

1678   The colony of Maine was embodied into Massachusetts.

1679   New Hampshire became a crown colony.

1680   An Anglo-Spanish treaty provided for real peace 'beyond the line' (i.e. in the New World colonies), thus ending the freedom of buccaneers to operate and, by implication, confirming the right of England to trade in the West Indies.

1681   The Quaker colony of Pennsylvania was founded by William Penn with authorisation for religious toleration. The Hudson's

Bay Company had by now established a line of defensible trading posts around the bay – forts which were repeatedly attacked by the French (1686–97). The Dutch in the East Indies expelled the English from their factory at Bantam (which was never restored).

1683   The East India Company's charter was renewed, granting it the right to coin money, to exercise jurisdiction over English subjects and to make peace, war and alliances.

1684   The Somers Island Company was abolished, thus making Bermuda a crown colony. The charter of Massachusetts was annulled.

1686   English forces occupied Calcutta. The charter of Rhode Island was annulled. In a treaty of peace between England and France, France restored the forts captured from the Hudson's Bay Company (except Fort Charles) and both parties agreed to a state of neutrality in America.

1687   The charter of Connecticut was annulled. The East India Company was granted a new charter with powers to raise large amounts of revenue from duties to maintain its military strength.

1688   War between the East India Company and the Moguls resulted in the loss of several English factories.

1689   Existing charters of all colonies were recognised by William and Mary. St Kitts was captured by the French.

1690   A British factory was set up in Calcutta, following the declaration of peace between the Moguls and the East India Company. St Kitts was recaptured by the English.

1691   Massachusetts received a new charter, which provided for the annexation of Plymouth and stipulated that the appointment of all main officials rested with the crown.

1693   An abortive attempt was made to capture Martinique from the French.

1694   An Act of Parliament sanctioned the sale of iron and copper abroad (except in France).

1695   The Company of Scotland was set up by the Scottish parliament to promote trade with Africa and the Indies.

1696   The Navigation Act stipulated that no merchandise was to be carried from or into any plantation, or to England, except in English-built and -owned ships with three-quarters of the crew English. The Royal Board of Trade and Plantations was established.

1697   The Hudson's Bay Company was limited to the factory of Fort Albany by the terms of the Treaty of Ryswick, losing its other forts to the French.

1698   A charter was granted to the New East India Company, consisting of private merchants or 'interlopers'. Fort William was built as a protection to Calcutta. The Company of Scotland sent out an abortive expedition to Darien with the aim of setting up a colony on the Isthmus of Panama.

1699   The Company of Scotland's second expedition to Darien was unsuccessful. By this date cloth exports had fallen to 47 per cent of England's total exports with re-exports of tobacco, sugar and Indian calicoes rising to 30 per cent.

1700   There were serious recriminations after the evacuation of survivors of the third Darien expedition, the Scottish parliament charging England with deliberate sabotage of the scheme.

1702   British troops in the War of Spanish Succession captured the French half of St Kitts. Agreement was reached between the two East India Companies over merger. Delaware was created a crown colony.

1703   The second Methuen Treaty with Portugal secured favourable trading terms for English cloths in exchange for similar terms for port and madeira.

1704   Gibraltar was captured by Admiral Sir George Rooke.

1708   Minorca was captured by General James Stanhope, thus securing the important naval base of Mahon.

1709   The Old and New East India Companies were merged into the 'United Company of the Merchants of England trading to the East Indies'.

1710   Nova Scotia (Acadia) was captured by British forces with militia from New England in support.

1711   The South Sea Company was established.

1712   The Royal Africa Company's monopoly of slave and ivory trade was abolished.

1713   Carolina was split into two colonies, North and South. In treaties signed at Utrecht with Britain, France ceded St Kitts, Newfoundland, Nova Scotia and Hudson Bay territory; and Spain not only ceded Gibraltar and Minorca, but also agreed to the Asiento contract for the supply of black slaves by the South Sea Company to the West Indies for 30 years and the dispatch of an annual ship to central America.

3 Chronology of relations with Scotland and Ireland

Note that the names of institutions and offices used in this section (e.g. parliament, privy council, chancellor) refer to those in Scotland or Ireland. Where the English equivalent is intended, this will be made clear in the text (e.g. English parliament, English chancellor).

Scotland: chronology of events

1603   Sir George Hume of Spott (later Earl of Dunbar) continued as Treasurer (appointed 1601), controlling all the revenue departments; John Spottiswoode continued as Archbishop of Glasgow.

1604   James I proclaimed himself King of Great Britain (though the English parliament continued to style him King of England, Scotland, France and Ireland); commissioners from the two kingdoms discussed the idea of a union of the two parliaments, but this was rejected by both parliaments; Alexander Seton, 1st Earl of Dunfermline, was appointed Chancellor to control administration in Scotland.

1605   An Anglo-Scottish border commission was established to help pacify the border regions; a policy of colonisation of the troublesome Western Isles commenced with the 'Gentlemen Adventurers of Fife', but ended in failure.

1606   A new union flag was adopted together with a new design of the royal arms; a regular postal service between London and Edinburgh was gradually established; the unification of the coinage was also undertaken; and customs rates were abolished. John Forbes and five other dissident ministers from Aberdeen were found guilty of treason and sentenced to exile; Andrew Melville and other presbyterian ministers were detained in London without trial. James was recognised by the Scottish parliament as the Supreme Governor in both temporal and spiritual matters – with the right to decide the timing of meetings of the General Assembly. Lordships of Erection were created out of the profits of former monastic land to fund additional patronage for the lesser nobility.

1607   Scottish nobles and councillors petitioned James against full-scale union.

1608   Judges in Calvin's case (the *post nati* case) ruled that all Scots born after 1603 had naturalisation rights in England as well as Scotland; an Anglo-Scottish naval expedition to the Western Isles under Lord Ochiltree captured numerous local chiefs, who later submitted to the responsibilities contained in the statutes of Iona.

1609   James tried unsuccessfully to introduce commissioners of the peace to counter the power of the nobility in their localities.

1610   Customs rates reintroduced between the two countries; the Scots began to take part in the colonisation of Ulster; the king's supremacy within the Church was formally ratified by parliament; the consistorial authority of bishops was restored; the courts of High Commission were restored at Glasgow and St Andrews; three Scottish bishops were consecrated in England; Dunbar appointed Comptroller, as well as Treasurer, to undertake a major reorganisation of crown finance.

1611   Death of Dunbar; succeeded as Treasurer by Sir Robert Carr, the king's new favourite – created Viscount Rochester.

1612   The General Assembly accepted the full authority of the bishops within the Church. Orkney was annexed to the crown.

1615   John Spottiswoode appointed Archbishop of St Andrews.

1616   John Erskine, 2nd Earl of Mar, appointed Treasurer with instructions to reduce the large deficit.

1617   James I visited Scotland; advocated an increase in ritual and ceremonial in the Church of Scotland. A policy was launched by the king of attempting to reduce the number of hereditary juridictions by buying up sheriffdoms – with little success.

1618   Prompted by James, the Perth General Assembly passed the Five Articles, making provision for the observance of holy days, confirmation by bishops, kneeling at communion, private baptism and private communion; *The Book of Sports* introduced, breaching the puritan ideal of the sabbath by permitting certain recreations on Sundays.

1621   Parliament sanctioned the Five Articles after fierce opposition on grounds of popery; growth of open air conventicling in the Lowlands. Parliament granted James £1,200,00 in taxation over four years – the largest sum ever – and a new tax on annual rents. The border commission was disbanded – followed by an increase in disorder.

1622   Death of Dunfermline; succeeded as Chancellor by Sir George Hay.

1623   Scotland was hit by the worst famine on record for the century.

1625   Death of James I and VI; accession of Charles I. Charles announced a royal revocation of lands secularised by the Church since 1540 – caused widepread hostility as an apparent threat to property rights. The king continued his father's policy of attempting to bring local government and justice under the control of the crown – but only 16 sheriffdoms were in royal hands by 1633.

1626   A committee of war established by Charles to circumvent the more ponderous Privy Council on vital matters. A Scottish deputation, including the Earl of Rothes and Lord Loudon, petitioned Charles in London against the revocation.

1627   A commission for surrenders and teinds was established to compensate landlords for the surrender of lands under the royal revocation – an indication that Charles was giving way to pressure.

1628   William Graham, 7th Earl of Menteith, appointed by Charles as President of the Privy Council and Justice General to provide an effective link with him at court.

1630   Parliament granted a £100,000 land tax and a continuation of the tax on annual rents. A common Anglo-Scottish fishing policy was established.

1632   The coinage was debased.

1633   Death of Hay; replaced as Chancellor by Archbishop Spottiswoode; he was joined on the council by 10 bishops to provide Charles with a malleable group. The national debt rose to £853,000; parliament granted an extension of the 1630 land tax for a further six years, a benevolence and an increase in the tax on annual rents. Charles visited Scotland for his coronation, accompanied by Archbishop Laud, and decided on the need for the reform of worship – ordered the Scottish bishops to prepare a liturgy. The king agreed to entrust the selection of the Lords of the Articles to the bishops.

1634   The Anglo-Scottish border commission was re-established. Lord Balmerino, a leading critic of government policies in Scotland, was found guilty of treason but spared execution.

1635   Diocesan courts were established.

1636   John Stewart, 1st Earl of Traquair, appointed Treasurer. Tariffs on Scottish exports to England raised by two and a half per cent, thus hitting the coal and salt industries. A new Book of Canons was introduced for use in the Church of Scotland.

1637   A new Prayer Book, based on the English liturgy and largely fashioned by Laud, was introduced by royal prerogative. Its use in St Giles' Cathedral in Edinburgh led to a riot (repeated in Glasgow) and a petition against the Prayer Book signed by many of the nobility and clergy. A committee, known as The Tables and composed of representatives from the four estates, was established to organise opposition.

1638   The Privy Council moved from Edinburgh to Stirling. The Tables drew up the National Covenant, which appealed to all classes of opposition, requiring subscribers to pledge themselves to remove the recent innovations. Charles sent the Marquess of Hamilton to negotiate with the Scots and subsequently accepted his advice to revoke the Prayer Book and canons, to remove the Court of High Commission and to suspend the Five Articles.

The king also authorised a meeting of the General Assembly, which met in Glasgow with a large majority of well-organised Covenanters; ignoring Hamilton's order for dissolution, it continued its session and, under the leadership of Alexander Henderson, overthrew royal supremacy, abolished episcopacy, the Five Articles, the Prayer Book and the canons, and restored the presbyterian system. The Covenanters began the task of gaining signatures for the Covenant throughout Scotland, raising money and establishing a military organisation ready for war.

1639   Charles marched north with an inadequate and ill-equipped army; confronted by a covenanter army under General Alexander Leslie, the king agreed to end the First Bishops' War; under the terms of the Truce of Berwick, the Scottish army was to be disbanded and Scottish parliaments were to be regularly called. The General Assembly passed the 'Barrier Act', which forbade changes in the laws of the Church until ratified by provincial synods and presbyteries; it also demanded compulsory adherence to the Covenant. Parliament formally sanctioned previous decisions taken by the General Assembly; and elected a Standing Committee of the Estates to replace The Tables and to supersede the Lords of the Articles as the effective organ of government. Charles formed in London a committee for Scottish affairs, which was dominated by Wentworth, Hamilton and Laud. The General Assembly appointed a Commission of the Assembly to control affairs while the Assembly itself was in recess.

1640   Parliament met without the king's authority, agreeing to triennial parliaments and other constitutional changes. Charles called the Short Parliament (May) in an unsuccessful bid to gain supply for his struggle against the Scots. The covenanter army of 18,000 invaded England and seized Newcastle, defeating the king's forces at Newburn; the king accepted the Treaty of Ripon, which concluded the Second Bishops' War, agreeing to pay the Scots £850 a day until a settlement was made. The king called the Long Parliament (November) in the forlorn hope that they would resist the Scots.

1641   Pro-Scottish MPs in the English parliament put forward the Root and Branch Bill and also commenced proceedings against Laud and Wentworth (now the Earl of Strafford). Charles visited Scotland, partly in the vain expectation of establishing a royalist party to assist him against opposition in England; he submitted to parliament's demands for greater control over appointments and policies, reviving the Privy Council with a largely covenanter membership (and thus replacing the Committee of Estates).

1642   Charles recruited a Scottish army of 10,000 troops to help suppress the catholic rebellion in Ireland; arriving in April, they successfully cleared the rebels from much of Ulster, where many Scottish immigrants lived. After the outbreak of civil war in England, both king and parliament made overtures to the Scots for assistance, but the king turned down an offer of mediation by the Covenanters under Argyll (April).

1643   Hamilton, strongly in favour of non-intervention, persuaded 41 members of the nobility to sign the Cross Petition (Jan.); but he was finally out-voted (June) by the interventionists under Argyll. John Pym sent Henry Vane the Younger to Edinburgh to negotiate terms for Scottish involvement in the war. The Solemn League and Covenant, which was accepted by the English parliament in September and imposed on the nation, provided for Scottish military assistance (financed by the English), closer working relationships and religious uniformity according to 'the Word of God' (a phrase which gave a certain flexibility of interpretation, not confined to the introduction of Presbyterianism in England). Scottish commissioners were sent to the Westminster Assembly to discuss the Covenant and the form of English religion.

1644   An army of 20,000 Scots crossed the border under General Alexander Leslie, Earl of Leven (Jan.), eventually gaining control of the North by occupying Newcastle upon Tyne, Carlisle, York and Durham; allied armies under Leven won a decisive victory at Marston Moor (July). A Committee of Both Kingdoms was established to co-ordinate the running of the war (Jan.). Montrose joined forces with Alastair MacColla's catholic mercenaries from Ireland to fight for the king in Scotland (Sept.), defeating the Covenanters at Tippermuir and Aberdeen.

1645   Montrose continued his run of victories by defeating the

Covenanters at Inverlochy, Dundee, Auldearn, Alford and Kilsyth, before suffering final defeat by David Leslie at Philiphaugh (Sept.). The king lost the final decisive battle in England at Naseby (June).

1646   The king surrendered to the Scottish army at Newark (May), hoping to exploit differences that were beginning to appear among the allies over the question of religious settlement; the Scots removed the king to Newcastle, where discussions took place for several months before finally collapsing over the king's refusal to accept a presbyterian system in England and parliamentary control of the militia. The Scottish army in Ulster was defeated by the catholic Irish confederates at Benburb (June).

1647   The Scots handed over the king to the English parliament (Jan.), which organised his transfer to Holmby House in Northamptonshire; the Scottish army returned to Scotland after agreement was made for the settlement of its pay arrears of £400,000. The king escaped to the Isle of Wight (Nov.), from where he made an 'engagement' with Scottish royalists and moderates, led by Hamilton, Loudoun (the Chancellor), Lauderdale and Lanark; the king agreed to respect the 1641 settlement and to sanction a three-year experiment of Presbyterianism in England in return for immediate military support; although the engagement was supported by the parliament, it was opposed by the General Assembly, led by Argyll, as a betrayal of the Covenant.

1648   Hamilton with difficulty raised an army of 20,000, in spite of obstruction by western Covenanters, but it was crushed by Cromwell at Preston (Aug.); Hamilton was captured and executed. Cromwell arrived in Edinburgh (Oct.), set up Argyll as the leader of a covenanter government and insisted that all engagers be removed from public office (enacted in Jan. 1649).

1649   Charles I was tried and executed (Jan.); Charles II was proclaimed King of Scotland, England, France and Ireland (Feb.), but this was conditional on his agreement to sign the Covenant and impose Presbyterianism on England; the Rump Parliament in England abolished the monarchy (Mar.). Parliament abolished lay patronage in the Church and increased ministers' stipends.

1650   Montrose led an abortive rising in the North in the hope of gaining concessions for the king, but was defeated at Carbisdale, captured and executed (Apr.). Charles II landed in Scotland (June) and signed the Covenant. Cromwell, having crushed the Irish rebellion, led an army to Scotland (July); advanced on Edinburgh, but was forced to retreat to Dunbar, where he decisively defeated David Leslie (Sept.) before capturing Edinburgh (Dec.). The Western Remonstrance of radical Presbyterians (Oct.) was undermined by the defeat of the army of the Western Association at the hands of Cromwell (Dec.). A royalist coup, known as 'The Start', was unsuccessful (Oct.). A coalition of Covenanters and engagers was formed (Dec.) to defend the king, country and Covenant from foreign invasion.

1651   Charles II was crowned at Scone by Argyll (Jan.); Cromwell's army captured Perth, Stirling and Dundee (Aug./Sept.); Charles marched south over the border with a weakened army and was routed by Cromwell at Worcester (Sept.); Charles fled to France (Oct.). A declaration by the English government regarding the settlement of Scotland indicated their desire for union through incorporation.

1652   An English government regime was established and a cess tax of £10,000 per month imposed.

1653   A royalist rising led by John Middleton and the Earl of Glencairn broke out in the West and the Highlands.

1654   General Monck's forces invaded the Highlands to crush the royalist rebels and to impose a repressive regime based on an occupying force of 10,000 troops and a network of fortresses. An Ordinance of the English government decreed the union of the two countries; the Scots were allocated 30 seats in the English parliament (though 16 of these were actually filled by Englishmen in the 1656 parliament). Regality and baronial courts were abolished, thus leaving the provision of local justice largely in the hands of the army. The General Assembly was abolished, thus removing clerical influence from government.

1655   A Scottish Council was established with two Scots included in its total of nine members. Lord Broghill, President of the Council of State in Scotland, launched a policy of involving acceptable

Scots in the control of local government and justice – thus reducing the size and cost of Monck's occupying army. A programme of social and economic reforms was instigated.

1657   The Protectorate Parliament in England formally passed the Act of Union.

1659   The Rump Parliament was recalled in England with Scottish members excluded. General Monck and his army marched into England with the aim of restoring parliamentary government, leaving the Earl of Glencairn in charge of affairs in Scotland.

1660   Charles II was restored as King of England. He preferred to keep English and Scottish affairs separate, giving considerable responsiblity to the Scottish government for domestic matters. All unlicensed meetings were outlawed in Scotland. The Navigation Acts in England deprived Scottish merchants of trade with Europe and the colonies.

1661   The Act Recissory was passed by parliament, repealing all legislation relating to Scotland since 1633 – thus completely restoring the king's authority and prerogatives, including the right to call and dissolve parliament and to nominate the Lords of the Articles. Parliament granted taxes of £480,000 per year based on customs and excise duties. The government consisted of Middleton (the King's Commissioner to parliament), Glencairn (the Chancellor), Lauderdale, Crawford, Rothes and Cassillis. James Sharp was appointed Archbishop of St Andrews. Persecution of Covenanters commenced – both James Guthrie and the Duke of Argyll were executed. Parliament imposed on all office-holders an oath of allegiance, which also rejected the Covenant and gave recognition to royal supremacy within the Church; episcopacy and lay patronage were restored; conventicling was outlawed; the first four new bishops were consecrated at Westminster. The Solemn League and Covenant was burnt in public on the orders of the English Cavalier Parliament.

1662   Crawford and Cassillis resigned after refusing to take the oath condemning the Covenant. The Act of Indemnity excluded over seven hundred people, who became subject to fines. An Act of Parliament demanded that all ministers appointed after 1649 should be re-presented by their patrons to the bishop – 268 ministers were deprived of their livings in consequence by 1663. All ministers and schoolmasters were required to gain a bishop's licence.

1663   Middleton was dismissed. Rothes was appointed Treasurer and King's Commissioner. Fines were imposed for non-attendance at church. The Church Commission was established. Archbishop Sharp was appointed to the Privy Council. England imposed increased customs duties on Scottish exports of coal, linen, salt and cattle.

1664   Death of Glencairn. Alexander Burnet appointed Archbishop of Glasgow.

1665   A land tax was imposed to help pay for the cost of the Anglo-Dutch War.

1666   The Pentland Rising, which took place in the South-West as a protest against the oppressive tax gathering methods employed by the military, was crushed at Rullion Green.

1667   The army was considerably reduced in size and replaced by a militia under the leadership of the local nobilty. The cess tax was reintroduced.

1668   Lauderdale, who was appointed to the English 'Cabal' government, controlled all Scottish affairs at court and also became a member of the committees for trade and colonies; he secured the demotion of his rival, Rothes. The English parliament passed the Irish Cattle Bill, which helped the cattle trade by restricting Irish exports to Scotland. The king's proposal to establish an Anglo-Scottish economic union failed.

1669   The Act of Supremacy formally recognised the king's absolute supremacy within the church. Lauderdale was appointed King's Commissioner with John Hay, 2nd Earl of Tweeddale, as his deputy. The duty on Scottish cattle exports was removed. Proposals for an Anglo-Scottish commercial union broke down, but the English Cabal started discussions for an Anglo-Scottish legislative union. With the first Declaration of Indulgence, Lauderdale launched a policy of indulgence towards moderate dissenters by permitting deprived ministers to regain their livings on acceptance of episcopacy on limited terms; this was only a modest success with a mere 42 ministers conforming. This measure and the Act of Supremacy were fiercely opposed by Archbishop Burnet, who was replaced by Robert Leighton.

1670   The Clanking Act was passed by parliament, making preaching at conventicles a capital offence. Negotiations for an Anglo-Scottish union broke down.

1671   Tweeddale was dismissed for his presbyterian sympathies.

1672   A second Declaration of Indulgence, issued by the Privy Council, increased the total of conforming ministers to 136, but also created a hard core of dissident clergy who held illegal conventicles, especially in the South-West.

1673   In parliament Hamilton and Tweeddale led protests against Lauderdale's government in relation to economic and religious grievances.

1674   The king continued to give support to Lauderdale, creating him earl; parliament was dissolved (until 1681) and Lauderdale's opponents, including Hamilton, removed from the Privy Council. Leighton, who was opposed to toleration, resigned as Archbishop of Glasgow after failing to gain comprehension for Presbyterians within the episcopal system; he was replaced by Burnet, heralding harsher policies towards dissenters; troops were employed to suppress conventicles in the South-West, but with little success.

1678   The government, fearing loss of control in the South-West, quartered there 'the Highland Host' militia of 8,000 men, whose methods were brutal.

1679   Archbishop Sharp was assassinated outside St Andrews Cathedral. The *Rutherglen Declaration* was issued condemning the systematic betrayal of the Covenant since 1648. After John Graham's government troops had been defeated in their attack on an armed conventicle at Drumclog, an Anglo-Scottish army under the Duke of Monmouth (recently appointed Captain-General in Scotland) overwhelmed the covenanter rebels at

Bothwell Brig. Lauderdale authorised the third indulgence, granting pardon to the majority of the rebels. James, Duke of York, began his stay in Scotland as the King's Commissioner to the Estates, gaining great popularity with the nobility.

1680   A rising of radical Covenanters, led by Richard Cameron, was suppressed at Aird's Moss (after their *Sanquar Declaration* had declared holy war on Charles II).

1681   Parliament was recalled. It sanctioned a further repressive policy to eliminate dissent, launching a period of brutal executions, imprisonments and fines; decreed that James, Duke of York, was the rightful heir; and passed the Test Act, which required all those in office to swear an oath recognising royal supremacy within the Church. A committee of trade was established. The Duke of Rothes died; William Douglas, 3rd Earl of Queensberry, was appointed Treasurer. The Marquess of Argyll fled abroad.

1682   Lauderdale died. George Gordon, Earl of Aberdeen, was appointed Chancellor. A commission for securing peace in the Highlands was established, heralding a more conciliatory policy.

1683   A secret committee of seven councillors was established in Edinburgh to liaise with the king.

1684   Sir George Mackenzie published his *Jus Regium* in favour of absolute monarchy. James Renwick, a supporter of the rebel Richard Cameron, published the *Apologetical Declaration*, a renunciation of allegiance to the king. James Drummond, 4th Earl of Perth, was appointed Chancellor; John Drummond was appointed Secretary.

1685   James II and VII succeeded to the throne. Queensberry was appointed King's Commissioner to the Estates. Parliament granted the king excise duty for life. Argyll landed in western Scotland to lead a rebellion, but the rebels were quickly crushed and Argyll was executed.

1686   John Drummond, Earl of Melfort, was appointed King's Commissioner to the Estates. Parliament's rejection of the king's offer of free trade with England in exchange for toleration for Catholics was followed by the dissolution of parliament and riots in Edinburgh. James appointed the catholic Earl of Dunbarton as army commander. By royal prerogative, James granted freedom of private worship to Catholics and Quakers.

1687   James II's first Declaration of Indulgence granted complete toleration and office-holding rights to Roman Catholics; rights of private worship to Presbyterians; and the relaxation of penal laws for conventiclers.

1688   William of Orange invaded England (Nov.); James II and VII fled to France (Dec.). The government in Edinburgh broke up with the Earls of Glencairn and Crawford conducting affairs. The king's control of the localities had already been lost.

1689   The Convention of the Estates met in Edinburgh (Mar.), eventually evolving into a parliament which sat until 1702. It elected a committee to be responsible for the government; declared the crown forfeit; proclaimed William and Mary joint sovereigns; approved the Claim of Right and the Articles of Grievance, which detailed the rights of parliament in its relationship with the crown (Apr.). William and Mary were crowned jointly (May), implicitly accepting the conditions. Episcopacy was abolished (July); in a presbyterian backlash, 152 ministers were deprived of their livings by the commission of the General Assembly. James Graham of Claverhouse, Viscount Dundee, led a Jacobite rising in the Central Highlands, defeating government forces at Killiecrankie (July) with the loss of his own life; his troops later were defeated at Dunkeld (Aug.).

1690   The second session of William's parliament met, dominated by Sir James Montgomery's faction of Whig/Presbyterians; it abolished the Committee of the Articles; restored the presbyterian church government and the Westminster Confession of Faith; vested church patronage in the heritors, elders and presbyteries; repealed the Act of Supremacy; and restored those ministers ejected in 1662. The General Assembly met, dominated by die-hard Presbyterians, and instituted a purge of episcopal sympathisers from parishes and universities.

1691   In the face of continued unrest in the Highlands, Sir John Dalrymple, the Scottish Secretary, gave the clans until the end of the year to recognise William as king (agreed with the chiefs at Achallader).

1692   Alastair McIan failed to meet Dalrymple's deadline; the MacDonalds of Glencoe were therefore subjected to punitive action with 38 people killed in the Massacre of Glencoe (Feb.). Scotland experienced the first of seven successive very poor harvests.

1694   The king agreed to let the General Assembly regulate its own affairs.

1695   Grain shortages were severe, this year marking the start of 'King William's III Years'. Prices began to rise sharply. The Bank of Scotland was founded. Parliament established the Company of Scotland with a monopoly of trade with Asia, Africa and the Indies – a move which was greeted with hostility by the English parliament and the East India Company.

1696   England imposed tighter restrictions on Scottish trade with the colonies.

1697   The Barrier Act granted to presbyteries the power of decision-making previously held by the General Assembly (thus removing some of the crown's influence). The Company of Scotland agreed to support the Darien Scheme in Panama.

1698   The Company of Scotland's expedition departed for Panama to establish the colony of Caledonia. The famine continued with widespread deaths due to starvation. James Douglas, 2nd Duke of Queensberry, was appointed King's Commissioner to parliament.

1699   The harvest again failed; nearly one-third of the population had either died or fled since the start of the crisis.

1700   The Darien Scheme collapsed in failure with the death of c 2,000 colonists and the loss of £1.8 million; great anger was expressed in parliament at the perceived undermining of the scheme by the English.

1701   Death of James II and VII; Louis XIV of France recognised his son, James Edward, as James III and VIII.

1702   The Privy Council ratified William's declaration of war on France over the Spanish succession – a potentially damaging blow to Scottish overseas markets. Death of William III. The Convention was dissolved. The first free election since the Revolution resulted in Queensberry's court party failing to secure a majority – an indication of mounting anger against English involvement. Negotiations commenced regarding a possible Union of the two parliaments (Nov.).

1703   Negotiations for Union broke down (Feb.). James Ogilvie, Earl of Seafield, was appointed Chancellor. The opposition gained the passing of the Act of Security, which stipulated that royal succession in Scotland would be controlled by parliament – a clear response to the passing of the Act of Settlement in England (1701) without consultation in Scotland; the measure failed to gain royal assent. Parliament passed the Act Anent [i.e. concerning] Peace and War, stipulating the right of the Scottish parliament to control these matters.

1704   The Bank of Scotland suspended payments. Queensberry was dismissed as the Queen's Commissioner to parliament and replaced by John Hay, 2nd Marquis of Tweeddale and leader of the 'new party' or 'squadrone'. The Act of Security received royal assent.

1705   The English parliament passed the Aliens Act (Feb.) stipulating that all Scots were to be treated as aliens and their exports to England banned unless, by the end of the year, they repealed their Act of Security and commenced negotiations for either Union or Hanoverian succession. Hostility to the English surfaced when the crew of an English ship on an alleged charge of piracy were hanged under pressure from the mob. Queensberry was reinstated as effective leader of the government with assistance from John Campbell, 2nd Duke of Argyll, as Queen's Commissioner. Parliament agreed to leave to the queen the choice of commissioners to negotiate Union. The Alien Act was repealed by the English parliament (Nov.).

1706   The Union Commissioners were appointed with Queensberry and his allies representing Scotland; negotiations commenced (Apr.); a draft treaty was agreed (July) – the two national parliaments were replaced with a parliament of Great Britain, including 45 MPs and 16 peers from Scotland; the Scots were granted free trade with England and the colonies, plus a concessionary rate of taxation; protestant succession through the House of Hanover was ratified; Scottish law and legal administration were to remain unchanged; compensation was granted to the Company of Scotland; a common flag and coinage were agreed together with unified weights and measures. Parliament passed the Kirk Act to secure the protestant religion and the presbyterian church – and an additional article was inserted into the draft treaty to guarantee the presbyterian church settlement of 1690.

1707   After extensive use of patronage by Queensberry, parliament ratified the Treaty of Union by a majority of 43 votes (Jan.); the Scottish parliament was dissolved (Apr.); and the royal assent given (May).

1708   The Privy Council was abolished. James Stuart led an expedition to Scotland with French support, but failed to land.

1711   Death of Queensberry. The Scottish peers boycotted the Lords after Hamilton, Duke of Brandon, was refused permission to sit as an English peer instead of a representative one.

1712   Parliament granted toleration in Scotland for Episcopalians and restored lay patronage in the Church of Scotland; riots took place in Edinburgh and Leith.

1713   Parliament imposed the malt tax on Scotland in contravention of the terms of the Act of Union. A proposal, made in the House of Lords with backing from Argyll, to dissolve the Union was narrowly defeated

1714   Death of Queen Anne (Aug.).

Scotland: major officers of state

Chancellors and Keepers of the Great Seal (KGS)

1599   John Graham, Earl of Montrose
1604   Alexander Seton, Lord Fyvie (Earl of Dunfermline, 1605)
1622   Sir George Hay (Earl of Kinnoull, 1633)
1634   John Spottiswoode, Archbishop of St Andrews

1638	John, Marquess of Hamilton (KGS; Duke, 1643)
1641	John Campbell, Earl of Loudoun
1652	Alexander Jaffray (KGS)
1656	Samuel Disbrowe (KGS)
1660	William Cunningham, Earl of Glencairn
1664	John Leslie, Earl of Rothes (KGS to 1667, when appointed Chancellor)
1681	Office vacant
1682	Sir George Gordon, Earl of Aberdeen
1684	James Drummond, Earl of Perth
1689	In commission
1692	John Hay, Earl of Tweeddale
1696	Patrick Hume, Lord Polwarth (Earl of Marchmont, 1697)
1702	James Ogilvy, Earl of Seafield
1704	John Hay, Marquess of Tweeddale
1705	James Ogilvy, Earl of Seafield (to 1708; then Chancellor again in 1713)

Chamberlains

1583	Ludovick Stewart, Duke of Lennox; granted hereditary office, 1603
1624	After the death of the duke, the office remained hereditary in his family until 1672, when it reverted to the crown
1673	James Scott, Duke of Buccleuch and Monmouth (to 1685)
1680	Charles Lennox, Duke of Richmond and Lennox, granted hereditary office after Monmouth's death; resigned 1705
1705	Office vacant
1711	In commission

Treasurers and Comptrollers

In the fifteenth century, the Chamberlain's financial functions were transferred to two new officials, the Comptroller (who was responsible for financing the royal household) and the Treasurer (who was responsible for the remaining revenue and expenditure). The two offices were united from 1610.

1599	Sir David Murray (Lord Scone, 1604); *Comptroller*
1601	Sir George Home, Earl of Dunbar (also *Comptroller* from 1610)
1608	Sir James Hay (Feb.–Aug.; *Comptroller*)
1611	Office vacant
1613	Robert Carr, Earl of Somerset
1616	John Erskine, Earl of Mar

1630	William Douglas, Earl of Morton
1636	John Stewart, Earl of Traquair
1641	In commission
1644	John Lindsay, Earl of Crawford
1649	In commission (to 1651)
1661	John Lindsay, Earl of Crawford
1663	John Leslie, Earl of Rothes
1667	In commission
1682	William Douglas, Marquess of Queensberry (Duke, 1684)
1686	In commission

Secretaries

1598	James Elphinstone (Lord Balmarino, 1603); to 1609
1608	Sir Alexander Hay; to 1612
1612	Sir Thomas Hamilton (Earl of Melrose, 1619); to 1627
1626	Sir William Alexander (Earl of Stirling, 1633); to 1640
1627	Sir Archibald Acheson; to 1634
1640	William Hamilton, Earl of Lanark (Duke, 1649); dismissed by king, but confirmed by parliament, 1644; to 1649
	Sir James Galloway (Lord Dunkeld, 1645); to 1646, but not recognised by parliament after 1641
1644	Sir Robert Spottiswoode; appointed by king, but not recognised by parliament; to 1645
1649	William Ker, Earl of Lothian; to 1660 (though not acting after 1651)
1660	John Maitland, Earl of Lauderdale (Duke, 1672); to 1680
1680	Alexander Stewart, Earl of Moray; to 1688
1682	Charles, Earl of Middleton; to 1684
1684	John Drummond (Earl of Melfort, 1686); to 1688
1689	George, Earl of Melville; to 1691
1691	John Dalrymple (Earl of Stair, 1703); to 1695
1692	James Johnston; to 1696
1696	John Murray, Earl of Tullibardine (Duke of Atholl, 1703); to 1698
	Sir James Ogilvy (Earl of Seafield, 1701); to 1702
1699	John, Lord Carmichael; to 1702
1702	James Douglas, Duke of Queensberry; to 1704
	George Mackenzie, Viscount Tarbat (Earl of Cromarty, 1703); to 1704
1704	John Ker, Earl of Roxburghe; to 1705
	James Ogilvy, Earl of Seafield; to 1705
1705	William Johnston, Marquess of Annadale (Mar.–Sept.)

	Hugh Campbell, Earl of Loudoun; to 1708
	John Erskine, Earl of Mar; to 1709
1709	James Douglas, Duke of Queensberry; to 1711
1713	John Erskine, Earl of Mar; to 1714

Justices General

The Earls of Argyll were granted the hereditary right to this office in the sixteenth century. However, the 8th Earl resigned it to the crown in 1628.

1628	William Graham, Earl of Menteith; to 1633
1635	Sir William Elphinstone
1641	Sir Thomas Hope; to 1643
1646	William Cunningham, Earl of Glencairn; to 1649
1649	John Kennedy, Earl of Cassillis; to 1651
1661	John Murray, Earl of Atholl
1675	Alexander Stewart, Earl of Moray
1676	Sir Archibald Primrose
1678	Sir George Mackenzie (Earl of Cromarty, 1703)
1680	William Douglas, Earl of Queensberry
1682	James Drummond, Earl of Perth
1684	George Livingston, Earl of Linlithgow
1689	Robert Ker, Earl of Lothian; to 1703
1704	George Mackenzie, Earl of Cromarty
1710	Archibald Campbell, Earl of Ilay (Duke of Argyll, 1743); to 1761

Scotland: Archbishops

Episcopal government in the Church of Scotland was abolished in 1638, restored in 1661 and abolished for a second time in 1689.

St Andrews		**Glasgow**	
1604	George Gledstanes	1603	John Spottiswoode
1615	John Spottiswoode (to 1638)	1615	James Law (to 1632)
		1633	Patrick Lindsay (to 1638)
1661	James Sharp	1661	Andrew Fairfoul
1679	Alexander Burnet	1664	Alexander Burnet (to 1669)
1684	Arthur Rose (died 1704)	1671	Robert Leighton
		1674	Alexander Burnet
		1679	Arthur Rose
		1684	Alexander Cairncross
		1687	John Paterson (died 1708)

Ireland: chronology of events

1603   James I was proclaimed in Dublin as King of Ireland (5 April); ratification of this was initially refused by the city of Cork. The Earl of Tyrone surrendered at Mellifont and pledged his loyalty to the king. Mountjoy, the Lord Deputy, sanctioned the private celebration of mass; was later appointed Lord Lieutenant and was succeeded as Lord Deputy by Sir George Carey. Rory O'Donnell was created Earl of Tyrconnell; and Sir John Davies Solicitor-General. A new Irish coinage was minted.

1604   Catholic clergy were expelled from Munster by order of the Lord President, Sir Henry Brouncker. Sir Arthur Chichester was appointed Lord Deputy.

1605   A general amnesty was issued for offences committed during the rebellion and the protection of the law granted to all inhabitants. A proclamation decreed that all persons were the free subjects of the king and not subjects of any lord. Attempts were made to enforce church attendance on Catholics and to expel Jesuit priests.

1606   Death of Mountjoy; appointment of Sir John Davies as Attorney-General. Establishment of a commission to remedy defective titles to land occupancy. St Anthony's Franciscan College was founded in Louvain.

1607   The Earls of Tyrone and Tyrconnell, having fled to the continent, were charged with high treason and subjected to the forfeiture of their lands. Donal Ballagh O'Cahan replaced them as Commissioner of Justice in Ulster and was knighted.

1608   Plans were formulated for the plantation of confiscated lands in six Ulster counties. Sir Richard Nugent was created Earl of Westmeath after pardon for involvement in a conspiracy to seize Dublin castle. A rebellion was staged in Derry by Sir Cahir O'Doherty, who was later killed. Death of the Earl of Tyrconnell in exile. Appointment of Sir Humphrey Winche as Lord Chief Justice.

1609   Plans for the plantation of the six Ulster counties (Armagh, Cavan, Coleraine, Donegal, Fermanagh and Tyrone) were completed with a detailed survey.

1610   Legal documentation was prepared for the settlement of 500,000 acres in Ulster and a proclamation issued outlining procedure for the removal of native inhabitants. Agreement was made between the crown and the city of London for the plantation of the town and the county of Coleraine, the barony of Loughinsholin and the city of Derry under the title of the county of Londonderry. Arrival of prospective settlers commenced.

1612   The Bishop of Down and Connar (Cornelius O'Devany) was executed for treasonable involvement with Tyrone. Dungannon was incorporated – the first of 40 new boroughs.

1613   The new county of Londonderry was incorporated. Christopher Hampton was appointed Archbishop of Armagh and Primate of All Ireland. A controversy over the Speakership erupted at the opening of the Irish parliament (the first since 1585) with the catholic members walking out in protest. The king summoned the first national convocation of the Church of Ireland in Dublin. The king agreed to the farming out of Irish customs for a yearly charge of £6,000.

1614   In a proclamation against the toleration of popery, the king ordered Lord Deputy Chichester to enforce the expulsion of Jesuit priests and to impose protestant worship on Catholics.

1615   Concern was expressed by Lord Deputy Chichester about the threat of conspiracy in Ulster. Parliament was dissolved. The Confession of Faith was adopted by the convocation of the Church of Ireland.

1616   Sir Oliver St John was appointed Lord Deputy in succession to Chichester, who was created Baron Belfast. Death of Tyrone in exile.

1617   Proclamations were issued for the expulsion of catholic clergy and the punishment of those guilty of harbouring Jesuits.

1618   Natives were threatened with fines for failure to vacate (by 1st May 1619) lands assigned for settlement.

1619   Death of the Lord Chancellor, Thomas Jones, who was replaced by Sir Adam Loftles.

1620   Richard Boyle was created Earl of Cork.

1621   Authorisation was given for the plantation of parts of King's County, Queen's County, Leitrim and Westmeath.

1622   Appointment as Lord Deputy of Henry Cary, Viscount Falkland.

1623   City officials were required to take the oath of supremacy. Appointment of Thomas Fleming as catholic Archbishop of Dublin.

1625   Appointment of James Ussher as Archbishop of Armagh. Charles I, who succeeded his father as king, ordered an end to the imposition of fines for recusancy.

1626   The king offered 'graces' (or concessions in religion) to catholic lords in exchange for army subsidies – a move condemned by Archbishop Ussher and 12 other bishops.

1627   Roger Boyle was created Baron Broghill. A 'great assembly' in Dublin was dissolved by Falkland when it proved hostile to the king's proposal of 'graces'. Sir William St Leger was appointed Lord President of Munster.

1628   A delegation of catholic old English lords guaranteed a subsidy of £120,000 over three years in exchange for concessions negotiated in the '51 Instructions and Graces'.

1629   Fears were expressed over a catholic plot in Leinster. Attempts to enforce a proclamation to close all catholic monasteries and churches provoked riots in Dublin.

1631   The Earl of Cork was appointed Lord High Treasurer.

1632   Appointment of Viscount Wentworth as Lord Deputy. The king ordered the reimposition of fines on Catholics for recusancy (as a plan to raise more money), but later revoked this on payment of £20,000 by the catholic old English lords.

1634   Charles I's first Irish parliament met and granted six subsidies to the king, each worth £50,000. The anglican 39 Articles and the Canons of 1604 were adopted by the Convocation of the Church of Ireland.

1635   The king secured title to lands in Boyle, Mayo and Sligo, but was resisted by jurors in Galway (who, in 1636, were imprisoned in consequence). The City of London and Irish Society was found guilty of mismanaging the Londonderry plantation, fined and made to forfeit its Irish property.

1637   The king finally secured title to lands in Galway.

1638   The Bishop of Down and Connor criticised the passing of the National Covenant in Scotland.

1639   All Scottish landowners in Ireland were forced to take the 'Black Oath', swearing allegiance. Lord Deputy Wentworth returned to England to become the king's chief adviser.

1640   Charles I's second Irish parliament met and granted £200,000 to help put down the rebellion in Scotland. Wentworth, who was created Earl of Strafford and appointed Lord Lieutenant, raised 9,000 troops in Ireland for the war against the Scots. The Irish House of Commons sent a remonstrance against Strafford to London.

1641   Strafford was executed after a Bill for his attainder was passed by the House of Commons in England. The Earl of Ormond was appointed to command the army in Ireland. The king granted 30 concessions in exchange for financial subsidies. An armed rising, planned by Hugh MacMahon, Conor Maguire and Sir Phelim O'Neill, began in Ulster when the latter seized Charlement fort (22nd Oct.). The rebellion quickly spread to Lowth, Fermanagh, Monaghan, Connaught, Wicklow and Armagh. Rebels under Rory O'More defeated government forces at Julianstown Bridge, near Drogheda. An alliance to protect their religion was formed between the Ulster Irish and the old English lords after a meeting at Knockcrofty, near Drogheda. Appointment of Sir Charles Coote as Governor of Dublin.

1642   The king sent 1,900 additional troops from England under Lt-Col. George Monck. Maj.-Gen. Robert Monro landed at Carrickfergus with a Scottish army to assist the government. Ormond laid waste the Boyne valley and County Kildaire. The Confederation of Kilkenny, with its own supreme council, was established by catholic clergy. The first properly constituted presbytery in Ireland, formed by Scottish soldiers, met at Carrickfergus. Catholics were expelled from parliament. After the outbreak of civil war in England, Ormond was appointed Lt-Gen. of the king's forces in Ireland. The General Assembly of the Confederation Catholics asserted the rights of a parliament, formed a government at Kilkenny and organised the confederate armies into a proper command structure.

1643   Ormond negotiated at Sigginstown a cessation of hostilities between the royalists and the Confederates (15th Sept.). The English parliament ordered that the Solemn League and Covenant was to be imposed on Ireland, a measure opposed by the king. Ormond was appointed Lord Lieutenant. The second and third meetings of the General Assembly of the Confederation were held.

1644   The trials were held of Hugh MacMahon and Conor Maguire (both were later executed). Parliament appointed Lord Inchiquin as Lord President of Munster. Negotiations between Ormond and the Confederates broke down. The fourth meeting of the General Assembly of the Confederation was held.

1645   Expiration of the cessation (10th Apr.). Appointment of Sir Charles Coote by parliament as Lord President of Connaught. The fifth meeting of the General Assembly of the Confederation was held. A secret treaty between the king and the Confederates was negotiated by Lord Glamorgan (25th Aug.) – followed by a second one (20th Dec.). Archbishop Giovanni Rinuccini, papal envoy to the Confederation, arrived at Kenmare. Glamorgan was arrested by Ormond on a charge of high treason.

1646   The sixth meeting of the Confederation was held. The king disowned the Glamorgan treaties. Ormond secured a peace with the Confederates. Rinuccini repudiated the Ormond peace and ejected his opponents from the supreme council. Lord Glamorgan joined the Confederation. The Civil War in England ended with Charles I held in custody.

1647   The seventh and eighth meetings of the General Assembly of the Confederation were held. The Ormond peace was rejected by the Confederation under Rinuccini's influence. Parliamentary commissioners from England negotiated a treaty with Ormond, who then surrendered Dublin. Parliamentary forces under Col. Michael Jones defeated the Confederates at Dungan's Hill, near Trim; and those under Lord Inchiquin defeated Confederates at Knockanuss, near Kanturk.

1648   Inchiquin, having deserted the parliamentary cause for that of the king, negotiated a truce with the Confederation – a move condemned by Rinuccini, who imposed excommunication on those involved. The ninth and last meeting of the General Assembly of the Confederation was held. Owen Roe O'Neill, commander of the Confederates' army in Ulster, broke with the Confederation's supreme council.

1649   A second peace with the Confederation was secured by Ormond. Charles I was executed. Rinuccini left Ireland. Oliver Cromwell was appointed commander of parliament's forces in Ireland and Governor-General. Ormond, who had been appointed Lord Lieutenant by Charles II in exile, was defeated by Jones at Rathmines. Henry Ireton landed from England with parliamentary reinforcements. Cromwell captured Drogheda and Wexford, massacring the garrisons and civilian occupants. Parliamentary forces also captured Belfast and New Ross. Death of Owen Roe O'Neill.

1650   Appointment of Ireton as Lord President of Munster. Cromwell captured Kilkenny, Cashel and Clonmel before returning to England and leaving Ireton in military command. Charles II landed in Scotland (28th June) and subsequently repudiated Ormond's peace terms to the rebels. Parliamentary forces captured Athlone, Carlow, Waterford and Duncannon. Parliament appointed commissioners to be responsible for civilian administration. Ormond and Inchiquin fled abroad.

1651   Parliament passed the Navigation Act, which limited the carriage of imported goods to English ships. Ireton, who had secured the surrender of Limerick, died and was succeeded by Edmund Ludlow as Commander-in-Chief. Parliament appointed commissioners to be responsible for both military and civilian administration, having abolished the positions of Lord Deputy and Lord Lieutenant.

1652   Roscommon, Galway, Ballyshannon and Ross Castle surrendered to parliament. Charles Fleetwood was appointed Commander-in-Chief and leading commissioner. The English parliament passed an Act for the settlement of Ireland, categorising the population according to guilt in the rebellion.

1653   The expulsion of catholic priests was ordered by the commissioners, who also made plans to transport 8,000 Irish vagrants to the West Indies. Ireland was granted representation by six MPs in the English Barebone's Parliament. Plans were formed for a land settlement commission to establish how much land (especially in the rebellious area) was available to satisfy debts incurred in the war; to finalise details for the transplantation of Irish into Connaught; and to establish valid titles to all land in Ireland.

1654   Cromwell's appointment as Lord Protector was proclaimed in Dublin. The tasks of mapping forfeited land and allocating land in settlement of debts to soldiers and adventurers commenced. Thirty Irish MPs sat in the 1st Protectorate Parliament. The government stipulated that all transplantation to Connaught should have been completed by March 1655. A ban was imposed on the celebration of Christmas.

1655   Those refusing to be transplanted were to be subject to court martial and the threat of the death penalty. The government ordered the clearance of papists from Dublin, the evacuation of inhabitants of Galway by November, the arrest of all Quakers and a ban on the celebration of Easter.

1656   Death of James Ussher, Archbishop of Armagh. Appointment of William Steele as Lord Chancellor.

1657   The English parliament passed an Act for the attainder of rebels and papists in Ireland, but pardoning those who had accepted transplantation. Appointment of Henry Cromwell as Lord Deputy.

1658   Richard Cromwell succeeded to the office of Lord Protector on the death of his father (3 Sept.).

1659   Robert Goodwin, John Jones and William Steele were appointed by the Long Parliament as commissioners for Ireland; later joined by Miles Corbett and Matthew Tomlinson. Dublin Castle was seized by Sir Hardress Waller in support of the Long Parliament (which had recently been expelled by the army).

1660   Lord Broghill and Sir Charles Coote came out in favour of the restoration of the monarchy. Charles II was proclaimed King of England (8th May) and King of Ireland in Dublin (14th May). Appointment of Coote as Lord President of Connaught – also created Earl of Mountrath. The Act of Oblivion excluded those involved in the Irish rebellion. Parliament passed the Navigation Act to regulate England's trade, dealing with England and Ireland as one entity. A royal declaration ratified the Cromwellian land settlement, but authorised the restoration of innocent papists to their land.

1661   The Church of Ireland was re-established and John Bramhall appointed as its Archbishop of Armagh. James Butler, Marquess of Ormond (from 1642), was created a duke and appointed to the offices of Lord High Steward in England and Lord Lieutenant in Ireland. Charles II's first Irish parliament met. Death of the 1st Earl of Mountrath.

1662   Export of Irish wool prohibited by the English parliament. The Act of Settlement was passed restoring 'innocent Catholics' to their land, but compensating current holders with lands elsewhere; a Court of Claims was established.

1663   A planned rising by Col. Thomas Blood to protect the interests of protestant landowners collapsed. Limits were imposed on exports of Irish cattle to England and on trade between Ireland and the colonies.

1665   The Act of Explanation was passed ratifying, but not increasing, the decrees of innocence issued in 1663.

1666   A second Court of Claims was established to hear further claims under the terms of the Act of Settlement. The Act of Uniformity made obligatory the use of the Book of Common Prayer; the licensing of schoolmasters by Church of Ireland bishops; and the taking of the oath of supremacy by all office-holders.

1667   Irish cattle and meat were prohibited from sale in English and Scottish markets.

1668   Appointment of Richard Jones as Chancellor of the Exchequer.

1669   Ormond was replaced as Lord Lieutenant by John, Lord Robartes. Appointment of Oliver Plunkett as catholic Archbishop of Armagh.

1670   Appointment of John, Lord Berkeley as Lord Lieutenant. The catholic bishops, led by Archbishop Plunkett, declared their loyalty to the king.

1671   A second Navigation Act banned direct imports to Ireland from the colonies. Richard Jones, Earl of Ranelagh, came to the 'Ranelagh Understanding' with the king concerning revenue farmers.

1672   In the Declaration of Indulgence, the king promised the suspension of restrictive legislation on Catholics and dissenters. Appointment of Arthur Capel, Earl of Essex, as Lord Lieutenant. The king made his first grant of money (*Regium Donum*) to presbyterian ministers.

1673   The exclusion of all non-Anglicans from office was effected under the terms of the Test Act. Roman Catholic priests were banished and religious houses closed by royal proclamation.

1677   The Duke of Ormond was reappointed as Lord Lieutenant.

1678   The Popish Plot was revealed by Titus Oates and Israel Tonge, who cited Peter Talbot, Archbishop of Dublin, for complicity. Ormond ordered the immediate enforcement of the closure of religious houses and the banishment of Roman Catholic clergy.

1679   Oliver Plunkett, catholic Archbishop of Armagh, was arrested on a charge of complicity in the Popish Plot.

1680   The trial of Plunkett in Ireland collapsed. Work commenced on the Royal Hospital for Irish soldiers at Kilmainham, Dublin.

1681   Plunkett was tried and executed in London.

1684   Establishment of the Dublin Philosophical Society.

1685   James II succeeded Charles II as King of England and Ireland. Richard Talbot was created Earl of Tyrconnell.

1686   Appointment of Henry Hyde, Earl of Clarendon, as Lord Lieutenant. The king authorised catholic bishops and archbishops to be paid from the Exchequer. Appointment of Sir Charles Porter as Lord Chancellor. Tyrconnell, who was appointed Lt-Gen. of the army in Ireland, began the mass recruitment of Roman Catholics.

1687   Porter was replaced as Lord Chancellor by a Catholic, Sir Alexander Fitton. Tyrconnell, who was appointed Lord Deputy, promised equal protection to subjects of all religions.

1688   The king authorised the appointment of Jesuits to fill teaching vacancies in all government schools. Death of the Duke of Ormond. William of Orange invaded England; James II was considered by parliament to have abdicated after his flight abroad. The gates of Derry were closed by apprentice boys against the catholic forces of Lord Antrim.

1689   William and Mary succeeded to the throne (13th Feb.). A royal proclamation offered security and toleration to Jacobites on their surrender. James II landed at Kinsale with an armed following (12th Mar.). The Jacobites defeated the Ulster Protestants at the 'Break of Dromore' in County Down (14 Mar.). Tyrconnell was created Duke of Tyrconnell by James, who called an Irish parliament (the 'Patriot Parliament'). The city of Derry, besieged by Jacobites for 105 days, was relieved by William's fleet. William's Enniskillen troops under William Wolseley defeated the Jacobites at Newtownbutler (31st July). An Anglo-Dutch army of reinforcements under Marshal Schomberg arrived (13th Aug.); captured Carrickfergus and successfully defended Dundalk against an attack by James.

1690   French troops arrived at Cork under the Comte de Lauzun; William arrived at Carrickfergus (14th June) and, with an army of 36,000, defeated James (with 25,000) at the Battle of the Boyne (1st July). William entered Dublin, offering pardon to all Jacobites except their leaders. James fled to France (4th July) followed later by Tyrconnell and Lauzun (12th Sept.). William's forces took Kilkenny, Clonmel and Waterford, but failed to capture Athlone and Limerick after siege. William returned to England (5th Sept.), leaving Baron von Ginkel as army commander. The Duke of Marlborough arrived at Cork (22nd Sept.), taking the city after siege (28th Sept.).

1691   Tyrconnell returned to Limerick from France (14th Jan.); a French army under the Marquis de St Ruth arrived in Limerick (8th May). Ginkell captured Athlone (30th June); and Galway (21st July). After a siege of Limerick, a truce was declared (24th Sept.) as a preliminary to peace negotiations. The Treaty of Limerick (3rd Oct.), which signalled the end of the war, permitted James's Irish army to leave for France and promised Roman Catholics similar privileges in religion as those enjoyed under Charles II. An Act of Parliament was passed in England which introduced a declaration against Roman Catholics in a new oath of supremacy, thus effectively excluding them from public office (24th Dec.). Death of Tyrconnell.

1692   Appointment of Henry, Viscount Sidney, as Lord Lieutenant. The Irish parliament, which met with a totally protestant membership, expressed hostility to William's plans to extend further concessions to Roman Catholics under the Act of Settlement. The lands of those outlawed for supporting James were confiscated (over one million acres).

1694   The maximum life of parliament was fixed at three years by the Triennial Act passed in England. Death of Queen Mary II.

1695   Appointment of Henry, Lord Chapel, as Lord Deputy; and Robert Rochfort as Attorney-General (who was also elected Speaker of the House of Commons). In contradiction to the spirit of the Treaty of Limerick, parliament passed an act banning Catholics from recruitment in the army, bearing arms without a licence, establishing schools or sending their children abroad for education.

1696   Deaths of Capel (the Lord Deputy), and Porter (the Lord Chancellor). Irish linen was admitted to England without duty.

1697   Appointment of John Methuen as Lord Chancellor. Acts were passed banishing papists who exercised an ecclesiastical jurisdiction; and forbidding burials in any suppressed religious buildings. A Huguenot settlement under Samuel-Louis Crommelin was established at Lisnagarvey to further the development of the Irish linen industry.

1698   Publication of William Molyneaux's tract, *The Case of Ireland's being Bound by Acts of Parliament in England stated*. Transportation of banned religious groups commenced.

1699   Acts of Parliament passed in England imposed duties on the export of Irish woollens and restricted their export exclusively to English ports. A further Act sanctioned the establishment of a standing army in Ireland of 12,000 men.

1700   A subsidy was granted to Crommelin to enable him to set up a linen manufactory. A start was made by the forfeiture trustees on the sale of confiscated lands.

1701   Death of James II in France. Appointment of Laurence Hyde, Earl of Rochester, as Lord Lieutenant. Building commenced on the Royal Barracks and Marsh's Library (Ireland's first public library). A severe economic recession commenced, lasting until 1706.

1702   Death of William III and accession of Queen Anne.

1703   Appointments of William King as Archbishop of Dublin; Narcissus Marsh as Archbishop of Armagh; James Butler, 2nd Duke of Ormond, as Lord Lieutenant; and Sir Richard Cox as Lord Chancellor. The Irish parliament, in an address to the queen, pledged its belief in the vital importance of maintaining the link with England; and, subsequently, advocated a full union between the two countries. The Abjuration Act was passed by the English parliament, which required all office-holders to swear allegiance to Queen Anne as the rightful ruler.

1704   An Act was passed imposing restrictions on Catholics regarding land purchase, leases and legacies; and a sacramental test for public office on both Catholics and protestant dissenters alike. Catholic priests in Ireland were required by the Registration Act to register in court, placing two bonds for £50 each for their good behaviour.

1705   An Act was passed by the English parliament sanctioning the direct export of Irish linen to the British colonies.

1707   Appointment of Thomas Herbert, Earl of Pembroke, as Lord Lieutenant.

1709   Appointment of Thomas, Earl of Wharton, as Lord Lieutenant. All registered priests were required to swear the oath of abjuration (but only 33 did so). The Irish House of Lords urged union with England, following the Act of Union with Scotland.

1710   A board of trustees was appointed for linen manufacture in Ireland. Severe penalties were introduced for the maiming (or houghing) of cattle.

1711   Appointment of Constantine Phipps as Lord Chancellor; and the 2nd Duke of Ormond as Lord Lieutenant. Government concern at widespread agrarian unrest and 'hougher' activities.

1712   Rewards were offered for the arrest of houghers, whose activities had spread through Galway, Sligo, Fermanagh, Roscommon, Leitrim and Clare; priests in those areas were accused of failing to preach to their congregations against such crimes.

1713   Jonathan Swift became Dean of St Patrick's in Dublin. Appointment of Charles Talbot, Duke of Shrewsbury, as Lord Lieutenant. Death of Narcissus Marsh, Archbishop of Armagh.

1714   Death of Queen Anne.

Ireland: Lord Lieutenants and Chief Governors

(LL = Lord Lieutenant; LD = Lord Deputy; LJ = Lord Justice; LC = Lord Chancellor)

James I
1603   Sir Charles Blount (LL); Sir George Cary (LD)
1604   Sir Arthur Chichester (LD)
1615   Thomas Jones and Sir John Denham (LJs); Oliver St John (LD)
1622   Sir Adam Loftus (LC); Richard, Viscount Powerscourt (LJ); Henry Cary, Viscount Falkland (LD)

Charles I

1629	Adam, Viscount Loftus (LC); Richard Boyle, Earl of Cork (LJ)
1633	Thomas, Viscount Wentworth (LD)
1640	Thomas Wentworth, Earl of Strafford (LL)
1641	Robert Sydney, Earl of Leicester (LL)
1643	Sir John Borlase and Sir Henry Tichborne (LJs *appointed by the king*)
1644	James Butler, Marquess of Ormond (LL *appointed by the king*)
1646	Philip Sydney, Lord Lisle (LL *appointed by parliament*)
1647	Arthur Annesley, Sir Robert King, Sir Robert Meredyth, Col. John Moore and Col. Michael Jones (commissioners of parliament)
1648	James, Marquess of Ormond (LL *appointed by the king*)

Interregnum

1649	Lt-Gen. Oliver Cromwell (LL)
1650	Ulick Burke, Marquess of Clanrickarde (LD *appointed by Charles II in exile*)
	Com.-Gen. Henry Ireton (LD *appointed by parliament*)
1652	Lt-Gen. Charles Fleetwood (C.-in-C.), Lt-Gen. Oliver Cromwell, Lt-Gen. Edmund Ludlow, Miles Corbet, Col. John Jones and John Weaver (parliamentary commissioners)
1654	Charles Fleetwood (LD); Henry Cromwell, Matthew Tomlinson, Miles Corbett, Robert Goodwin and William Steele (parliamentary commissioners)
1656	William Steele (LC)
1657	Henry Cromwell (LD); then LL in 1658
1659	John Jones, William Steele, Robert Goodwin, Matthew Tomlinson and Miles Corbet (parliamentary commissioners); Edmund Ludlow (C.-in-C.)
1660	John Weaver, Robert Goodwin, Sir Charles Coote, Sir Hardress Waller and Col. Henry Markham (parliamentary commissioners)

Charles II

1660	Lt-Gen. George Monck, Duke of Albermarle (LL); Sir Maurice Eustace (LC); Roger, Earl of Orrery (LJ)
1662	James, 1st Duke of Ormond (LL)
1668	Thomas, Earl of Ossory (LD)
1669	John, Lord Robartes (LL)
1670	John, Lord Berkeley (LL)
1672	Arthur, Earl of Essex (LL)
1677	James, 2nd Duke of Ormond (LL)

James II
1685   Michael Boyle (LC); Arthur, Earl of Granard (LJ); Henry, Earl of Clarendon (LL)
1687   Richard, Earl of Tyrconnell (LD)

William III and Mary
1689   James II in Ireland
1690   William III in Ireland; Henry, Lord Sydney, and Thomas Coningsby (LJs); Sir Charles Porter (LC)
1692   Henry, Viscount Sydney (LL)
1693   Sir Charles Porter (LC); Henry, Lord Capel, Sir Cyril Wyche and William Dunscombe (LJs)
1695   Henry, Lord Capel (LD)
1696   Sir Charles Porter (LC); Charles, Earl of Mountrath, and Henry, Earl of Drogheda (LJs)
1697   Charles, Marquess of Winchester, Henry, Earl of Galway, and Edward, Viscount Villiers (LJs)
1699   Charles, Duke of Bolton, Charles, Earl of Berkeley, and Henry, Earl of Galway (LJs)
1700   Laurence, Earl of Rochester (LL)

Anne
1703   James, 2nd Duke of Ormond (LL)
1707   Thomas, Earl of Pembroke (LL)
1708   Thomas, Earl of Wharton (LL)
1710   James, 2nd Duke of Ormond (LL)
1713   Charles, Duke of Shrewsbury (LL)

Ireland: Archbishops

	Church of Ireland Archbishops		Catholic Archbishops	
Armagh	1595	Henry Ussher	1601	Peter Lombard
	1613	Christopher Hampton	1626	Hugh MacCaghwell
	1625	James Ussher (to 1656)		(Apr.–Sept.)
	1660	John Bramhall	1628	Hugh O'Reilly
	1663	James Margetson		(to 1652)
	1679	Michael Boyle	1657	Edmund O'Reilly
	1703	Narcissus Marsh	1669	Oliver Plunkett
	1713	Thomas Lindsay		(to 1681)
		(to 1724)	1683	Dominic Maguire
				(to 1707)

Cashel	1571	Miler Magrath	1603	David Kearney
	1623	Malcolm Hamilton	1626	Thomas Walsh
	1629	Archibald Hamilton		(to 1654)
	1660	Thomas Fulwar	1669	William Burgat
	1667	Thomas Price (to 1685)		(to 1674)
	1690	Narcissus Marsh	1677	John Brenan
	1694	William Palliser		(to 1693)
		(to 1727)	1695	Edward Comerford
			1711	Christopher Butler
				(to 1757)

Dublin	1567	Adam Loftus	1600	Matthew de Oviedo
	1605	Thomas Jones	1611	Eugene Matthews
	1619	Lancelot Bulkeley	1623	Thomas Fleming
		(to 1650)		(to 1651)
	1661	James Margetson	1669	Peter Talbot (to 1680)
	1663	Michael Boyle	1683	Patrick Russell
	1679	John Parker	1693	Piers Creagh
	1682	Francis Marsh		(to 1705)
	1694	Narcissus Marsh	1707	Edmund Byrne
	1703	William King (to 1729)		(to 1724)

Tuam	1595	Nehemiah Donnellan	1609	Florence Conry
	1609	William Daniel	1630	Malachy O'Queely
	1629	Randolph Barlow		(to 1645)
	1638	Richard Boyle	1647	John de Burgo
	1645	John Maxwell (to 1647)		(to 1667)
	1660	Samuel Pullen	1669	James Lynch
	1667	John Parker	1713	Francis de Burgo
	1679	John Vesey (to 1716)		(to 1723)

SECTION THREE

Lists of major officers of state

All key appointments for the period are listed below. A more comprehensive list of office holders will be found in E.B. Fryde, D.E. Greenway, Stephen Porter and Ian Roy, eds, *Handbook of British Chronology*, 3rd edn, (London, 1986).

Lord Chancellors and Lord Keepers of the Great Seal

(LC = Lord Chancellor; LK = Lord Keeper)

The Lord Chancellor, whose office seems to have originated in the reign of William I, was Keeper of the Great Seal, Speaker of the House of Lords, head of Chancery and judge in the popular equity Court of Chancery (which dealt with petitions outside the scope of common law). His staff of nearly 50 secretaries and clerks were responsible for the final issue of instruments authorised by the Great Seal, although the Chancellor had the power to delay or veto the issue of these instruments, which served as a check on the advice given by the Secretaries of State. The seal itself, which depicted on one side the sovereign enthroned and on the other the sovereign mounted, was used to authenticate most state documents on receipt of a Privy Seal warrant.

James I
1603	Sir Thomas Egerton (later Lord Ellesmere, then Viscount Brackley), LK – later LC (1603)
1617	Sir Francis Bacon (later Lord Verulam, then Viscount St Albans), LK – later LC (1618)
1621	Seal was briefly placed in commission (Sir Julius Caesar, Sir John Ley, etc.)
1621	John Williams, Dean of Westminster, LK

Charles I
1625	Sir Thomas Coventry (later Lord Coventry), LK
1640	Sir John Finch (later Lord Finch), LK

1641   Sir Edward Lyttleton (later Lord Lyttleton), LK
1645   Sir Richard Lane, LK

Civil War and Interregnum
(A new great seal was authorised and entrusted to commissioners)

1643   John, Earl of Rutland (later replaced by Henry, Earl of Kent);
         Oliver, Earl of Bolingbroke; Oliver St John; John Wylde; Samuel
         Browne; Edmund Prideaux
1646   William, Earl of Salisbury, replaced Bolingbroke
1646   Edward, Earl of Manchester, and William Lenthall (Speakers of
         the two Houses) replaced the above
1648   Henry, Earl of Kent; William, Lord Grey of Warke; Sir Thomas
         Widdrington; Bulstrode Whitelocke
1649   (A new Commonwealth seal created) Bulstrode Whitelocke;
         John Lisle; Richard Keeble
1654   Bulstrode Whitelocke; Sir Thomas Widdrington; John Lisle
1655   John Lisle; Nathaniel Fiennes
1659   John Bradshaw; Thomas Terryll; John Fountaine
1660   Thomas Terryll; Sir Thomas Widdrington; John Fountaine;
         Edward, Earl of Manchester (the seal was broken up in May)

Charles II
1649   Sir Richard Lane, LK
1653   Sir Edward Herbert, LK
1658   Sir Edward Hyde (later Lord Hyde, then Earl of Clarendon), LK
         – later LC (1658). Hyde was appointed Lord Chancellor in 1658
         at Charles II's Court in exile, but he was only effectively in the
         government of the country after the Restoration in 1660.
1667   Sir Orlando Bridgeman, LK
1672   Anthony Ashley Cooper, Earl of Shaftesbury, LC
1673   Sir Heneage Finch (later Lord Finch, then Earl of Nottingham),
         LK – later LC (1675)
1682   Sir Francis North (later Lord Guildford), LK

James II
1685   Sir George Jeffreys (later Lord Jeffreys), LC

William III and Mary
1689   The seal was placed in commission
1693   Sir John Somers (later Lord Somers), LK – later LC
1700   Sir Nathan Wright, LK

Anne

1705   William Cowper (later Lord Cowper), LK – later LC of Great
           Britain (1707)
1708   The seal was placed in commission
1710   Sir Simon Harcourt (later Lord Harcourt), LK – later LC (1713)

Keepers of the Privy Seal

The Privy Seal Office, over which the Lord Privy Seal presided, consisted
of four Masters of Requests and four Clerks of the Privy Seal, who were
responsible for receiving documents from the Signet Office and
preparing documents for the Great Seal. The privy seal itself was a small
seal bearing the royal coat of arms, applied on a red wax; it was used by
the king when replying to various petitions and authorising special
money transactions. The Lord Privy Seal was also responsible for the
Court of Requests (a prerogative court offering cheap and speedy justice
to the poor in civil law cases).

James I

1603   Sir Robert Cecil (appointed 1601; later Lord Cecil, then Earl of
           Salisbury)
1608   Henry Howard, Earl of Northampton
1614   Robert Carr, Earl of Somerset
1616   Edward Somerset, Earl of Worcester

Charles I

1628   Sir John Coke (Mar.)
           Sir Robert Naunton (May)
           Henry Montagu, Earl of Manchester (July); to 1642
1643   Lucius Carey, Viscount Falkland (Apr.)
           Sir Edward Nicholas (Nov.)
1644   Henry Bourchier, Earl of Bath; to 1654

The Protectorate

1655   Nathaniel Fiennes (sole commissioner)
1658   Nathaniel Fiennes (Keeper of the Privy Seal); to 1659

Charles II

1661   John, Lord Robartes (later Earl of Radnor)
1673   Arthur Annesley, Earl of Anglesey
1682   George Savile, Marquess of Halifax

James II

1685   Henry Hyde, Earl of Clarendon
1686   Henry, Lord Arundel; to 1688

William and Mary

1689   George Savile, Marquess of Halifax
1690   The seal was placed in commission
1692   Thomas Herbert, Earl of Pembroke
1699   John Lowther, Viscount Lonsdale
1700   Ford Grey, Earl of Tankerville
1701   The seal was placed in commission

Anne

1702   John Sheffield, Marquess of Normanby (later Duke of Buckinghamshire)
1705   John Holles, Duke of Newcastle
1711   John Robinson, Bishop of Bristol (later Bishop of London)
1713   William Legge, Earl of Dartmouth

Lord Treasurers and First Lords of the Treasury

(Lord Treasurer = LT; First Lord = FL; Treasury Commissioners = TC)

The office of Treasurer originated in the twelfth century, when he began to preside over the Exchequer, a central financial organisation dealing with crown revenue. The title 'Lord Treasurer' was used more commonly from the sixteenth century, by which time he had also become an important officer of state and adviser to the king. During the Interregnum and again later in the seventeenth century, the office was put in commission. If the first commissioner was a member of the Commons, he also undertook the duties of Chancellor of the Exchequer; if, however, he was a member of the Lords, he was styled 'First Lord' and a separate Chancellor of the Exchequer was appointed from the Commons.

James I

1603   Sir Thomas Sackville, Lord Buckhurst (later Earl of Dorset), LT
1608   Robert Cecil, Earl of Salisbury, LT
1612   Henry Howard, Earl of Northampton, FL
1613   Sir Thomas Egerton, Lord Ellesmere, FL
1614   Thomas Howard, Earl of Suffolk, LT
1618   George Abbot, Archbishop of Canterbury, FL

1620   Sir Henry Montagu, Viscount Mandeville (later Earl of Manchester), LT

1624   James, Lord Ley (later Earl of Marlborough), LT

Charles I

1628   Richard, Lord Weston (later Earl of Portland), LT
1635   William Laud, Archbishop of Canterbury, FL
1636   William Juxon, Bishop of London, LT
1641   Sir Edward Lyttleton (later Lord Lyttleton), FL
1643   Francis, Lord Cottington, LT

The Protectorate

(The financial system was not properly operational until 1654)

1654   Bulstrode Whitelocke; Sir Thomas Widdrington; John Lisle; Henry Rolle; Oliver St John; Edward Montagu; William Sydenham; William Matham; TC

1658   Whitelocke; Montagu; Sydenham; Widdrington; TC

1659   John Disbrowe; William Sydenham; Richard Salway; Cornelius Holland; John Clerke; John Blackwell; TC

Charles II

1660   Sir Edward Hyde (later Earl of Clarendon), FL
         Thomas Wriothesley, Earl of Southampton, LT
1667   George Monck, Duke of Albermarle, FL
1672   Thomas, Lord Clifford, LT
1673   Sir Thomas Osborne, Viscount Latimer (later Earl of Danby), LT
1679   Arthur, Earl of Essex, FL
         Laurence Hyde (later Earl of Rochester), FL
1684   Sidney, Lord Godolphin, FL

James II

1685   Laurence, Earl of Rochester, LT
1687   John, Lord Belasyse, FL

William and Mary

1689   Charles, Viscount Mordaunt (later Earl of Peterborough), FL
1690   Sir John Lowther (later Viscount Lowther), FL
         Sidney, Lord Godolphin, FL
1697   Charles Montagu (later Lord Halifax), FL
1699   Lord Grey, Earl of Tankerville, FL

| 1700 | Sidney, Lord Godolphin, FL |
| 1701 | Charles Howard, Earl of Carlisle, FL |

Anne

1702	Sidney, Lord Godolphin, LT
1710	John, Earl of Poulett, FL
1711	Robert Harley, Earl of Oxford, LT
1714	Charles Talbot, Duke of Shrewsbury, LT

Chancellors and Under-Treasurers of the Exchequer

1603	Sir George Home (later Earl of Dunbar)
1606	Sir Julius Caesar
1614	Sir Fulk Greville (later Lord Brooke)
1621	Sir Richard Weston (later Earl of Portland)
1628	Edward, Lord Barrett
1629	Francis Cottington (later Lord Cottington)
1642	Sir John Culpeper (later Lord Culpeper)
1643	Sir Edward Hyde (later Earl of Clarendon)

(The Treasury was in commission during the Interregnum)

1661	Anthony Ashley Cooper, Lord Ashley (later Earl of Shaftesbury)
1672	Sir John Duncombe
1676	Sir John Ernle
1689	Henry Booth, Lord Delamer (later Earl of Warrington)
1690	Richard Hampden
1694	Charles Montagu (later Lord Halifax)
1699	John Smith
1701	Henry Boyle
1708	John Smith
1710	Robert Harley (later Earl of Oxford)
1711	Robert Benson (later Lord Bingley)
1713	Sir William Wyndham

Masters of the Court of Wards

The Court of Wards and Liveries, which originated in the sixteenth century, was independent of the Exchequer and was responsible for administering the profits produced by the king's feudal rights to wardship. The Master controlled an office which included a Receiver General, a Surveyor, an Attorney and several auditors and clerks. Highly unpopular, the court was abolished in 1646.

1603	Robert Cecil (appointed 1599; later Earl of Salisbury)
1612	Sir George Carew
	Sir Walter Cope
	William Knollys (later Viscount Wallingford)
1618	Lionel Cranfield (later Earl of Middlesex)
1624	Sir Robert Naunton
1635	Francis, Lord Cottington
1641	William Fiennes, Lord Saye and Sele (acting for parliament)
1644	Francis, Lord Cottington (acting for the king with a new seal in Oxford)

Secretaries of State

The Secretaries of State were responsible for dealing with the king's personal and official correspondence, taking decisions on many matters of state and advising the king on both domestic and foreign affairs. They controlled the Signet Office, where Signet Clerks prepared correspondence for the Signet Seal (a smaller seal than the Privy Seal; used for personal letters as well as major communications). Although two secretaries had been appointed from 1640, their work was more formally divided from 1660, when one became responsible for the Northern (N) Department of foreign affairs (i.e for protestant countries) and the other for the Southern (S) Department (for catholic countries). The Northern Secretary, who was the junior partner, was always promoted to the Southern Department on the resignation of its holder. By the seventeenth century, the office had grown in stature to rival those of the Lord Treasurer and the Lord Chancellor.

James I

1603	Sir Robert Cecil (later Earl of Salisbury); appointed 1596; to 1612
	John Herbert; appointed 1600; to 1616
1612	Robert Carr, Viscount Rochester (later Earl of Somerset); to 1614
1614	Sir Ralph Winwood; to 1617
1616	Sir Thomas Lake; to 1619
1618	Sir Robert Naunton; to 1623
1619	Sir George Calvert (later Lord Baltimore); to 1625
1623	Sir Edward Conway (later Lord Conway); to 1628

Charles I

1625	Sir Albertus Morton; to 1625
	Sir John Coke; to 1640

1628	Dudley, Viscount Carleton (later Viscount Dorchester); to 1632
1632	Sir Francis Windebank; to 1641
1640	Sir Henry Vane, senior; to 1642
1641	Sir Edward Nicholas
1642	Lucius Carey, Viscount Faulkland; to 1643
1643	George Digby (later Earl of Bristol); to 1645; reappointed 1658.

Secretaries of State under the Protectorate

1653	John Thurloe; to 1659
1660	Thomas Scott (Jan.–Feb.)
	John Thurloe and John Thompson (jointly; Feb.–June)

Charles II

1660	Sir Edward Nicholas; to 1662 (S)
	Sir William Morice; to 1668 (N)
1662	Sir Henry Bennet (later Lord Arlington); to 1674 (S)
1668	Sir John Trevor; to 1672 (N)
1672	Henry Coventry; to 1674 (N), then to 1680 (S)
1674	Sir Joseph Williamson; to 1679 (N)
1679	Robert Spencer, Earl of Sunderland; to 1680 (N), then to 1681 (S)
1680	Sir Leoline Jenkins; to 1681 (N), then to 1684 (S)
1681	Edward, Earl of Conway; to 1683 (N)
1683	Robert Spencer, Earl of Sunderland; to 1684 (N), then to 1688 (S)
1684	Sidney Godolphin (later Lord Godolphin); to 1684 (N)
	Charles, Earl of Middleton; to 1688 (N), then to 1688 (S)

James II

1688	Richard, Viscount Preston; to 1689 (N)

William III and Mary

1689	Charles Talbot, Earl of Shrewsbury; to 1690 (S)
	Daniel Finch, Earl of Nottingham; to 1690 (N)
1690	Earl of Nottingham; sole secretary, June–Dec., then to 1692 (S)
	Henry, Viscount Sidney (later Earl of Romney); to 1692 (N)
1692	Earl of Nottingham; sole secretary to Mar. 1693, then to Nov. 1693 (S)
1693	Sir John Trenchard; to 1693 (N); then sole secretary to 1694; then to 1695 (S)
1694	Charles, Duke of Shrewsbury, to 1695 (N); then to 1698 (S)
1695	Sir William Trumbull; to 1697 (N)

1697   James Vernon; to 1698 (N); then sole secretary to 1699; then to
        1700 (N)
1699   Edward Villiers, Earl of Jersey; to 1700 (S)
1700   James Vernon; sole secretary (June–Nov.); then to Jan. 1702 (S);
        then to May 1702 (N)
        Sir Charles Hedges; to 1701 (N)
1702   Charles Montagu, Earl of Manchester; Jan.–May (S)
        Sir Charles Hedges; to 1704 (N); then to 1706 (S)
        Earl of Nottingham; to 1704 (S)
1704   Robert Harley, Earl of Oxford; to 1708 (N)
1706   Charles Spencer, Earl of Sunderland; to 1710 (S)
1708   Henry Boyle (later Lord Carleton); to 1710 (N)
1710   William Legge, (later Lord Dartmouth); to 1713 (S)
        Henry St John (later Viscount Bolingbroke); to 1712 (N); then
        to 1714 (S)
1713   William Bromley; to 1714 (N)

Chief Justices of the King's Bench

The King's Bench was the highest common law court, originating in the
Court of the King's Council. By the sixteenth century, it had become a
type of appeal court in criminal cases and some civil cases.

1603   John Popham
1607   Thomas Fleming
1613   Edward Coke
1616   Henry Montagu
1621   James Ley
1625   Ranulphe Crewe
1627   Nicholas Hyde
1631   Thomas Richardson
1635   John Bramston
1642   Robert Heath (disabled 1645)
1648   Henry Rolle
1655   John Glynne
1660   Richard Newdigate (Jan.)
        Robert Foster (Oct.)
1663   Robert Hyde
1665   John Kelyng
1671   Matthew Hale
1676   Richardson Rainsford
1678   William Scroggs

1681	Francis Pemberton
1683	Edmund Saunders (Jan.)
	George Jeffreys (Sept.)
1685	Edward Herbert
1687	Robert Wright
1689	Sir John Holt
1710	Sir Thomas Parker (Lord Macclesfield); to 1718

Chief Justices of the Court of Common Pleas

The Court of Common Pleas originated in the thirteenth century as a court which was independent of both king and Council. Dealing with civil suits between subjects, it developed a reputation as both the busiest and the slowest of the common law courts. Much of its business was therefore taken over by the King's Bench.

1603	Edmund Anderson
1605	Francis Gawdy
1606	Edward Coke
1613	Henry Hobart
1626	Thomas Richardson
1631	Robert Heath
1634	John Finch
1640	Edward Lyttelton
1641	John Banks (to 1644)
1648	Oliver St John
1660	Orlando Bridgeman
1668	John Vaughan
1675	Francis North
1683	Francis Pemberton (Jan.)
	Thomas Jones (Sept.)
1686	Henry Bedingfield
1687	Robert Wright (Apr.)
	Edward Herbert (Apr.)
1689	Sir Henry Pollexfen
1692	Sir George Treby
1714	Sir Peter King

Attorney-Generals

1603	Edward Coke
1606	Henry Hobart

1613	Francis Bacon
1617	Henry Yelverton
1621	Thomas Coventry
1625	Robert Heath
1631	William Noy
1634	John Banks
1641	Edward Herbert
1645	Thomas Gardner
1649	William Steele (Jan.)
	Edmund Prideaux (Apr.)

(Edward Herbert was appointed to this post by Charles II in exile, 1649–53)

1660	Geoffrey Palmer
1670	Heneage Finch
1673	Francis North
1675	William Jones
1679	Creswell Levinz
1681	Robert Sawyer
1687	Thomas Powys
1689	Henry Pollexfen (Feb.)
	George Treby (May)
1692	John Somers
1695	Thomas Trevor
1701	Edward Northey
1707	Simon Harcourt
1708	James Montagu
1710	Simon Harcourt (Sept.)
	Sir Edward Northey (Oct.)

Solicitor-Generals

1603	Thomas Flemming
1604	John Doderidge
1607	Francis Bacon
1613	Henry Yelverton
1617	Thomas Coventry
1621	Robert Heath
1625	Richard Shilton
1634	Edward Lyttleton
1640	Edward Herbert
1641	Oliver St John *(continued as a parliamentary appointee until 1648)*
1643	Thomas Gardner

1645	Geoffrey Palmer
1648	Edmund Prideaux
1649	John Cook
1650	Robert Reynolds
1654	William Ellis
1660	Heneage Finch
1670	Edward Turnour
1671	Francis North
1673	William Jones
1674	Francis Winnington
1679	Heneage Finch
1686	Thomas Powys
1687	William Williams
1689	George Treby (Feb.)
	John Somers (May)
1692	Thomas Trevor
1695	John Hawles
1702	Simon Harcourt
1707	James Montagu
1708	Robert Eyre
1710	Robert Raymond
1714	Nicholas Lechmere

Lord Admirals and First Lords of the Admiralty

The title was first used in 1540, thus replacing the former style 'Admiral of England'. From 1619, the Lord Admiral also took control of the Navy Board, which was responsible for the maintenance of ships in the royal navy in peacetime as well as war. In 1628, the office was placed in commission for the first time (and frequently thereafter) under the leadership of the First Lord of the Admiralty. After the Union with Scotland (1707), the title was changed to 'Lord High Admiral of Great Britain'.

1585	Charles, Lord Howard of Effingham (Earl of Nottingham, 1597)
1619	George Villiers, Marquess of Buckingham (Duke of Buckingham, 1623)
1628	Richard, Lord Weston (Earl of Portland, 1633)
1635	Robert Bertie, Earl of Lindsey
1636	William Juxon, Bishop of London
1638	Algernon Percy, Earl of Northumberland
1643	Francis, Lord Cottington (for the king)
	Robert Rich, Earl of Warwick (for parliament)

1645	Committee of 6 peers and 12 MPs to undertake the work of the Lord High Admiral; later increased by 5 additional peers and 10 MPs
1648	Earl of Warwick
1649	Powers of the Lord High Admiral transferred to the Council of State
1652	Admiralty and Navy Commissioners appointed to undertake the work
1660	James, Duke of York
1673	King Charles II
1679	Sir Henry Capell
1681	Daniel, Lord Finch (Earl of Nottingham, 1682)
1684	King Charles II
1685	King James II
1689	King William III; then Arthur Herbert, Earl of Torrington
1690	Thomas Herbert, Earl of Pembroke
1692	Charles, Lord Cornwallis
1693	Anthony Carey, Viscount Falkland
1694	Edward Russell, Earl of Orford
1699	John Egerton, Earl of Bridgwater
1701	Earl of Pembroke
1702	Prince George of Denmark
1708	Queen Anne (Oct.)
	Earl of Pembroke (Nov.)
1709	Earl of Orford
1710	Sir John Leake
1712	Thomas Wentworth, Earl of Strafford

Archbishops of Canterbury

1583	John Whitgift
1604	Richard Bancroft
1611	George Abbot
1633	William Laud (to 1645; episcopacy abolished by parliament, 1646)
1660	William Juxon
1663	Gilbert Sheldon
1677	William Sancroft (deprived 1690)
1691	John Tillotson
1694	Thomas Tenison (to 1715)

Archbishops of York

1595	Matthew Hutton
1606	Tobias Matthew
1628	George Montaigne
1629	Samuel Harsnett
1632	Richard Neile
1641	John Williams (episcopacy abolished, 1646)
1660	Accepted Frewen
1664	Richard Sterne
1683	John Dolben
1688	Thomas Lamplugh
1691	John Sharp
1714	William Dawes (to 1724)

Bishops of London

1597	Richard Bancroft
1604	Richard Vaughan
1607	Thomas Ravis
1610	George Abbot
1611	John King
1621	George Montaigne
1628	William Laud
1633	William Juxon (episcopacy abolished, 1646)
1660	Gilbert Sheldon
1663	Humfrey Henchman
1675	Henry Compton
1713	John Robinson (to 1723)

SECTION FOUR

Glossary of constitutional, political and religious terms

Addled Parliament, 1614: The parliament, which had been called by James I to grant financial aid, was dissolved after just two months before it had passed any measure. The frustration of the king's attempts to secure the return of a favourable House of Commons, through the interference of his 'undertakers' in the elections, ensured a hostile attack on his policies led by Wentworth, Eliot, Pym and others.

Agitators: In April 1647, these representatives of the ordinary soldiers in the New Model Army were elected to discuss grievances with the officers.

Agreement of the People, **1647:** A proposal of constitutional ideas drawn up by the Agitators and Levellers in the army on 28th October 1647 and presented to the Army Council in the Putney Debates. It proposed: (1) dissolution of the present parliament on 30th September 1648; (2) biennial parliaments; (3) equal electoral areas; (4) freedom of conscience in religion; (5) sovereignty of the Commons; (6) an end to impressment for military service; (7) equality of all citizens before the law. An amended version was presented to the Rump in 1649.

Anabaptists: Extreme religious reformers, who also advocated radical social and political ideas. Appearing on the continent in the sixteenth century, they believed in complete religious independence and were persecuted in England from 1534. They influenced the Brownists and later separatists.

Apology of the Commons, 1604: This 'Form of Apology and Satisfaction', drawn up by the Commons (but never formally presented to James I), restated their privileges, which were 'of right, not of grace'. They particularly stressed their right to freedom of speech, freedom from arrest and freedom of elections – and their right to vote on any proposed alterations in religion.

Archpriest: The office was established by the Pope in 1598 to provide leadership for those priests in England who were not members of a religious order (i.e. 'secular' priests). The Archpriest had no authority over the Jesuits (i.e. 'regular' priests) or the laity. The office lapsed in 1621, after a dispute between the regulars and the seculars, and the Archpriest was eventually replaced by a bishop with special responsibility for the secular clergy.

Arminianism: The doctrine was based on the beliefs of the Dutch theologian Jacob Arminius, which emphasised free will and salvation by works at the expense of predestination, the doctrine favoured by the Calvinists. Arminianism gained strength in the Church of England in the early seventeenth century, supported by Archbishop Laud's high church group. Their opponents perceived it with great suspicion as part of a return to Catholicism.

Articles of Grievance, 1689:   The Convention of the Estates in Scotland, which met in Edinburgh and proclaimed William and Mary joint sovereigns, also passed the Articles of Grievance (April) which listed their concerns. These included demands that the king should rule according to the law (i.e. an end to the manipulation of the courts, the use of torture and the crown's appointment and control of judges); and that episcopacy should be abolished.

Assessment: A tax to raise money for the war effort, imposed by parliament on 24th February 1643. It was levied on everyone; based on the value of property and the income from land; collected at first on a weekly basis ('the weekly assessment'), but later monthly; intended to produce a weekly revenue of £33,518 nationally, allocated between the counties and local parishes.

Augmentations: To counter the low salaries available to ministers in many churches (*see* Lay impropriation), parliament attempted to 'augment' or increase their earnings through money raised by the sale of lands belonging to bishops, deans and chapters and by the confiscation of tithes held by convicted royalists. The policy, which was first established by the Bill for the Better Maintenance of Ministers (1641), was not wholly successful.

Barebone's Parliament July–December 1653 (also called the Parliament of the Saints, the Little Parliament or the Nominated Parliament): Popularly styled after one of its members, Praise-God Barebone, it was called by Cromwell after the expulsion of the Rump. Aiming to establish a 'godly' parliament, the Council of the Army selected 140 members from lists of candidates submitted by independent congregations throughout the country. However, the more moderate members, who were soon alarmed by radical proposals for reform, met early one morning to agree to a dissolution.

Bate's Case, 1606:   This concerned the imprisonment of a merchant, John Bate, for refusing to pay the imposition on currants. Judgment was given in favour of James I in the Court of the Exchequer by Chief Baron

Fleming, who emphasised the king's right to levy duties on any merchandise with the aim of controlling trade – but not with the aim of raising taxes.

Bill of Rights, 1689: This included the clauses in the Declaration of Rights which had already been accepted by William and Mary. The Bill also set out that the throne should in future only be occupied by a Protestant; that the succession was to go (1) to Mary's heirs and (2) to Anne and her heirs; that an oath of allegiance to William and Mary was to be administered.

Billeting (or free quarter): An unpopular system of accommodating soldiers in civilian households with the promise (often unfulfilled) of future payment. Used extensively by Charles I, it resulted in violent protests in affected areas – followed by the imposition of martial law (especially in 1627–28). The practice was condemned in the Petition of Right (1628) and outlawed (1679), but reintroduced by both Charles II and James II before being again outlawed in the Bill of Rights (1689).

Bloody Assizes, 1683: The trials in Exeter and elsewhere of those charged with involvement in Monmouth's Rebellion were heard by Lord Chief Justice, Judge Jeffreys, and four other judges on the Western Circuit. As a result, some 320 people were condemned to death and nearly 800 sentenced to transportation to the West Indies in judgments notorious for their brutality and injustice.

Book of Rates: These contained the official valuations of items which were liable to customs duties. In 1604, James I ordered the first major revision since 1558. In 1608, following a favourable judgment in Bate's Case (1606), impositions were extended to most imports and rates increased in a new Book of Rates. Devised by the Lord Treasurer, Robert Cecil, this was intended to raise an additional £70,000 in non-parliamentary income for the crown – a move which brought furious opposition from the Commons when it next met in 1610.

***Book of Sports*, 1618, 1633:** This was issued by James I in 1617 for Lancashire (and in 1618 for the rest of the country) to legalise morris dancing and other sports after divine service on Sundays, following attempts made by local puritan magistrates to enforce observance of the sabbath through the suppression of these activities. The Book was reissued in 1633 by Charles I, after an attempt by Puritans in Somerset to ban church ales, wakes and similar celebrations on Sundays – the declaration to be read by clergy from the pulpits in all churches on pain of expulsion or imprisonment.

Books of Orders: These consisted of detailed instructions (first issued in 1578) from the Privy Council to local justices concerning the handling of a specific crisis – e.g. plague in 1603, 1609, 1625, 1630, 1636, 1646; and dearth in 1608, 1622, 1630. The Book of Orders of 1631, however, provided continuity of action and supervision over a broad range of local government, involving the justices, sheriffs and assize judges – especially in relation to the poor law and vagabondage.

Bye Plot, 1603: This plot to kidnap James I and enforce his redress of grievances was devised by William Watson, a catholic priest. After betrayal to the Privy Council by a Jesuit, those implicated were tried alongside the conspirators in the Main Plot; Watson was executed.

Cabal, 1667–73: The inner group of ministers appointed by Charles II after the fall of Clarendon; named 'The Cabal' as a combination of the first letters in their names – Clifford, Arlington, Buckingham, Ashley Cooper, Lauderdale. The group collapsed after opposition in parliament to the French alliance (1670) and the Declaration of Indulgence (1672).

Calvinism: The doctrine was based on the beliefs of a theologian from Geneva, John Calvin, who emphasised predestination – i.e. the idea that some people ('the elect') are chosen by God for salvation and that others are foreordained to damnation. The doctrine gained strength in the Church of England during Elizabeth's reign, but was strongly challenged later during the 1620s and 1630s by the supporters of William Laud.

Case of the Army Truly Stated, **1647:** Drafted by John Lilburne, this document was the work of army Levellers. It called for an indemnity for those involved in the war, the payment of arrears to the army, the dissolution of the present parliament, biennial parliaments elected by free-born males over 21, the redress of social grievances and the sovereignty of the people.

Cavalier Parliament, 1661: This met in May after a landslide royalist victory in the elections, which saw the return of only 60 presbyterian or independent members (and no Scottish or Irish MPs). The parliament was dissolved in 1679.

Cess tax: A tax resulting from a local 'assessment' on land values. It was used controversially in Scotland after the Restoration, prompting a refusal to pay by some of the Covenanters.

Cessation, 1643: An agreement made with the Irish rebels on 15th September by the Marquess of Ormond (on behalf of Charles I) to suspend hostilities for one year, pending detailed discussions on a permanent peace. This in theory resulted in the immediate release of the king's English army in Ireland for service against parliament in the Civil War (although not all returning soldiers by any means enrolled for the king). The Irish rebels granted Charles £30,000, but declined to send their own troops to support his war effort in England.

Chancery, Court of: The consistory court of the Archbishop of York, which heard appeals from the church courts. It was abolished with other church courts in 1641, but restored in 1661 under the terms of the Ecclesiastical Commission Act.

Clarendon Code, 1661–65: Named after the Chancellor, Clarendon (though not actually drafted or even fully approved by him), the Code consisted of four measures enacted by the Cavalier Parliament, which sought to restrict the influence of nonconformists – the Corporation Act (1661), the Act of Uniformity (1662), the Conventicle Act (1664) and the Five Mile Act (1665).

Classis: In the presbyterian system of church government, 'provinces' (usually counties) were divided into *classes.* Each *classis* consisted of a group of parishes under the control of a committee of local ministers and elders drawn from local congregations.

Clubmen: Armed 'Clubmen' or 'peacekeeping associations' made their appearance in many southern and western counties in 1645 as a form of self-defence against the atrocities of war. Although they did not represent a unified movement, local Clubmen often shared certain characteristics – an emphasis on neutralism, a desire for peace and an organisation led by the humbler yeomen farmers rather than the gentry.

Cockayne Project, 1614: James I (given financial incentives) accepted the scheme put forward by Alderman Cockayne and a group of London merchants to ban the export of unfinished cloth, withdraw the Merchant Adventurers' cloth trade monopoly and authorise them to establish a new company for the dyeing and export of cloth. The project failed (thanks to a lack of technical and marketing skills) and a trade crisis ensued (1614–17). The Merchant Adventurers were reinstated in 1617.

Committee for Compounding: (*See* Goldsmiths' Hall Committee, 1644–50.)

Committee for Plundered Ministers, 1642:   This was set up in 1642 to relieve ministers whose estates had been plundered by royalists and, at the same time, to consider the confiscation of the estates of royalist clergy. From 1643, it also dealt with clergy suspected of Catholicism or scandalous living.

Committee of Both Kingdoms, 1644:   After the agreement reached between parliament and the Scots in the Solemn League and Covenant (1643), this committee was set up to organise the war effort, consisting of 14 MPs, 7 members of the Lords and 4 Scottish commissioners. Its work was taken over in 1648 by the Derby House Committee.

Committee of the Estates: The Scottish parliament appointed this committee (1640–51, 1660–61, 1688–89) composed of lairds and burgesses who were not members of the parliament itself, granting it independent powers to take decisions on parliament's behalf. In practice, it became the effective government in Scotland, 1640–51, before its capture *en bloc* by General Monck.

Commonwealth: The Rump, having abolished the monarchy and the House of Lords (17th–19th March 1649), proceeded to declare England a 'Commonwealth and Free State' (19th May) with government by the Rump and a Council of State of 41 members chosen by them. Cromwell's dismissal first of the Rump (20th April 1653) and then of the Barebone's Parliament (12th December 1653) effectively ended the Commonwealth. It was replaced by the Protectorate, established by the Instrument of Government (16th December).

Composition: (*See* Goldsmiths' Hall Committee, 1644–50.)

Comprehension: The policy of those who, in a search for unity, favoured the development of the Church of England as an umbrella to shelter a wide range of beliefs and practices.

Confederation of Kilkenny, 1642:   After the catholic rising in Ireland (1641), the Confederation of Kilkenny was established by catholic clergy (1642). Its General Assembly claimed the rights of a parliament and its

Supreme Council undertook the duties of government, organising confederate armies into a proper command structure against the king's forces under Ormond.

Conventicle Act, 1664:   Banned religious meetings (i.e. not conforming to the Prayer Book) of more than five people, who were not members of the household, in an attempt to prevent ejected clergy from holding their own private services with members of their old congregations. The Act lapsed in 1668, but was renewed in 1670.

Conventicles: The term was used to denote unauthorised meetings for religious worship, especially following the Act of Uniformity (1662) and the Conventicle Acts (1664, 1670).

Convention of the Estates: In Scotland, the Three Estates of the realm (the clergy, nobility and burgesses – with the lesser crown tenants added after 1587 to form a Fourth Estate) met from time to time as a 'convention' – but more informally than when in session as the parliament – to conduct legislative and financial (but not judicial) business.

Convention Parliament, 1660:   Summoned in April to work out the details of the Restoration settlement, it invited Charles II to resume the throne, having resolved that he had been king 'by inherent birthright' since 1649; government was henceforth to be by King, Lords and Commons, but all legislation passed in 1641 was confirmed. The parliament was dissolved in December.

Convocation: A meeting of the clergy in the provinces of either Canterbury or York.

Corporation Act, 1661:   A measure of the Cavalier Parliament aimed at facilitating the election of anglican MPs by excluding Presbyterians, Catholics and other dissenters from membership of corporations; henceforth all office-holders in boroughs were to receive the Church of England sacrament, to renounce the Covenant and to swear oaths of allegiance, supremacy and non-resistance.

Council of State: The Rump established a council of 41 members as its executive committee in the new 'Commonwealth and Free State', which it set up on 19th May 1649, following the abolition of the monarchy and House of Lords.

Council of the North: Based in York, the Council's original function had been to deal with problems of law and order in the border counties. By the seventeenth century, however, it was used increasingly by the crown to exercise authority by employing Star Chamber techniques. Under its president, Viscount Wentworth (1628–31), it became an instrument of arbitrary rule in his policy of 'Thorough'. It was abolished by the Long Parliament in 1641.

Covenant (*See* National Covenant, 1638.)

Darien Scheme: The Company of Scotland was established in 1695 with authority to establish colonies in Africa and the Indies. Its attempt to set up a colony on the Isthmus of Darien, however, ended in disaster after three unsuccessful expeditions (1698–1700). There were bitter recriminations, based on the belief that the project had been deliberately undermined by the English.

Declaration of Breda, 1660:   A statement issued by Charles II from Breda on the advice of Monck, which granted pardon and indemnity to all former enemies (other than those excepted by parliament), religious toleration, arrears of army pay and a land settlement to protect previous purchasers of delinquents' lands; the clauses were subject to parliamentary ratification, thus making it responsible for their implementation.

Declaration of Indulgence, 1662, 1672, 1687, 1688:   The Declaration of 1662, a promise by Charles II to remove all laws against nonconformists, was rejected by parliament. The Declaration of 1672, which suspended the penal laws and permitted protestant dissenters to worship in public and Roman Catholics in private, was withdrawn after parliament's protest and quickly followed by the Test Act (1673). In James II's Declaration of 1687, all penal laws were suspended and freedom of worship in public was granted to both protestant dissenters and Roman Catholics alike. The Declaration of 1688 stipulated that the terms of 1687 were to be read in churches, thus provoking the Seven Bishops' Case.

Declaration of Rights, 1689:   A summary of the conditions on which the throne was offered to William and Mary, including their acceptance of free elections, freedom of speech in parliament and freedom to petition the king; and their rejection of standing armies in peacetime, ecclesiastical courts, unauthorised taxes and the suspending and dispensing powers. William and Mary were declared joint sovereigns

(23rd February 1689), following their acceptance of the terms, and the Declaration embodied into the Bill of Rights.

Defective titles: In an attempt to raise further revenue, Charles I appointed in 1628 the 'commission for defective titles' with powers to 'compound with', or fine, (1) those crown tenants who lacked an effective title to their land or who could not prove continuous occupation for the last 60 years, (2) those who had illegally enclosed wastes or commons, and (3) those who had encroached on royal forests.

Deists: These believed in a 'supreme being' who was a remote creator of the natural world rather than an omnipotent force involved with the individual destinies of mankind. Rationalist in outlook, they rejected the Christian idea of the revelation of God on earth and were opposed to the authority of the organised Church.

Delinquent: The term was first used by parliament in 1642 when it referred to the king's advisers and royalist supporters as 'delinquents, malignants and disaffected persons'. These terms were increasingly used after the Second Civil War in 1648.

Derby House Committee: Following Charles I's Engagement with the Scots, this committee (which met at Derby House in London and without Scottish representatives) was established by parliament in January 1648 to take over responsibility for the conduct of military affairs from the Committee of Both Kingdoms.

Diggers (or True Levellers): A group of radicals, led by Gerrard Winstanley, who established a small agricultural community on St George's Hill in Surrey in 1649. Their ideas, outlined in Winstanley's book *Law of Freedom*, were based on a social revolution which would give back the land to the people. Opposed to violent methods, they were quickly crushed by the authorities.

Directory of Worship, 1645: In January 1645, parliament passed an Ordinance which abolished the Book of Common Prayer, replacing it with the Directory for the Public Worship of God, compiled by the Westminster Assembly. This was the first step in the establishment of Presbyterianism, although the Directory met with only partial acceptance throughout the country.

Dispensing power: This use of the royal prerogative to dispense with a law for the benefit of a particular individual was particularly employed by

James II to permit Roman Catholics to hold high office. It was made illegal by the Bill of Rights (1689).

Dissent: Members of Parliament who took 'The Dissent' made a declaration that they had dissented from or, if they had been present in the Commons at the time of the vote, they *would* have dissented from (i.e. voted against) the decision taken by the Long Parliament on 5th December 1642 in favour of further negotiations with Charles I. It did not necessarily indicate their willingness (in December 1648 or January 1649) to bring the king to trial and execution, but rather their willingness afterwards (in February 1649) to accept what had already happened.

Divine right of kings: A theory particularly advocated by James I (e.g. in his book *True Law of Free Monarchies*, 1598), which reasoned that kings were appointed by God and , therefore, answerable only to Him for their actions. This view was consistently opposed by parliament and finally rejected by the Bill of Rights (1689).

Ejectors: In August 1654, the 1st Protectorate Parliament appointed commissioners for ejecting scandalous, ignorant and insufficient ministers from churches. These became known as 'Ejectors'.

Engagement, 1647: Charles I signed a secret Engagement with the Scots on 26th December, having intrigued with them for several weeks from his refuge at Carisbrooke Castle on the Isle of Wight. It was agreed that the two kingdoms would be united, that the king would establish Presbyterianism for a three-year trial period and that the Scots would disband the English army, suppress the independent sects and restore Charles to the throne.

Episcopalians: The term used to describe those who believed in government of the church by bishops (i.e. episcopacy).

Erastianism: The notion that the state should maintain responsibility for the church.

'Et cetera oath', 1640: The canons of 1640, published by Convocation (June) as a codification of Laud's innovations, contained one controversial canon. This required all clergy to swear that that they would not alter the government of the Church 'by archbishops, bishops, deans and archdeacons etc., as it stands now established'. Set against fears of a popish plot, this 'et cetera oath' was the final proof to some that Laud intended to introduce the Pope to the list by stealth. Parliament declared the canons illegal (Dec.).

Ex officio oath: An oath, which was employed especially in the prerogative courts to compel a person to indict him- or herself on his or her own evidence. This was regarded by opponents of the crown as a basic infringement of common law principle.

Exchequer, Court of: From 1579, the Court of Exchequer (or Exchequer of Pleas) formally became the common law court dealing with financial cases.

Excise: The Excise Ordinance of 1643 authorised a new duty on home-produced beer, cider and perry, and on a range of imported luxury goods. Introduced to raise money for the war effort, the tax was without precedent in England and very unpopular – the right of search granted to commissioners was seen as a threat to personal liberty. Nevertheless, the excise was retained at the Restoration.

Exclusion Bills, 1679, 1680, 1681: These measures to exclude the catholic Duke of York from the succession were introduced by Shaftesbury's Whig party after their success in the 1679 elections. The 1679 Bill failed when Charles II immediately dissolved parliament; the 1680 Bill was rejected by the Lords, after passing the Commons; the 1681 Bill was again thwarted by parliament's dissolution.

Feoffees for impropriations: In 1625, a group of 12 puritan 'feoffees' (lawyers, clergy and London citizens) began to buy up any lay impro-priations which became vacant. This then enabled them to appoint 'godly' clergy to those livings with salaries paid by the feoffees. Surplus money was used to set up puritan lectureships. The feoffees were disbanded by Archbishop Laud in 1633.

Fifteenths and tenths: A tax on movable property (except personal clothing etc.), which was paid by all; originated in the thirteenth century. After 1640, this type of tax tended to be replaced by taxes on income.

Fifth Monarchists: A puritan sect (including Maj.-Gen. Thomas Harrison), which based its ideas on the prophesy in Nebuchadnezzar's dream that 'the fifth monarchy' of Christ's own kingdom on earth would appear after the collapse of four other kingdoms. Believing that it was the task of the 'saints' to prepare immediately for this kingdom, they scored their greatest success in 1653 with the establishment of Barebone's Parliament (or the Parliament of the Saints). After its dissolution, they became bitter enemies of Cromwell, planning his overthrow in Venner's abortive rising of 1657.

Five Articles, 1618: The General Assembly of the Church of Scotland, meeting at Perth and prompted by James VI & I, passed the Five Articles, which made provision for the observance of holy days, confirmation by bishops, kneeling at communion, private baptism and private communion. These measures were seen by many as indicative of a drift to popery.

Five Knights' Case, 1627: About 80 gentry were imprisoned for refusing to pay a forced loan levied by Charles I to help finance the war against France. Five of these (Darnel, Corbet, Erle, Hampden and Hevingham), in bringing their cause to the High Court, argued that they should either be charged or released on bail. The judgment of Lord Chief Justice Hyde against their release was taken as a sign that the judges had given legal sanction to both the loan and their indefinite imprisonment on the king's orders.

Five Members, 1642: Charles I attempted to impeach six of his leading opponents for high treason – Hampden, Haselrig, Holles, Pym and Strode from the Commons and Mandeville from the Lords. Failing to secure the co-operation of the two Houses in their arrest, the king (accompanied by 300 troops) went to the Commons himself to arrest the Five Members – an action seen as a breach of parliamentary privilege. The members, however, had been secretly alerted and had already made good their escape by boat to the city of London.

Five Mile Act, 1665: This banned nonconformist clergy from teaching; and from coming within five miles of a corporate town or a place where they had previously worked as ministers.

Forced knighthood: In an attempt to raise further revenue during his rule without parliament, Charles I appointed a commission (1630) to fine those in possession of land worth £40 per annum who had failed to take up knighthood (according to feudal custom) at his coronation. This device, which raised £165,000 (1630–35), was declared illegal by the Long Parliament in 1641.

Forced loans (or benevolences): A device used by English monarchs (including most of the Tudors and James I) to raise additional revenue from their wealthy subjects for emergencies. Charles I, however, met with considerable opposition to his attempts to impose loans in 1627 and 1628 (*see* Five Knights' Case), including a formal protest from the Commons in the Petition of Right (1628). Another loan was demanded in 1640.

Form of Apology and Satisfaction, 1604: Drafted by a group of MPs in the face of perceived threats to the liberties of parliament, the document expressed anxieties about 'the prerogatives of princes', which 'do daily grow', and the diminution of the privileges of the subject. The Commons eventually decided against presenting it to the king.

General Assembly: The governing body of the Church of Scotland (established *c*.1560), which had originally contained representatives from the three estates of the realm. By the seventeenth century, however, it consisted of ministers and elders elected by the local presbyteries.

General Baptists: Originated in the Netherlands, first appearing in England in 1612; believed in the baptism of adult believers, toleration and salvation for all by good works. They were active around London during the 1640s and forged links with radical groups. During the 1660s, they became politically inactive, but steadfastly refused to take any oath required by governments.

***Godden* v. *Hales*, 1686:** Godden sued his master, Sir Edward Hales (a Catholic), for breaching the Test Act by failing to take the sacrament and the specified oaths. The king's right to grant dispensations to individuals, however, was upheld by 11 of the 12 appeal judges on the King's Bench. Hales was subsequently appointed Governor of the Tower of London.

Goldsmiths' Hall Committee, 1644–50: Following the sequestration of royalist estates by parliamentary Ordinance (March 1643), this committee was set up (meeting in London at the Goldsmiths' Hall under the chairmanship of John Ashe) to compound with royalists for the return of their estates (i.e. to impose fines to the value of one-tenth, one-sixth, one-third or even two-thirds of their estates).

***Goodwin* v. *Fortescue*, 1604:** This concerned a disputed election for Buckinghamshire in which the return of Sir Frances Goodwin (an outlaw) had been declared void by the Court of Chancery. The Commons, insisting on their own privilege in the face of the crown's prerogative, ruled that Goodwin should take his seat (even though the by-election had been won by Sir John Fortescue). Although James insisted that all privileges stemmed from him, he finally accepted their right to be arbiters of disputed elections.

Grand Remonstrance, 1641: An address presented the king (1st December) and drafted by Pym; this catalogued grievances before demanding that Charles should only appoint ministers approved by parliament and that the Church should be reformed according to the recommendations of the Assembly of Divines. The Remonstrance, which passed the Commons by just 11 votes, served to force many moderates onto the king's side.

Great Contract, 1610: A plan devised by Salisbury, the Treasurer, to alleviate the crown's financial problems by granting the king a regular supply of £200,000 per annum (from land tax and excise) in return for his surrender of feudal rights (e.g. purveyance and wardship) and impositions. Negotiations, however, collapsed.

Gunpowder Plot, 1605: A plan to blow up the king and parliament, devised by Robert Catesby as a prelude to a catholic rising. The plotters were betrayed to Lord Cecil by Lord Monteagle, who had been taken into confidence; Guido Fawkes was caught red-handed as he prepared to light the fuse. The conspirators were executed and the penal laws against Catholics strictly enforced.

Habeas Corpus Amendment Act, 1679: This Act was introduced to safeguard personal liberty against threats from the royal prerogative, especially freedom from indefinite arrest without a formal charge being made in a court of law. It also declared illegal certain devices used by the crown's officers to evade the implications of the *habeas corpus* writ.

Hampden's Case, 1637: A group of the king's opponents, led by Lord Seye and Sele, decided to fight a test case through John Hampden, who refused to pay the ship money tax (which many feared would become a permanent tax). It was, however, ruled by 7 out of 12 judges in the Court of Exchequer that the king had the right to levy a tax for defence in time of danger and that he alone was the arbiter of what constituted danger.

Hampton Court Conference, 1604: James I reacted to the Millennary Petition by providing a platform for John Reynolds and three puritan ministers to debate in his presence their case for moderate reform with Archbishop Whitgift and eight bishops. Their use of the term 'presbytery', however, led him to fear that they were challenging his supremacy of the Church. He therefore warned them that they must conform, or he would 'harry them out of the land'.

Heads of Proposals, 1647: Moderate peace proposals, drafted by Henry Ireton and submitted to the king by the New Model Army (23rd July), including biennial parliaments with control of the army and navy for 10 years; free elections and reform of the franchise; foreign policy conducted by the Council of State for seven years; the end of insistence on either the Prayer Book or Covenant; easy composition terms for royalists. Rejected by the king.

High Commission, Court of: A prerogative court, it was the senior church court, which was summoned at the sovereign's discretion to administer penalties outside the common law. It was particularly used by Archbishop Laud in the 1630s to coerce opponents and to implement his religious policy in an arbitrary manner. Abolished by the Long Parliament in 1641, it was revived by James II (1686) under the name of the Court of Ecclesiastical Commission.

High Court of Justice, 1649: The name given to the court, which was formed to try Charles I on charges of high treason and levying war against his people. Appointed by the Rump Parliament, it consisted of 135 commissioners (although less than half of these attended) under the presidency of John Bradshaw.

Highland Host, 1678: Troops, consisting of both highlanders and lowland militia, who were sent to Ayreshire and Renfrewshire in 1678 and quartered on local people in an attempt to suppress resistence to the ecclesiastical settlement.

Humble Petition, 1648: A petition presented to parliament (11th September) from the citizens of London, but drafted by Lilburne as a full statement of Leveller beliefs. It stressed that the Commons were the supreme authority and that the king was accountable to them; and it listed their unfulfilled expectations of the present parliament.

Humble Petition and Advice, 1657: In its first draft (31st March), the petition urged Cromwell to accept the crown and restore the House of Lords in an end to arbitrary rule. After opposition from senior army officers, Cromwell rejected the kingship (8th May), but accepted an amended petition (25th May), which gave him power to nominate his successor and members of an Upper House – and made provision for the meeting of parliament at least once every three years.

Impeachment: A long-standing procedure (revived in 1621 after lapsing in 1459) to enable a person to be tried by the House of Lords on criminal charges, following a petition from the Commons. This made possible the trial of ministers and high-ranking officials, charged with offences against the state, in cases where ordinary courts would be unreliable (e.g. Buckingham, 1626; Strafford and Laud, 1640).

Impositions: The crown traditionally exercised the right to impose import duties for the regulation of trade and the protection of domestic industry. 'New Impositions' of this kind were imposed by Elizabeth I on currants and tobacco (1601) and extended by James I to most imports (1608) after a favourable ruling in Bate's Case (1606). In the face of parliament's angry protests in 1610, the tax was amended to ensure that the greatest impact fell on foreign merchants.

Indemnity and Oblivion, Act of, 1660: A general pardon, granted by the Convention Parliament in response to promises made in the Declaration of Breda, to all those involved in the Civil War or governments of the Interregnum - except 50 named individuals. Sir Henry Vane and 13 regicides were subsequently executed.

Independents: In religion, the term is often used as a collective name to describe puritan sects (especially Baptists and Congregationalists); but is used more precisely to denote those who believed in freedom of conscience and freedom of congregations to choose their their own forms of worship; they opposed national systems of organisation which anglican bishops and Presbyterians alike tried to impose. In politics, the term is used to denote those who usually identified with the 'war party', which stood for vigorous prosecution of the Civil War and outright defeat of the king. With their main strength in the army, they were also largely instrumental in bringing about Pride's Purge and the trial of Charles I. It cannot be assumed, however, that the 'political' Independents necessarily shared the religious views outlined above.

Instrument of Government, 1653: Drafted by John Lambert and the council of army officers, it represented England's first written constitution (16th December). It made provisions for a Lord Protector (Cromwell), triennial parliaments of 460 MPs, franchise reform, a Council of State, £200,000 to support the civil administration, exclusion

of royalists for the first four parliaments, an army of 30,000 and freedom of worship (except for Papists and Prelatists).

Interregnum: The term used to denote the period between the execution of Charles I (30th January 1649) and the Restoration of Charles II (8th May 1660), including the Commonwealth (19th May 1649 to 16th December 1653) and the Protectorate (to 25th May 1659).

Intruded Ministers: Clergy who were put into churches as replacements for those clergy who had been ejected either for scandal or for supporting the royalist cause in the Civil War.

Jacobites: The term used to denote the supporters of James II & VII after his deposition from the thrones of England and Scotland in the Glorious Revolution of 1688–89; and later, the adherents of his son, James Francis, and his grandson, Charles Edward.

Jesuits: Members of the Society of Jesus, a religious order established in 1534 to fight heresy and disseminate the catholic faith. Arriving in England in 1580, they became involved in political conspiracies against Elizabeth I and internal conflicts with the catholic secular priests. Their presence caused the penal laws against Catholics to be made more severe and they were banished in 1604, 1606 and 1610.

Junto: A term used to describe the Whig leaders who formed the administration under William III between 1696 and 1697 (i.e. Montagu, Russell, Somers, Wharton), and under Anne between 1708 and 1710 (i.e. Halifax, Orford, Somers, Sunderland, Wharton).

Kirk Act, 1706: Set against the background of debates on the union with England, this 'act for securing the protestant religion and presbyterian church government' was passed by the Scottish parliament. An additional article was subsequently added to the Act of Union (1707), guaranteeing the presbyterian church settlement of 1690.

Latitudinarianism: A belief, prevalent in ecclesiastical thought in the seventeenth century, that reason and personal judgment were of greater value than church doctrine.

Laudianism: The religious policies of Archbishop Laud in the 1630s, which combined Arminian views on salvation by works with Laud's own ideas on the beauty of holiness and the importance of episcopacy. This

led to the implementation of strict uniformity in worship and an increased emphasis on ceremony, the sacrament and the priesthood.

Lay impropriation: Tithes (i.e. tax payments of one-tenth of income to the church) had gradually been 'appropriated' or taken over by monasteries and bishops. After the dissolution of the monasteries in 1536–39, the tithes were often granted by the king to laymen, who therefore became 'lay impropriators' or 'lay rectors'. These regarded the tithes as personal income and only paid a small fraction of the value in the form of salary to the vicar, who performed the religious duties in the church. The lay impropriator often kept the 'great tithes' of corn, hay and wool for himself, leaving only the 'small tithes' for the vicar.

Lecturers: These had been established after the Reformation to supplement the work of parish clergy. During the 1620s and early 1630s, the Puritans exploited the system by gaining the appointment of calvinist preachers to these posts (often funded by puritan corporations or individuals) to counter the growth of Arminianism. Lecturers were difficult to control by bishops, because they were not bound by the oath imposed on beneficed clergy by the Canons of 1604. Laud therefore attempted to regulate the activities of such lecturers by imposing tight conditions on their operations (e.g. the need to read from the Book of Common Prayer in surplice and hood before the sermon was preached).

Levellers: A party of extreme radicals, active mainly in 1647–49, with support initially from the London mob and later from the ranks of the New Model Army. Led by Lilburne, Wildman and Rainsborough, they demanded manhood suffrage, abolition of both monarchy and House of Lords, religious toleration, social reform and equality before the law. The argued their beliefs with army officers in the Putney Debates (1647) and outlined them in their publications *The Case of the Army Truly Stated* (1647) and, *The Agreement of the People* (1647) and in The Humble Petition (1648).

Long Parliament, 1640: Called by Charles I on 3rd November 1640 and sat without dissolution until 16th March 1660, when it dissolved itself prior to the call of the Convention Parliament. Its presbyterian members were excluded in Pride's Purge (6th December 1648); thereafter it became known as the Rump Parliament, which was forcibly ejected by Oliver Cromwell (20th April 1653), but later recalled after Richard Cromwell's failure as Protector (7th May 1659). Those members excluded in Pride's Purge were restored after intervention by Monck (21st February 1660).

Lords of Erection: From 1606, these new lordships were created in Scotland based on former monastic lands – part of the policy of both James I and Charles I to expand the peerage and thus win political support through the widespread use of patronage.

Lords of the Articles: A committee (first established *c.*1467) appointed by the Scottish parliament; composed of the chief officers of state and representatives from all the estates with reponsibility for drawing up the agenda for the full parliament. Largely under the influence of the crown, its unpopularity ensured its abolition in 1641. The committee was revived at the Restoration in 1660.

Main Plot, 1603: A plot to overthrow James I in favour of Lady Arabella Stuart (a descendent of Mary Tudor); devised by Lord Cobham, who eventually turned king's evidence and implicated Sir Walter Raleigh. The latter was condemned to death, but reprieved; other conspirators were executed or imprisoned.

Major-Generals, 1655: The system of direct rule devised by Cromwell after the outbreak of Penruddock's Rising. The country was divided into 10 (later 11) areas, each controlled by a major-general with a cavalry-militia and financed by a decimation tax (i.e. a 10 per cent levy on land) imposed on royalists. Their task was to keep law and order, collect in the decimation, search out plots, suppress vice and encourage virtue. The system was abolished in January 1657.

Martial law: The term used to describe the system of maintaining law and order through use of the army and army courts, when ordinary courts had been suspended by royal proclamation. The practice was condemned in the Petition of Right (1628), following the imposition of martial law in certain districts by Charles I in 1627–28, after disturbances in protest at the billeting of soldiers.

Meal Tub Plot, 1679: This ficticious plot to prevent the succession of the catholic Duke of York was 'uncovered' by Thomas Dangerfield, after incriminating evidence had allegedly been found under a meal tub belonging to a Mrs Cellier. Aimed at bringing discredit to the Whigs and Presbyterians, the plot was quickly proved to be unauthentic.

Militia Acts, 1662–63: Parliament granted the king control of the militia, which was to be recruited from the the ranks of the wealthier citizens by the lord lieutenant of each county – with a possible demand for service anywhere in the country.

Militia Bill, 1642: This gave parliament the power to nominate the lord lieutenant of each county, thus gaining effective control of the trained bands. When Charles I refused to give assent to the Bill, parliament passed the Militia Ordinance (5th March), which legalised the measure without royal assent. The king then issued a proclamation (27th May) forbidding observance of the Ordinance by the militia.

Millenarianism: The belief that the second coming of Christ would herald his reign on earth for a period of one thousand years. Although most believers awaited this coming passively, others (including the Fifth Monarchists and Ranters) strove actively to prepare for it. Barebone's Parliament of 1653 consisted of many who believed that rule by the godly ('the saints') offered a vital period of preparation for this millennium.

Millenary Petition, 1603: This was presented to James I shortly after his accession, on his way to London from Scotland. Allegedly supported by over a thousand puritan ministers, it outlined their moderate demands for the reform of certain catholic practices in church worship (e.g. the sign of the cross in baptism, bowing to the altar, the positioning of the altar, the wearing of the surplice, etc.). James later called the Hampton Court Conference to debate these issues.

Monopolies: These enabled individuals or institutions to purchase, by royal favour, the exclusive right to produce or sell specific merchandise, or to issue licences. In spite of their unpopularity, James I revived the practice in 1612. Although monopolies were made illegal (except for inventors, boroughs and trading companies) by the Monopolies Act (1624), Charles I issued new monoplies to individuals in 1632 – before withdrawing them in 1639.

National Covenant, 1638: This manifesto was drawn up by Alexander Henderson and Archibald Johnston and signed in Greyfriars' Church, Edinburgh (February), to unite Scottish resistance to Charles I's innovations in religion (especially the introduction of a new Scottish Prayer Book) and opposition to the corrupt government of the Kirk.

New Model Army, 1645: Parliament's professional army, established by Ordinance (15th February 1645) on a suggestion by Waller and Cromwell. Numbering 22,000 troops in all, it consisted of 12 infantry regiments, 11 cavalry regiments, a regiment of dragoons, two regiments of fusiliers, a company of pioneers and a strong artillery unit. It was well trained, regularly paid and strictly disciplined. Commander-in-Chief was

Sir Thomas Fairfax, assisted by Oliver Cromwell (commander of cavalry) and Philip Skippon (commander of infantry).

Newport Treaty, 1648: Much to the annoyance of the army, negotiations between parliament (with its presbyterian majority) and the king resumed at the end of the Second Civil War. Held at Newport, Isle of Wight, they finally collapsed over details of a religious settlement.

Nineteen Propositions, 1642: This summary of parliament's demands, which centred on the question of sovereignty, was sent to the king at his headquarters in York. Parliament insisted on control of all major appointments, foreign policy, church reform and the education and marriage of the king's children. For his part, the king was required to enforce penal laws against Catholics, surrender all 'delinquents' to justice and sign the Militia Ordinance. Charles rejected these proposals.

Non-jurors: The term was used to describe the 400 high church clergy, including Archbishop Sancroft, who refused to swear oaths of allegiance to William III and Mary on the grounds that James II was still king *de jure.* They were, in consequence, deprived of their livings.

Occasional Conformity Act, 1711: This measure was designed to thwart evasion of the Test and Corporation Acts by many nonconformists who merely took the anglican communion once in order to retain office. Occasional Conformity Bills were introduced by the Tories in 1702, 1703 and 1704 to stop this practice, but were defeated by the Lords and opposed by the Whigs. The 1711 Act was passed by the Whigs unopposed, but was not strictly enforced.

Ordinances: The term used to denote legislation which passed through parliament, but lacked the royal assent (particularly during the period 1642–60). Such measures, therefore, could not strictly be described as 'Acts of Parliament', but rather 'Parliamentary Ordinances'.

Oxford Negotiations, 1643: These proposals for a settlement, which were put to the king in Oxford by commissioners sent by parliament (March), included punishment of key royalist advisers, abolition of episcopacy and enforcement of penal laws against Catholics. For his part, Charles I demanded surrender of all garrisoned strongholds, disbandment of parliament's army and removal of parliament to an area free from the intimidation of the London mob. The negotiations ended in stalemate.

Oxford Parliament: This was effectively Charles I's own alternative parliament, consisting of both MPs and peers, which met in the Great Hall of Christ Church College, Oxford, from January 1644 to March 1645.

Particular Baptists: These originated in the independent calvinist congregations on the continent and first appeared in England during the 1630s; believed in the baptism of adult believers, toleration and pre-destination. They grew rapidly in the 1640s and 1650s, developing links with radical groups and establishing an organisation. Unwilling to co-operate with the General Baptists, they became politically inactive after the Restoration, despite persecution.

Penruddock's Rising, 1655: The Sealed Knot conspirators had planned a general royalist rising in England, supported by a Scottish invasion and a personal appearance of Charles II from the continent (8th March). Although this rising was totally frustrated by the vigilance of government spies, a small rising did take place in the West, led by Wagstaffe, Penruddock, Jones and Grove (12th March). The rebels failed to raise sufficient support, after seizing the sheriff and judges in Salisbury, and were finally captured at South Molton.

Personal Rule: The term used to denote the period when Charles I ruled without parliament (10th March 1629–13th April 1640). It was particularly associated with the growth of Arminianism and the high church reforms of Archbishop Laud; the imposition of taxes which parliament later judged to be 'illegal'; Strafford's policy of 'Thorough' in Ireland; and the enforcement of policy through the unpopular courts of Star Chamber and High Commission.

Petition of Right, 1628: Before agreeing to the grant of subsidies at the start of the new parliament, the two Houses jointly presented Charles I with a petition embodying four resolutions, which requested a reaffirm-ation of their ancient rights and liberties together with a redress of their present grievances (especially martial law, forced loans, billeting and imprisonment without trial). To ensure supply, Charles gave assent to the Bill accommodating these resolutions.

Plantation: The method used from 1556 to subdue the Irish by removing natives and planting English and Scottish protestant settlers within certain counties (schemes organised by authorised 'undertakers' or 'adventurers'). Six counties in Ulster were extensively replanted after confiscations of land (1608–11); further large-scale confiscations took place under Cromwell (1653–55) with the transplantation of Irish rebels into Connaught.

Pluralities/Pluralism: The practice of holding more than one church living simultaneously (pluralism) was widespread in the sixteenth and early seventeenth centuries, thanks in part to the poor remuneration of clergy. The Canons of 1604, however, prohibited the holding of benefices in plurality, if they were more than 30 miles apart.

Poll tax: A tax on individuals which, in 1641, fixed contributions according to rank, occupation or income – ranging from £100 for a duke to 6d a head for poorer people.

Popish Plot, 1678: Rumours were spread by Titus Oates and Israel Tonge of a catholic plot to assassinate Charles II, massacre Protestants and install James, Duke of York, as king. In the resulting scare, which lasted until 1681, Lord Chief Justice Scroggs and other judges condemned 35 men to death for treason; all Catholics were banned from coming within 10 miles of London; the Test Act was passed and Shaftesbury's 'Country Party' introduced Exclusion Bills. Oates was later convicted of perjury.

Predestination: This formed the central doctrine to the teaching of John Calvin, namely that salvation through the atonement of Christ on the cross was pre-ordained by God from the beginning for a minority of mankind only (i.e. the 'elect'). He therefore rejected the doctrines of universal salvation and free will by stressing that the majority were pre-ordained to damnation.

Presbyterians: In religion, the term is used to denote those Puritans who believed in a system of church government (similar to that in Scotland) by ministers and lay elders (or 'presbyters') elected by all who had taken the Covenant. Opposed therefore to rule by bishops, they favoured strict uniformity of beliefs and rules for worship on a national basis with local *classes*, regional assemblies and national synods responsible for formulating policy. In politics, the term is used to denote those who identified with the moderate 'peace party' which desired a settlement with the king after the ending of the Civil War. Conservative and opposed to social revolution, they were not in favour of religious toleration and were increasingly distrustful of the New Model Army. It cannot be assumed, however, that political and religious views always merged. It was, for instance, possible to be a Presbyterian in religion, but an Independent in politics – or a member of the 'middle group'.

Presbyteries: These provincial assemblies of ministers and elders, drawn from local churches, formed part of the mechanism of government within the national presbyterian system.

Pride's Purge, 1648:   The officers of the New Model Army, furious at the resumption of negotiations with the king at Newport by the presbyterian majority in the Commons, ordered a purge of parliament. Colonel Thomas Pride, with a group of musketeers, forcibly removed 143 presbyterian MPs, leaving a remnant or 'rump' of about 50 who supported the army (6th December). This Rump Parliament, as it became known, immediately proceeded with the establishment of a court to try the king.

Privy Council: This smaller body of court advisers had emerged by the fourteenth century from the King's Council (or parliament); by the sixteenth century, it had developed important political, administrative and judicial functions, giving advice to the sovereign and undertaking much detailed business of central government. By the seventeenth century, various standing committees had been formed to handle specific areas; and the standing committee on foreign affairs had evolved into an 'inner cabinet council'.

Prophesyings: The term used to denote gatherings of clergy to discuss and expound the scriptures, usually in the presence of the laity.

Propositions of Newcastle, 1646:   Parliament summarised its terms for a settlement with the king and his return to the throne in these proposals, which were sent to him in captivity with the Scots at Newcastle – namely, his agreement to abolish episcopacy, reform the Church, take the Covenant, authorise parliament's control of foreign policy and the army for 20 years and accept the punishment of his supporters. These were rejected by Charles.

Prorogation: The term used to denote the bringing of a session of parliament to an end without actually dissolving it (i.e. keeping open the possibility of further sessions).

Protectorate: This was established by the Instrument of Government (16th December 1653), which stipulated that government was to consist of a Protector, a Council of State and the House of Commons. From May

1657, a 'Second Chamber' was added and the Protector was given the right to nominate his successor. The 1st Protectorate Parliament met in 1654; the 2nd betweeen 1656 and 1658. Richard Cromwell succeeded his father (3rd September 1658), but soon abdicated (25th May 1659).

Protestation, 1621: James I, furious at parliament's intrusion into matters concerning what he believed was the royal prerogative (i.e. foreign policy and the marriage of his children), threatened action against those who interfered in his business. The Commons, angrily reminding him of their traditional privilege of freedom of speech, entered the Protestation in their Journal (18th December). Their liberties and privileges were, it stated, 'the ancient and undoubted birthright and inheritance of the subjects of England'. James tore out the offending page and dissolved parliament.

Puritans: Originally the term denoted those people inside the Church of England who wanted to 'purify' it after the 1559 settlement with further reforms of doctrine and church practices (as outlined in the Millenary Petition of 1603). By 1640, they had added a call for the abolition of episcopacy. The term is used more generally to denote all those, whether inside or outside the Church, who wanted further reform of a protestant nature. After the outbreak of civil war, the Puritans broke up into a variety of sects, which became more distinct and exclusive. Later, after the Act of Uniformity in 1662, they tended to be classed as nonconformists.

Purveyance: The traditional right of the crown to purchase supplies for the royal household at prices below market level.

Putney Debates, 1647: Representatives of the officers and Agitators from each regiment in the New Model Army met with the senior officers in Putney church (28th October–8th November) to debate Leveller ideas, as expressed in the *Agreement of the People*. Fundamental differences in opinion emerged, the debate ending in stalemate.

Quakers (or Friends): The movement began in the 1650s under its leader, George Fox. They believed in revelation of God to the individual through an 'inner light', which brought greater authority than scripture, laws or institutions. They opposed the concept of an organised church with buildings, clergy and formal prayers. They attracted persecution, partly because of their perceived mysticism and partly because of their policy of breaking up church services.

Quo Warranto: This was a writ which demanded that the owner of a particular charter should surrender it for legal scrutiny. Charles II and James II employed these frequently against boroughs incorporated by royal charter, which usually submitted meekly in view of the expense incurred in fighting the royal will.

Ranters: The movement developed during the 1650s as part of the growth of radicalism after the ending of the Civil War. They believed that God was present in every person and that the gaining of salvation provided them with the freedom to violate God's laws. They therefore became notorious for sexual excesses and blasphemy – hence the passing of the Blasphemy Act of 1650.

Rector: A clergyman of a parish who performed the religious duties and enjoyed the tithes (i.e. they had not been appropriated by a lay rector – *see* Lay impropriation). A vicar or 'substitute' was a clergyman appointed by a lay rector to perform the religious duties on his behalf at a salary (i.e. instead of tithes).

Recusancy: Those who refused to attend services of the Church of England were called recusants and, from 1552, were subject to weekly fines (increased to £20 per month in 1581). Catholics were in addition subject to a number of penal laws (resulting in imprisonment or banishment), which were extended in 1606 and 1610.

Regality Courts: These courts in Scotland were landlords' courts, which were free from the operation of justiciars and sheriffs and had the power to try all cases (except treason) in their own 'little kingdom' associated with particular lands.

Regicides: The term used to denote the 59 commissioners who signed Charles I's death warrant (1st January 1649). Later (October 1660), 29 of these were tried and convicted of treason, although only 13 were actually executed. The bodies of three, who had died earlier (Cromwell, Bradshaw and Ireton), were exhumed and ceremonially hung, drawn and quartered at Tyburn.

Remonstrance of the Army, 1648: A petition to parliament from the council of army officers (20th November), which demanded sovereignty of the people, payment of army arrears, removal of Presbyterians from parliament and the trial of the king. Influenced in part by Leveller opinion, it was instantly rejected. Pride's Purge followed shortly afterwards.

Restoration, 1660:   Charles II was invited to resume the throne by the Convention Parliament, after he had issued the Declaration of Breda. In the agreed settlement, parliament ratified the king's right to dissolve parliament, appoint his own ministers, conduct foreign policy, command the armed forces and veto legislation. He was, however, denied the right to continue with some practices adopted earlier in the century – namely, to employ the courts of Star Chamber and High Commission, to impose taxes without parliament's consent and to amend the law by royal proclamation.

Revocation of Lands, 1625:   In Scotland, the king could – before reaching his 25th birthday – legally and traditionally revoke all grants made by him during his minority. In 1625, Charles I revoked all grants made since 1540 in a move to recover the teinds (tithes) from lay impropriators and thus fund clerical salaries. The move aroused widespread alarm and opposition from property owners.

Root and Branch Bill, 1641:   The Bill (27th May), which resulted from a petition from 15,000 London citizens and clergy urging the abolition of episcopacy 'with all its dependencies, roots and branches' (11th December 1640), advocated the abolition of bishops, deans and chapters and the setting up of county commissions of clergy and laity to organise church affairs. The Bill was shelved after deep divisions had been revealed in the debate.

Rump Parliament: A remnant or 'rump' of about 50 MPs had been left in the Commons after the expulsion of Presbyterians and their allies by the army in Pride's Purge (6th December 1648). Although later additions were made, membership was never greater than 125, with attendance usually around 80. After the abolition of the monarchy (19th May 1649), the Rump governed with a Council of State until its ejection by Cromwell (20th April 1653). It was recalled briefly (7th May 1659).

Rye House Plot, 1683:   A plot, devised by Richard Rumbold, to ambush and assassinate Charles II and the Duke of York on their return from the races at Newmarket. Having been thwarted by the royal couple's premature departure, the conspirators were betrayed by Josiah Keeling. Members of the Council of Six (Whig exclusionists Grey, Sydney, Monmouth, Essex, Howard and Russell) were also unfairly implicated.

Savoy House Conference, 1660:   This conference of 12 bishops and 12 Presbyterians at the Savoy Palace assembled in response to Charles II's

Declaration on Ecclesiastical Affairs, in which he put forward his preference for a comprehensive settlement in religion. It ended in deadlock with the bishops rejecting presbyterian proposals for Prayer Book modifications and acceptance of a 'Savoy Liturgy'.

Sealed Knot: In 1653, Charles II in exile appointed a group of six royalists in England (Villiers, Compton, Belasyse, Russell, Willys and Loughborough) to work out details for a royalist rising. This 'Sealed Knot', as they were called, made plans for a rising in the spring of 1655 to be led by the Earl of Rochester, but were thwarted by the work of government spies. Penruddock's Rising was an isolated episode in this affair.

Sectaries: The term was used to denote those protestant sects which emerged during and after the Civil War and were more radical than the Independents and Presbyterians. They included Baptists, Fifth Monarchists, Quakers, Ranters and Seekers, as well as many more groups with extreme theological ideas. They were all opposed to the parochial structure of a national church, most preferring independent congregations with elected ministers.

Security, Act of, 1703: This was passed by the Scottish parliament in response to the passing of the Act of Settlement in England (1701) without any consultation in Scotland. Through the Security Act, the parliament claimed for itself the right to control the royal succession in Scotland, including its own protestant nominee to succeed Queen Anne.

Self-Denying Ordinance, 1645: Set against the background of growing dissatisfaction inside parliament with the conduct of the Civil War, this Ordinance (3rd April) demanded the resignation, within 40 days, of members of both Houses from all military or civil offices held since 20th November 1640. By adding a rider that individuals might be reappointed later at the will of parliament, the measure ensured quality leadership for the New Model Army.

Separatists: The term was used to denote those who separated from the established Church in the belief that each 'gathered congregation' should control its own affairs. They therefore rejected the idea of a national church organised on a parochial system. These congregational separatists, who had strong links with the continent, first emerged in England in Elizabeth's reign, but had largely disappeared by the 1640s.

Sequestration: The term used to denote the confiscation of royalist estates during and after the Civil War (authorised by the Ordinance of 27th March 1643) with the income being used to maintain parliament's forces. Royalists were later permitted to pay a composition (or fine) for the return of their estates (*see* Goldsmiths' Hall Committee, 1644–50).

Settlement, Act of, 1701: This stipulated that the succession was to pass to the Electress Sophia of Hanover or her protestant heirs, if William III and Anne both died without heirs. Future sovereigns were required to receive the anglican communion and to agree not to leave the country or to become involved in wars to defend continental territory without parliament's permission.

Seven Bishops' Case, 1688: Archbishop Sancroft and six bishops submitted a petition to James II, requesting him to withdraw his order that clergy should read the Declaration of Indulgence in churches on two consecutive Sundays (on the grounds that parliament had ruled against the legality of the royal dispensing power). Although the bishops were prosecuted for seditious libel on the king's instructions, they were acquitted amid popular acclaim.

Ship money: The tax, paid traditionally by coastal towns and counties for their protection against threats from sea, was revived by Charles I in 1634 – and then extended one year later, amid great unpopularity, to inland areas according to wealth and size. Ship money, which was imposed for six years (1635–40), proved increasingly difficult to collect (e.g. only £43,417 was received in 1639 out of £214,000 assessed). The Long Parliament made the tax illegal (1641).

Short Parliament, 1640: In the face of a war with the Scots, Charles I called this parliament (13th April) to secure financial support. However, the Commons (under the guidance of Pym) insisted first on a consideration of their grievances relating to recent abuse of royal power and the king's infringement of their liberties. Charles quickly dissolved parliament (5th May).

Solemn Engagement, 1647: This resolution was unanimously adopted by the army when it staged a mutiny at Newmarket (29th May) in protest at parliament's threat to disband them without payment of arrears. The troops pledged themselves to resist disbandment until the army's council (consisting of the general officers with two officers and two soldiers from each regiment) had negotiated satisfactory terms.

Solemn League and Covenant, 1643: This consisted of an alliance between the English parliament and the Scots in their struggle against Charles I. In return for the immediate help of a Scottish army, parliament agreed to pay a monthly sum of £30,000 for its upkeep and to establish the presbyterian church system in England and Ireland.

Star Chamber, Court of: This body, which met in the Star Chamber at the Palace of Westminster, had gradually emerged from the Privy Council in the sixteenth century as a court specialising in political or public order cases. Operating outside common law, it was used increasingly by Charles I to deal ruthlessly and speedily with his political opponents. Abolished by the Long Parliament (1641), it had become unpopular as an instrument of arbitrary rule.

Stop of the Exchequer, 1672: The government, faced with enormous debts and the need to raise immediate cash to finance the Third Anglo-Dutch War, ordered the cessation of interest payments on part of its outstanding loans from bankers. The bankruptcy of five city financiers which ensued led to a collapse of confidence. The payments were later made up at 6 per cent interest.

Subsidy: This was a tax on income for landowners, office-holders and wage-earners and on movable property for merchants, tenant farmers and artisans. Subsidies were granted by parliament as part of the sovereign's 'extraordinary' revenue for specific needs, such as war. By the seventeenth century, the tax was often based on outdated assessments and was therefore not very productive.

Suspending power: James II claimed the right, through the royal prerogative, to suspend the operation of any particular law. Thus, in 1687, he suspended the penal laws against Roman Catholics and nonconformists in his Declaration of Indulgence. This enabled them to practise their own religion openly. However, the use of the suspending power without parliamentary sanction was made illegal by the Bill of Rights (1689).

Synod: A gathering of elected ministers and elders, which formed part of the mechanism of government within the national presbyterian system. The synod stood midway between the regional presbytery and the General Assembly.

Tables: A committee set up in 1637 in Scotland to lead the opposition to Charles I and the new Scottish Prayer Book; composed of four representatives from each estate of the realm. The National Covenant resulted from its deliberations.

Teinds: The term used in Scotland to denote the tithe or tenth part of income, which parishioners were obliged to pay for the maintenance of the local church and minister.

Test Act, 1673, 1678: The 1673 Act stipulated that all office-holders were to take the oaths of allegiance and supremacy, a declaration against transubstantiation and the sacrament as used in the anglican church. In the 1678 Act, all Roman Catholics were banned from taking up seats in parliament (except the Duke of York).

Thorough: The term used to describe the ruthlessly efficient system of government during Charles I's personal rule (1629–40) aimed at central-ised control. It was employed particularly by Strafford as President of the Council of the North (1628–33) and Lord Deputy of Ireland (1632–39) and Laud as Archbishop of Canterbury (1633–45). Their high-handed use of the crown's prerogative courts (i.e. the courts of Star Chamber and High Commission) was deeply resented.

Three Resolutions, 1629: Charles I ordered an adjournment of the Commons in response to their repeated criticism of his ministers and the growth of Arminianism. However, after Eliot had secured the agreement of an angry House to lock the king's bodyguard outside, the Speaker was forcibly held down in his chair while the Three Resolutions were passed against innovations in religion or extension of popery, and the levying or payment of unauthorised tunnage and poundage.

Tithes: A tax amounting to one-tenth of the personal income, profits or agricultural produce of the laity, given in support of the clergy. After the dissolution of the monasteries, the right to many of these was bought up by lay impropriators, who paid vicars to fulfil the ecclesiastical duties within the parish.

Trained bands (also called the militia): Originally established in 1573 in the face of an expected invasion from Spain, they consisted of ordinary citizens (formed into companies of foot and horse) who trained at weekends in readiness to defend their counties. Deputy lieutenants were required to call musters and ensure that armouries were stocked. At the start of the Civil War, both sides tried hard to seize control of these bands.

Transplantation: After the suppression of the 1641 Irish rebellion, parliament passed an Act for the Settlement of Ireland (1652), categorising the population according to guilt in the rebellion. Many subsequently had their lands confiscated and were transplanted to Connaught (1653–55).

Triennial Act, 1641, 1664:   The 1641 Act stipulated that the king should summon parliament every three years for a session of at least 50 days; and that, in cases of non-compliance, parliament should automatically be summoned through writs issued by the Lord Chancellor and the Lord Keeper. The 1664 Act repealed the previous act and, though stating that parliament should meet at least once every three years, relied entirely on the king to ensure that this happened. The 1694 Act not only reiterated that parliament must meet 'once in three years at the least', but also added a new stipulation that no parliament was to last more than three years at most without dissolution.

Triers: A commission of 35 Triers, consisting of presbyterian, independent and baptist ministers, was appointed by Cromwell (20th March 1654) to examine and approve clergy who had been nominated by private patrons.

Tonnage and Poundage: These customs duties were imposed on every tun of wine imported and every pound's worth of merchandise either imported or exported. Although, from the fifteenth century, they had been traditionally granted to the monarch for life by the first parliament of the reign, the 1625 parliament granted them to Charles I for one year only.

Uniformity, Act of, 1662:   This required all clergy and schoolmasters to swear an oath agreeing to use the newly revised Prayer Book, rejecting the Covenant and denouncing rebellion. In addition, all parish clergy were to be ordained by a bishop and all schoolmasters licensed by a bishop. Two thousand clergy were ejected from their livings in consequence for non-compliance.

Union, Act of, 1707:   Under the terms of this Act, which safeguarded the presbyterian church in Scotland and the Scottish judicial system, 16 peers and 45 MPs were to represent Scotland in the Parliament of Great Britain.

Unitarians: The term was used to denote those who believed in the unity of the Godhead, as opposed to the doctrine of the Trinity.

Uxbridge Negotiations, 1645: These peace discussions took place at Uxbridge between commissioners from the king (led by Richmond), the Scots (led by Loudon) and parliament (led by Vane and St John). The so-called Uxbridge Treaty was to be based on the establishment of a presbyterian church system, control of foreign affairs and the forces by parliament and punishment of leading royalists. Charles rejected the proposals.

Venner's Rising, 1661: Thomas Venner, a winecooper, was leader of the more militant wing of the Fifth Monarchists. After his plans for a plot to overthrow the government had been uncovered in 1657, he led an armed rising in London in 1661. With no more than 50 men, he held the trained bands at bay for four days before his inevitable defeat. Venner and 10 others were executed.

Vote of No Addresses, 1648: This decision of the Long Parliament (17th January) was passed in the face of an impending 'engagement' between the king and the Scots. They resolved to halt all further approaches to the king regarding a settlement and to replace the Committee of Both Kingdoms with the Derby House Committee. The vote was repealed after the ending of the Second Civil War (September), when negotiations recommenced.

Wardship: This was the king's feudal right to act as guardian to those tenants who inherited estates as minors (i.e. for boys, under 21; for girls, under 14). Wardship could either be undertaken directly by the king through the Court of Wards, which supervised the welfare and education of the minors and administered their estates (with the king enjoying the revenue); or sold to the highest bidder, who could abuse the trust and waste the inheritance.

Westminster Assembly, 1643–49: In 1643, parliament established the 'Assembly of Learned and Godly Divines' to settle the government of the Church according to the Solemn League and Covenant. Consisting of 120 puritan clergy (including representatives from each county, each university and the city of London) and 30 laymen (including 10 peers and 20 Members of Parliament) and (later) 8 Scottish commissioners, it issued the Directory of Worship to replace the Book of Common Prayer, the catechism, the calvinist Westminster Confession of Faith and a plan for a presbyterian system of church government.

SECTION FIVE

Biographies

These biographical notes on influential political, military and religious leaders detail the most important points in each life, but do not attempt a full-scale biographical study with critical comment. For more comprehensive coverage, reference should be made to either the relevant works listed in the bibliographical section of this book or the compact assessments contained in the *Dictionary of National Biography*, C.P. Hill, *Who's Who in Stuart Britain* (London, 1988) and Edwin Riddell, ed., *Lives of the Stuart Age, 1603–1714* (London, 1976).

Abbot, George (1562–1633): Son of Maurice Abbot, cloth worker of Guildford; educated at Guildford Grammar School and Oxford; appointed Master of University College, Oxford (1597), Vice-Chancellor (1600), Bishop of Lichfield (1609), Bishop of London (1610) and Archbishop of Canterbury (1611). A moderate Puritan, he accompanied James I to Scotland (1608) and assisted in restoring episcopacy there. His anti-Spanish and anti-arminian views brought him into opposition at court to Robert Carr (over the divorce of the Countess of Essex), the Howards and George Villiers (over the Spanish marriage proposal). His reputation suffered over the killing of Lord Zouch's gatekeeper in a shooting accident (1621). His conflict with Charles I over Arminianism was brought to a head when Abbot refused to authorise the publication of Robert Sibthorp's sermon justifying the forced loan (1627); he was suspended in consequence with Laud heading a commission to take over his powers.

Albermarle, Duke of (1608–70) – *see* Monck, George.

Anne (1665–1714): Daughter of James, Duke of York (James II) and Anne Hyde; married Prince George of Denmark (1683), but all 18 children died either at birth or in early childhood; educated as a Protestant; developed an early friendship at court with Sarah Jennings (later Duchess of Marlborough), who became Lady of the Bedchamber. Anne deserted her father and fled to Nottingham on the invasion of William of Orange (1688), quickly recognising William and her sister, Mary, as joint sovereigns. Decreed as the next-in-line by the Declaration of Rights in 1688 (a fact confirmed by the Act of Settlement (1701), she succeeded to the throne on 8th March 1702, appointing Sarah as Keeper of the Privy Purse and Marlborough as Captain-General of the army. Her limited intellect and poor health made her largely dependent upon her ministers and the Marlboroughs, who dominated her decision-making until 1710. A keen advocate of the High Church, she established a fund (known as Queen Anne's Bounty) to supplement the stipends of poorly-paid clergy (1704), supported an act to build 50 new churches in London (1711) and strove to control appointments within the Church. Otherwise she played little personal role in the Act of Union (1707), the Treaty of Utrecht (1713) or major acts of policy. Patriotic by nature, she nevertheless gloried in the success of Marlborough's armies in the War of Spanish Succession. From 1707, her relationship with the Duchess of Marlborough became strained as Abigail Masham (a relative of Robert Harley) gradually grew in personal influence at court. After the death of her husband, Prince George (1708), Anne turned for support increasingly to Abigail (appointed Keeper of the Privy Purse, 1711) and Harley (created Earl of Oxford, 1711). The return of a Tory ministry under Harley (1710) precipitated the break with both Sarah (1710) and Marlborough (1711).

Argyll, 8th Earl & 1st Marquess (1598–1661) – *see* Campbell, Archibald.

Argyll, 9th Earl of (1629–85) – *see* Campbell, Archibald.

Argyll, 1st Duke of (1651–1703) – *see* Campbell, Archibald.

Arlington, 1st Earl of (1616–85) – *see* Bennet, Henry.

Bacon, Francis (1561–1626): Son of Lord Keeper Bacon; educated at Cambridge and Gray's Inn; called to the Bar (1582). MP for Melcombe Regis (1584), Taunton (1586), Liverpool (1589), Middlesex (1593), Southampton (1597). Appointed Queen's learned counsel (1596); failed to support the Earl of Essex in his treason trial (1601). Knighted by James I (1603); supported union with Scotland (1607); appointed Solicitor-General (1607), Attorney–General (1613), Privy Councillor (1616), Lord Keeper (1617) and Lord Chancellor (1618). Took part in the prosecution of Somerset (1616), Raleigh (1618) and Suffolk (1619). Backed James in his quarrel with Sir Edward Coke. Created Baron Verulam (1618) and Viscount St Albans (1621). Charged with bribery as Chancellor (1621) and dismissed, but granted a royal pardon. Publications included *Essays* (1597), *A Confession of Faith* (1603), *Advancement of Learning* (1605), *Novum Organum* (1620), *History of Henry VII* (1622) and *Maxims of the Law* (1630).

Baillie, Robert (1599–1662): Son of a Glasgow merchant; educated at Glasgow University; married (1) Lilias Fleming and (2) Mrs Wilkie; ordained into the Episcopal Church (1622), but later joined a presbyterian congregation; refused to preach in favour of Laud's new

Scottish Prayer Book (1637). Elected to the General Assembly (1638); chaplain to the covenanter armies (1639–40); appointed member of the Scottish delegation to London to assist in the indictment of Laud (1640). A moderate anti-Arminian, he recorded the events of these years and his own presbyterian views in his *Letters and Journals* (1637–62), *Antidote against Arminianism* (1641), *The Unlawfulness and Danger of Limited Prelacie and Episcopacie* (1641), etc. Appointed Professor of Divinity at Glasgow University (1642); member of the Westminster Assembly; member of the General Assembly's embassy to the court of Charles II at The Hague with the aim of offering him the crown in return for acceptance of the Covenant. Appointed Principal of Glasgow University (1660), having refused a bishopric.

Bancroft, Richard (1544–1610): Son of John Bancroft, gentleman of Farnworth, Lancs.; educated at Farnworth Grammar School and Cambridge; appointed one of 12 licensed preachers to the university (1576); member of Whitgift's Ecclesiastical Commission (1586); canon of Westminster Abbey (1587). He preached a fiercely anti-puritan sermon at Paul's Cross (1589) and assisted in the detection of the printers of the Marprelate Tracts (1589). Appointed Chaplain to Archbishop Whitgift (1592); Bishop of London (1597); and Archbishop of Canterbury (1604). Met with puritan leaders at Hampton Court (1604), showing uncompromising hostility towards them. Published his Book of Canons (1604), compelling acceptance by the clergy of the Thirty-Nine Articles, kneeling at communion and the wearing of the cope and surplice; resulted in fierce opposition by common lawyers and the House of Commons – and the loss of livings by many clergy. Issued his Articles of Abuse (1605), protesting at the interference by civil judges with the proceedings of ecclesiastical courts. Elected Chancellor of Oxford University (1608).

Bastwick, John (1593–1654): Born at Writtle, Essex; educated at Cambridge (briefly) and Padua; practised as a doctor in Colchester (from 1623). A keen Puritan, he wrote *Flagellum Pontificis* (1634) in support of Presbyterianism, for which he was convicted of scandalous libel by the Court of High Commission, fined and imprisoned; and the *Litanie of Dr John Bastwicke* (1637), a denunciation of bishops, for which (in the company of William Prynne and Henry Burton) he was sentenced by Star Chamber to the loss of his ears, a £5,000 fine and imprisonment for life. He received much popular support; was imprisoned on St Mary's, Scilly Isles, until 1640, when he was released by the Long Parliament. Fought for parliament in the Civil War, later writing pamphlets in support of the Presbyterians against the Independents, who largely controlled the army.

Baxter, Richard (1615–91): Son of Richard Baxter of Eaton Constantine, Shropshire; educated privately and through reading at Ludlow Castle; a Puritan by conviction, he was ordained (1638); appointed headmaster of a school in Dudley (1638); and assistant minister in Bridgnorth (1639). He led opposition in Shropshire to the 'et cetera oath', imposed by Convocation on all professionals (1640); appointed lecturer in Kidderminster (1641–60), transforming the spiritual life of the town. Supported parliament in the Civil War, despite his natural conservatism and belief in the monarchy; appointed chaplain in the army, where he disapproved of increasing sectarianism; opposed the Solemn League and Covenant, the Engagement, the execution of the king and all forms of arbitrary rule. Wrote *Aphorisms of Justification* (1649), which described his dealings with the sectaries; and *The Saints' Everlasting Rest* (1650), a pioneering work in popular Christian literature. Moved to London (1660), where he worked for the Restoration of Charles II; was appointed a royal chaplain, but declined a bishopric; was excluded from the Church by the restrictions contained in the Act of Uniformity (1662), retiring to Acton, Middlesex. On the accession of James II, was arrested, tried and imprisoned on a charge of libelling the Church in his *Paraphrase of the New Testament* (1685); released (1686) and preached to large congregations; supported the revolution of 1688. His *Reliquiae Baxterianae*, a narrative of his own life, was published in 1696.

Bennet, Henry, 1st Earl of Arlington (1618–85): Son of Sir John Bennet, a lawyer of Saxham, Suffolk; educated at Westminster School and Oxford; married Isabella von Beverweert, daughter of Louis of Nassau (1666); fought for the king in the Civil War and served as adviser to Charles II in exile; appointed royalist representative to the Spanish court in Madrid (1658). After the Restoration, was appointed Keeper of the Privy Purse (1661); and Secretary of State for the Southern Department (1662), with particular responsibility for foreign affairs; supported war against the United Provinces. Created Lord Arlington (1665). Supported the dismissal and impeachment of his rival Clarendon (1667). A member of the Cabal government (1667–74). Instrumental in the establishment of the Triple Alliance with the United Provinces and Sweden (1668); but also heavily involved in the Secret Treaty of Dover (1670) with France for a war against the Dutch and the reintroduction of Catholicism to England. Created earl (1672). His policies were attacked by parliament (1673), which also passed the Test Act, forcing his ally, Clifford of the

Cabal, to resign. Increasingly overshadowed by Danby, the new Treasurer, he was sent on an abortive peace mission to Holland (1673). Resigned his Secretaryship and was appointed Lord Chamberlain (1674); retired to Suffolk (1675); assisted in the impeachment of Danby (1678); confessed to Catholicism on his death bed. Unpopular with his contemporaries, he was widely distrusted as being totally lacking in principle.

Bentinck, William, 1st Earl of Portland (1649–1709): Son of Bernhard Bentinck of Diepenheim, a Dutch nobleman; appointed Page-of-Honour (1664) and then Gentleman of the Bedchamber to William of Orange; served with the prince in the Third Dutch War, nursing him when sick with smallpox (1675). Negotiated in England the prince's marriage with Mary, daughter of the Duke of York (1678); trusted by William to prepare for the invasion of England (1688), negotiating the neutrality of the German princes, organising the navy and encouraging support inside England. Created Earl of Portland (1688); fought with William in Ireland (1690) and the Netherlands (1691). His diplomatic skills helped to secure the Treaty of Ryswick (1697) and the two Partition Treaties (1698, 1700), concerning the Spanish Succession. His close friendship with the king caused envy and unpopularity, as did his Dutch origins. He felt increasingly overshadowed by van Keppel, the king's new favourite; resigned his offices at court (1699); but survived an attempt by the Commons to impeach him (1701); withdrew from public affairs on the death of William (1701).

Blake, Robert (1599–1657): Son of Humphrey Blake, a Bridgwater merchant; educated at Bridgwater Grammar School and Oxford. MP for Bridgwater in the Short Parliament (1640) and the Long Parliament (from 1645). Fought for parliament in the Civil War, distinguishing himself in the siege of Bristol (1643); defended Lyme against siege (1644); captured and, as Governor, rebuilt Taunton after siege (1644–45). Appointed joint Commander of the Fleet (1649); then Warden of the Cinque Ports and sole Commander of the Winter Fleet at Plymouth. Blockaded Prince Rupert in the Tagus (1650) and destroyed most of his fleet at Malaga (1651). Appointed to the Council of State (1651). In the First Anglo-Dutch War, fought indecisive battles off Dover and the Kentish Knock (1652); was defeated off Dungeness (1652); but won victories off Portland and the Gabbard (1653). In the Spanish War, he commanded the Mediterranean Fleet (1656). Died at sea (1658); buried in Westminster Abbey, but disinterred later by royalists.

Booth, George (1622–84): Son of William Booth of Cheshire; MP for Cheshire (1645, 1654, 1656); fought for parliament in the Civil War; appointed military commissioner for Cheshire (1655). Later joined a group of Presbyterians and cavaliers supportive of Charles II; led a rebellion in Cheshire, North Wales and Lancashire in favour of a free parliament (Aug. 1659) – captured Chester, but eventually defeated by Lambert at Nantwich Bridge; after a brief imprisonment, resumed his seat in parliament and was a member of the delegation sent to The Hague to negotiate for the return of Charles II. At the Restoration, was created Baron Delemere (1661) and appointed Keeper of the Rolls in Cheshire; thereafter, played no further part in public affairs.

Bolingbroke, 1st Viscount (1678–1751) – *see* St John, Henry.

Boyle, Richard, 1st Earl of Cork (1566–1643): Son of Roger Boyle, gentleman of Canterbury; educated at King's School, Canterbury, Cambridge and the Middle Temple. Emigrated to Ireland (1588); appointed assistant to the Escheator-General (1590); married (1) Joan Appsley (1595) and (2) Catherine Fenton (1603); returned to London on the outbreak of revolution (1598). Returned to Ireland on appointment as Clerk to the Council of Munster (1599); chosen to convey to the Queen the news of the rebels' defeat at Kinsale (1601); knighted (1603). Helped by Cecil to purchase cheaply substantial lands in Munster belonging to Raleigh; settled these lands with armed English colonists; established iron, woollen and shipbuilding industries; built towns, defences and the necessary infrastructure; became wealthy and powerful. Appointed to the Privy Council of Ireland (1612); created Lord Boyle (1616) and Earl of Cork (1620); appointed Lord Justice of Ireland (1629) and Lord High Treasurer (1631). From 1633, he was subject to Wentworth's (later Strafford's) policies of high taxation and subjugation of the powerful in Ireland; moved to England (1638) and assisted in bringing Strafford to trial and execution (1641).

Boyle, Roger, 1st Baron Broghill & 1st Earl of Orrery (1621–79): Son of Richard Boyle, 1st Earl of Cork; educated at Trinity College, Dublin, and through the Grand Tour of Italy and France (1636–39); created Baron Broghill (1627). Second-in-command to the Earl of Inchiquin in Munster at the start of the 1641 Irish rebellion; retired to Somerset, after failing to be appointed Lord President of Munster (1647); following the execution of the king, his correspondence with Charles II was intercepted – accepted Cromwell's offer of a pardon in return for military service in Ireland (1649); defeated royalist and catholic forces in

Munster (1650–51); promoted to Lieutenant-General (1651). MP for Cork (1654) and Edinburgh (1656); appointed President of the Council of Scotland (1655–56) and member of the new Upper Chamber (1657); supported first Richard Cromwell and then General Monck (1659); in favour of the Restoration; MP for Arundel (1660, 1661); created Earl of Orrery (1660); appointed member of the Privy Council, Lord President of Munster and Lord Justice of Ireland (1660); but fell out of favour after 1672. Developed his talent as a dramatist and poet; his publications include *The General, or Altemira* (1660–61), *Mustapha* (1665), *Henry the Fifth* (1668), *The Black Prince* (1669) and *Treatise on the Art of War* (1677).

Bradford, William (1590–1657): Son of William Bradford, a Yorkshire yeoman; married (1) Dorothy May (1613) and (2) Alice Carpenter (1623); a member of a puritan separatist (Brownist) congregation, he fled with them to Holland in the face of persecution; established a cloth business with the proceeds of his English property, moving to Leyden with the community (1609). Became a leader of a group which sailed from Plymouth in *The Mayflower* (Sept. 1620) with a royal patent to establish a colony in North America (i.e. the Pilgrim Fathers); and signed the Mayflower Compact, outlining the form of government agreed. Succeeded John Carver as Governor of the Plymouth colony (1621); established good relations with the Indians and drafted the colony's constitution. A scholarly man, he wrote diaries, works of theology and *The History of the Plymouth Plantation, 1620–47* (1856).

Bradshaw, John (1602–59): Son of Henry Bradshaw of Marple, Cheshire; educated at Stockton Grammar School and Gray's Inn; called to the Bar (1627), practised in Cheshire; moved to London (by 1643); appointed judge of the sheriffs' court (1643); helped to prosecute Lord Maguire and Hugh MacMahon for their involvement in the 1641 Irish rebellion (1644); counsel for John Lilburne in his successful appeal against a Star Chamber sentence (1645); appointed bencher at Gray's Inn (1647), Chief Justice of Chester (1647) and Sergeant-at-Law (1648). Nominated by the Rump as a member of the special commission appointed to try the king – and subsequently elected its president (Jan. 1649); banned the king from speaking at the trial, after his refusal to plead; pronounced sentence of death (Jan. 1649). Later involved in other trials of royalist leaders; appointed President of the Council of State, Chancellor of the Duchy of Lancaster and Attorney-General for Cheshire and North Wales (1649). An ardent republican, he opposed the expulsion of the Rump, disagreed with the appointment of Cromwell as Lord Protector and, when elected MP for Stafford (1654), declined to sign the 'recognition', pledging members to support the government. Withdrew from public life, but served on the Council (1659) after Cromwell's death; buried in Westminster Abbey, but disinterred by royalists after the Restoration.

Broghill, 1st Baron (1621–79) – *see* Boyle, Roger.

Buckingham, 1st Duke of (1592–1628) – *see* Villiers, George.

Buckingham, 2nd Duke of (1628–87) – *see* Villiers, George.

Burnet, Gilbert (1643–1715): Son of Robert Burnet, an Edinburgh advocate; educated at Marishal College, Aberdeen; married Lady Margaret Kennedy (1671); became friendly with Lauderdale, supporting a policy of reconciliation between Presbyterians and Episcopalians; appointed minister of Saltoun parish (1664) and Professor of Divinity at Glasgow University (1669); opposed Lauderdale's change to a policy of religious persecution – moved to England (1672). Appointed royal chaplain (1673) and Chaplain of the Rolls Chapel (1675). During the crisis over the Popish Plot, he published his *History of the Reformation in England* (1679), which argued against the catholic case, but spoke forcefully against the persecution of Catholics. Became friendly with Whig leaders involved in the Rye House Plot (1683); and preached against popery (1684). On the accession of James II (1685), joined William of Orange in Holland, becoming his close adviser; landed with William at Brixham and preached at St Paul's on their arrival in London (Dec. 1688). Appointed Bishop of Salisbury (1689), supporting in the Lords the policy of toleration. Later publications: *Exposition of the Thirty-Nine Articles of the Church of England* (1698) and *History of My Own Time* (1723, 1734).

Burton, Henry (1578–1648): Son of William Burton of Birdsall, Yorkshire; educated at Cambridge; appointed Clerk to the Closet to Prince Henry and later to Prince Charles (1612); entered the ministry (1618); lost favour with Charles I (1625) after accusing William Laud and Richard Neile of Catholicism. Appointed Rector of St Matthew's, Friday Street – launched attacks on episcopacy in his sermons; published *The Baiting of the Pope's Bull* (1627), for which he was summoned before the Privy Council; but continued to write tracts and preach sermons against popery and bishops; refused a summons to appear before a Court of High Commission (1636) – suspended and arrested after a house search; appeared before Star Chamber (with Prynne and Bastwicke) – sentenced to be deprived of his living, fined £5,000, pilloried with the loss of his ears and imprisoned for life (1637); received widespread popular demonstrations of support on his way to imprisonment in Guernsey; released by the Long Parliament (1640). Returned as minister to St Matthew's (1642), reorganising it along independent lines.

Butler, James, 12th Earl & 1st Duke of Ormond (1610–88): Born at Clerkenwell; son of Thomas, Viscount Thurles; as a royal ward, educated at Lambeth; married Elizabeth Preston (1629). Succeeded to the earldom of Ormond and Ossory (1632); moved to Ireland (1633); appointed Commander-in- Chief in Ireland during Wentworth's absence (1640); appointed Lieutenant-General of the king's forces there once the rebellion started (1641); won victories at Killslaghen, Kilrush and Ross; Marquess (1642); completed the Cessation with the rebels (1643). Appointed Lord Lieutenant of Ireland (1644); surrendered Dublin to parliamentarian forces, signing a treaty with their commissioners (1647); fled to France (1648), but returned in an abortive attempt to retake Dublin (1649); thereafter, remained with Charles I in exile as a member of his Privy Council. After the Restoration, created Baron Butler and Earl of Brecknock (1660); Duke of Ormond and Lord High Steward (1661); reappointed Lord Lieutenant of Ireland (1661–68 and 1677–85); appointed Chancellor of Oxford University (1669). Buried in Westminster Abbey.

Butler, James, 2nd Duke of Ormond (1665–1745): Son of Thomas, Earl of Ossory; educated in France and at Oxford; succeeded his father as Earl of Ossory (1680); married Anne, daughter of Lord Hyde (1682); succeeded his grandfather as Duke of Ormond (1688). Fought for James II against Monmouth (1685); elected to succeed his grandfather as Chancellor of Oxford University (1688); although appointed Knight of the Garter by James, he supported William of Orange (1688); fought at the Battle of the Boyne, commanding William's life guard (1690); commanded the soldiers in Rooke's Cadiz expedition (1702); appointed Lord Lieutenant of Ireland (1703–7, 1710–13). Suspected of Jacobite sympathies – dismissed from his command by George I (1714); impeached, fled to France, joining the court of the Old Pretender; actively involved in the 1715 rebellion; retired to Spain.

Campbell, Archibald, 8th Earl & 1st Marquess of Argyll (1598–1661): Son of Archibald, 7th Earl of Argyll; educated at St Andrews University; took charge of the family estates on the conversion of his father to Catholicism (1619); appointed Privy Councillor (1626); succeeded his father as Earl (1638). After early hesitation, he opposed Charles I's attempt to impose a new Prayer Book on Scotland and joined the Covenanters (1638); a powerful leading figure in the General Assembly of Scotland, he supported the abolition of episcopacy and helped to gain concessions from the king concerning the powers of the Scottish parliament; created a marquess (1641). Negotiated the Solemn League and Covenant with the English parliament (1643); fought in the Scottish army at Marston Moor (1644); returned to Scotland to oppose the royalist rising led by his old adversary, Montrose; but suffered the devastation of his lands and defeat at Inverlochy and Kilsyth (1645). Opposed the Engagement between the king and the Scottish parliament (1647) and supported Cromwell's victory over Hamilton at Preston (1648); but he opposed the execution of Charles (1649) and personally crowned Prince Charles King of Scotland at Scone (1650). Opposed the Scottish invasion of England (1651); made his peace with Cromwell's regime and sat as MP for Aberdeenshire in the 1659 parliament. At the Restoration (1660), he was arrested for high treason, having collaborated latterly with Cromwell, and executed.

Campbell, Archibald, 9th Earl of Argyll (1629–85): Son of Archibald Campbell, 8th Earl of Argyll; married Lady Mary Stuart (1650). Supported the young Prince Charles as captain of his Scottish life guard (1650) and member of the highland royalists (1653); imprisoned in Edinburgh on suspicion of complicity in a royalist plot (1657–60); released at the Restoration, but imprisoned and sentenced to death for involvement in his father's treasonable activities; finally restored to his earldom (1663). Worked on the restoration of his estates; appointed commissioner to help re-establish law and order in the Highlands (1667) and extraordinary Lord of Session (1674–80). After the Duke of York's appointment as High Commissioner in Scotland (1680), Argyll's power and ardent Protestantism were viewed with suspicion – found guilty of treason (1681) and sentenced to death with the confiscation of his estates; rescued from prison by his stepdaughter; fled to Holland; involved in the Rye House Plot (1683). Led a small expedition to Scotland in favour of the Duke of Monmouth – but not widely supported; captured at Inchannan and executed (1685).

Campbell, Archibald, 1st Duke of Argyll (1651–1703): Son of Archibald Campbell, 9th Earl of Argyll; married Elizabeth Talmarsh; dissociated himself from his father's treasonable activities (1685); tried to win back his estates by a conversion to Catholicism, but eventually joined William III for his invasion of England (1688). He was restored to the earldom and the Scottish Convention (1689); administered the coronation oath to William and Mary in Scotland and was appointed Privy Councillor (1689). Took vengeance on the family's longstanding enemies in the Highlands, especially the MacDonald clan, by seizing on Alexander MacDonald's failure to take the oath of submission; his own regiment helped to inflict brutal treatment on the clan in the massacre of Glencoe (1692). Appointed extraordinary Lord of Session (1694), a Lord of the Treasury (1696) and Duke of Argyll (1701).

Carr (or Ker), Robert, Earl of Somerset (1585?–1645): Son of Thomas Ker of Ferniehurst, Scotland; accompanied James I to England (1603), who quickly became infatuated with him; was knighted and appointed Gentleman of the Bedchamber (1607). Advised by Sir Thomas Overbury at court, Carr quickly rose in influence and power; was granted the manor of Sherborne, previously owned by Raleigh (1608); created Viscount Rochester (1611); appointed the King's Secretary on the death of Salisbury (1612); created Earl of Somerset (1613), Treasurer of Scotland (1613) and Lord Chamberlain (1614). Married the recently-divorced Frances Devereux, Countess of Essex (1613), coming thereby under the influence of the Howard family; but, with the arrival of George Villiers at court, suffered a decline in power. Was implicated with his wife in the murder in the Tower of Thomas Overbury, who had opposed their marriage – both were tried and found guilty by the Lords, but were eventually pardoned by James and released (1622). Thereafter, he played no further part in public life.

Cary, Lucius, 2nd Viscount Falkland (1610–43): Son of Sir Henry Cary, 1st Viscount Falkland; educated at Trinity College, Dublin; married Letice Morrison (c.1630); inherited estates at Burford and Great Tew (1625), where he enjoyed a circle of literary friends, including William Chillingworth, Edward Hyde, Edmund Waller and Ben Jonson. Fought for the king in the First Bishops' War (1639); was elected MP for Newport, Isle of Wight in both the Short and the Long Parliaments (1640), speaking against both Laud and Strafford, opposing Ship Money and favouring the Triennial Bill. However, fearing a drift towards extremism, he opposed the Root and Branch Bill and voted against the Grand Remonstrance (1641); was persuaded by Hyde to accept the king's appointment as Secretary of State (1642). Accompanied the king to York; supported the protestation against war; and negotiated unsuccessfully with parliament for peace (1642). Became totally despondent on the outbreak of war, desiring not victory, but peace; believed that differences could be settled by reason in open discussion; present at the siege of Gloucester (1643), where he hoped for death;

killed at the Battle of Newbury (1643), where he deliberately rode into musket fire.

Catesby, Robert (1573–1603): Son of Sir William Catesby of Lapworth, Warwickshire, a catholic recusant; educated at Oxford; married Catherine Leigh (1592); inherited vast estates at Lapworth and Chastleton in Oxfordshire by 1598. Gave support to the Earl of Essex at his execution (1601), but was imprisoned for his violent protest and only released from prison on payment of a crippling fine. Became embittered by the savagery of the anti-catholic laws and disillusioned by James I's unwillingness to offer relief. Readily assisted Thomas Winter and Guy Fawkes, therefore, in their plan to assassinate the king and the government by blowing up the House of Lords (1605); fled with other plotters to Holbeche in Staffordshire on the arrest of Fawkes and the betrayal of their plot; was discovered there and killed in the subsequent fighting.

Catherine of Braganza (1638–1705): Daughter of John IV, Duke of Braganza and King of Portugal (from 1640); married Charles II (1662), bringing a valuable dowry of Tangier, Bombay and £330,000 in cash. Unprepared for the licentiousness of court life, she became deeply unhappy at the appearance of Lady Castlemaine, Charles II's mistress, only accepting the situation after Clarendon's appeasement. The king tolerated her inability to produce an heir; defended her against charges of plotting his death during the Popish Plot scare (1678); and refused to consent to proposals put forward by Buckingham and Shaftesbury for divorce in order to ensure a protestant consort (1679). She exercised little religious or political influence at court; returned to Portugal after the king's death (but not until 1692); contributed to the formation of an Anglo-Portuguese alliance through the Methuen Treaty (1703); and was appointed regent for her brother in Portugal (1704).

Cavendish, William, Duke of Newcastle (1592–1676): Son of Sir Charles Cavendish; educated at Cambridge; married Elizabeth Bassett (*c.*1617) and Margaret Lucas (1645); appointed Viscount Mansfield (1620), Earl of Newcastle (1628) and Privy Councillor (1638). Fought for the king in the Civil War, being appointed Governor of Hull and commander of the four northern counties; raised an army and took control of the port of Newcastle (1642). In 1643, he won the battle of Adwalton Moor, captured Bradford and controlled all Yorkshire (except Hull); took Gainsborough and Lincoln; refused to march south on London; failed in his attempt to take Hull by siege. Created marquess (1643). In the face of an advancing Scottish army (1644), he retreated to York, which he defended against prolonged siege until relieved by Prince Rupert; defeated at the Battle of Marston Moor; fled abroad, losing much of his fortune and spending exile in Paris (1645–48), Rotterdam (1648) and Antwerp (1648–60) as a member of Charles II's Privy Council. After the Restoration, appointed Chief Justice in Eyre north of Trent (1661) and Duke of Newcastle (1665); played no further part in politics, devoting his time to riding and writing poetry and comedies. Buried in Westminster Abbey.

Cecil, Robert, Earl of Salisbury (1563–1612): Son of William Cecil, Lord Burghley; educated at Cambridge; married Elizabeth Brooke (1589). MP for Herfordshire and High Sheriff (1589); knighted and appointed Privy Councillor (1591); appointed Secretary of State (1596); headed the embassy to France in an attempt to halt any alliance with Spain (1598); his influence at court reduced by the death of his father (1598); participated in the trial of the Earl of Essex for treason (1601); obtained subsidies for the Spanish War from Elizabeth's last parliament. Read the proclamation declaring James I king (1603); reappointed Secretary of State; appointed Lord High Steward to the Queen (1603), Baron Cecil of Essingden (1603), Viscount Cranbourne (1604), Earl of Salisbury (1605), Knight of the Garter (1605), Lord Treasurer (1608).

Charles I (1600–49): Second son of James I and Anne of Denmark; created Duke of York (1605), Duke of Cornwall (1613), Prince of Wales (1616) and Privy Councillor (1621). Was frustrated in his plans to marry the Spanish Infanta (1623); succeeded to the throne (1625); married Henrietta Maria of France (1625). Conducted a war with Spain (1625); dissolved his first parliament after a controversy over tonnage and poundage (1625); declared war with France (1627); quarrelled with his third parliament, which passed the Petition of Right (1628) and the Three Resolutions (1629); ruled without parliament (1629–40); made peace with France (1629) and Spain (1630); undertook a number of questionable expedients to raise money; appointed William Laud as Archbishop of Canterbury (1633), supporting his High Church practices; appointed Wentworth as Lord Deputy of Ireland (1632); attempted to impose a new Prayer Book on Scotland (1637), resulting in the First and Second Bishops' Wars (1639, 1640); called the abortive Short Parliament (April 1640) and the Long Parliament (Nov. 1640) after a Scottish invasion. Gave his reluctant sanction to the execution of Strafford, the Triennial Act and the abolition of prerogative courts (1641). Thwarted in his plan to arrest the Five Members (Jan. 1642); left London for York

(Mar. 1642); raised his standard at Nottingham (Aug. 1642); established his headquarters at Oxford; failed in his strategy to retake London (1643); defeated by the New Model Army at Naseby (1645); surrendered to the Scots at Newark (1646). In 1647, he was handed over to parliament (Jan.); captured by the army from Holmby House (June), escaped to Carisbrooke Castle (Nov.); signed the Engagement with the Scots (Dec.), which prompted the outbreak of the Second Civil War (1648); negotiated with parliamentary commissioners at Newport (Sept. 1648). He was arrested by the army and transferred to Hurst Castle (Nov. 1648); escorted to Windsor (Dec. 1648); tried in Westminster Hall (20–27 Jan. 1649); and executed (30 Jan. 1649).

Charles II (1630–85): Son of Charles I and Henrietta Maria; created Prince of Wales (1639); married Catherine of Braganza (1662). Appointed commander of the king's western forces in the Civil War (1644); subsequently fled abroad. Assumed the title of King of England (Jan. 1649); proclaimed King of Scotland (Feb. 1649) – took the Covenant and was crowned at Scone (Jan. 1651); defeated at Worcester (Sept. 1651); again fled abroad, setting up his own court in exile, taking refuge in France, Germany and Holland (1651–60). Invited to return as king, after the intervention of General Monck; signed the Declaration of Breda; entered London (May 1660). Under the influence of Clarendon as Lord Chancellor (1660–67: see also p. 220), pursued a war policy against the Dutch (1665–67) and a persecution policy against the Puritans. Under the influence of the Cabal ministry (1667–73), he abandoned the Triple Alliance and signed the Secret Treaty of Dover (1670) in return for French subsidies; endeavoured to gain toleration for dissenters and Roman Catholics by the Declaration of Indulgence (1673), but was forced to accept the Test Act (1673). Under the influence of Danby as chief minister (1673–79), he moved towards a Dutch alliance and sanctioned the marriage of Princess Mary to William of Orange (1677). He was forced to accept severe retribution on Roman Catholics after the Popish Plot and to sanction the Parliamentary Test Act (1678); but refused to endorse the Exclusion Bill (1679–81).

Churchill, John, 1st Duke of Marlborough (1650–1722): Son of Sir Winston Churchill, a Dorset gentleman; educated at the City Free School, Dublin, and St Paul's; page at court to James, Duke of York (1666); commissioned (1667), served in the Tangier garrison (1668), fought in Flanders in the Third Anglo-Dutch War under Monmouth and Turenne (1673–74); married Sarah Jennings (1678); went into exile with his patron, the Duke of York, during the Exclusion Crisis (1679); created

Baron Churchill of Aymouth (1682). On the accession of James II, he was second-in-command of the king's forces in the Battle of Sedgemoor (1685); but, expressing doubts over the king's religion, he corresponded with William of Orange and joined his cause at the Revolution (1688). Created Earl of Marlborough (1689); commanded British forces in the Netherlands (1689); appointed Commander-in-Chief in England during William's absence in Ireland (1690); captured Cork and Kinsale (1690). William gradually distrusted his influence over Princess Anne and his contacts with James II – briefly imprisoned (1692) and out of office (1692–98). Appointed Governor to the Duke of Gloucester (1698) and Commander-in-Chief in the Netherlands (1701), from where he negotiated the Grand Alliance. On the accession of Anne, he was appointed Captain-General of all British forces, his wife Mistress of the Robes and his friend, Lord Godolphin, Lord Treasurer (1702). Created Duke of Marlborough (1702). His military successes in Germany and the Netherlands culminated in victories against the French at Blenheim (1704), Ramillies (1706), Oudenarde (1708) and Malplaquet (1709). He was granted the royal manor of Woodstock and funds with which to construct Blenheim Palace (1704); but gradually lost favour with Anne through his increasing reliance on Whig support and his inability to bring about peace (1709–10); dismissed as commander (1711), as was his wife from all court offices (1711); retired to the continent (1712), but returned on George I's accession (1714) – reappointed Commander-in-Chief; but suffered two strokes and played little further part in public life.

Churchill, Sarah, Duchess of Marlborough (1660–1744): Daughter of Richard Jennings, a Hertfordshire landowner; appointed attendant at court to Princess Anne (1673), who became her close friend; married John Churchill (1678); appointed Lady of the Bedchamber to Anne (1683), whom she influenced in her flight to Nottingham and her support of William of Orange during the Revolution (1688). On Anne's accession, she was appointed Mistress of the Robes and Keeper of the Privy Purse (1702), also becoming Duchess of Marlborough. But relationships gradually became soured, partly through Sarah's ill-tempered and overbearing behaviour and partly through the growing support she gave to the Whigs; from 1707 her influence at court (which she had used on behalf of her husband) was overshadowed by that of her cousin, Abigail Masham, and Robert Harley, a staunch Tory. After a series of hysterical outbursts and quarrels, Sarah was dismissed from her offices (1711); retired to the continent with her husband (1712), but returned on George I's accession to Woodstock; after Marlborough's death (1622), she completed the building of Marlborough Palace.

Clarendon, Earl of (1609–74) – *see* Hyde, Edward.

Clifford, Thomas, 1st Baron Clifford of Chudleigh (1630–73): Son of Hugh Clifford, a catholic landowner from Devon; educated at Oxford and the Middle Temple; elected MP for Totnes in the Convention and Cavalier Parliaments (1660, 1661). An ardent royalist, he was supported in his rise to prominence by Henry Bennet, Lord Arlington; appointed commissioner for the care of wounded seamen (1664), commissioner of prizes (1665), Privy Councillor (1666), Commissioner of the Treasury (1667) and Treasurer of the Household (1668). A member of the Cabal Ministry (1667), he defended the royal cause vigorously in the Commons; pro-French, anti-Dutch and pro-Catholic in outlook; helped to negotiate the Secret Treaty of Dover (1670); advised Charles to stop payments from the Exchequer and to publish the Declaration of Indulgence (1672). Created First Baron Clifford of Chudleigh and appointed Lord Treasurer (1672). Charles rejected his advice to dissolve parliament in the face of hostile attacks (1673); strongly opposed the Test Act (1673); resigned as Lord Treasurer and Privy Councillor (1673); died through possible suicide.

Coke, Sir Edward (1552–1634): Born at Mileham, Norfolk; educated at Norwich Free School, Cambridge, and Clifford's Inn; called to the Bar (1578); married Bridget Paston (1582) and Lady Elizabeth Hatton (1598). MP for Aldborough (1589), Norfolk (1592), Coventry (1624), Norfolk (1625), Buckinghamshire (1628). Recorder of Norwich (1586); Bencher of the Inner Temple (1590); Solicitor-General (1592); Recorder of London (1592); Speaker (1592–3); Attorney-General (1593–4); Treasurer of the Inner Temple (1596); knighted (1603); Chief Justice of the Court of Common Pleas (1606); Chief Justice of the King's Bench (1613); Privy Councillor (1613). Acted for the prosecution in the cases against Essex (1600), Southampton (1600), Raleigh (1603), the Gunpowder Plotters (1605). Argued against any increase of James I's prerogative and refused the king's demand that he should cease action in the case of Commendams (1616); was suspended from the Council in consequence and dismissed as Chief Justice (1616). Gradually regained favour, but emerged as leader of the 'popular party' in the 1620–21 parliament; opposed monopolies and the Spanish marriage; spoke strongly in favour of the liberties of parliament; was arrested and imprisoned. Vigorously opposed the imposition of oppressive taxation (1624); attacked the forced loan and Buckingham's influence, also leading the call for the Petition of Right (1628). His publications included *Reports* (1600–15) and *Institutes* (1628).

Compton, Henry (1532–1713): Son of Spencer Compton, 2nd Earl of Northampton and an ardent royalist; educated at Oxford; commissioned in the Royal Horse Guards (1660); ordained (1660). Danby's influence aided his advancement in the Church; appointed Bishop of Oxford (1674); Bishop of London and Dean of the Chapel Royal (1675); a wholehearted Protestant, he was made responsible for the spiritual education of Princess Anne and Princess Mary. Appointed Privy Councillor (1676). An opponent of the Exclusion Bill, he nevertheless spoke vigorously against James II's pro-catholic policies and his attempt to use a royal dispensing power in relation to the Test Act; in consequence, was dismissed from the Privy Council (1685). Refused to suspend John Sharp for preaching anti-papal sermons and was himself suspended as bishop in consequence (1686); supported the Seven Bishops in their petition against the Declaration of Indulgence (1688); a signatory of the invitation sent to William of Orange to invade (1688); personally escorted Anne's flight from London. Reappointed Privy Councillor (1689); crowned William and Mary at their coronation (1689); but failed to gain appointment as Archbishop of Canterbury (1691, 1695); supported the Toleration Act. After Anne's accession, he opposed Occasional Conformity, but his influence gradually diminished.

Cooper, Anthony Ashley, 1st Earl of Shaftesbury (1621–83): Son of John Cooper of Wimborne St Giles, Dorset; educated at Oxford and Lincoln's Inn; married (1) Margaret Coventry (1639) and (2) Lady Frances Cecil (1650). MP for Tewkesbury (1640) and Wiltshire (1653, 1654, 1659). At first supported the king in the Civil War, commanding the garrison of Weymouth (1643), but changed sides (1644) and was appointed commander of parliament's forces in Dorset. Appointed High Sheriff of Wiltshire (1646); and member of the Council of State (1653), but quarrelled with Cromwell; joined the opposition of Republicans and Presbyterians. A member of the delegation to The Hague, which conveyed the invitation to Charles II to return (1660). A member of the Convention Parliament (1660); appointed Chancellor of the Exchequer and created Lord Ashley (1661); a member of the Cabal ministry (1672); created Lord Shaftesbury and appointed Lord Chancellor (1672); in favour of the Declaration of Indulgence (1672) and the Test Act (1673); dismissed on the fall of the Cabal (1673), becoming leader of the opposition; started to intrigue with the Duke of Monmouth regarding the succession to the throne; in favour of the attacks on Catholics during the Popish Plot scare (1678); helped to gain the passing of the Habeas Corpus Act (1679); unsuccessful in his efforts to impeach the Duke of York as a popish recusant (1680); played a leading part in the debates on the Exclusion Bill (1681); indicted for high treason, but released (1681); planned an armed rising (1682), but fled abroad when it failed to materialise. Died in exile.

Cork, 1st Earl of (1566–1643) – *see* Boyle, Richard.

Cranfield, Lionel, 1st Earl of Middlesex (1575–1645): Son of a London merchant; educated at St Paul's; apprenticed to Richard Sheppard, a textile trader (1590); made a member of the Mercers' Company (1597), exporting cloth to Germany and the Netherlands; married (1) Elizabeth Sheppard (1599) and (2) Anne Brett (1620); made a fortune through trade, money-lending, customs farming and land speculation. Introduced to court by his patron, the Earl of Northampton; knighted (1613); appointed Surveyor-General of the Customs (1613); adviser to the Privy Council on trade (1614–16). With help of his new patron, George Villiers, his promotion was rapid – Master of Requests (1616); Keeper of the Great Wardrobe (1618); Master of the Court of Wards and Liveries (1619); and member of the Privy Council (1620). His reforms in the household, navy and exchequer increased James I's income by controlling wastefulness. Elected MP for Arundel (1621); appointed Lord Treasurer (1621); created Earl of Middlesex (1622). He exercised a policy of curbing expenditure in all areas, but offended Buckingham when, for financial reasons, he opposed the latter's demand for war with Spain (1624); impeached for corruption, fined, dismissed and imprisoned – but later pardoned on the accession of Charles I (1625). Retired and played little further part in public life.

Cromwell, Oliver (1599–1658): Son of Robert Cromwell; educated at Huntingdon Free School and Cambridge; married Elizabeth Bourchier (1620); MP for Huntingdon (1628) and Cambridge (1640); moved the second reading of the Triennial Bill (1640). Fought for parliament in the Civil War, raising a double regiment of cavalry in 1643 and winning battles at Grantham, Gainsborough and Winceby. In 1644, was appointed Lieutenant-General in Manchester's Eastern Association; stormed Lincoln; fought at Marston Moor and Newbury; attacked Manchester's leadership of the army and supported the Self-Denying Ordinance. In 1645, was appointed Lieutenant-General of Horse in the New Model Army under Fairfax; fought at Naseby, Bridgwater, Bristol, Winchester and Basing House. In 1647, after the war, he used his influence as an MP to support the army in its quarrel with the Presbyterians in parliament; rejoined the army when it mutinied (May); gave support to the seizure of the king from Holmby House (June);

helped to draft the Heads of Proposals, which the king rejected (July); led the march on London to eject presbyterian leaders from parliament (Aug.); chaired the Putney Debates and opposed the Levellers (Oct.). In 1648, during the Second Civil War, he besieged Pembroke Castle; won the Battle of Preston (Aug.); and gave his support to Pride's Purge (Dec.). In 1649, he approved the trial of the king and signed the death warrant (Jan.); became a member of the Council of State (Feb.); was appointed commander of the army sent to Ireland to put down the rebels (Aug.); stormed Drogheda (Sept.) and Wexford (Oct.). In 1650, he was appointed Captain-General of the army sent to Scotland (June); won the Battle of Dunbar (Sept.); and pursued the royalist army into England, winning the Battle of Worcester (Sept. 1651). Expelled the Rump Parliament (1653); appointed Lord Protector by the Instrument of Government (1653); suppressed Penruddock's Rising (1655); appointed Major-Generals to govern the country locally (1655); engaged in war with Spain (1655); signed treaty with France (1657); refused offer of the crown (1657), but accepted proposal for a new Upper House. Buried in Westminster Abbey, but disinterred by royalists in 1661.

Cromwell, Richard (1626–1712): Son of Oliver Cromwell; educated at Felstead School and Lincoln's Inn; married Dorothy Mayor (1649); MP for Hampshire (1654) and Cambridge (1656); appointed Chancellor of Oxford University (1657); member of the Council of State (1657); commander of a regiment (1658); and member of the new Upper House (1658). Nominated by his father as his successor just prior to his death; proclaimed Protector (3rd Sept. 1658). Although Fleetwood's army soon became alienated, Cromwell refused to arrest their leaders when they disobeyed orders to return to their regiments after delivering army grievances – 'I will not have a drop of blood spilt for the preservation of my greatness, which is a burden to me.' After the rendezvous of the army at St James, he agreed to dissolve parliament and abdicate in return for personal protection (Apr. 1659). Fled almost penniless to Paris under the name of John Clarke (1660); moved to Italy (1666); returned to Cheshunt in England (1680).

Danby, Earl of (1632–1712) – *see* Osborne, Sir Thomas.

Defoe, Daniel (1660–1731): Son of James Foe, a London butcher and dissenter; educated at a Dissenting Academy in Newington; set up in business as a merchant (1685), but became bankrupt (1692); fought for Monmouth at Sedgemoor (1685) and supported William of Orange at the Revolution (1688). Wrote *The Essay on Projects* (1698), a far-sighted survey of banking and insurance; *The True-Born Englishman* (1701), a defence of William's Dutch background; and *The Shortest Way with Dissenters* (1702), a brilliant parody of Tory and Anglican extremists, which brought him imprisonment and instant popular acclaim. Again in debt, he was released from prison through the efforts of Harley (1703) and employed as a government agent up and down the country to assess public opinion on major issues and encourage dissenters to back the ministry. Founded *The Review* (1703–13), a thrice-weekly political journal with his own 'leader' article offering comment and advocating social reform; although consistent in his belief in toleration and moderation, he tended to change the tone of *The Review* to support each new government (1708, 1710). After the death of Anne and the fall of Harley, he was imprisoned for libelling Lord Annesley (1715), but freed after making an agreement to work for the Whigs as editor of both the Tory *News Letter* (1715) and the Jacobite *Mist's Weekly Journal* (1717), toning down opinion and encouraging a more sympathetic attitude to the government. He wrote over 80 pamphlets (1715–18); several novels, including *The Life and Surprising Adventures of Robinson Crusoe* (1719), *The Life of Captain Singleton* (1720), *The Fortunes and Misfortunes of the Famous Moll Flanders* (1722), *A Journal of the Plague Year* (1722) and *Roxana, or the Fortunate Mistress* (1724); and an economic and social review of the country, *Tour Through the Whole Island of Britain* (1724–27).

Desborough or Disbrowe, John (1608–80): Son of James Desborough, a Cambridgeshire gentleman; a lawyer by training; married Jane Cromwell (1636), Oliver Cromwell's sister; appointed quartermaster to Cromwell's troop of horse on the outbreak of civil war (1642); promoted to Major, he saw action at Langport (1645) and Bristol (1645); promoted to Colonel (1648); and Major-General (1651), taking part in the Battle of Worcester; and General of the Fleet (1653). Appointed to the Council of State (1653); elected MP for Cambridgeshire (1654) and Somerset (1656). After helping to suppress Penruddock's Rising (1655), he was appointed one of 11 Major-Generals with the personal task of administering the South-West (1655–56). A loyal Republican, he opposed the move to make Cromwell king; with Fleetwood and Lambert, he opposed the continuation of Richard Cromwell's regime; assisted in the expulsion of the Rump (1659); was arrested on trying to flee abroad and briefly imprisoned at the Restoration (1660); fled to Holland, where he intrigued with Republicans, but was ordered to return to England (1666); released after a brief imprisonment (1667) and retired to Hackney, playing no further part in public life.

Devereux, Robert, 3rd Earl of Essex (1591–1646): Son of Robert, 2nd Earl, and Frances, daughter of Sir Francis Walsingham; educated at Eton and Oxford; married (1) Frances Howard (1606) and (2) Elizabeth Paulet (1631). MP and member of the Council of War (1621); refused to pay the forced loan; supported the popular party in the Petition of Right (1628); appointed Lieutenant-General in the First Bishops' War (1639); allied with Pym and St John in the Long Parliament (1640); appointed Lord Chamberlain and commander of southern forces by Charles I in a vain effort to secure his loyalty (1641); but he declined to join the king in York (1642). Appointed General of parliament's army, commanding it at the battles of Edgehill and Turnham Green (1642). In 1643, captured Reading, relieved Gloucester and won the First Battle of Newbury. In 1644, failed to take Oxford and was defeated by the king at Lostwithiel with the surrender of his entire infantry; opposed Cromwell's attack on Manchester in parliament and the formation of a New Model Army. Resigned his command (Apr. 1645) in anticipation of the Self-Denying Ordinance.

Dundee, 1st Viscount – *see* Graham, John of Claverhouse (1649–89).

Eliot, Sir John (1592–1632): Son of Richard Eliot of Port Eliot, Cornwall; educated at Oxford and the Inns of Court; married Rhadagund Gedie (1611); MP for St Germans in the Addled Parliament (1614); knighted (1618); MP for Newport, Cornwall (1624) – gave his support to the Spanish War and the strict enforcement of the laws against Catholics. MP for St Germans (1626) – emerged as a leader of the popular party; made a bitter attack on Buckingham and commenced impeachment proceedings against him; introduced a remonstrance insisting on the right of parliament to cross-examine ministers; arrested and sent to the Tower. Again imprisoned for refusal to pay the forced loan (1627). MP for Cornwall (1628) – led the opposition to illegal taxation; responsible, with Coke, for the Petition of Right; launched further onslaughts against Buckingham's policies; faced with the certain adjournment of parliament, he read out the Three Resolutions with the Speaker held down in the Chair (2nd Mar. 1629). Arrested with eight other leaders; tried (1630), fined £2,000 and imprisoned. Publications include *Negotium Posterorum* (1881) and *The Monarchy of Man* (1871). Died in prison.

Essex, 3rd Earl of (1591–1646) – *see* Devereux, Robert.

Fairfax, Ferdinando, 2nd Baron Fairfax (1584–1648): Son of Thomas, 1st Baron Fairfax of Yorkshire; married (1) Mary, daughter of Lord

Sheffield (1607), and (2) Rhoda Chapman (1646); inherited his title (1640); elected MP for Boroughbridge (1622–29) and Yorkshire (1640). Supported the opposition in the Long Parliament, assisting in the presentation of the Grand Remonstrance; but nevertheless endeavoured to maintain Yorkshire's neutrality at the start of the Civil War (1642). He eventually raised a regiment to fight for parliament (1642); though outnumbered, bravely resisted the advance of Newcastle's royalist army in Yorkshire at the Battles of Tadcaster (1642) and Adwalton Moor (1643); and, as Governor, held firm throughout the siege of Hull (1643). Captured Selby (1644), forcing Newcastle to return to York from the North-East, where he had been opposing the advance of the Scottish army into England. Joined forces with the Scots to besiege York and commanded an infantry brigade at the Battle of Marston Moor (1644); appointed Governor of York (1644–5), until the Self-Denying Ordinance forced his resignation (1645); appointed member of the committee responsible for the government of the northern counties (1644–48).

Fairfax, Sir Thomas, 3rd Baron Fairfax (1612–71): Son of Fernando, 3rd Baron, of Denton, Yorkshire; educated at Cambridge; married Anne Vere (1637); commanded a troop in the First Bishops' War (1639); knighted (1640); helped father at the start of the Civil War to lead parliament's forces in Yorkshire (1642). In 1643 regained Leeds and Wakefield, suffered a reverse at Adwalton Moor and assisted the garrison in Hull. In 1644, he defeated royalists at Nantwich and Selby, gained control in Cheshire and commanded cavalry in the victory at Marston Moor. In 1645 he was appointed Commander-in-Chief of the New Model Army, winning battles at Naseby and Langport and capturing Bridgwater, Bath, Bristol and Tiverton. In 1646 he completed the conquest of the West with the surrender of Exeter, before capturing both Oxford and Raglan to end the war. He supported the army in its quarrel with parliament (1647). In the Second Civil War, he defeated royalists at Maidstone and captured Colchester after siege (1648). He supported the trial and deposition of the king, but refused to be a member of the High Court of Justice. Resigned his commission (1650) after declining to lead the invasion of Scotland. He took no active military or political role under Cromwell, but became MP for Yorkshire in 1659; negotiated with Monck; supported the idea of a free parliament and the restoration of the king; led the commission depatched to the king at The Hague (1660). Took no part in public affairs after the Restoration.

Falkland, 2nd Viscount (1610–43) – *see* Cary, Lucius.

Fawkes, Guy (1570–1606); Son of Edward Fawkes, a protestant lawyer from Yorkshire (though his mother's second husband, Sidonis Baynbrigge, was a Catholic); educated at St Peter's School, York, where the catholic influence was strong. He was later converted to Catholicism; sold his inherited property and joined the Spanish army in the Netherlands as a soldier of fortune (1593); fought at the siege of Calais (1596). He became obsessed with the idea of restoring Catholicism to England; tried, on a visit to Madrid, to gain the involvement of Philip III (1603); was bitterly disappointed with other Catholics that the accession of James I had failed to produce any relaxation in the recusancy laws. He therefore readily agreed to join the plot devised by Robert Catesby and Thomas Winter to blow up the king and the House of Lords (1605); but, after the betrayal of their plans, was arrested as he stood watch in the cellar which contained the explosives; signed a confession after severe torture and was executed (1606).

Finch, Daniel, 2nd Earl of Nottingham (1647–1730): Son of Heneage Finch, 1st Earl; educated at Westminster School and Oxford. Entered parliament in 1673; appointed to the Admiralty Commission (1679) and the Privy Council (1680); succeeded to the earldom (1682). A High Tory by inclination, though independent in practice, he opposed the Exclusion Bills and James II's policy of catholicisation. He was not involved in the invitation to William of Orange to invade (1688); tried unsuccessfully to establish a regency after James's flight; supported the Toleration Act, but failed to gain comprehension for dissenters within the Church of England; loyally supported William and Mary as Secretary of State (1689–93). Reappointed to that office by Anne in the Tory ministry (1702–4); helped to secure the Methuen Treaty with Portugal (1703); advocated a foreign policy centred on maritime rather than land-based wars, as envisaged by Marlborough. A champion of the High Church, he supported bills against occasional conformity, finally succeeding with Whig support in 1711. Opposed the Jacobites, the Act of Union (1707) and the Schism Act (1714); supported Dr Sacheverell (1710) against his impeachment. Appointed Lord President by George I in the Whig ministry (1714), but dismissed (1716) after pleading leniency for Jacobite peers.

Fleetwood, Charles (1618–92): Son of Sir Miles Fleetwood of Aldwinkle, Northants; educated at Gray's Inn; married (1) Frances Smith, (2) Bridget Cromwell (1652) and (3) Mary Hartopp (1664). In the Civil War fought for parliament at the First Battle of Newbury (1643) and Naseby (1645). MP for Marlborough (1646); supported the army in its quarrel with parliament (1647); one of the commissioners sent by parliament to negotiate with the army; but was not involved in the trial of the king (1649). Appointed Governor of the Isle of Wight (1649); took part in Cromwell's Scottish campaign as Lieutenant-General of Horse (1650), fighting at Dunbar. Appointed a member of the Council of State and commander of forces in England, playing a crucial part in the defeat of Charles II at Worcester (1651). Appointed Commander-in-Chief in Ireland (1652–55) and Lord Deputy (1654); persecuted catholic priests and transplanted catholic landowners to Connaught. Keenly supported Cromwell in the Protectorate; appointed a member of the Council of State (1654) and a Major-General (1655); opposed to Cromwell becoming king, but in favour of the amended Humble Petition and Advice; was appointed to the new Upper House. Supported the accession of Richard Cromwell (1658), but later led a military demonstration defying Cromwell's orders (1659). Appointed Commander-in-Chief by the restored Rump; but used the army to expel the Rump, after disagreements (Oct. 1659); lost his command when parliament was recalled on the advance of Monck into England (Dec. 1659). Banned for life from all offices of trust once the Restoration had taken place.

Fox, George (1624–91): Born in Leicestershire; son of Christopher Fox, a puritan weaver; apprenticed to a shoemaker; left home and wandered the country (1643–47), discussing religion in a search for faith; finally discovered the 'Inner Light', whereby man had direct access to God. After a vision on Pendle Hill in Lancashire, he spent almost 40 years as a travelling preacher, visiting Scotland, Ireland, America, the West Indies and Holland. A born organiser, he gradually established a system of regular meetings for his converts (called Quakers or Friends) throughout the country with an emphasis on religious silence; central control was provided by the executive of the Society of Friends. He endured violent attacks from town mobs and persecution from the authorities, suffering imprisonment on eight occasions. He married Margaret Fell from Swarthmoor Hall in Lancashire (1669); and published his autobiography, *The Journal,* in 1694. A pacifist and believer in sexual equality, he also campaigned for the abolition of slavery.

Godolphin, Sidney, 1st Earl of Godolphin (1645–1712): Born in Cornwall; son of Sir Francis Godolphin. Appointed a king's page (1662); elected MP for Helston (1668); appointed Commissioner of the Treasury (1679), First Lord of the Treasury and Baron Godolphin (1684); Lord Chamberlain to the queen (1685) and James II's commissioner to negotiate with William of Orange (1688). The marriage of his son,

Francis, to Marlborough's daughter, Henrietta, led to his own promotion on Anne's accession (1702). Appointed Lord Treasurer (1702–10), he successfully managed the ministry, the parliament and the country's finances during the lengthy War of Spanish Succession; he also steered through the Act of Union (1707) and the restructuring of the East India Company (1708). A moderate Tory, he was forced to rely increasingly on Whig support after High Tory attempts to limit the war. Loss of popularity over the trial of Dr Sacheverell (1710) and his inability to end a costly war – combined with Anne's gradual shift towards the High Tories – brought about his dismissal (1710).

Goring, Lord George (1608–57): Son of George Goring, Earl of Norwich; married Lettice, daughter of Richard, Earl of Cork. A courtier under Charles I, he fought for the Dutch at the siege of Breda (1637); was appointed Governor of Portsmouth (1639); supported the king in the Civil War (1642), having first attempted to play both sides off against each other. Ambitious and largely unprincipled, he proved himself an inspirational cavalry commander during the war; was captured by Sir Thomas Fairfax at Wakefield (1643), but later released (1644); commanded the royalist left wing cavalry at Marston Moor (1644); was subsequently appointed Lieutenant-General of Horse in the royalist army; fought at both Lostwithiel and Newbury (1644). He failed to obey Prince Rupert's order to join him for the Battle of Naseby (1645); was appointed commander of all royalist forces in the west, but failed to prevent the New Model Army from relieving Taunton (1645); became notorious for his own debauchery, idleness and drunkenness and the indiscipline of his troops; defeated by Fairfax at Langport; eventually abandoned his demoralised army in north Devon, fleeing to the continent (1645).

Graham, James, 1st Marquess & 5th Earl of Montrose (1612–50): Born at Montrose; educated at St Andrews University; succeeded his father as earl (1626); married Magdalene, daughter of Lord Carnegie (1629). An elder of the Kirk, he opposed Archbishop Laud's attempt to impose the new Prayer Book on Scotland (1637); signed the National Covenant (1638); fought for the Covenanters at the battles of the Bridge of the Dee (1639) and Newburn (1640). His moderate views brought him into conflict with the extremism of the Earl of Argyll (leader of the rebellious Scottish parliament); signed the Cumbernauld Bond to resist this (1640); wrote the *Discourse of Sovereignty* (1641) in support of the monarchy; was arrested and imprisoned (1641); met Queen Henrietta Maria (1643), warning her of Argyll's plans to ally with the English parliament. The signing of the Solemn League and Covenant (1643) caused him to throw his support onto the side of the king; was appointed Lieutenant-General to recruit forces for the king in Scotland (Mar. 1644); raised his standard at Blair Atholl (Aug.) with just 2,000 supporters. However, by exploiting clan rivalry, he won a series of victories at Tippermuir (Aug.), Aberdeen (Sept.), Inverlochy (Feb. 1645), Aldearn (May) and Alford (June). Having entered Glasgow, he planned a march into England, but was heavily defeated at Philiphaugh (Sept.) by David Leslie's Covenanters. After the king had ordered him to lay down his arms at the end of the war (July 1646), he fled abroad. Although he was later sent by Charles II to raise Scotland for the royal cause (1650), his small army was defeated by Leslie at Carbisdale; he was captured and hanged without trial (1650).

Graham, John of Claverhouse, 1st Viscount Dundee (1649–89): Son of Sir William Graham; educated at St Andrews University; married Jean, daughter of Lord Cochrane (1684). Served on the continent under Turenne and William of Orange, before receiving a commission to serve in Scotland under the Duke of York against the Covenanters (1677); was defeated at Drumclog, but assisted the Duke of Monmouth in a decisive victory over the rebels at Bothwell Brig (1679) and led a ruthless follow-up search for survivors. He persuaded the government to grant him a commission (1682) to launch a campaign of terror against the Covenanters in south-west Scotland. Appointed commander of a regiment (1682) and a member of the Scottish Privy Council (1683). He supported James II and his pro-catholic policies; was appointed Provost of Dundee (1688); joined the king at Salisbury in the face of William of Orange's invasion; created Viscount Dundee (1688); but failed to persuade James to fight to the last. After William's arrival, Dundee was granted permission to return to Scotland; sat briefly in the Edinburgh Convention (1689); but then attempted to raise the Highlands in support of James. Deemed a traitor by the Convention, he was pursued by government forces under Hugh Mackay; although these were heavily defeated in a successful ambush at the pass of Killiecrankie (1689), Dundee himself was killed in the battle – thus ending any hopes held by the Jacobite Scots of restoring James to the throne.

Hale, Sir Matthew (1609–76): Born at Alderley, Gloucestershire; son of Robert Hale, a barrister; educated at Oxford and Lincoln's Inn; called to the Bar (1637). In spite of his own puritan beliefs, he maintained a neutral stance during the Civil War, acting with great impartiality for the defence in the trials of Archbishop Laud (1643), the Duke of Hamilton

(1649) and Christopher Love (1651). He was elected a member of the Westminster Assembly of Divines (1644); appointed judge in the Court of Common Pleas (1654); and elected MP for Gloucestershire (1654, 1660) and Oxford (1659). He was appointed by Charles II Chief Baron of the Exchequer (1660) and Chief Justice of the King's Bench (1671), exercising his duties with great integrity and fairness. His many publications include *Historia Placitorum Coronae* (1685) and *History of the Common Law of England* (1713).

Halifax, 1st Marquess of (1633–95) – *see* Savile, George.

Halifax, Earl of (1661–1715) – *see* Montagu, Charles.

Hamilton, James, 3rd Marquess & 1st Duke of Hamilton (1606–49): Son of the 2nd Marquess; married Mary, daughter of Lord Fielding (1620); educated at Oxford; inherited the title (1625). Appointed Master of the Horse (1628) and commander of an abortive expedition to bring aid to Gustavus Adolphus on the continent (1631). As the King's Commissioner in Scotland (12638), he failed to subdue the Covenanters, resorting instead to contemptible intrigue, which created considerable distrust. He took command in the Bishops' Wars (1639, 1640) in support of the king, but his efforts lacked enthusiasm and he temporarily allied with the Earl of Argyll (1641). On the outbreak of civil war (1642), Hamilton tried to resist the signing of the Solemn League and Covenant (1643) but also intrigued against the king's main ally in Scotland, Montrose, in an attempt to enhance his own influence at court. On returning to Oxford, he was therefore arrested and imprisoned (1644). After his release and the king's surrender (1646), he rejoined Charles in Newcastle, trying in vain to persuade him to accept Presbyterianism as the price for Scottish support. As opinion hardened against the extremism of the army, the Scottish parliament finally gave its backing to Hamilton's scheme for intervention. In July 1648, he therefore brought a poorly equipped and badly led army of 20,000 troops into England. These were crushed at Preston by Cromwell (17th–18th Aug,). Hamilton was captured and executed for treason (9th Mar. 1649).

Hampden, John (1594–1643): Son of William Hampden of Great Hampden, Bucks.; educated at Thame Grammar School, Oxford and the Inner Temple; married (1) Elizabeth Symeon (1619) and (2) Letitia Knollys; MP for Grampound (1621), Wendover (1626) and Buckinghamshire (1640). Refused to pay the forced loan (1627) and was imprisoned; allied in parliament with Eliot in his opposition to the king's policies; refused to pay ship money for inland counties (1637). In the Short Parliament (1640) served on various committees discussing grievances; was briefly arrested at the dissolution of parliament. In the Long Parliament (1640) he actively supported Pym, helping to draft the indictment of Strafford and manage his impeachment; advocated a settlement with the king and the reform of episcopacy; was one of the Five Members whom the king attempted to arrest (1642); proposed that parliament should take control of the Tower and the militia. In 1642 he was appointed to the Committee of Public Safety; raised a regiment for parliament when the Civil War broke out; seized control of Buckinghamshire. He became a staunch member of the 'war' party in opposition to peace proposals put forward by the king; favoured an outright assault on the king's headquarters in Oxford; was mortally wounded at Chalgrove Field (18th June 1643).

Harley, Robert, 1st Earl of Oxford (1661–1724): Born in London; son of Sir Edward Harley, squire; educated at presbyterian dissenting academies and the Inner Temple; appointed sheriff of Herefordshire (1688); elected MP for Tregoney (1689) and New Radnor (1690 on). During William III's reign, he became a most influential member of the moderate Country Whigs, opposed to corruption at court, high taxes and standing armies; was instrumental in securing the Triennial Act (1694) and reductions in the army (1697); elected Speaker (1701–4). Under Anne, he was appointed Secretary of State, joining with Godolphin and Marlborough to form a powerful, but moderate triumvirate, which dominated policy (1704–8); was largely instrumental in securing the Act of Union (1707). His influence at court was increased by the arrival there of his relative, Mrs Abigail Masham, as the Queen's new favourite (1707). Godolphin and Marlborough, who suspected him of undermining their position, forced his resignation (1708); but, with the growing unpopularity of the ministry, Anne brought him back as Chancellor of the Exchequer (1710) in a largely tory government, which included Henry St John; Harley was created Earl of Oxford (1711) and appointed Lord Treasurer (1711). In spite of increasing tension both inside and outside the government, he was prominent in the establishment of the South Sea Company (1711); successfully secured peace at the Treaty of Utrecht (1713) and gained the dismissal of Marlborough. Suspected (wrongly) of Jacobitism and increasingly undermined by St John (now Viscount Bolingbroke), he was dismissed by Anne in 1714 and later, on the accession of George I, impeached and imprisoned for his handling of the peace negotiations (1715).

Harrison, Thomas (1616–60): Born in Newcastle-under-Lyme: son of Richard Harrison, butcher; educated at Clifford's Inn. Fought for parliament in the Civil War, serving initially in Essex's life guards; later fought at Marston Moor (1644), Naseby (1645), Preston (1648), Dunbar (1650) and Worcester (1651), eventually reaching the rank of Major-General. Elected MP for Wendover (1646); strongly supported the army in its clash with parliament; advocated the abolition of the House of Lords and the trial of the king; a signatory of the death warrant (1649). Appointed commander of forces in Wales (1649) and in England (1650), during Cromwell's absence; a member of the Council of State and a close colleague of Cromwell (1651); actively supported the expulsion of the Rump (1653). A member of the Fifth Monarchy sect, he became a leading member of the Barebone's Parliament (1653), envisaging 'the rule of the saints'; their radical policies, however, alarmed Cromwell's moderate supporters, who dismissed the parliament and established the Protectorate. Harrison refused to serve, was stripped of his army commission and was twice imprisoned on suspicion of subversive activities. At the Restoration, he was tried and executed as a regicide (1660).

Haselrig, Sir Arthur (1610–61): Born in Leicestershire; son of Sir Thomas Haselrig; elected MP for Leicestershire (1640). Strongly Puritan, he was actively involved in the attack on Laud, the attainder of Strafford, the Root and Branch Bill and the Militia Bill (1641); he was one of the Five Members whom Charles I tried to arrest (1642). In the Civil War, he raised a regiment of cuirassiers, known as the Lobsters, who fought at Edgehill (1642), Lansdown (1643) and Roundway Down (1643). An Independent in politics, he supported Cromwell in his clash with Essex and Manchester over army leadership (1644), resigning his own commission under the terms of the Self-Denying Ordinance (1645). Appointed Governor of Newcastle (1647); in favour of the trial and execution of Charles I (1649), though he refused to serve personally as a member of the court; a prominent leader of the Independents in parliament (1647–53) and a member of the Council of State, he eventually broke with Cromwell over the expulsion of the Rump. He opposed the Protectorate and was consequently banned from sitting in the Commons, though he himself refused the offer of a seat in the 'Second Chamber' (1657). He took a leading part in the restored Rump (1659); supported Monck (1659) and became a member of the Council of State (1660) – though, as a Republican, he did not favour the Restoration, which saw his arrest and imprisonment.

Henrietta Maria (1609–69): Daughter of Henry IV of France and Marie de Medici; married Charles I (1625); their initial unhappiness was largely overcome after the assassination of Buckingham (the king's favourite) in 1625. During the 1630s, she aroused unpopularity with the Puritans over her love of dramatic entertainments at court and her devotion to Catholicism, which saw the arrival of a papal agent and the open celebration of mass in her chapel. Increasingly she became more involved in politics, raising money for the king's army in the Bishops' War (1639), encouraging him to arrest the Five Members (1642), exploring the possibility of foreign intervention, pressing Charles into uncompromising resistance of parliament and raising arms for the royalist cause in Holland (1642). Joining the king in Oxford on her return from the continent (1643), she eventually moved into the South-West to give birth to a daughter at Exeter (1644) before escaping to France. She continued to intrigue in support of Charles until his execution (1649), after which she retired from all political activity. Returning to England after the Restoration (1660), she lived in Somerset House but exercised no influence on the policies of her son, Charles II.

Holles, Denzil, 1st Baron Holles of Ifield (1599–1680): Born at Houghton, Nottinghamshire; son of John Holles, 1st Earl of Clare; educated at Cambridge and Gray's Inn; elected MP for St Michael, Cornwall (1624); immediately supported the opposition to Buckingham's policies, led by his brother-in-law, Wentworth; helped in holding the Speaker down in the chair while the Three Resolutions were passed (1629) – was fined and imprisoned in consequence (released 1630). Refused to pay ship money; sat in the Short and the Long Parliaments (from 1640) as one of the king's leading opponents (though he tried to save his brother-in-law from prosecution); was one of the Five Members whom Charles attempted to arrest (1642); led the cry for control of the militia by parliament. During the Civil War, after commanding a regiment at Edgehill, his views moderated; emerged as a leader of the presbyterian 'peace party' in opposition to the views of Cromwell, whom he unsuccessfully attempted to impeach (1644). After the war, he clashed with the army, which impeached him (1647); fled to France (1648). Returned to England during the Protectorate, but played no part in public life. Resumed his seat in the recalled Long Parliament (1660); appointed a member of the Council of State. At the Restoration, appointed to the Privy Council and created baron by Charles II (1661); appointed ambassador to France (1663); involved in drawing up the Treaty of Breda (1667). Dismissed (1668) after opposing the banishment of Clarendon; joined the opposition against Danby, assisting Shaftesbury in his impeachment (1678); in the debate over the Duke of York, opposed the notion of exclusion, preferring instead the idea of limitations.

Hopton, Ralph, 1st Baron Hopton (1596–1652): Son of Ralph Hopton of Witham Friary, Somerset; educated at Oxford and the Middle Temple; married Elizabeth Lewin (1623). Campaigned (1620) as a volunteer (with William Waller) in the service of the Elector Palatine in the Thirty Years War. Elected MP for Bath (1625), Wells (1628 and Long Parliament, 1640) and Somerset (Short Parliament, 1640); created Knight of the Bath (1626); fought in the Bishops' War (1639). Puritan in religion, he joined the attack on Strafford and supported the Grand Remonstrance (1641); moderate in politics, he opposed the extremism of the leaders of the Commons, demonstrated by the Militia Ordinance (1642), and defended the king's attempt to arrest the Five Members – briefly imprisoned in consequence and expelled from parliament (1642). Supported the king in the Civil War; raised a new Cornish army, which won victories at Braddock Down and Stratton on its march through Cornwall and Devon; fought his old friend Waller in the indecisive battle of Lansdown and defeated him at Roundway Down, before assisting in the capture of Bristol (1643). Appointed Governor of Bristol and Field Marshal of the king's western army (1643); defeated by Waller at Cheriton (1644); again appointed commander of the western forces (1646), but defeated by Fairfax at Torrington, before surrendering at Tresilian Bridge (1646). In retirement, he lived in Jersey, Holland and Bruges, playing no part in the intrigues of Charles II's court.

Hyde, Edward, Earl of Clarendon (1609–74): Son of Henry Hyde of Dinton, Wilts; educated at Oxford and the Middle Temple; married (1) Anne Ayliffe (1629) and (2) Frances Aylesbury (1634); MP for Wootton Bassett in the Short Parliament (1640) and Saltash in the Long Parliament (1640); closely involved with the popular party in its attacks on ship money and the Star Chamber; helped to prepare charges for Strafford's impeachment, but opposed 'root and branch' measures against episcopacy. Emerged as leader of the king's party in the Commons (1641) in an attempt to discourage Charles from further unconstitutional actions; objected to his attempted arrest of the Five Members, but nevertheless joined him in York (1642). Knighted, appointed Privy Councillor and Chancellor of the Exchequer (1643); advocated the setting up of the Oxford Parliament (1643); became the king's chief peace negotiator. Accompanied the Prince of Wales into exile (1645); ambassador of the king in exile to Madrid (1649–51); Charles II's chief minister (1652–60); appointed Lord Chancellor (1658); helped to formulate the Declaration of Breda (1660). At the Restoration became head of government; appointed Chancellor of Oxford University (1660) and Earl of Clarendon (1661); his daughter, Anne, married the Duke of York. He supported the persecution of Puritans in the Corporation Act (1661), the Act of Uniformity (1662), the Conventicle Act (1664) and the Five Mile Act (1665). He continued the French alliance, selling back Dunkirk to Louis XIV (1662); opposed the outbreak of the Dutch War, but was blamed for its unimpressive conduct. Dismissed as Chancellor (1667) and impeached by the Commons for corruption and arbitrary government; fled to France; sentenced to exile for life. During his exile he wrote *History of the Great Rebellion* (1702–4) and *The Life of Edward, Earl of Clarendon* (1759).

Hyde, Laurence, Earl of Rochester (1641–1711): Son of Edward Hyde, Earl of Clarendon; married Harrietta Boyle (1665); MP for Newport, Cornwall (1660), Oxford University (1661–79) and Wootton Bassett (1679). Appointed Master of the Robes (1662–75) and First Lord of the Treasury (1679); created Viscount Hyde (1681) and Earl of Rochester (1682). Gaining in influence following the dismissal of Shaftesbury, he defended the Duke of York in the Exclusion Bill debates, negotiated the secret subsidy treaty with France and supported a close alliance with France at the expense of the Triple Alliance; was dismissed as First Lord of the Treasury (1684). Created Lord Treasurer and Knight of the Garter by James II (1685), he largely controlled the government; served on the Ecclesiastical Commission, where he supported the suspension of Henry Compton, Bishop of London (1686); but he was a loyal Anglican and objected to the king's plans to restore Catholicism; dismissed after declining to change his religion (1687). Supported the idea of a regency in the Revolution (1688), but backed William III and Mary after their accession. Readmitted to the Privy Council and the cabinet, as leader of the High Church party (1700); appointed Lord Lieutenant of Ireland (1700) under Anne; opposed the war with France; resigned (1703); opposed the Regency Bill (1705) and the Act of Union (1707); appointed Lord President in Harley's ministry (1710).

Inchiquin, 1st Earl of (1614–74) – *see* O'Brien, Murrough.

Ireton, Henry (1611–51): Son of German Ireton of Attenborough, Notts.; educated at Oxford and the Middle Temple; married Bridget Cromwell (1646). At the start of the Civil War, he led the parliamentarians in Nottinghamshire (1642); fought at Edgehill (1642) and Gainsborough (1643); was appointed Quartermaster-General in Manchester's army at the Second Battle of Newbury (1644); allied with Cromwell in his criticism of Manchester; appointed Commissary-General of Horse in the New Model Army (1645); commanded cavalry at Naseby (1645) and took part in the sieges of Bristol (1645) and Oxford (1646). MP for Appleby (1645); supported the army in its dispute with parliament (1647); a parliamentary commissionary in its negotiations with the army. Drafted the Declaration of the Army, the Remonstrance of the Army and the Heads of Proposals (1647). In the Putney Debates (1647), advocated moderation in opposition to the radical demands of the Levellers as outlined in their *Agreement of the People*. In the Second Civil War (1648), fought with Fairfax in Kent and Essex; supported the trial of the king; closely involved in Pride's Purge (1648); a member of the High Court of Justice and a signatory of the death warrant (1649). Appointed second-in-command to Cromwell in Ireland (1649); appointed President of Munster (1650) and Lord Deputy of Ireland on Cromwell's return to England (1650); pursued policies in favour of the replantation of the country with English and Scottish colonists and against the toleration of Catholics. Buried in Westminster Abbey, but disinterred by royalists at the Restoration.

James I (1566–1625): Son of Mary, Queen of Scots and Lord Darnley; became James VI of Scotland (24th July 1567); assumed personal power (1578); captured by nobles at the Raid of Ruthven (1582); tried unsuccessfully to thwart the abolition of episcopacy by the General Assembly. Married Anne of Denmark (1589); survived Bothwell's assassination attempts (1591, 1593); defeated the catholic nobility at Glenlivet (1594); published *Basilikon Doron* (c.1598) in support of episcopacy; revived the appointment of bishops (1599); survived Ruthven's Gowrie Conspiracy (1600). Succeeded to the English throne (24th Mar. 1603); rebuked the Puritans at the Hampton Court Conference (1604); expelled the Jesuits (1604); survived the Gunpowder Plot (1605); arranged the marriage of his daughter, Elizabeth, to Frederick V, Elector Palatine (1613). He promoted George Villiers (later Duke of Buckingham) as court favourite in place of Robert Carr (Earl of Somerset) (1615); pursued a peace policy with Spain (1615); was unsuccessful in his use of 'managers' to control the Addled Parliament (1614); attempted to augment his revenue through benevolences, sale of peerages and monopolies; rejected involvement in the Thirty Years War on behalf of the Elector Palatine (1618). Dissolved the 1621 parliament after it had launched attacks on his policies and impeached Bacon;

declared war on Spain after his abortive attempt to marry Prince Charles to the Spanish Infanta (1625); planned, instead, the marriage of Charles to Henrietta Maria of France.

James II (1633–1701): Son of Charles I and Henrietta Maria; Married (1) Anne Hyde (1660) and (2) Mary of Modena (1673); created Duke of York (1633). During the Civil War, was captured at Oxford (1646), but escaped to Holland (1648). Appointed Lord High Admiral at the Restoration (1660); ably commanded the fleet against the Dutch (1665); converted to Roman Catholicism (1669) and resigned his command on the passing of the Test Act (1673). Following an attempt to prevent his succession by the Exclusion Bill, he was sent abroad by Charles II to allow the controversy to subside; returned as Lord High Commissioner to Scotland; survived attempts to impeach him as a popish recusant (1680) and assassinate him in the Rye House Plot (1683); reappointed Lord High Admiral and member of the Council (1684). Succeeded to the throne (6 Feb. 1685); survived rebellions by Monmouth in England and Argyll in Scotland (1685). Pursued a policy aimed at the restoration of Catholicism; used his dispensing power to appoint Catholics to office, freeing them from the conditions of the Test Act; established a new Court of Ecclesiastical Commission (1686), which suspended the Bishop of London; succeeded in gaining the judges' agreement to the legality of the dispensing power; assembled an army of 13,000 on Hounslow Heath under catholic officers; issued the Declaration of Indulgence (1687) to relieve dissenters; ordered the trial of seven bishops who refused to enforce the Declaration (1688). After the invasion of William of Orange, he was deserted by his own army and escaped to France (1688); was supported by Louis XIV of France in an expedition to Ireland (1689), but suffered a setback by the raising of the siege of Londonderry and defeat at the Battle of the Boyne (1690). Returned to France, where he remained until his death.

Jeffreys, George, 1st Baron Jeffreys of Wem (1645–89): Born in Acton, near Wrexham; son of John Jeffreys, gentleman; educated at Shrewsbury, St Paul's and Westminster Schools, Cambridge University and the Inner Temple; called to the Bar (1668). Cultivated connections at court; knighted (1677); appointed Recorder of London (1678). He gained a reputation for his vindictive and insulting manner as council for the prosecution in the trials of Archbishop Plunkett (1681), Lord Russell (1683) and others – and for the brutal punishments imposed on the flimsiest of evidence as an Old Bailey judge in the trials of Algernon Sidney (1683), Titus Oates (1685) and Richard Baxter (1685).

Appointed Chief Justice of Chester (1680); Lord Chief Justice (1683); member of the Privy Council (1683). He gained notoriety for his trials of the Monmouth rebels (1685), many of whom were either executed or deported. Created Baron Jeffreys and Lord Chancellor by James II (1685); defended the king's use of the dispensing power; helped to purge municipal corporations; chairman of the Ecclesiastical Commission. He was arrested while attempting to flee abroad after the Glorious Revolution (1688) – died in prison.

Juxon, William (1582–1663): Born in Chichester; Son of Richard Juxon; educated at Merchant Taylor's School and Oxford; ordained (1615); appointed president of St John's College, Oxford (1621); a friend and supporter of Laud. Appointed Dean of Worcester (1627), Bishop of Hereford (1632), Bishop of London (1633); Lord Treasurer (1636); member of the Privy Council (1636). After the start of the Civil War, largely withdrew from political life; ministered to Charles I (1646–49) and was present with him on the scaffold. Retired to Little Compton in Gloucestershire (1649–60). At the Restoration, was appointed Archbishop of Canterbury (1660), but was too old and weak to play a major role.

Ker, Robert (1585?–1645) – *see* Carr, Robert.

Lambert, John (1619–83): Born at Calton, Yorkshire; married Francis Lister (1639). Fought for parliament in the Civil War, seeing action at Hull (1643), Nantwich (1644), Marston Moor (1644) and Pontefract (1645); commanded the infantry in the New Model Army; helped to secure the surrender of Exeter and Oxford (1646). Led the army's protest against parliament (1647); assisted Cromwell at the Battle of Preston (1648); sent to Scotland in support of the Duke of Argyll (1648); in favour of the trial of the king (1648/49). He was appointed second-in-command on Cromwell's Scottish campaign (1650), fighting at the Battle of Dunbar and pursuing Charles II to his defeat at Worcester. He refused appointment as Commander-in-Chief in Ireland (1652); in favour of Cromwell's dissolution of the Rump (1653); appointed a member of the subsequent Council of State; assisted in the drafting of the Instrument of Government (1653); loyally supported Cromwell (1653–57), but opposed the offer of kingship; resigned all offices following his refusal to take the oath for councillors (1657). Supported the accession of Richard Cromwell (1658); MP for Pontefract (1659); appointed to the Committee of Safety and Council of State (1659); restored to his army command; assisted in the dissolution of the Rump (1659); marched north in an attempt to prevent Monck's march on

London from Scotland; deprived of his command by the restored parliament; imprisoned in the Tower (1660), but escaped to lead an abortive rising (1660); condemned for treason (1662), but reprieved by Charles II; exiled to Jersey.

Laud, William (1573–1645): Son of William Laud, a Reading clothier; educated at Reading Free School and Oxford; ordained (1601). Appointed Archdeacon of Huntingdon (1615); Dean of Gloucester (1616); and Bishop of St David's (1621). Having accompanied James I on his visit to Scotland (1617), he became a close friend of the Duke of Buckingham and thereby secured significant influence on the accession of Charles I (1625). He was a staunch supporter of the king in his disputes with parliament, drafted his speeches in defence of Buckingham and advocated the importance of giving priority to the promotion of arminian clergy. He was appointed Dean of the Chapel Royal and Bishop of Bath and Wells (1626); Privy Councillor (1627); Bishop of London (1628); Chancellor of Oxford University (1630); and Archbishop of Canterbury (1633). He revived metropolitan visitations (1634); stipulated that all communion tables were to be fixed at the east end and all clergy to conform to the Prayer Book; enforced standards through the Court of High Commission; supported Charles I in his reissue of *The Book of Sports* (1633) in opposition to the puritan sabbath. He was actively involved in the prosecution of Prynne in the Court of Star Chamber (1634, 1637); was appointed member of the Commission of the Treasury and the Committee for Foreign Affairs (1635). Urged the vigorous imposition of the new canons and Prayer Book in Scotland and the recall of parliament to vote supply for the Scottish war (1639). Impeached by the Long Parliament (1640); imprisoned in the Tower for over two years without trial; was finally tried (1644) for endeavouring to subvert the laws and overthrow the protestant religion; condemned to death by ordinance; executed (1645).

Lauderdale, 2nd Earl & 1st Duke of (1616–82) – *see* Maitland, John.

Leslie, Alexander, 1st Earl of Leven (1580–1661): Son of George Leslie; gained military experience on the continent (1628–38) under Gustavus Adolphus in the Thirty Years War. Took the Covenant (1638); appointed Lord General of Scottish forces (1639); seized Edinburgh Castle; gained a negotiated settlement in the First Bishops' War (1639). In the Second Bishops' War (1640), crossed into England and seized Newcastle; in the ensuing settlement, was created Earl of Leven by Charles I and appointed Captain of Edinburgh Castle. Appointed General of the

Scottish army sent from Scotland to quell the Irish rebellion (1641) – but returned to lead the Scottish army into England in support of parliament (1644); commanded the infantry at Marston Moor, but fled the field; captured Newcastle by storm (1644); was host to Charles I after his surrender to the Scots (1646), but returned to Scotland after the king was handed over to parliament. During the Second Civil War (1648), Leslie did not take part in the abortive invasion of England, but was responsible for the security of Scotland. Was nominally commander of the army which was defeated by Cromwell at Dunbar (1650), but by then old age had reduced him to a mere figurehead. Captured by English forces (1651) and imprisoned; released (1654) into retirement.

Leslie, David, 1st Baron Newark (d. 1682): Son of Sir Patrick Leslie; gained military experience on the continent under Gustavus Adolphus in the Thirty Years War; appointed Major-General of Horse in the Scottish army, which invaded England in support of parliament (1644); fought with distinction at Marston Moor (1644); captured Carlisle (1645). After his recall to Scotland, he inflicted a heavy defeat on Montrose at Philiphaugh (1645). At the end of the Civil War, he was appointed Lieutenant-General, but declined to join the army which invaded England in support of the king (1648); again defeated Montrose at Carbisdale following the latter's declaration for Charles II (1650). After Charles II had taken the Covenant, Leslie commanded the forces to resist Cromwell's invasion with the New Model Army (1650); but was defeated at Dunbar (1650). Then, on the orders of Charles II, he crossed with his army into England, marched south, but was defeated by Cromwell at Worcester (1651); was captured at Chester and imprisoned (1651–60). At the Restoration, he was created Baron Newark and awarded a pension by Charles II.

Leven, 1st Earl of (1580–1661) – *see* Leslie, Alexander.

Lilburne, John (1614–57): Son of Richard Lilburne of County Durham; educated at Bishop Auckland Grammar School and the Royal Grammar School, Newcastle-upon-Tyne; married Elizabeth Dewell; apprenticed to a clothier in London (1630), where he came under puritan influence; helped to publish and distribute John Bastwick's *Litany*, for which he was tried by the Star Chamber and sentenced to a fine, public whipping, time in the pillory and imprisonment, having refused to take the oath or recognise the legality of the court (1638); won much popular support through his suffering and the nickname of 'Freeborn John'; spent his imprisonment in writing pamphlets; released by the Long Parliament

(1640). During the Civil War, he was appointed captain in Lord Brooke's regiment, fighting at Edgehill and Brentford (1642), and later Lieutenant-Colonel in Manchester's army, fighting at Marston Moor (1644); supported Cromwell's attack on Manchester's handling of the war (1644); resigned his commission after refusing to take the Covenant (1645). He attacked the presbyterian majority in the Commons for intolerance; published *England's Birthright Justified* (1645), which listed grievances and demanded freedoms; frequently questioned the authority and procedure of parliamentary committees and the House of Lords – for which he was imprisoned (1646). He allied with radical groups and the army Levellers, condemning the tyranny of parliament and calling for constitutional reform. Released from prison (1648); attacked the tyranny of Cromwell and the army in *England's New Chains* (1649); arrested with his co-leaders of the Leveller movement, Overton and Walwyn, and tried for high treason (1649), but acquitted by the jury amid popular acclaim. He was later banished by the Rump for a pamphlet directed against Sir Arthur Haselrig (1651), living in Amsterdam and Bruges (1652). Returned without authority (1653); was arrested, tried and acquitted – but sent into custody first in Jersey (1654) and then in Dover Castle (1655), where he became a Quaker.

Maitland, John, 2nd Earl & 1st Duke of Lauderdale (1616–82): Born in East Lothian; Son of John Maitland, 1st Earl; educated as a Presbyterian; trained as a lawyer; supported the Covenant; appointed a member of the Committee of Both Kingdoms (1644); took part in the Uxbridge Negotiations (1645); reacted against the growing extremism of the Independents in the army; led the Scottish delegation which arranged the Engagement with Charles I (1647); influenced the Covenanters to support the king in the Second Civil War (1648). After the king's execution (1649), he accompanied Charles II to Scotland, supported his coronation at Scone (1650) and fought for him at Worcester (1651); was captured and imprisoned (1651–60). At the Restoration, was appointed Secretary of State for Scotland (1660), thereafter dominating its government and becoming a loyal member of the Cabal; appointed Lord High Commissioner (1669); created a duke (1672). He purged opposition from parliament and launched a period of persecution of Presbyterians; an attempt at moderation through the Letter of Indulgence (1669) was quickly abandoned and he resorted again to the suppression of conventicles with some brutality (e.g. the use of the 'Highland Host' to subdue the South-West in 1678). Mounting opposition to him centred on Hamilton in Scotland and Shaftesbury in England. He resigned on grounds of ill health (1680).

Manchester, 2nd Earl of (1602–71) – *see* Montagu, Edward.

Marlborough, 1st Duke of (1650–1722) – *see* Churchill, John.

Marlborough, Duchess of (1660–1744) – *see* Churchill, Sarah.

Marten, Henry (1602–80): Born at Oxford; son of Sir Henry Marten, lawyer; educated at Oxford; MP for Berkshire (1640). Although far removed from Puritanism, he was fiercely republican and anti-royalist from the outset. Fought for parliament in the Civil War, after which he led the call for the king's punishment, proposing the motion for 'no further addresses' to the king (1647). He gave support to the army in its struggle with parliament; allied with the Levellers, supporting their call for reform and helping to draft *The Agreement of the People* (1647); and published *England's Troublers Troubled* (1648), an attack on capitalism. He was a member of the court which tried Charles I, a signatory of the death warrant and a member of the Council of State (1649). He disagreed with Cromwell over the expulsion of the Rump and was expelled from the Commons (1653). At the Restoration, he was tried as a regicide, but escaped with imprisonment for life.

Mary II (1662–92): Eldest daughter of James, Duke of York and Anne Hyde; married her cousin, William of Orange (1677), but without issue; educated as a Protestant under the guidance of Bishop Compton, on the orders of Charles II, in spite of the opposition of her catholic parents. Lived rather unhappily in Holland (1677–88), seeing little of her husband and playing no part in political affairs. A devout Protestant, she supported William nevertheless in his condemnation of the Declaration of Indulgence (1687), his support of the Seven Bishops (1688) and his acceptance of the invitation to invade Britain (1688). She rejected all her father's attempts to convert her to Catholicism; refused Danby's suggestion that she should become sole sovereign, but accepted the offer of joint sovereignty and coronation (1689); took control over affairs during William's frequent absences on military campaigns, but otherwise willingly left political matters in his hands; became responsible, however, for ecclesiastical appointments; and instigated the establishment of Greenwich Hospital. Her close relationship with her sister, Anne, was strained by the latter's attachment to the Marlboroughs and finally broken by Marlborough's disgrace and imprisonment (1692). She died of smallpox.

Maurice, Prince (1620–52): Son of Frederick V, Elector Palatine and King of Bohemia, and Elizabeth, daughter of James I; educated at universities in France and Holland. Campaigned in the Thirty Years War, before volunteering (with his brother, Prince Rupert) to help his uncle, Charles I, in the Civil War. Appointed to command royalist forces in safeguarding Gloucestershire, he defeated Waller at Ripple Field (1643); was appointed Lieutenant-General of Horse to the Marquess of Hertford and accompanied the latter to the West in an attempt to strengthen Hopton's advancing Cornish army; fought in the Battles of Lansdown and Roundway Down and the successful siege of Bristol (1643). Appointed Lieutenant-General of the king's western army, he captured Dorchester, Exeter and Dartmouth (1643), but abandoned the siege of Lyme on the approach of the Earl of Essex's army (1644). Appointed Major-General to defend Worcestershire and the Welsh border, he lost Shrewsbury, but relieved Chester (1645); took part in the storming of Leicester and the defeat at Naseby (1645). At the end of the war, he fled abroad and later joined Rupert in a career of piracy on the high seas, but was eventually lost at sea in a storm.

Middlesex, 1st Earl of (1575–1645) – *see* Cranfield, Lionel.

Milton, John (1608–74): Son of John Milton, scrivener of London; educated at St Paul's School and Cambridge; married (1) Mary Powell (1643), (2) Catherine Woodstock (1656) and (3) Elizabeth Minshull (1663). He was involved in controversy with the Bishop of Exeter, following the publication of his pamphlets attacking episcopacy (1641–42). Supported parliament's cause in the Civil War and its subsequent victory; wrote *Areopagitica* on the censorship of the press (1644); sympathised with the army in their quarrel with parliament (1647); showed approval of the execution of the king, writing *Tenure of Kings and Magistrates* (1649), which advocated the right of the people to judge their rulers. He was appointed Latin Secretary to the Council of State (1649); and, at the request of the Council, wrote *Eikonoklastes* (1649 – a reply to Gauden's *Eikon Basilike*), *Pro Populo Anglicano Defensio* (1651) and *Defensio Secunda* (1654). Having lost his sight (1652), he was assisted by Philip Meadows and Andrew Marvell; supported the Protectorate and the accession of Richard Cromwell; favoured the separation of Church and State. Lived in hiding at the Restoration, his *Defensio* having been burnt by the common hangman; was arrested, but pardoned under the Indemnity Act. He wrote his most famous works in retirement – *Paradise Lost* (1667); *Paradise Regained* (1671) and *Samson Agonistes* (1671).

Monck, George, Duke of Albermarle (1608–70): Son of Sir Thomas Monck of Devon. Took part in expeditions to Cadiz (1625) and the Isle of Ré (1627); present at the siege of Breda (1637). He served against the rebels in both Scotland (1640) and Ireland (1642); was appointed Major-General by the king in the Civil War (1644), but was captured at Nantwich and imprisoned for two years on charges of high treason. After the Civil War, he took the Covenant and served parliament in Ireland as commander of forces in Ulster (1647–49). He accompanied Cromwell to Scotland (1650), leading a brigade of foot at Dunbar; was appointed Lieutenant-General of Ordinance and Commander-in-Chief in Scotland on Cromwell's departure (1651), completing its reduction by the capture of Stirling, Dundee, Aberdeen, etc.; appointed one of the commissioners responsible for the civil settlement there (1651). On the outbreak of the First Anglo-Dutch War, was appointed one of three Generals of the Fleet (1652), taking part in the victories off Portland and the Gabbard (1653). Elected MP for Devon (1653); returned to command the army in Scotland (1654–58); favoured the accession of Richard Cromwell (1658). With the outbreak of disorder after Lambert's army had expelled parliament by force, he marched into England (1660); was appointed member of the Council of State and Commander-in-Chief of all forces; demanded the election of a new parliament; commenced negotiations with Charles II, informing him of the proposals contained in the Declaration of Breda; presented the king's letters to parliament, which voted the Restoration; received a commission as Captain-General; met the king at Dover; created Baron Monck and Duke of Albermarle (1660). Supervised the government of London during the plague (1665) and the Great Fire (1666); joined Rupert and the navy in the war against the Dutch (1666–67); appointed First Lord of the Treasury (1667).

Monmouth, Duke of (1645–85) – *see* Scott, James.

Montagu, Charles, Earl of Halifax (1661–1715): Born in Northamptonshire; son of George Montagu, gentleman; educated at Westminster School and Cambridge, where he was appointed Fellow of Trinity College. A witty author, he wrote *The Town and County Mouse* (1687) with Matthew Prior, a burlesque of Dryden's *The Hind and the Panther.* He was a signatory of the letter inviting William of Orange to invade (1688); and was elected MP for Malden (1689). Appointed Commissioner of the Treasury (1691), Privy Councillor (1694), First Lord of the Treasury (1697) and Chancellor of the Exchequer (1694–97), he established vital financial reforms which successfully funded a period of war and gave security to individual investors – the National Debt (1693), the Bank of England (1694), the Consolidated Fund (1696), the Re–coinage Act (1695) and the issuing of exchequer bills. A member of the Whig Junto, he resigned after election reverses (1699); was created Baron Halifax (1700). Unsuccessfully impeached for corruption and involvement in the Partition Treaty (1701), he held no major office under Anne – although he was appointed a commissioner in the negotiations for the Union with Scotland (1707). Nominated a regent by George I on his accession to handle administration until his own arrival from Germany, he was again appointed First Lord of the Treasury, created an earl and awarded the Order of the Garter (1714).

Montagu, Edward, 2nd Earl of Manchester (1602–71): Son of Sir Henry Montagu, 1st Earl; educated at Cambridge; elected MP for Huntingdon (1623); created Baron Montagu (1626) and granted the courtesy title of Viscount Mandeville (1626); married five times; his second wife, daughter of the Earl of Warwick, introduced him to puritan circles; thereafter, he became a close associate of Pym and the king's target for arrest (along with the Five Members) on a charge of high treason (1642). Succeeded his father as Earl of Manchester (1642); appointed by parliament Major-General of the Eastern Association army (1643); fought at Marston Moor (1644) and the Second Battle of Newbury (1644), but became increasingly cautious and reluctant to engage; was horrified by the prospect of total victory, favouring a negotiated settlement and a constitutional monarchy. This prompted a breach with Cromwell, his second-in-command, who accused him in the Commons of incompetency; resigned his commission under the terms of the Self-Denying Ordinance (1645). A member of the House of Lords, he often took the Speaker's chair; supported moves to draw up a peaceful settlement with Charles; opposed the trial and execution of the king; withdrew from public life during the Commonwealth and Protectorate; actively supported the Restoration. He was appointed by Charles II Chancellor of Cambridge University, Lord Chamberlain, Privy Councillor and Knight of the Garter (1660–61).

Montagu, Edward, 1st Earl of Sandwich (1625–72): Born in Northamptonshire; son of Sir Sydney Montagu, a royalist sympathiser; married Jemimah Crewe (1642). Fought for parliament in the Civil War, raising a regiment in Cambridgeshire (1643) and joining the army of his cousin (the Earl of Manchester) at Marston Moor (1644); later commanded a regiment at Naseby (1645) and the siege of Bristol (1645) in Fairfax's New Model Army. Elected MP for Huntingdonshire (?1645), but was largely inactive during the turbulent years, 1646–49. Deeply loyal to Cromwell, he was appointed a member of the Council of State (1653), Commissioner of the Treasury (1654), joint commander (with Blake) of the fleet (1656) and a member of the new 'Second Chamber' (1657). Supported Richard Cromwell; but after the latter's fall, intrigued with Charles II and used the navy to escort him to England at the Restoration (1660). He was created Earl of Sandwich and granted the Order of the Garter by Charles, who also appointed him Lieutenant-Admiral of the navy under the Duke of York. Fought in the Second Anglo-Dutch War at the Battle of Lowestoft (1665), but resigned after criticism of his plundering of Dutch East India Company vessels (1665). Appointed ambassador to Spain (1666); fought in the Third Anglo-Dutch War, but was killed in action in the Battle of Solebay (1672).

Montrose, 1st Marquess & 5th Earl (1612–50) – *see* Graham, James.

Newark, 1st Baron (d. 1682) – *see* Leslie, David.

Newcastle, Duke of (1592–1676) – *see* Cavendish, William.

Nicholas, Sir Edward (1593–1669): Born in Wiltshire; son of John Nicholas; educated at Oxford and the Middle Temple; appointed Secretary to the Warden of the Cinque Ports under both Lord Zouch and the Duke of Buckingham (1618–25); Secretary of the Admiralty (1625); Clerk to the Council in extraordinary (1626); Clerk to the Council in ordinary (1635), dealing with ship money problems; elected MP for Winchelsea (1620–21, 1623–24) and Dover (1627–28); was made responsible for updating the king on affairs in London during Charles I's visit to Scotland (1641–42). Appointed Secretary of State (1641), he advised the king during the Civil War, represented him during the Uxbridge Negotiations (1645) and organised his surrender terms (1646). Went into exile on the continent after the war, serving Charles II as Secretary of State (from 1654), though his influence was gradually undermined by Queen Henrietta Maria in favour of Edward Hyde. At the Restoration (1660), he returned with Charles, but was soon dismissed from office (1662).

Nottingham, 2nd Earl of (1647–1730) – *see* Finch, Daniel.

Oates, Titus (1649–1705); Son of Rev. Samuel Oates; born at Oakham; educated at Cambridge; ordained (1673); curate to his father in Hastings (1674); imprisoned for perjury (1675), but escaped to become naval chaplain. Met Israel Tonge (1676) and began to scheme ways of making profit by unearthing catholic plots, real or imaginary; attempted to infiltrate their ranks by joining a Jesuit college in Spain (1677) and an

English seminary in the Netherlands (1678). Oates and Tonge then devised the Popish Plot, which was outlined to a London magistrate (Sir Edmund Godfrey) and then the Privy Council; the alleged plot was to include the assassination of the king and Council, the massacre of Protestants, an invasion of Ireland by the French and the establishment of the Duke of York as king. Although based on lies, the plot was believed by the London mob, who feted Oates as a hero. After the mysterious death of Godfrey, over 30 people were tried and executed for complicity in the plot, largely on the evidence of Oates and his accomplices. From 1681, however, his popularity declined and, following his attempt to denounce the Duke of York as a traitor, he was arrested and charged damages (1684), before being tried for perjury (1685) and sentenced to public humiliation, whipping, a fine and imprisonment. Released in 1688 with a modest pension, he became a baptist preacher (1698), but was later expelled for disorderly behaviour.

O'Brien, Murrough, 1st Earl of Inchiquin (1614–74): Son of Dermod, 5th Baron Inchiquin; married Elizabeth St Leger. After military service on the continent, he was appointed Vice President of Munster by Charles I (1640), fighting against the catholic rebels and defeating them at Liscarrol (1642); he supported the Cessation (1643); but was refused the title of Lord President on a visit to the king in Oxford (1644). Thereafter, he switched his support to parliament, realising that they had more resources to assist the Protestants in Ireland; was confirmed by them as Lord President; with reinforcements provided by Lord Lisle (1647), he recovered control of the South-West, defeating the rebels at Knocknannus (1647). He switched back to support the king (1648); was appointed Lieutenant-General of the royalist army under Ormond; but was unable to withstand the onslaught of Cromwell's New Model Army (1649). Fled from Ireland (1650); was appointed a member of Charles II's Council; and was converted to Catholicism. After the Restoration (1660), he was appointed general of an expedition to Lisbon (1662); returned to Ireland (1663); and was again appointed Vice President of Munster (1664).

Ormond, 1st Duke of (1610–88) – *see* Butler, James.

Ormond, 2nd Duke of (1665–1745) – *see* Butler, James.

Orford, Earl of (1653–1727) – *see* Russell, Edward.

Orrery, 1st Earl of (1621–79) – *see* Boyle, Roger.

Osborne, Sir Thomas, 1st Earl of Danby (1632–1712): Son of Sir Edward Osborne of Yorkshire; married Lady Bridget Bertie (1654); elected MP for York (1665). Appointed Treasurer of the Navy (1668); Privy Councillor (1673); Lord High Treasurer (1673). Created Viscount Osborne (1673), Baron Osborne (1673) and Earl of Danby (1674). A High Tory, he was chief minister of Charles II (1673–79); revived the persecution laws against Catholics and dissenters (1676); made peace with the Dutch; opposed the aggressive policies of Louis XIV; secured the marriage of Princess Mary to William of Orange (1677); agreed to the secret deal between Charles II and Louis XIV for England's neutrality in return for subsidies. He was impeached when his part in the secret negotiations became known (1678) and imprisoned without trial until 1684; impeachment removed (1685). He greatly disliked James II's catholic tendencies and arbitrary actions; signed the invitation to William of Orange (1688); seized control of York for William; helped to persuade the Lords to support the joint offer of the crown to William and Mary (1688). Created Marquess of Carmarthen (1689); President of the Council (1689); Lord Lieutenant of the Three Ridings (1690); and Duke of Leeds (1694). On the retirement of Lord Halifax (1690), he emerged in almost total control of the government. He was impeached (1695) for receiving a bribe from the East India Company; escaped punishment, but gradually lost influence; resigned his offices (1699).

Oxford, 1st Earl of (1661–1724) – *see* Harley, Robert.

Penn, Sir William (1621–70): Born in Bristol; son of Sir Giles Penn, merchant; married Margaret Jasper. He fought at sea for parliament in the Civil War in Warwick's fleet; appointed Rear Admiral (1647), seeing action against Rupert's pirate ships (1650). Appointed Vice Admiral under Blake in the First Anglo-Dutch War (1652), fighting in the battles of Kentish Knock (1652) and Portland (1653). Appointed General of the Fleet (1653); commanded an expedition to the West Indies (1654–55), capturing Jamaica – but was later briefly imprisoned in disgrace for his hasty withdrawal from Hispaniola. Retired to his estates in Ireland; secretly corresponded with Charles II throughout the 1650s; at the Restoration, was granted a knighthood and appointed a naval commissioner. Appointed Captain of the Fleet in the Second Anglo-Dutch War, fighting at Solebay (1665).

Penn, William (1644–1718): Born in London; son of Sir William Penn; educated at Chigwell School, Oxford, the Huguenot College of Saumur and Lincoln's Inn; converted to Quakerism (1667); married (1)

Gulielma Springett (1672) and (2) Hannah Callowhill (1696). Imprisoned on three occasions (1667–70) for attending Quaker meetings and writing controversial pamphlets, including *Truth Exalted* (1668), *No Cross, No Crown* (1669) and *The Great Case of Liberty of Conscience* (1671). He continued to preach in England, Ireland, Germany and Holland during the 1670s and supported the Whigs in the Exclusion Crisis (1678–81). He gradually drew up plans to set up a 'holy experiment' in Christian living in a new Quaker colony in America; gained from Charles II a grant of land as repayment for a debt owed to his father (1680), calling the colony Pennsylvania (1681) and establishing it on the 'Frame of Government', a personally drafted constitution. He was its first Governor, making a peace treaty with the local Indians (1683) and masterminding the construction of Philadelphia. Returned to England (1684); became a supporter of James II, gaining the release of Quakers from prison; but was regarded with suspicion in William III's reign for his correspondence with the exiled king; revisited his colony (1699–1701). His later writings included *Some Fruits of Solitude* (1693) and *Essay towards the Present and Future Peace of Europe* (1693).

Penruddock, John (1619–55): Born in Compton Chamberlayne, Wiltshire; son of Sir John Penruddock; educated at Blandford School, Oxford University and Gray's Inn; fought for the king in the Civil War. In 1655, the Sealed Knot (a royalist group of conspirators) had devised a plan for a general rising to bring about the restoration of Charles II. Their plans, however, were largely uncovered by Cromwell's espionage system with the result that the general rising failed to materialise. Nevertheless, in Wiltshire, Penruddock's band of 400 followers pressed ahead by capturing Salisbury and proclaiming Charles king at Blandford; disappointed by the lack of popular support, they headed towards Cornwall, but were intercepted and defeated at South Molton in Devon. Penruddock was captured, tried for treason at Exeter and executed (1655). Penruddock's Rising was followed by the imposition of rule by the Major-Generals.

Pepys, Samuel (1633–1703): Born in London; son of John Pepys, tailor; educated at Huntingdon Grammar School, St Paul's School and Cambridge; married Elizabeth Marchand de St Michel (1665). Appointed clerk to George Downing, a teller of the Exchequer (1658); secretary to his cousin, Edward Montagu, in the fleet which escorted Charles II back to England; Clerk of the Privy Seal (1660); Treasurer of the commission responsible for Tangier (1662); and Clerk to the Victualling Office (1665). Started work on his *Diary* in shorthand

(1660–69), covering personalities, social life and events (including the Plague and the Great Fire). He strongly defended the navy from adverse criticism in the Commons (1668); was elected MP for Castle Rising (1673) and Harwich (1679, 1685). He was appointed Secretary of the Admiralty (1673–79, 1684–88), after it had been put into commission by Charles II, following the removal of the Duke of York as Lord High Admiral (i.e. in consequence of the Test Act); commenced an effective programme of naval reforms, including the revision of naval contracts, the construction of 30 new battleships, the establishment of the convoy system and the restructuring of ranks. He was elected President of the Royal Society (1684). The inevitable opposition to his reforms was led by Shaftesbury; was accused of popery (1673) and complicity in Godfrey's murder (1678) – briefly imprisoned (1679). Served loyally under James II and continued his naval reforms in the admiralty (1684–88); dismissed by William III (1689), after which he concentrated on writing (including *Memoirs of the Navy* in 1690) and his work as a governor of Christ's Hospital.

Peter, Hugh (1598–1660): Born at Fowey; son of Thomas Peter; educated at Cambridge; ordained (1623); married Elizabeth Read (1624). A Puritan, he became a controversial nonconformist preacher in London and was suspended for his attacks on Queen Henrietta Maria's catholic beliefs (1628); emigrated to Rotterdam in Holland (1629), serving as a minister to English merchants (1629–35); emigrated to New England (1635), after Archbishop Laud had investigated his activities in Holland; appointed minister of the church at Salem (1639), which he ran on congregational lines; assisted in the establishment of the Massachusetts Bay colony and Harvard College. Returned to England (1641) to gain financial assistance, but became engulfed in the Civil War; served parliament as an inspiring preacher/propagandist and chaplain/chronicler in the New Model Army (1645–46); strongly supported the Independents in the army in their quarrel with parliament, Pride's Purge (1648) and the trial of the king (1649); preached sermons which were hostile to Charles during the king's trial, including one on 'the terrible denunciation to the king of Babylon' on the eve of his execution. During the Commonwealth, he accompanied Cromwell's army to Ireland (1649); was appointed chaplain to the Council of State (1650) and a Trier to license clergy in the Church (1654). Poor health and later disillusionment made him largely withdraw from public affairs during the Protectorate. At the Restoration, he was exempted from the Act of Oblivion and Indemnity, tried as a regicide and executed for high treason.

Portland, 1st Earl of (1649–1709) – *see* Bentinck, William.

Prynne, William (1600–69): Son of Thomas Prynne of Somerset; educated at Bath Free School, Oxford and Lincoln's Inn. Launched an outspoken attack on stage plays in his *Histriomastix* (1632); tried before the Star Chamber for his implied criticism of the queen and sentenced to life imprisonment, a £5,000 fine and the loss of both ears (1634). Wrote pamphlets in the Tower attacking bishops, especially *News from Ipswich* (1636), for which he was again tried, with similar punishments. Released by the Long Parliament (1640), he wrote further pamphlets attacking bishops (e.g. *The Antithapy of the English Lordly Prelacy*, 1641) and in favour of parliament (e.g *The Sovereign Power of Parliaments and Kingdoms*, 1643). He took an important role in the prosecution of Nathaniel Fiennes (1643) and Archbishop Laud (1645), subsequently writing pamphlets on Laud's trial – *Hidden Works of Darkness* (1644) and *Canterburies Doom* (1646). Wrote pamphlets against Independency, urging parliament to defeat the sectaries (e.g. *Independency Examined, Unmasked and Refuted*, 1644). Supported the Presbyterians in parliament in their dispute with the army (1647). Appointed Recorder of Bath (1647) and elected MP for Newport, Cornwall (1648). Vigorously opposed the army and supported a settlement with the king; was expelled and arrested in Pride's Purge (1648); strongly objected to the king's trial. On his release (1649), he fiercely attacked the new Commonwealth in *A Legal Vindication of the Liberties of England* (1649); was arrested and imprisoned without trial (1650–53). Resumed his seat on the recall of the Long Parliament (1660); elected MP for Bath in the Convention and Cavalier Parliaments (1660, 1661); campaigned against the regicides, attempting to restrict the Act of Indemnity. Reprimanded for his pamphlet against the Corporation Bill (1661); a manager in Mordaunt's impeachment (1667); opposed the banishment of Clarendon. Appointed Keeper of the Records in the Tower (1660–69). Wrote *Brevia Parliamentaria Rediviva* (1662).

Pym, John (1584–1643): Son of Alexander Pym of Somerset; educated at Oxford and the Middle Temple; married Anna Hooker. Appointed Receiver-General for Gloucestershire, Hampshire and Wiltshire (1607–38); elected MP for Tavistock (1620). Favoured strict implementation of laws against Catholics (1625); a manager of Buckingham's impeachment (1626); supported the Petition of Right and spoke vigorously against Buckingham (1628). Emerged as a leader of the popular party in the Short Parliament (1640), making a telling speech which summarised the nation's grievances. In the Long Parliament, he played a leading part in the impeachment and trial of Strafford (1641); moved the impeachment of Laud (1640); supported the Root and Branch Bill (1641), although opposed to the presbyterian church system; largely responsible for the Grand Remonstrance (1641); supported the Militia Bill (1641). He was offered the position of Chancellor of the Exchequer in an attempt by the king to secure his support (1642), but was one of the Five Members whom the king tried unsuccessfully to arrest (1642). Appointed a member of parliament's Committee of Safety (1642), he proposed that parliament should assume powers of taxation (1642) and that the excise tax should be imposed, after the breakdown of the Oxford Negotiations (1643). He became leader of the 'war party', criticising Essex's lack of energy in pursuing the war; urged an alliance with Scotland; was appointed Lieutenant-General of Ordnance (1643), but died shortly afterwards of an internal abscess.

Rainsborough, Thomas (1610–48): Son of William Rainsborough, naval captain; fought for parliament in the Civil War, first as a Vice-Admiral at sea (1643) and then as a colonel in the army, after he had joined the Hull garrison (with other members of his crew) to stiffen its resistance to siege (1643). Raised an infantry regiment in Manchester's army – helped to garrison Cambridge; captured Crowland Abbey after siege (1644). He was appointed colonel in the New Model Army, fighting at Naseby, Sherborne and Bristol; and capturing Berkeley Castle (1645); appointed Governor of Worcester (1646). Elected MP for Droitwich (1646), he emerged as a leading Republican, who advocated a more democratic suffrage and opposed any negotiated settlement with the king. Led the advance party in the army's march on London (1647), after its quarrel with parliament. In the army's Putney Debates on constitutional issues (1647), Rainsborough (who sympathised with the Levellers) clashed with Cromwell (whose views were conservative). After reconciliation, he was appointed Vice-Admiral, but his fleet mutinied after the outbreak of the Second Civil War (1648); he resumed his army career, capturing Colchester; but was murdered by royalists as he prepared to command the siege of Pontefract (1648).

Rochester, Earl of (1641–1711) – *see* Hyde, Laurence.

Rooke, Sir George (1650–1709): Born at Canterbury; son of Sir William Rooke. He served at sea from 1665; commanded his first ship in 1673, subsequently fighting in the battles of Bantry Bay (1689), Beachy Head (1690) and La Hogue (1692). Appointed Rear Admiral (1690), Vice-Admiral (1692), Admiral (1694), Commander of the Mediterranean

fleet (1695) and commander of a fleet sent to the Sound to support
Sweden (1700). He was knighted (1693); appointed a Lord
Commissioner of the Admiralty (1694); and elected MP (1698). In the
War of Spanish Succession, he commanded an unsuccessful expedition
to Cadiz (1702), but captured a Spanish treasure fleet in Vigo Bay
(1702); commanded a fleet which assisted the Archduke Charles in
abortive attacks on Toulon and Barcelona, before capturing Gibraltar
and driving away Toulouse's French fleet off Malaga (1704). Rivalry with
Marlborough, however, brought about his retirement in 1705.

Rupert, Prince (1619–82): Son of Elizabeth, Queen of Bohemia, and
Frederick V, Elector Palatine. Fled with his parents to Holland (1621);
campaigned in the Thirty Years War, including the siege of Breda (1637)
and the invasion of Westphalia (1638). On the outbreak of the Civil War,
he joined the king at Nottingham (1642) and was appointed General of
the Horse. In 1642, he fought at Edgehill, Reading and Brentford. In
1643, he took Cirencester, Birmingham, Lichfield and Bristol; besieged
Gloucester; and fought at Aldbourne Chase and Newbury. In 1644, he
was created Earl of Holderness and Duke of Cumberland; appointed
Captain-General and later Commander-in-Chief; relieved Newark, York
and Donnington Castle; but was defeated at Marston Moor. In 1645, he
relieved Chester and captured Leicester, but was defeated at Naseby;
became Governor of Bristol, but quickly surrendered it to Fairfax and
was temporarily banished by the king in consequence. At the end of the
Civil War, he fled to France (1646); sailed in the company of Prince
Charles with the rebellious ships from Warwick's fleet (1648);
commanded the royalist fleet sent to assist Ormond in Ireland; relieved
Kinsale and the Scilly Isles (1649); captured merchant ships in the
Mediterranean, but was pursued by Blake, who destroyed most of his
fleet in Cartagena (1652); returned to the court of Charles II in Paris
(1653); lived in Germany (1654–60). At the Restoration, he was
appointed Privy Councillor (1662); Admiral under the Duke of York at
the Battle of Solebay (1665); joint Commander of the Fleet with Monck
in battles against the Dutch (1666); Constable of Windsor Castle (1668);
Vice-Admiral (1672); Admiral of the Fleet in the Third Anglo-Dutch War
(1673); and First Lord of the Admiralty (1673–79).

Russell, Edward, Earl of Orford (1653–1727): Son of Edward Russell and
cousin to Sir William Russell; married his cousin Mary Russell (1691);
saw service at sea from 1671, commanding his first ship in 1672. He
supported William of Orange after the persecution of the Whigs in the
1680s; signed the letter of invitation to William (1688); and

accompanied his invasion from Holland. Elected MP for Launceston (1689), Portsmouth (1690) and Cambridgeshire (1695); became a member of the Whig Junto (1689–1709). He was appointed Treasurer of the Navy (1689) and Admiral in Torrington's fleet (1689); replaced the latter as commander after the defeat off Beachy Head (1690); won the battle of La Hogue against the French (1692), but was briefly dismissed for failing to follow up the victory; recalled as Admiral (1693), leading the first fleet ever to winter abroad in the Mediterranean (1694–95); appointed First Lord of the Admiralty (1694–99; 1709–10; 1714–17); created Earl of Orford (1697). He survived an attempt to impeach him for his involvement in the Partition Treaties (1701); was appointed a commissioner to negotiate the Union with Scotland (1706) and one of the Lords Justices to administer affairs until the arrival of George I (1714).

Russell, Lord William (1639–83): Son of Francis Russell, 5th Earl of Bedford; educated at Cambridge; married Rachel Wriothesley (1669); twice changed sides in the Civil War. Elected MP for Tavistock (1661–78) and Bedfordshire (1679–81); gradually became a leading member of Shaftesbury's Country Party in opposition to the corruption at court and its pro-French and pro-catholic tendencies; joined in vigorous attacks on the Cabal, Buckingham and Danby, whom he tried to impeach (1675). During the Popish Plot scare (from 1678), he proposed in the Commons the withdrawal of the Duke of York from the king's presence; helped to secure the dismissal of Danby and was appointed to the Privy Council with other opposition leaders (1679). He became a leading advocate of the unsuccessful Exclusion Bill (1680); resigned from the Privy Council (1680); and joined the 'Council of Six', after the dismissal of parliament (1681), to discuss other ways of achieving their aims, including support for the Duke of Monmouth as heir to the throne. When the Rye House Plot to assassinate the king and the Duke of York was uncovered (1683), the government seized the opportunity to implicate and arrest the Council of Six. Russell was executed for treason.

St John, Henry, 1st Viscount Bolingbroke (1678–1751): Son of Sir Henry St John; educated at Eton; MP for Wootton Bassett (1701) and Berkshire (1710); rose rapidly in the Tory hierarchy – appointed Secretary at War (1704–8); helped Harley to bring about Marlborough's dismissal (1710); played a major part in ending the War of Spanish Succession and drafting the Treaty of Utrecht (1713); created Viscount Bolingbroke (1712); appointed head of the Tory ministry (replacing Harley) shortly before Anne's death (1714), but dismissed by George I; fled to France to escape impeachment; appointed Secretary of State to the Old Pretender (1715), but dismissed (1716). Returned to England (1723) and became a focus for opposition to Walpole's government – especially through his contributions to *The Craftsman*. Returned to France (1736) to write; his publications included *The Idea of a Patriot King* (1749). Unscrupulous and largely unprincipled.

St John, Oliver (1598–1673): Son of Oliver St John, gentleman; educated at Cambridge and Lincoln's Inn; joined the Bar (1626). A Puritan he quickly identified with the opposition to the court; briefly imprisoned for seditious libel (1629); joined with other puritan leaders (John Pym, the Earl of Warwick and Lord Saye) in the management of the Providence Island Company; twice married into Cromwell's family. He gained national fame as defence counsel for John Hampden in the case over ship money (1637). Elected MP for Totnes (Short and Long Parliaments, 1640), he quickly emerged as leader of the opposition with Pym; was appointed Solicitor-General by Charles I in an attempt to silence him (1641) – but he remained prominent, calling for the attainder of Strafford and the passing of the Militia Bill. He was appointed Commissioner of the Great Seal by parliament (1643); increasingly loyal to Cromwell, he led the war party and the Independents (with Vane) in the Commons; supported the establishment of the New Model Army (1645) and its quarrel with parliament (1647). He was appointed Chief Justice of the Common Pleas (1648), after which he left the Commons and receded from politics; supported Pride's Purge (1648), but refused to serve in the court at the trial of the king (1649); opposed the Instrument of Government (1653), but urged Cromwell to accept the crown (1657). Tried to reconcile the factions and supported Monck before the Restoration (1659–60).

Salisbury, Earl of (1563–1612) – *see* Cecil, Robert.

Sancroft, William (1617–93): Born at Fresingfield, Suffolk; educated at Bury St Edmund's Grammar School and Cambridge – but ejected from his fellowship at Emmanuel College (1651) for failure to subscribe to the Commonwealth. After the Restoration, he was appointed Royal Chaplain (1661), Master of Emmanuel College (1662), Dean of St Paul's (1664) and Archbishop of Canterbury (1677); was heavily involved in the rebuilding of St Paul's Cathedral; tried in vain to convert the Duke of York to Anglicanism. After the accession of James II, he refused to stay on as a member of the Ecclesiastical Commission with Judge Jeffreys as its chairman (1686); led the Seven Bishops in their open opposition to the Declaration of Indulgence – was arrested, in consequence, for seditious libel, but was acquitted (1688); advised the king to call a free parliament. He did not become involved in the Glorious Revolution (1688), retiring instead to his palace at Lambeth and refusing, on principle, to swear an oath of allegiance to William and Mary, having already done so to James; was therefore suspended (1689), deprived (1690) and ejected from his palace (1691).

Sandwich, 1st Earl of (1625–72) – *see* Montagu, Edward.

Savile, George, 1st Marquess of Halifax (1633–95): Son of Sir William Savile of Yorkshire; educated at Shrewsbury School; married (1) Dorothy Spencer (1656) and (2) Gertrude Pierrepont (1672); elected MP for Pontefract (1660). Appointed captain in Prince Rupert's regiment of horse (1667); created Baron Savile and Viscount Halifax (1668); appointed Commissioner of Trade (1669) and Privy Councillor (1672). Opposed the Test Act (1673) and the policies of the Cabal; member of the new Council of Thirty (1679) and the Committee of Foreign Affairs; created Earl of Halifax (1679), Marquess of Halifax and Lord Privy Seal (1682). Opposed the Exclusion Bill in the Lords (1680), but was increasingly anxious about James's growing influence. Wrote *Character of a Trimmer* (1685, printed 1688) and *Character of King Charles II* (1685). Was appointed President of the Council by James II, but was dismissed after his opposition to the repeal of the Test and Habeas Corpus Acts (1686). Wrote *Letter to a Dissenter* (1686). Following the invasion of William of Orange, he was sent by James II to negotiate – but pledged his support to William instead (1688); elected Speaker of the Lords in the Convention Parliament and Lord Privy Seal (1689), but resigned his offices in the face of bitter criticism (1689–90). Continued to attend the House of Lords, opposing the renewal of press censorship (1692).

Scott, James, Duke of Monmouth (1649–85): Son of Charles II by Lucy Walter; during the exile of the royalist court, he adopted the name of James Crofts; married Lady Anne Scott (1663). Returned to England after the Restoration (1662); created Duke of Monmouth and Orkney (1663); officially recognised by the king as his son. He fought at sea against the Dutch (1665); appointed captain in the life guards (1668); commanded troops in the Third Anglo-Dutch War (1672); served under Prince William of Orange (1678); fought at Bothwell Bridge against the Covenanters (1679). Nominated by Shaftesbury and the protestant party as the next heir to the throne; banished to Holland by Charles II, who then proclaimed his illegitimacy (1679); returned without authority

(1680), making a triumphant tour throughout England; arrested at Stafford, but reconciled to the king; joined the Rye House Plot to mount a revolution (1683); again banished to Holland, from where he was expelled on the accession of James II. Landed at Lyme Regis with a small invasion force (1685); proclaimed his own legitimacy and right to the throne; marched through Somerset, but disappointed at the lack of popular support; routed by the king's forces under Faversham and Churchill at Sedgemoor (1685); captured near Ringwood and executed.

Shaftesbury, Earl of (1621–83) – *see* Cooper, Anthony Ashley.

Shovel, Sir Cloudesley (1650–1707): Born at Cockthorpe, Norfolk; son of John Shovel, gentleman; married Elizabeth Narbrough (1691); served an apprenticeship at sea under relatives from 1664, gaining a reputation for courage; appointed captain (1677); commanded the fleet assembled to resist William of Orange's invasion (1688), but accepted the Glorious Revolution when it came. Knighted (1689); appointed Rear-Admiral (1690), achieving distinction under Russell in the battle of La Hogue (1692); Vice-Admiral (1693) and Admiral (1696) with command of the Channel. Elected MP for Rochester (1698). In the War of Spanish Succession, he joined Rooke in the Mediterranean, taking part in the capture of Gibraltar and the Battle of Malaga (1704). Appointed Admiral of the Fleet (1705); commanded the fleet which escorted Peterborough's troops in the capture of Barcelona (1705); and the fleet involved in the unsuccessful attempt to seize Toulon (1707). Returning from the latter, his ship was wrecked on the rocks of the Scilly Isles; cast ashore, he was allegedly murdered by a native woman (1707).

Sidney or Sydney, Algernon (1622–83): Son of Robert Sidney, 2nd Earl of Leicester; fought in Ireland against the rebels (1641–43); and then for parliament in the Civil War, taking part at Marston Moor (1644) and commanding a cavalry regiment in the New Model Army (1645); appointed Governor of Colchester (1645). Elected MP for Cardiff (1646); appointed Governor of Dublin (1647) and Governor of Dover (1648–51). Refused to participate in the trial of Charles I (1649); appointed a member of the Council of State (1652), but opposed the Protectorate and withdrew from public life. Although he was reappointed to the Council of State (1659), he was, as a Republican, opposed to the Restoration and therefore went into exile on the continent (1660–77), where he was involved in various intrigues against Charles II. His return to England was viewed with deep suspicion by the authorities, as he became a central figure in Whig opposition to the government, allegedly supported by French subsidies. After the dissolution of parliament (1681), Whig leaders (including Sidney) turned to consider other methods of opposition, forming the Council of Six (1683). The government seized the opportunity to implicate them in the Rye House Plot (1683), an attempt by others to assassinate the king and the Duke of York. He was arrested, tried by Jeffreys for high treason and executed.

Skippon, Philip (d. 1660): Born at West Lexham, Norfolk; son of Luke Skippon; married (1) Maria Comes (1622) and (2) Katherine Phillips (after 1655); served his military apprenticeship on the continent, fighting in Germany and Holland (1622–39) and gaining the rank of captain. He fought for parliament in the Civil War; was appointed Major-General with responsibility for the security of London and training the city's trained bands (1642); fought with them at Turnham Green (1642) and the First Battle of Newbury (1643); campaigned with Essex in the South-West, surrendering his infantry at Lostwithiel (1644), but fighting again in the Second Battle of Newbury (1644). Appointed Major-General of Infantry in the New Model Army, he was made responsible for training; was badly injured at Naseby (1645). During the army's quarrel with parliament, he acted as one of its spokesmen (1647); in the Second Civil War, he again commanded the London militia (1648). He avoided any involvement as a judge in the trial of Charles I, but supported the Commonwealth; was appointed a regular member of the Council of State; elected MP for Lyme (1654, 1656); appointed Major-General for London and district (1655); appointed member of Cromwell's Upper House (1657); and reappointed Major-General of the London militia (1659).

Somerset, Earl of (1585?–1645) – *see* Carr, Robert.

Spencer, Robert, 2nd Earl of Sunderland (1641–1702): Son of Henry Spencer, 1st Earl of Sunderland; educated at Oxford; married Anne Digby (1665); succeeded to the title (1643). Appointed ambassador extraordinary to Louis XIV (1672) and at the Nijmegen peace negotiations (1678). Appointed Privy Councillor and Gentleman of the Bedchamber (1674); Secretary of State (North) and member of the inner cabinet with Essex, Halifax and Temple (1679); member of the triumvirate (with Godolphin and Hyde) known as 'The Chits', who directed affairs during Charles II's illness (1679). An opportunist, he responded to public opinion by supporting the Exclusion Bill, but was dismissed from the Council (1681). Reconciled with Charles II (1682);

readmitted to the Council and appointed Secretary of State (North) in 1683; signed the proclamation of James II (1685); agreed to support the repeal of the Test Act; appointed Lord President (1685); in favour of severe punishment for the Monmouth rebels (1685); appointed Knight of the Garter (1687); supported the dismissal of Rochester as Treasurer (1687); signed the committal of the Seven Bishops (1688); publicly renounced the protestant religion and took mass (1688). Dismissed on the approach of the Revolution; fled to Rotterdam (1688); excepted from the Act of Indemnity (1690). Returned to England, declaring himself to be a Protestant (1691); took the oath of loyalty to William and attended both court and parliament (1692); appointed Lord Chamberlain and member of the regency, but resigned in the face of public opinion (1697).

Strafford, Earl of (1593–1641) – *see* Wentworth, Thomas.

Strode, William (1599–1645): Son of Sir William Strode; born at Newnham, Devon; educated at the Inner Temple and Oxford. He was elected MP for Bere Alston (1624); a prominent opponent and vehement critic of Charles I, he was implicated in the holding down of the Speaker during the passing of the Three Resolutions (1629); imprisoned in consequence (1629–40). With the recall of parliament (1640), he became a leading and embittered member of the opposition, demanding annual parliaments, parliamentary control of the militia and the destruction of Strafford. He supported the Grand Remonstrance (1641); and was one of the Five Members whom Charles attempted to arrest in parliament (1642). During the Civil War, he fought at Edgehill (1642) and strongly supported the trial and execution of Laud.

Sunderland, 2nd Earl of (1640–1702) – *see* Spencer, Robert.

Swift, Jonathan (1667–1745): Born in Dublin; son of Jonathan Swift, barrister; educated at Kilkenny Grammar School and Trinity College, Dublin. Became clerk to and a member of the household of Sir William Temple (1689), who became his patron; ordained in Ireland (1694); appointed to the prebend of Kilroot, near Belfast (1685); returned into Temple's service (1696), preparing the latter's memoirs for publication; wrote a mock heroic, *The Battle of the Books* (published in 1704 along with *Tale of the Tub*). On the death of Temple, he secured the livings of three small parishes near Dublin (1699), but also developed contacts in England with politicians (like Halifax) and writers (like Steele and Addison). A Whig in politics by inclination, his hopes of preferment were frustrated until 1710, when the new Tory ministry under Harley and St John realised his potential as a political journalist. His articles in *The Examiner*, which he helped to edit (1710–11), and his pamphlets, *The Conduct of the Allies* (1711) and *The Public Spirit of the Whigs* (1714), did much to influence public opinion against the Whigs and in favour of Tory foreign policy. He was appointed Dean of St Patrick's Cathedral, Dublin (1713), to where he retired from politics after the death of Anne and the dismissal of the Tory ministry (1714). His later writings included *Journal to Stella* (1710–13), *Drapier's Letters* (1724) and *Gulliver's Travels* (1726).

Talbot, Richard, Earl of Tyrconnel (1630–91): Son of Sir William Talbot; fought at Drogheda (1649) against Cromwell's army; fled to Spain and lived as a mercenary in Europe until he became acquainted in Flanders with James, Duke of York (1653); went to England in 1655 to assist the proposed royalist rising, was captured but made good his escape; appointed commander of the Duke of York's regiment in exile. After the Restoration, he was appointed Gentleman of the Bedchamber to the Duke; but was twice imprisoned for insulting Ormond (1661, 1670) and again for alleged complicity in the Popish Plot (1678). On the accession of James II, he was created Earl of Tyrconnel and commander of the army in Ireland (1685); quickly made plans to disarm Protestants, dismantle the land settlement and promote Catholics to to positions within the army, judiciary, town corporations and government. He was appointed a member of the Privy Council (1686) and Lord Deputy (1687); recruited a new army (1688); worked closely with James during his visit to Ireland (1689–90); commanded operations in the defeat at the Battle of the Boyne (1690); was appointed by James Lord Lieutenant and Commander-in-Chief in Ireland (1691) shortly before his sudden death.

Tenison, Thomas (1636–1715): Born at Cottenham, Cambridgeshire; son of John Tenison, anglican minister; educated at Norwich Free School and Cambridge University, where he became Fellow of Corpus Christi College; ordained (1659); appointed university reader and vicar of St Andrew the Great, Cambridge (1665); following other clerical appointments, he was appointed rector of St Martin-in-the-Fields, London (1680), gaining a fine reputation for preaching and pastoral work. He also published *The Creed of Mr Hobbes Examined* (1670), *Baconia* (1678) and *Discovery of Idolatry* (1678). He ministered to the Duke of Monmouth on the scaffold (1685). Gained fame for his controversy with Andrew Pulton over the beliefs of the Jesuits (1687) and his attack on the system of indulgences (1687). He supported the Seven Bishops over their opposition to the Declaration of Indulgence (1688); and William of Orange in his plans for invasion (1688). Appointed Bishop of Lincoln (1691) and Archbishop of Canterbury (1694). Philanthropic by nature, he built the first public library in London (1695), endowed a school on the same site, distributed relief during periods of distress and supported the establishment of the Society for the Propagation of the Gospel in Foreign Parts (1701). He held liberal views in doctrine, favoured toleration and supported the Whigs in politics. Although he crowned Queen Anne (1702), he fell out of favour because of his religious views, his opposition to the Occasional Conformity Bill (1703) and his correspondence with the Electress Sophia concerning Hanoverian Succession. He regained favour with the accession of George I (1714) and was the first of the justices to be appointed.

Thurloe, John (1616–68): Son of Thomas Thurloe, rector of Abbot's Roding, Essex; married (1) Miss Peyton and (2) Anne Lytcott; studied law. Secretary to the parliamentary commissioners at the Treaty of Uxbridge (1645); appointed secretary to Strickland and St John on their mission to Holland (1651); Secretary to the Council of State (1652); clerk to the Committee for Foreign Affairs (1652); member of the Council of State (1653); Controller of Intelligence (1653); bencher at Lincoln's Inn (1654); Controller of the Post (1655). Elected MP for Ely (1654, 1656) and for Cambridge University (1659). His network of spies provided vital intelligence about the schemes of foreign states and domestic conspirators; responsible for expounding government policy to parliament, but seldom influenced Cromwell's decisions to any great degree; believed that Cromwell should accept the kingship (1657). Supported the accession of Richard Cromwell (1658), leading his group of sympathisers in the 1659 parliament, where he was attacked for his espionage system; advised Richard against dissolution. Reappointed Secretary of State by the restored Rump; opened negotiations with Hyde for a possible restoration, but was suspected by the royalists. Arrested at the Restoration and charged with high treason (1660), but released on condition that he should make available his advice to the new Secretaries of State; retired to Great Milton.

Tonge (or Tongue), Israel (1621–80): Son of Henry Tonge, minister; born near Doncaster; educated at Oxford, later being elected Fellow of University College (1648); married Jane Simpson (1649); appointed rector of Pluckley, Kent (1649), and Fellow of Durham College (1657); after various other positions, he was appointed rector of St Michael's,

Wood Street, London (1672); began writing pamphlets against the Catholics and Jesuits; was persuaded by Richard Greene of a catholic plot to assassinate the king (1675). Having joined Titus Oates in the latter's plans to uncover catholic intrigues (1676), he incorporated the views of both of them into a fictional narrative of the Popish Plot, drawn up in documentary form under 43 heads of indictment (1678). He then presented the evidence to Danby and the king, before arranging for Oates to give his evidence on oath before a magistrate, Sir Edmund Godfrey (1678); then, with Oates, he appeared before the Privy Council and the Commons (1679) to relate the story. Many Catholics were arrested in consequence and over 30 executed on flimsy evidence (*see also* Oates, Titus for a fuller account of the sequel). Tonge died at the height of the panic, having written a self-justification of his own involvement.

Tyrconnel, Earl of (1630–91) – *see* Talbot, Richard.

Vane, Sir Henry (1613–62): Son of Sir Henry Vane, Comptroller of the King's Household; educated at Westminster School and Oxford; married Frances Wray (1640). Appointed joint Treasurer of the Navy (1639); granted a knighthood (1640); elected MP for Hull in the Long Parliament (1640), joining the popular party; gave evidence at the trial of Strafford (1641). A prominent member of the 'war party', he was sent as a commissioner to negotiate the Scottish alliance (1643), inserting the vital phrase 'according to the word of God' into the Solemn League and Covenant. Led parliament, with St John, after the death of Pym (1643); proposed the establishment of the Committee of Both Kingdoms to organise the war (1644); seconded Tate's motion for the Self-Denying Ordinance (1644) and supported army reorganisation. Sympathised with the army in its quarrel with parliament (1647), but opposed the vote of no further addresses to the king (1648); voted for non-alteration of government by King, Lords and Commons (1648). Absent from the Commons immediately after Pride's Purge; opposed the trial and execution of the king. Elected to the Council of State, but unwilling to take the oath (1649); supported the Commonwealth as a close friend of Cromwell; appointed Treasurer of the Navy (1650), but disagreed with Cromwell over the dissolution of the Long Parliament (1653); retired to Lincolnshire; wrote *A Healing Question Propounded and Resolved* (1656), for which he was imprisoned. MP for Whitchurch in Richard Cromwell's parliament (1659); opposed the government and supported Lambert's forcible dissolution of the Rump. Arrested after the Restoration (1660); wholly excepted from pardon; tried and executed (1662).

Villiers, George, 1st Duke of Buckingham (1592–1628): Son of Sir George Villiers of Leicestershire; educated at Billesdon School; married Lady Catherine Manners (1620). Appointed Cupbearer to the king (1614), Gentleman of the Bedchamber and knight (1615), Lord High Admiral (1617); created Viscount Villiers (1616), Earl of Buckingham (1617), Marquess of Buckingham (1618) and Duke of Buckingham (1623). He became influential at the court and favourite of the king after the fall of Somerset (1615) and the removal of the Howards. Supported James I's plan for a marriage alliance between Prince Charles and the Spanish Infanta; accompanied Charles on an unsuccessful visit to Spain (1623). Advocated a war against Spain to recover the Palatinate for the king's son-in-law. Supported the marriage of Charles to Henrietta Maria, daughter of Louis XIII of France, but infuriated parliament by a promise of concessions to English Catholics (1624). Criticised by parliament for the failure of Mansfeld's expedition to the Palatinate (1625); organised alliances with Denmark and the United Provinces (1625); planned the abortive expedition to Cadiz (1625); personally led the disastrous expedition to the Isle of Ré (1627). Saved from dismissal by the dissolution of parliament (1626), after it had criticised and impeached him for mismanagement of the war. Singled out as 'the cause of all our miseries' by Eliot and Coke in the 1628 parliament, which passed a remonstrance demanding his dismissal; saved again by its dissolution. Assassinated by John Felton, a disgruntled ex-army officer, at Portsmouth (1628).

Villiers, George, 2nd Duke of Buckingham (1628–87): Born in Westminster; son of the 1st Duke; educated at court with Princes Charles and James, and at Cambridge University; fought briefly under Rupert in the Civil War, before going into exile on the continent; returned to England (1647); fought in the Second Civil War (1648), but escaped to Holland after defeat, entering the court of Charles II; accompanied Charles to Scotland (1650) and fought at Worcester (1651); fled with Charles abroad, but became unpopular at court after quarrels with Hyde and therefore returned to England (1657); having married Mary Fairfax, daughter of Sir Thomas (regaining his sequestered estates through that means, 1657), he was imprisoned until 1660. After the Restoration, he was appointed a member of the Privy Council (1662); helped to bring about the fall of Hyde (Lord Clarendon) in 1667; became notorious for his outrageous behaviour. He was a member of the Cabal (1667); supported the Declaration of Indulgence (1672); was sent on missions to Louis XIV (who gave him a generous pension) to help secure the Treaty of Dover (1670) and William of Orange (1673) to attempt peace negotiations. He gradually lost his influence to Arlington and, after the Commons had blamed Buckingham for the king's recent policies, he was dismissed from all offices at their insistence (1674). Eventually, he joined Shaftesbury's opposition country party, supporting the case of the dissenters and attacking Catholics during the Popish Plot scare; was briefly imprisoned (1677); finally broke with Shaftesbury, failed to support the Exclusion Bill (1680) and withdrew from public life. He wrote a popular play, *The Rehearsal* (1671).

Waller, Sir William (1597–1668): Son of Sir Thomas Waller, Lieutenant of Dover; educated at Oxford University and Gray's Inn; married (1) Jane Reynell (1622), (2) Lady Anne Finds (1634) and (3) Lady Anna Harcourt (1652). He served his military apprenticeship on the continent fighting for the Venetian republic and the King of Bohemia; knighted (1622); elected MP for Andover (1640). He actively supported parliament in the Civil War, fighting at Edgehill and capturing Portsmouth, Farnham Castle, Winchester and Chichester (1642). In 1643, he was appointed Major-General of parliament's western army; gained control of the Severn Valley by capturing Malmesbury, Monmouth, Chepstow, Tewkesbury and Hereford, but suffering defeat by Maurice at Ripple Field; successfully halted the advance of Hopton's Cornish army at Lansdown, before losing the decisive Battle of Roundway Down – and, with it, the control of the West. In 1644, as commander of a new southern army, he defeated Hopton' s forces at Cheriton, lost to the king at Cropredy Bridge and fought in the indecisive Second Battle of Newbury. He resigned his commission under the terms of the Self-Denying Ordinance (1645); became a leader of the presbyterian party and a critic of the Independents inside parliament and the army outside; was briefly forced into exile through their bitter enmity (1647), but returned to support the proposed Treaty of Newport with the king (1648); was arrested by the army in Pride's Purge (1648) and imprisoned for three years. He was again arrested on suspicion of intrigues with the royalists (1658), but released. Readmitted to the restored Rump, he was appointed to the Council of State and supported the Restoration; was elected as MP for Westminster in the Convention Parliament (1660), but retired shortly afterwards.

Wentworth, Thomas, 1st Earl of Strafford (1593–1641): Son of Sir William Wentworth; educated at Cambridge and the Inner Temple; married (1) Margaret Clifford (1611) and (2) Arabella Holles (1625); knighted (1611); elected MP for Yorkshire (from 1615). Initially supported the 'popular party' in parliament; defended parliament's privileges as their 'ancient and undoubted right' (1621); imprisoned for non-payment of the forced loan (1627); vigorously defended the liberties of the subject (1628); attempted to bring about a settlement between king and Commons; opposed the growth of Puritanism and parliament's attempts to control executive power. Switched to support the king – created Baron Wentworth and Viscount Wentworth (1628); appointed President of the Council of the North (1628); Privy Councillor (1629); Lord Deputy of Ireland (1632), where he introduced a programme of reforms through his policy of 'Thorough' – unpopular with English colonists for his strict regime and with native Irish for his plans to commence the plantation of Connaught. Recalled to England (1639) as head of a commission to deal with the Scottish problem; became chief adviser to the king. Created Earl of Strafford, Lord Lieutenant of Ireland and Lieutenant-General of the army (1640). Advocated the summoning of the Short Parliament (1640) to provide supplies for the Scottish war. Intended to gain the impeachment of the popular party for their treasonable correspondence with the Scots, but was himself impeached by Pym following the assembly of the Long Parliament (1640). Tried in Westminster Hall, but convicted by a Bill of Attainder; Charles gave his assent, fearing a popular rising; executed (1641).

Wharton, Thomas, 1st Marquis of Wharton (1648–1715): Son of 4th Baron Wharton; married (1) Anne Lee (1673) and (2) Lucy Loftus (1692); elected MP for Wendover (1673) and Buckinghamshire (1679); gained a reputation as a rake, a lover of race horses and a formidable duellist. A strongly principled Whig in politics, he firmly supported the Exclusion Bill (1679), but was not implicated in the Rye House Plot (1683); an opponent of James II, he corresponded with William of Orange, joining his invasion force at Exeter and composing the Revolution song, *Liliburlero* (1688). He helped to draft the Bill of Rights (1689); was appointed member of the Privy Council and Comptroller of the Household (1689–1702); succeeded to the barony (1696); was appointed warden of the southern royal forests (1697) and Lord Lieutenant of Buckinghamshire (1702). He developed a reputation as a party organiser, arranging meetings of the Whig Junto, controlling voting in the Commons and managing propaganda at elections. He was dismissed by Anne (1702); opposed the Occasional Conformity Bill (1702–4); supported Matthew Ashby from Aylesbury in his case to secure the franchise (*Ashby* v. *White*, 1703). He worked closely with the Whig Junto after their election success (1705); was appointed commissioner to negotiate the Act of Union (1706); was created earl (1706) and appointed Lord Lieutenant of Ireland (1708). He organised fierce opposition to the Tory government after 1710, opposing the Schism Bill (1714) and the Treaty of Utrecht (1714). He was created marquess by George I (1715).

Wildman, Sir John (1621–93): Educated at Cambridge; fought for parliament under Fairfax in the Civil War. A member of the Levellers, he represented (as a civilian) ordinary disgruntled soldiers in discussions with the officers' Council of the Army in the Putney Debates (1647); helped to pen *The Agreement of the People* (1647) and *The Case of the Army Truly Stated* (1647), an outline of Leveller views, including the abolition of the monarchy and the Lords and a more democratic franchise based on the power of the Commons. He was arrested with Lilburne and imprisoned for seven months (1648); eventually withdrew from the controversy (1649) and made a fortune from property speculation (1650–55). Elected MP for Scarborough (1654), he was refused entry to parliament by Cromwell; spent the following years intriguing with royalists, Levellers and Republicans to bring down the government; his planned republican insurrection in 1655 (for which he was imprisoned) failed, as did an assassination plot against Cromwell (1657). After the fall of Richard Cromwell (1659), he was requested by Fleetwood and the army to draw up a new constitution. After the Restoration, he controlled the post office, but was arrested for interference with the mail as part of a republican plot to bring down the monarchy (1661). Imprisoned for six years in the Scillies (1661–67), he was appointed trustee and solicitor to his friend, Buckingham (1667–79). Elected MP for Great Bedwin (1681), he supported Shaftesbury's Whigs in their attempt at Exclusion; was arrested (but released) on suspicion of complicity in the Rye House Plot (1683); supported Monmouth initially, but took no part in the rising and fled to Holland to avoid arrest (1685); actively supported William of Orange's invasion (1688); was elected MP for Wootton Bassett (1689) and appointed Post-Master General (1689–91); knighted (1692).

William III (1650–1702): Born at The Hague; son of William II and Mary (daughter of Charles I). He was appointed Captain-General, Admiral-General and Stadholder in Holland (1672); married Mary, daughter of James, Duke of York (1677); fought a defensive war against France and her allies (1672–78). His relationship with James II worsened after William had given sanctuary to the Huguenots after the Revocation of the Edict of Nantes (1685). He accepted an invitation to invade England, which prompted the flight of James II abroad (1688). The Convention Parliament offered the throne to William and Mary jointly, who accepted it along with the Declaration of Right concerning parliament's privileges and the succession. William declared war on France (1689); and took an army to Ireland, where he defeated French and Irish catholic forces at the Battle of the Boyne (1689). Supported by a Whig majority in parliament, he led the allied armies on the continent against the French, securing a favourable treaty at Ryswick (1697). He signed two partition treaties with France and the United Provinces concerning the future of the Spanish Empire (1698, 1700). Mary died in 1694 and the Duke of Gloucester (son of Anne and heir to the throne) in 1700; the Act of Settlement (1701) named the Electress Sophia of Hanover as the new heir. He clashed seriously with parliament over standing armies (1697–98), the Darien Scheme, Irish land settlements and foreign officials (1699). He formed the Grand Alliance (1701) to resist French designs on the Spanish Empire after the death of Charles II of Spain (1700); but died, following a riding accident, shortly afterwards.

Winstanley, Gerrard (1609?–60?): Born in Wigan; brought up under the influence of anabaptist teaching; became a London cloth merchant but, after the Civil War had undermined his business, he lived with friends in the country. He commenced writing a series of pamphlets in 1648 on theology, in which he discounted the doctrines of restricted salvation, resurrection and eternal damnation, and advocated his theory of the revelation of the truth by an inner light. His views on communism were first outlined in *The New Law of Righteousness* (1649) – views which were put into practice through the short-lived Digger movement, of which he became leader (1649–50); their action of digging up and cultivating common land at St George's Hill and Cobham in Surrey was meant not as a violent attack on private property, but as the start of a peaceful revolution in self-sufficiency; their efforts were quickly destroyed by local landlords and soldiers. He continued writing pamphlets, which detailed the principles of the Diggers; in *The Law of Freedom in a Platform* (1652), he described his ideal of a communist, classless society based on co-operation and without private property or money.

SECTION SIX

Bibliography

Abbreviations

AgHR	*Agricultural History Review*
AHR	*American Historical Review*
Alb.	*Albion*
BIHR	*Bulletin of the Institute of Historical Research*
CH	*Cheshire History*
CHR	*Catholic Historical Review*
EcHR	*Economic History Review*
EHR	*English Historical Review*
HAP	*Historical Association Pamphlets*
Hist.	*History*
HJ	*Historical Journal*
HT	*History Today*
IHS	*Irish Historical Studies*
JBS	*Journal of British Studies*
JEccH	*Journal of Ecclesiastical History*
JMH	*Journal of Modern History*
MH	*Midland History*
MM	*Mariner's Mirror*
NH	*Northern History*
PBA	*Proceedings of the British Academy*
PH	*Parliamentary History*
PP	*Past and Present*
RSCHS	*Records of the Scottish Church History Society*
SH	*Southern History*
SHR	*Scottish Historical Review*
TBGAS	*Transactions of the Bristol and Gloucestershire Archaeological Society*
TRHS	*Transactions of the Royal Historical Society*
WHR	*Welsh History Review*
WS	*War and Society*

The aim in this bibliographical essay is to highlight, from the mass of material available, those works which will be of greatest value to any undergraduate, sixth form student or teacher engaged in a study of this period. An attempt has been made to clarify the content of each work, where this is not self-apparent, thereby assisting students in identifying what is relevant to their needs and not leaving too much to the imagination.

The writings of some of the earlier historians have been superseded, at least in part, by the vast amount of recent research, particularly on the first half of the century. While definitive works of an earlier vintage have not been ignored, there is nevertheless an emphasis on the publications of the last twenty or so years and the main areas of debate which have emerged. The place of publication is London unless otherwise stated.

1. General books on the period

There are three **bibliographies** which are invaluable to the serious student. Godfrey Davies and Mary F. Keeler, eds, *Bibliography of British History: Stuart Period, 1603–1714* (Oxford, 1970) is a comprehensive description of publications up to 1969 with helpful pointers to the location of primary sources. J.S. Morrill, *Seventeenth Century Britain, 1603–1714* (Folkestone, 1980) supplements this by surveying, with perceptive comments, the latest research up to 1980 and listing relevant articles in learned journals. G.R. Elton, *Modern Historians on British History, 1485–1945: A Critical Bibliography, 1945–1969* (1970) is less exhaustive in range, but contains a concise bibliographical essay as a guide to vital reading on the seventeenth century. For the latter half of the period, C.L. Grose, *A Select Bibliography of British History, 1660–1960* (Chicago, 1967) and W.L. Sachse, *Restoration England, 1660–1689* (Cambridge, 1971) are also worthwhile.

Good, **general surveys of the century** are somewhat thin on the ground. The twin volumes in the old Oxford History of England series, Godfrey Davies, *The Early Stuarts, 1603–1660* (Oxford, 1937,1959) and G.N. Clark, *The Later Stuarts, 1660–1715* (Oxford, 1934, 1955) have, to a great extent, been superseded in the light of recent research, although the latter is still worth reading as a clear, well-written account. They have largely been replaced by two books in the new History of England series: Derek Hirst, *Authority and Conflict: England, 1603–1658* (Cambridge, Mass., 1978), a sound textbook which covers intellectual, economic, social and political aspects; and J.R. Jones, *Country and Court: England, 1658–1714* (Cambridge, Mass., 1978), which is particularly lucid and perceptive on the post-1688 period and contains several chapters giving a useful analysis of the nature and working of government. The first half of the century is also well covered in Robert Ashton, *Reformation and Revolution, 1558–1660* (1984), a lively if somewhat uneven book with good coverage of royal finance, foreign policy and colonial affairs; and Alan G.R. Smith, *The Emergence of a Nation State: The Commonwealth of England, 1529–1660*, 2nd edn (1997), which provides a valuable introduction to the period with a concise survey of all the major issues.

Fortunately, there are a number of fairly recent one-volume surveys of the century at large, which take into account recent debate. Barry Coward, *The Stuart Age: A History of England, 1603–1714*, 2nd edn (1994) gives a thorough and readable account of the period while, at the same time, offering an excellent source of reference material. J.P. Kenyon, *Stuart England*, 2nd edn (1985), a revised, corrected and improved version of his 1978 volume, remains a lively and thought-provoking description of political events. Blair Worden, ed., *Stuart England* (Oxford, 1986), lavishly illustrated, provides a concise, lucid narrative with scholarly analysis by a team of eminent historians. Of earlier studies, G.E. Aylmer, *The Struggle for the Constitution, 1603–1689*, 2nd edn (1968) gives a sound, basic introduction to the period with emphasis on social, economic and religious factors; Christopher Hill, *The Century of Revolution, 1603–1714* (1961) combines a brief narrative of events with a brilliantly argued analysis of social and economic problems, though his portrayal of the Civil War as a class struggle has been hotly disputed; D.L. Farmer, *Britain and the Stuarts, 1603–1714* (1965) is a basic textbook, giving a clear chronological survey of the century; and Roger Lockyer, *Tudor and Stuart England* (1964) remains one of the best introductory over-views for first-time readers wishing to get the century into perspective.

One feature of recent years has been the proliferation of **essay collections**. Four of the most important of these are H.R. Trevor-Roper, *Religion, the Reformation and Social Change* (1967), a series of outstanding pieces based around the problem of the crisis in government, society and ideas, including 'The general crisis of the seventeenth century', 'The philosophers of the puritan revolution', 'The fast sermons of the Long Parliament', 'Oliver Cromwell and his parliaments' and 'Scotland and the puritan revolution'; Christopher Hill, *A Nation of Change and Novelty: Radical Politics, Religion and Literature in Seventeenth-Century England* (1990), which includes new essays on 'Government and public relations' and 'The place of the seventeenth- century revolution in English history', as well as previously published ones on Archbishop Laud, the Ranters and the Restoration and literature; Timothy Eustace, ed., *Statesmen and Politicians of the Stuart Age* (1985), a series of 10 short, well-written biographies (Cranfield, Strafford, Buckingham, Vane, Clarendon, Pym,

Sunderland, Danby, Laud and Shaftesbury) which, although sometimes lacking in historical context, provide a synthesis of modern research and interpretation; and K.H.D. Haley, ed., *The Stuarts* (1973), a valuable collection of Historical Association pamphlets by eminent historians, including C.V. Wedgwood ('Charles I: the case for execution'), Christopher Hill ('Oliver Cromwell'), Alan Everitt ('The local community and the Great Rebellion'), Austin Woolrich ('Penruddock's Rising'), K.D.H. Haley ('Charles II'), Charles Wilson ('Mercantilism') and Ralph Davis ('A commercial revolution'). It is of course important to read these latter essays in conjunction with more recent books reflecting the latest research.

There are several useful **reference books** which cover a variety of fields. Chris Cook and John Wroughton, *English Historical Facts, 1603–1688* (1980) and Chris Cook and John Stevenson, *British Historical Facts, 1688–1760* (1988) contain a mine of key facts and statistical information on every aspect of life within the period, together with selected biographies. Edwin Riddell, ed., *Lives of the Stuart Age, 1603–1714* (1976) and C.P. Hill, *Who's Who in Stuart Britain*, 2nd edn (1988) provide a series of short biographies of leading figures based on modern research. Biographical studies of members of parliament at two key points in the century are given in M.F. Keeler, *The Long Parliament, 1640–41* (New York, 1954); Donald Brunton and D.H. Pennington, *Members of the Long Parliament* (Cambridge, 1954); and Basil Duke Henning, ed., *The History of Parliament: The House of Commons, 1660–1690*, 3 vols (1983).

2. Biographies

Early Stuart England, 1603–1640

Really good biographies for this century are still in short supply. This is particularly true of the reigns of the first two Stuart kings. **James I** lacks a full-scale biography which overcomes traditional prejudice and takes account of the revisionism of recent years. D.H. Willson, *James VI and I* (1956, 1961), though in need of update, gives a solid account of the reign, whereas S.J. Houston, *James I*, 2nd edn (1995), in the Seminar Studies series, provides a much more stimulating, discerning and concise introduction. However, Christopher Durston, James I (1993), in the Lancaster Pamphlets series, points the way to future development by offering a balanced reassessment of the king's real achievements and his relations with parliament based on the latest evidence. Maurice Lee, Jnr, *Great Britain's Solomon: James VI and I in his Three Kingdoms* (Urbana, Ill.,

1990) presents a series of thought-provoking essays, including a defence of James against the charge that he was a contributory factor in the later outbreak of civil war. One article, too, is well worth reading: Jenny Wormald, 'James VI and I: two kings or one?', *Hist.* 68 (1983) explores the differences in attitude shown over the years to James as King of Scotland and as King of England.

Although the definitive biography of **Charles I** is still awaited, the two most recent studies are to be recommended. Pauline Gregg, *Charles I* (1981), while based mainly on existing material, gives, nevertheless, some penetrating insights, while Charles Carlton, *Charles I: The Personal Monarch* (1984) is a scholarly and readable book which presents a convincing picture of this elusive personality. Roy Strong, *Charles I on Horseback* (1970) is hardly a biography, but offers a fascinating assessment based on portraits of the king. Brian Quintrell, *Charles I, 1625–1640* (1993), in the Seminar Studies series, examines his problems and policies in the light of recent reassessments of the more traditional views of the reign. Essays and articles worth reading in this context include G.E. Aylmer, *The Personal Rule of Charles I, 1629–1640 (HAP* New Appraisals in History 14, 1989); M.J. Havran, 'The character and principles of an English king: the case of Charles I', *CHR* 69 (1983); and Judith Richards, 'His nowe majestie and the English monarchy: the kingship of Charles I before 1640', *PP* 113 (1986).

A number of sound biographies of **ministers and courtiers of the pre-Civil War period** have appeared in recent years. Roger Lockyer, *Buckingham: The Life and Political Career of George Villiers, First Duke of Buckingham, 1592–1628* (1981) is an impressively researched book which gives a reassessment of Buckingham's statesmanship, particularly in foreign policy. Alongside this, it is worth reading G.E. Aylmer, 'Buckingham as an administrative reformer?', *EHR* 105 (1990). Archbishop William Laud is well served by H.R. Trevor-Roper, *Archbishop Laud,* 2nd edn (1962), a brilliant biography; Charles Carlton, *Archbishop William Laud* (1987), which, though lacking to some extent in detailed discussion of major issues, provides a useful summary of his career and a sensitive appreciation of both its personal and political aspects; and Kevin Sharpe, 'Archbishop Laud', *HT* (August, 1983). Menna Prestwich, *Cranfield: Politics and Profit under the Early Stuarts* (1966) is a substantial work which gives a convincing portrait of the minister and the government organisation in which he operated. C.V. Wedgwood, *Thomas Wentworth, First Earl of Strafford* (1961) is a lucid and valuable assessment of this key figure.

Other commendable biographies of **important personalities** during this period include M.J. Havran, *Caroline Courtier: The Life of Lord*

Cottingham (1973); J. Epstein, *Francis Bacon: A Political Biography* (1977) and Daniel Coquillette, *Francis Bacon* (Edinburgh, 1992); P.E. Kopperman, *Sir Robert Heath, 1575–1649* (1989); M. Van Cleave Alexander, *Charles I's Lord Treasurer: Sir Richard Weston, Earl of Portland* (1975); and Gervase Huxley, *Endymion Porter: The Life of a Courtier, 1587–1649* (1959). Although a convincing biography of Sir Edward Coke is still awaited, S.D. White, *Sir Edward Coke and the 'Grievances of the Commonwealth', 1621–1628* (1979) offers a first-rate assessment of the man's attitudes, beliefs and political career. Sir John Eliot and the Earl of Salisbury have also suffered from the lack of modern full-length biographies. However, Alan Haynes, *Robert Cecil, 1st Earl of Salisbury: Servant of Two Sovereigns* (1989) gives a brief, but helpful introduction to the latter, based mainly on secondary sources. A similar service is provided for another neglected character in Rosalind K. Marshall, *Henrietta Maria: The Intrepid Queen* (1990), which is concise, readable and lavishly illustrated.

The Revolution, 1640–1660

Out of the many biographies of **Oliver Cromwell** which have been published over the years, two have not only stood the test of time, but have remained at the top of the list. C.H. Firth, *Oliver Cromwell and the Rule of the Puritans in England* (Oxford, 1900) is based on Firth's close familiarity with vital source material and is probably the best short introduction. John Buchan, *Oliver Cromwell* (1934), beautifully written with imaginative insights into human nature and the issues of the time, is the best detailed study. C.V. Wedgwood, *Oliver Cromwell*, 2nd edn (1973) offers a short, readable and shrewd assessment, providing a useful guide for any new student. Christopher Hill, *God's Englishman: Oliver Cromwell and the English Revolution* (1970) is not a detailed biography in the usual sense, but a stimulating survey which views the Revolution through Cromwell's personality, giving emphasis to religious ideas. Later publications include Pauline Gregg, *Oliver Cromwell* (1988), which presents a sound, balanced portrait based mainly on printed sources; Peter Gaunt, *Oliver Cromwell* (Oxford, 1996), a re-examination of his life and career, which provides a convincing and lively assessment; and two books which offer an excellent synthesis of the most recent research by British and European historians – Bernard Cottret, *Cromwell* (Paris, 1993) and Barry Coward, *Cromwell* (1991), a political biography and a most useful starting point for students of the period. To supplement these biographies, there are four valuable collections which should not be ignored: Maurice Ashley, ed., *Great Lives Observed: Oliver Cromwell* (Englewood Cliffs, NJ 1969) examines Cromwell's character and achievement through a selection of his letters and speeches, the writings of contemporaries and the views of later historians; Ivan Roots, ed., *Cromwell: A Profile* (1973) brings together important articles by eminent historians on various aspects of his work, including H.R. Trevor-Roper, 'Cromwell and his parliaments'; John Morrill, ed., *Oliver Cromwell and the English Revolution* (1990) presents 10 essays by leading authorities on specific areas of his career, including his dealings with members of the Long Parliament and his treatment of Scotland and Ireland; R.C. Richardson, ed., *Images of Oliver Cromwell* (Manchester, 1993) consists of papers by Roger Howell and others on the changing interpretations over the centuries of Cromwell's life and work.

There are several important biographies of those **contemporaries of Cromwell** who played a vital part in the Revolution. William M. Lamont, *Marginal Prynne, 1600–1669* (1963) is a most readable and convincing portrait, which does not entirely replace E.W. Kirby, *William Prynne: A Study in Puritanism* (Cambridge, Mass., 1931), a scholarly account based mainly on Prynne's own pamphlets. John Adair, *A Life of John Hampden the Patriot, 1594–1643* (1976) is the only modern full-length study of this influential character in the early stages of the Revolution. We still lack a substantial modern biography of John Pym, although J.H. Hexter, *The Reign of King Pym* (1941) deals with his skilful political contribution during the crucial years 1641–43, and Conrad Russell, 'The parliamentary career of John Pym, 1621–9', in Peter Clark, A.G.R. Smith and Nicholas Tyacke, eds, *The English Commonwealth, 1547–1640* (1979) gives some valuable insights into his personality, ideas and methods. Fortunately, the first real study of Pym's colleague Oliver St John has now been published. William Palmer, *The Political Career of Oliver St John* (Newark, Del., 1993) describes his key role, following the death of Pym, in the revolutionary events of the 1640s and his subsequent loss of control after 1645. Two leading figures in the Leveller movement are well covered in Pauline Gregg, *Free-born John: A Biography of John Lilburne* (1961) and Maurice Ashley, *John Wildman, Plotter and Postmaster* (1947). The best study so far of the work of John Thurloe in national security is contained in Philip Aubrey, *Mr Secretary Thurloe: Cromwell's Secretary of State, 1652–1660* (1990), which also emphasises his contribution to policy. Other useful biographies of this period include Violet Rowe, *Sir Henry Vane the Younger* (1970); Nancy Matthews, *William Sheppard: Cromwell's Law Reformer* (Cambridge, 1984); Ruth Spalding, *The Improbable Puritan: A Life of Bulstrode Whitelocke, 1605–75* (1975); R.W. Ramsey, *Richard Cromwell: Protector of England* (1935); and Christopher Hill, *Milton and the English Revolution* (1977).

Biographies are also available for a number of **military leaders** who played a prominent part in the Civil War or Restoration. Vernon Snow, *Essex the Rebel* (1971) deals with the earl's political as well as military career; John Wilson, *Fairfax* (1985) is a well-documented, concise and readable account; F.T.R. Edgar, *Sir Ralph Hopton: The King's Man in the West, 1642–52* (Oxford, 1968) and John Adair, *Roundhead General: A Military Biography of Sir William Waller* (1976) are good, straightforward accounts of military commanders at work; John Stucley, *Sir Bevill Grenvile and His Times* (Chichester, 1983) succeeds in putting this royalist leader into the background of his West Country life; Frank Kitson, *Prince Rupert: Portrait of a Soldier* (1994), although based entirely on printed sources and lacking in an appreciation of the Prince's involvement in court politics, is valuable not only in providing a most lucid narrative of Rupert's major battles, but also in highlighting the opportunities lost by the royalists in the conflict; Patrick Morrah, *Prince Rupert of the Rhine* (1976), on the other hand, is an impressive, scholarly and better balanced study which is far more than a military biography; R.W. Ramsey, *Henry Ireton* (1949) is also based on sound scholarship, but fails to be entirely convincing in its portrayal; Maurice Ashley, *General Monck* (1977) is a clear and readable account of his career, but lacks penetrating analysis of his motivation and ideas; W.H. Dawson, *Cromwell's Understudy: The Life and Times of General John Lambert and the Rise and Fall of the Protectorate*, 2nd edn (1942) is a scholarly and persuasive book; and Maurice Ashley, *Cromwell's Generals* (1954) contains a series of brief biographies of Cromwell's leading commanders and major-generals between 1650 and 1660, set in a well-written narrative of the period.

Three **other key figures** must be mentioned. Edward Hyde, Earl of Clarendon, is well served, at least in part, in B.H.G. Wormald, *Clarendon: Politics, History and Religion, 1640–1660* (Cambridge, 1951), a brilliant account of his statesmanship during those years. Later works include R.W. Harris, *Clarendon and the English Revolution* (1983), which, although somewhat lacking in originality and placing too great an emphasis on narrative, provides a useful introduction for first-time students; and Richard Ollard, *Clarendon and His Friends* (1987), which concentrates on Clarendon the writer and moralist, but also includes a vivid account of his social and domestic life. For a study of the Puritan Richard Baxter, Geoffrey F. Nuttall, *Richard Baxter* (Edinburgh, 1965) gives an impressive account of his life and work, whereas William M. Lamont, *Richard Baxter and the Millennium* (1979), a somewhat difficult and unorthodox biography, offers a stimulating reappraisal of Baxter's personality and life – but not for beginners! The Quaker George Fox has at last been served by a modern biographer. H. Larry Ingle, *First Among Friends: George Fox and the Creation of Quakerism* (Oxford, 1994) makes maximum use of primary material in a scholarly portrayal, placing Fox in the setting of the Civil War, the Revolution and the Restoration.

The later Stuarts, 1660–1714

After countless complaints by generations of historians about the lack of a truly convincing biography of **Charles II**, no fewer than three appeared within the space of four years. Ronald Hutton, *Charles II* (Oxford, 1989) is a comprehensive, stimulating and definitive work, which covers his entire life and involvement in all three kingdoms; John Miller, *Charles II* (1991) in some ways complements the latter by concentrating on the politics of court and foreign policy during the years 1670–85, emphasising that there was no master-plan in the mind of this weak, vacillating king; J.R. Jones, *Charles II: Royal Politician* (1987) is again a study of Charles's role in politics and policy-making, although the author perhaps assumes too much prior knowledge on the part of the reader. Alongside these biographies, it is worth reading two articles: Joyce Lee Malcolm, 'Charles II and the reconstruction of royal power', *HJ* 35 (1992); and John Miller, 'Charles II and his parliaments', *TRHS* 5th series 32 (1982). On **James II**, John Miller, *James II: A Study in Kingship* (1978, 1991) is worthwhile, not only for its assessment of the king, but also for its insights into political activity during the period; Maurice Ashley, *James II* (1978) is scholarly, straightforward and concise.

There is no shortage of sound, readable **biographies of leading political figures** for these two reigns. Andrew Browning, *Thomas Osborne, Earl of Danby and Duke of Leeds, 1632–1712*, 3 vols (Glasgow, 1944–51) is an excellent and substantial study of the man and, at the same time, a useful guide to political life in the 1670s; Richard Ollard, *Cromwell's Earl: A Life of Edward Montagu, 1st Earl of Sandwich* (1994), based on the earl's own journal, is a beautifully written and balanced portrait of a soldier, admiral and diplomat who served both Cromwell and Charles II; R.L. Ollard, *Pepys: A Biography* (1974); J.P. Kenyon, *Robert Spencer, Earl of Sunderland* (1958) is one of the most outstanding biographies based within the century; K.D.H. Haley, *The First Earl of Shaftesbury* (Oxford, 1968) gives a clear and detailed account of the earl's career in a massive book; H.C. Foxcroft, *The Character of the Trimmer* (Cambridge, 1946) is an account of the life of Sir George Savile, 1st Marquess of Halifax; and C.H. Hartman, *Clifford of the Cabal, 1630–1673* (1937) uses family papers to trace the career of Thomas Clifford, Lord High Treasurer. Algernon Sidney has attracted the interest of two historians over recent years. Jonathan Scott's two volumes, *Algernon Sidney and the English Republic, 1623–1677* (Cambridge, 1988) and *Algernon Sidney and the Restoration*

Crisis, 1677–1683 (Cambridge, 1991), based on detailed research, are lively and witty and shed new light on Sidney's political ideas; John Carswell, *The Porcupine: The Life of Algernon Sidney* (1989) is a clearly written general biography, including discussion of the creation of the Sidney myth in the years following his death.

There are several excellent **biographies based largely on the period after 1688**. Stephen B. Baxter, *William III* (1966) is a first-rate study, which is scholarly in its use of archive material and sympathetic in its balanced portrayal of the king; Edward Gregg, *Queen Anne* (1980) is a most impressive and lucid work, which has become the definitive biography on the subject; Angus McInnes, *Robert Harley, Tory Politician* (1970) gives a clear, well-researched view of one the most important politicians of his age – a book to be read alongside two articles also by Angus McInnes, 'The appointment of Harley in 1704', *HJ* 11 (1968) and 'The political ideas of Robert Harley', *Hist.* 50 (1965); a more recent publication, Brian Hill, *Robert Harley, Speaker, Secretary of State and Premier Minister* (New Haven and London, 1988) provides a political study which, though omitting much of his early life, gives a particularly good account of his career to 1708; Henry Horwitz, *Revolution Politics: The Career of the Second Earl of Nottingham* (Cambridge, 1968) is an excellent survey written in a most lucid style; Roy A. Sundstrom, *Sidney Godolphin: Servant of the State* (Newark, Del., 1992), which shows Godolphin to be a major force in his own right, is a most welcome addition to the range of seventeenth-century biographies and provides the only scholarly life of the Lord High Treasurer written during the last hundred years; W.L. Sachse, *Lord Somers: A Political Portrait* (Manchester, 1975) is workmanlike, but not entirely satisfactory in providing a deep understanding of the man; and H.T. Dickinson, *Bolingbroke* (1970) gives a full and concise picture of Henry St John, Viscount Bolingbroke and has now become the standard work. Other worthwhile biographies include Frances Harris, *A Passion for Government: The Life of Sarah, Duchess of Marlborough* (Oxford, 1991) and J.R. Jones, *Marlborough* (Cambridge, 1993), which is a short, readable introduction to his opportunist rise, his decisive role in the 1688 Revolution and his dramatic fall. Marlborough's military prowess is well covered in Correlli Barnett, *Marlborough* (1976) and David Chandler, *Marlborough as a Military Commander* (1979).

In **religious and cultural life**, E.F. Carpenter, *The Protestant Bishop, being the Life of Henry Compton, Bishop of London, 1632–1713* (1956); Norman Sykes, *William Wake, Archbishop of Canterbury, 1657–1737*, 2 vols (Cambridge, 1957); E.F. Carpenter, *Thomas Tenison, Archbishop of Canterbury: His Life and Times* (1948); G.V. Bennett, *White Kennett, Bishop of Peterborough* (1957); G.V. Bennett, *The Tory Crisis in Church and State,*

1688–1730: The Career of Francis Atterbury, Bishop of Rochester (1975);
R.L. Greaves, *John Bunyan* (1969); Rosalind Miles, *Ben Jonson* (1986);
J.A. Downie, *Jonathan Swift: Political Writer* (1984); Michael Hunter, *John Aubrey and the Realm of Learning* (1975); David Tylden-Wright, *John Aubrey: A Life* (1991); Alan Cromartie, *Sir Matthew Hale, 1609–1676: Law, Religion and Natural Philosophy* (Cambridge, 1995); R.T. Peterson, *Sir Kenelm Digby* (1956); R.C. Bald, *John Donne: A Life* (1970); John Summerson, *Inigo Jones* (1966); Kerry Downes, *Christopher Wren* (1971); Jonathan Keates, *Purcell: A Biography* (1995); Frank Manuel, *A Portrait of Isaac Newton* (1968) and A. Rupert Hall, *Isaac Newton: Adventurer in Thought* (Oxford, 1992) are all worthy of consultation.

3. English political history
Early Stuart England, 1603–1642

In addition to the general books already cited above, the following are recommended as a preliminary guide to the period before the outbreak of civil war. Roger Lockyer, *The Early Stuarts: A Political History of England, 1603–1642* (1989) gives a substantial introduction which will be of particular value to students seeking a clear explanation of recent research. A more concise guide to the latest ideas is available in the Access to History series in Katherine Brice, *The Early Stuarts, 1603–1640* (1994), which considers how far the Civil War was inevitable, setting the areas of controversy within a British context. Richard Cust and Ann Hughes, eds, *Conflict in Early Stuart England: Studies in Religion and Politics, 1603–1642* (1989) is a stimulating series of essays on sources of friction, making a valuable contribution to the debate on the origins of the Civil War. Another collection, Howard Tomlinson, ed., *Before the Civil War: Essays on Early Stuart Politics and Government* (1983) provides a readable update on the structure of the early Stuart state, the Hampton Court Conference, the nature of parliament, the county communities, developments in finance and administration, foreign policy and the Personal Rule. Two books offer a background to political theory and ideology in the first part of the century: Glenn Burgess, *The Politics of the Ancient Constitution: Introduction to English Political Thought, 1600–1642* (1992) and J.P. Sommerville, *Politics and Ideology in England, 1603–1640* (1986), which is an excellent and concise survey of the ideological debates which raged before the outbreak of civil war and their impact on it. Although outdated in terms of its Whig interpretation of the period, S.R. Gardiner, *A History of England from the Accession of James I to the Outbreak of the Civil*

War, 10 vols, 2nd edn (1883–84) still remains the fullest and best narrative of events and is therefore a vital source of reference.

One of the most lively areas of controversy to exercise the minds of scholars in recent years has been **the debate over the nature and power of parliament** in the early Stuart period and the origins of the Civil War. There are of course specific studies on individual parliaments, including Wallace Notestein, *The Parliament of 1604–1610* (1971); T.L. Moir, *The Addled Parliament of 1614* (Oxford, 1958); Robert E. Zaller, *The Parliament of 1621: A Study in Constitutional Conflict* (Berkeley, Cal., 1971); Robert E. Ruigh, *The Parliament of 1624: Politics and Foreign Policy* (Cambridge, Mass., 1971) and Conrad Russell, *Parliaments and English Politics, 1621– 1629* (Oxford, 1979), which sets out a survey of the English political system and a detailed description of each parliament. Whereas the first four of these authors adhere to the traditional view that constitutional conflict was inevitable and that England was on the high road to civil war, Russell has been at the forefront of the revisionist debate. This has seen an onslaught on the traditionalist interpretation of the power of an emerging House of Commons locked in bitter conflict with an absolutist monarchy as expressed in Wallace Notestein, 'The winning of the initiative by the House of Commons', *PBA* (1924/25) and D.H. Willson, *The Privy Councillors in the House of Commons, 1604–1629* (Minneapolis, 1946).

Revisionist writings which question the Whig and Marxist views of the long-term causes of the Revolution and set out a radical reinterpretation of early Stuart politics include the following early articles: G.R. Elton, 'Parliament in the sixteenth century: functions and fortunes', *HJ* 22 (1979); G.R. Elton, 'A high road to civil war?', in Charles H. Carter, ed., *From the Renaissance to the Counter-Reformation: Essays in Honour of Garrett Mattingly* (New York, 1956); Conrad Russell, 'Parliamentary history in perspective, 1604–1629', *Hist.* 61 (1976); and three articles which appeared in *JMH* 49 (1977) – Mark Kishlansky, 'The emergence of adversary politics in the Long Parliament'; Paul Christianson, 'The peers, the people and parliamentary management in the first six months of the Long Parliament'; and James F. Farnell, 'The social and intellectual basis of London's role in the English Civil War'. Two books which came out in the late 1970s continued and expanded the revisionist theme by emphasising the lack of deep ideological divisions and the large degree of consensus which characterised relations between parliament and the court : Kevin Sharpe, ed., *Faction and Parliament: Essays in Early Stuart History* (1978) and (already mentioned) Conrad Russell, *Parliaments and English Politics, 1621–1629* (Oxford, 1979), a brilliant reassessment. Complementary to this is Russell's article, 'The parliamentary career of

John Pym, 1621–1629', in Peter Clark, Alan G.R. Smith and Nicholas Tyacke, eds, *The English Commonwealth, 1547–1640: Essays in Politics and Society presented to Joel Hurstfield* (Leicester, 1979). This piece is also reprinted in Conrad Russell, *Unrevolutionary England, 1603–1642* (1990), a collection of his essays published between 1962 and 1988, which set out in full his revisionist ideas on the nature of the clash between crown and parliament before 1629 and the lack of an organised opposition. To be read alongside this is Kevin Sharpe, *Personal Rule of Charles I, 1629–1640* (1992), a lavish and impressive volume. Sheila Lambert has also contributed to the debate in two articles: 'The opening of the Long Parliament', *HJ* 27 (1984), a reassessment of the view that that parliament was united against the king from the start; and 'Committees, religion and parliamentary encroachment on royal authority in early Stuart England', *EHR* 105 (1990), which deals with the nature of parliamentary opposition to the crown and its willingness to compromise backstage.

A sustained counter-attack on the ideas of the revisionists has been launched in recent years by a number of heavy-weight historians (styled the **post-revisionists**), commencing with two articles in *JMH* 50 (1978): J.H. Hexter, 'Power struggle, parliament and liberty in early Stuart England' and Derek Hirst, 'Unanimity in the Commons, aristocratic intrigue and the origins of the English Civil War'. These were followed by three further articles in *PP* 92 (1981) – one by Christopher Hill, 'Parliament and people in seventeenth-century England' and two under the heading 'Revisionism revised': Theodore K. Rabb, 'The role of the Commons' and Derek Hirst, 'The place of principle'. Other important contributions to the mounting criticism of the revisionists' interpretation of the 1620s and 1630s are Thomas Cogswell, *The Blessed Revolution: English Politics and the Coming of War, 1621–1624* (Cambridge, 1989), which is an impressive survey of the contribution of court, parliament and public opinion to the outbreak of war with Spain and a counter to the view that parliament was largely powerless; and L.J. Reeve, *Charles I and the Road to Personal Rule* (Cambridge, 1989), which is a study of the years 1628–32 with a critical assessment of Charles I's weaknesses. The following articles should also be consulted: Richard Cust, 'Charles I, the Privy Council and the forced loan', *JBS* 24 (1985), which examines how far new counsels were involved and the traditional order threatened; Richard Cust, 'Charles I, the Privy Council and the parliament of 1628', *TRHS* 6th series 2 (1992); Thomas Cogswell, 'A low road to extinction? Supply and redress of grievances in the parliaments of the 1620s', *HJ* 33 (1990); Perez Zagorin, 'Did Strafford change sides?', *EHR* 101 (1986), an examination of the nature of opposition to the crown in the 1620s;

P.G. Lake, 'Constitutional consensus and puritan opposition in the 1620s: Thomas Scott and the Spanish marriage', *HJ* 25 (1982); L.J. Reeve, 'The legal status of the Petition of Right', *HJ* 29 (1986) and John A. Guy, 'The origins of the Petition of Right reconsidered', *HJ* 25 (1982), which considers the duplicity of the king and its contribution to an explosive situation.

Students wishing to seek further clarification of this complex debate are recommended to read the following articles, which survey the latest trends in research: Glenn Burgess, 'On revisionism: an analysis of early Stuart historiography in the 1970s and 1980s', *HJ* 33 (1990); Glenn Burgess, 'Revisionism, politics and political studies in early modern England', *HJ* 34 (1991); Thomas Cogswell, 'Coping with revisionism in early Stuart History', *JMH* 62 (1990); and John Kenyon, 'Revisionism and post-revisionism in early Stuart history', *JMH* 64 (1992).

This reassessment of early Stuart politics has of course made a major impact on historians' views concerning **the causes of the Civil War**. Ann Hughes, *The Causes of the English Civil War* (1991) is a scholarly, well-researched book which highlights the remaining areas of disagreement among historians on this hotly debated topic and is therefore an ideal starting point for students. Anthony Fletcher, *The Outbreak of the English Civil War* (1981) is a fascinating and lucidly written account with a persuasive analysis of the reasons for a war which was both unforeseen and unwanted. Conrad Russell, *The Causes of the English Civil War: The Ford Lectures Delivered in the University of Oxford, 1987–1988* (Oxford, 1990), a reflection of his own revisionist views, is a brilliant and readable survey of the short- and long-term causes of the war, including the personality of the king, which stresses that there was nothing inevitable about the outbreak of hostilities. His earlier book, Conrad Russell, ed., *The Origins of the English Civil War* (1973), though in some respects now outdated, is still worth reading. In a series of essays by leading authorities the arguments on major central themes are summarised, including those of government, the king's finances, Puritanism, popery, court and country, economic issues and political thought. The earlier writings of two other historians are also worthy of reference, even though their views have long since been overtaken in the current debate. Lawrence Stone, *The Crisis of the Aristocracy, 1558–1641* (1965) is an attempt to attribute the long-term causes of the war to the decline in power, authority and wealth of the aristocracy. A second book, Lawrence Stone, *Social Change and Revolution in England, 1540–1640* (1965), puts into focus the gentry controversy, which raged in the 1950s over R.H. Tawney's theory linking the causes of the war to the rise of the gentry, by giving a series of key extracts from the writings of the main combatants. Christopher Hill's theory that 'the Civil War was a class war' is clearly outlined in Christopher Hill, *The English Revolution, 1640*, 3rd edn (1955) and in an article which has already been mentioned, 'Parliament and people in seventeenth-century England', *PP* 92 (1981).

More will be said in the next section about theories of allegiance in the Civil War, but it is relevant here to mention several articles which deal with **the context in which the war broke out:** J.S.A. Adamson, 'The baronial context of the English civil war', *TRHS* 5th series 40 (1990), which stresses the role of the peerage, including that of Lord Saye and Sele, but which is challenged by Mark Kishlansky in 'Saye no more', *JBS* 30 (1991); J.S. Morrill, 'The religious context of the English Civil War', *TRHS* 5th series 34 (1984) and 'Sir William Brereton and England's wars of religion', *JBS* 24 (1985); Robin Clifton, 'The popular fear of Catholics during the English Revolution', *PP* 52 (1971); David Underdown, 'What was the English revolution?', *HT* (March 1984), which sees the revolution as cultural as well as political – a conflict over the moral basis of English society; and Conrad Russell, 'The British problem and the English civil war', *Hist.* 72 (1987), which considers the causes of the war in the context of the problems of Britain as a multiple kingdom. This theme is expanded in Conrad Russell, *The Fall of the British Monarchies, 1637–42* (Oxford, 1991), an impressive and convincing reconstruction of these crucial years, giving a new perspective on the events which led to war and the inter-relationship of England, Scotland and Ireland. Further consideration of the mounting crisis which finally brought down the king's government is given in Caroline Hibbard, *Charles I and the Popish Plot* (1983), a scholarly investigation into the presence and influence of Catholics at court; Conrad Russell, 'Why did Charles I call the Long Parliament?', *Hist.* 69 (1984); Valery Pearl, *London and the Outbreak of the Puritan Revolution* (Oxford, 1964); Robert Ashton, *The City and the Court, 1603–1643* (Cambridge, 1979), which builds on Pearl's work to give a refined interpretation of the Revolution in the capital, 1641–42; and John Fielding, 'Opposition to the Personal Rule of Charles I: the diary of Robert Woodford, 1637–1641', *HJ* 31 (1988), which gives an insight into the growing crisis as viewed by a provincial townsman. The best narrative account of the events bringing the country to the eve of war is still C.V. Wedgwood, *The King's Peace, 1637–1641* (1955).

Two other specific themes need to be mentioned, because they in turn contribute to the debates on allegiance and the causes of war. The first concerns **the growth of popular involvement in elections** and the extent of influence enjoyed by the gentry – a subject covered with great authority in Derek Hirst, *The Representative of the People?* (Cambridge, 1975) and echoed in J.H. Plumb, 'The growth of the electorate in

England from 1600–1715', *PP* 45 (1969), which makes the point that the growth of larger borough electorates resulted in the growth of political propaganda and canvassing on a wide scale. The demands of the electorate on one Member of Parliament are well illustrated in S.P. Salt, 'Sir Thomas Wentworth and the Parliamentary representation of Yorkshire, 1614–1628', *NH* 16 (1980). The importance of political propaganda with an electorate which was increasing in political awareness is emphasised in Thomas Cogswell, 'The politics of propaganda: Charles I and the people in the 1620s', *JBS* 29 (1990), which argues that the government responded to the threat of an underground system of uncensored news by distributing propaganda of its own; and in Pauline Croft, 'The reput-ation of Robert Cecil: libels, political opinion and popular awareness in the early seventeenth century', *TRHS* 6th series 1 (1991). The second theme to be explored is that relating to **patronage and corruption at court.** Linda Levy Peck in *Patronage and corruption in Early Stuart England* (1990) gives a fascinating insight into corruption and patronage both at court and elsewhere in the country; and in ' "For a king not to be bountiful were a fault": perspectives on court patronage in early Stuart England', *JBS* 25 (1986) explores changes in court patronage and reasons why it came under increasing attack. This whole matter is developed further in Pauline Croft, 'Patronage and corruption, parlia-ment and liberty in seventeenth century England', *HJ* 36 (1993), while Linda Levy Peck gives an interesting reassessment of the role played in this by the Earl of Northampton in *Northampton: Patronage and Policy at the Court of James I* (1982). Two essays are also relevant in David Starkey, ed., *The English Court from the Wars of the Roses to the Civil War* (1987), namely Neil Cuddy, 'The bedchamber of James I, 1603–1625' and Kevin Sharpe, 'The court and household of Charles I, 1625–1642'. Another useful essay on this subject by Pauline Croft, 'Robert Cecil and the Early Jacobean Court', can be found in Linda Levy Peck, ed., *The Mental World of the Jacobean Court* (Cambridge, 1991).

Articles and books which could be useful in researching **particular aspects of the period** include Jenny Wormald, 'Gunpowder, treason and Scots', *JBS* 24 (1985), but also see Mark Nicholls, *Investigating Gunpowder Plot* (Manchester, 1991), a fascinating and well-researched reassessment of the plot, the government's investigation, the role of Henry Percy and the 'conspiracy theory'; Mark H. Curtis, 'The Hampton Court Conference and its aftermath', *Hist.* 46 (1961); Linda Levy Peck, 'The Earl of Northampton, merchant grievances and the Addled Parliament of 1614', *HJ* 24 (1981); Clayton Roberts and Owen Duncan, 'The parliamentary undertaking of 1614', *EHR* 93 (1978); Eric N. Lindquist, 'The king, the people and the House of Commons: the problem of early Jacobean purveyance', *HJ* 31 (1988); Richard Cust, *The Forced Loan and English Politics, 1626–1628* (Oxford, 1987); Linda S. Popfsky, 'The crisis over tonnage and poundage in parliament in 1629', *PP* 126 (1990); George Hammersley, 'The revival of the forest laws under Charles I', *Hist.* 45 (1960); Michael Mendle, 'The ship money case: The case of ship money and the development of Henry Parker's parliamentary absolutism', *HJ* 32 (1989); Conrad Russell, 'The ship money judgments of Bramston and Davenport', *EHR* 77 (1962); S.P. Salt, 'Sir Simon D'Ewes and the levying of ship money, 1635–1640', *HJ* 37 (1994); Lindsay Boynton, 'Martial law and the Petition of Right', *EHR* 79 (1964); E.R. Foster, 'Petitions and Petitions of Right', *JBS* 14 (1974); J.S. Flemion, 'The struggle for the Petition of Right in the House of Lords: the study of an opposition party victory', *JMH* 45 (1973); V.F. Snow, 'Essex and the aristocratic opposition to the early Stuarts', *JMH* 32 (1960); Glenn Burgess, 'The divine right of kings reconsidered', *EHR* 107 (1992); T.G. Barnes, 'County politics and a puritan *cause célèbre*: Somerset Churchales, 1633', *TRHS* 5th series 9 (1959); Peter Clark, 'Thomas Scott and the growth of urban opposition to the early Stuarts', *HJ* 21 (1978); Conrad Russell, 'The theory of treason in the trial of Strafford', *EHR* 80 (1965); and R.M. Smutts, 'The puritan followers of Henrietta-Maria in the 1630s', *EHR* 93 (1978).

The Revolution, 1642–1660

The best general account, for reference purposes at least, is Edward Hyde, Earl of Clarendon, *History of the Great Rebellion*, 6 vols (Oxford, 1958 edn), although for a reassessment of its value consult Ronald Hutton, 'Clarendon's History of the Rebellion', *EHR* 97 (1982). The most readable and authoritative narrative is to be found in two works by S.R. Gardiner: *History of the Great Civil War, 1642–1649*, 4 vols (1893) and *History of the Commonwealth and Protectorate*, 4 vols (1903); and one by C.H. Firth, which completed Gardiner's mammoth task: *The Last Years of the Protectorate*, 2 vols (1909). More manageable for most requirements are Ivan Roots, *The Great Rebellion, 1642–1660* (1966), an impressive and lucid account of the Civil War with one of the best surveys yet written of the Interregnum; and G.E. Aylmer, *Rebellion or Revolution? England from Civil War to Restoration* (Oxford, 1986), a clear, balanced but briefer account of the period with a helpful analysis of important themes. Three other books will help in a more general way to understand the background to this hotly debated phase in history: R.C. Richardson, *The Debate on the English Revolution Revisited* (1988, revised edn), an indispensable guide to changing interpretations in the study of the Revolution over the past three hundred years, including three new chapters which take account of the most recent developments; John Morrill, *The Nature of the English Revolution* (1993), a collection of his most stimulating essays over twenty years, including 'The making of Oliver Cromwell' and 'England's war of religion'; and John Sanderson, *'But the People's Creatures': The Philosophical Basis of the English Civil War* (Manchester, 1989), a clear summary of the political thinking behind the years of conflict, 1642–49.

Students of the period would do well to gain access to a number of **essay collections** which have appeared in recent years, containing the latest research on various key topics. The following are recommended: John Morrill, ed., *The Impact of the Civil War* (1991), which provides an excellent update by leading historians on the war's impact on government, political thought, Puritanism, the New Model Army, literature and ordinary people; Colin Jones, ed., *Politics and People in Revolutionary England* (Oxford, 1986), which covers such topics as the Putney Debates, the Major-Generals, the sects, the social background of the royalist generals, the committee of indemnity and ecclesiastical problems in South Wales; J.S. Morrill, ed., *Reactions to the English Civil War* (1982), a valuable set of essays on the coming of the war, including responses within the towns and within the church, the impact on ordinary people and the politicisation of the army; and R.H. Parry, ed., *The English Civil War and After, 1642–1658* (1970), which gives a useful introduction to important themes (but now in need of more recent update), including the causes of the war, the rebels of 1642, the trial of Charles I, the rule of the Saints, the Major-Generals and the class struggle.

Although the **military aspects** of the Civil War, 1642–46, will be covered separately in part 6 of this essay, it is worth mentioning here that the best and most readable one-volume commentary on the course of the war is C.V. Wedgwood, *The King's War, 1641–1647* (1958). The story is effectively continued in Robert Ashton, *Counter Revolution: The Second Civil War and its Origins, 1646–8* (New Haven, 1994), which demonstrates why the uneasy peace of 1646 was broken and how the royalists found support to resume their hostilities. Martyn Bennett, *The English Civil War* (1995, Seminar Studies in History series) provides students with a valuable introduction to the period of conflict. The most helpful guide to **the political divisions within parliament** at the start of the war and Pym's skilful management of them is J.H. Hexter, *The Reign of King Pym* (Cambridge, Mass., 1941), which should be read in conjunction with Lotte Glow, 'Pym and parliament: the methods of moderation', *JMH* 36 (1964) and Lotte Glow, 'The manipulation of committees in the Long Parliament, 1640–1642', *JBS* 5 (1965). David Wootton, 'From rebellion to revolution: the crisis of the winter of 1642/3 and the origins of civil war radicalism', *EHR* 105 (1990) argues, contrary to revisionist views, that a significant group on parliament's side considered the possibility of revolution much earlier than 1646. Five other articles carry on this theme of division and attempts at moderation: Valery Pearl, 'The Royal Independents in the English Civil War', *TRHS* 5th series 18 (1968); J.H. Hexter, 'The problem of the Presbyterian-Independent', *AHR* 44 (1938); Lawrence Kaplan, 'Presbyterians and Independents in 1643', *EHR* 84 (1969); Valery Pearl, 'Oliver St John and the middle group in the Long Parliament', *EHR* 81 (1966); and Christopher Thomson, 'The origins of the politics of the parliamentary middle group', *TRHS* 22 (1972). J.T. Cliffe, *Puritans in Conflict* (1988) studies the role of the puritan gentry at Westminster during and after the Civil War, explaining reasons for their rebellion and their later disagreements. His earlier book, *The Puritan Gentry* (1984), describes how puritan influence gained ground among the gentry before the war, ensuring that godliness was not the exclusive preserve of the 'middling sort'. On **the royalist side**, too, the situation of support was not entirely clear-cut, judging by the evidence of three further articles: Ronald Hutton, 'The structure of the royalist party, 1642–1646', *HJ* 24 (1981); J.S.A. Adamson, 'Politics and the nobility in civil war England', *HJ* 34 (1991); and David L. Smith, ' "The more posed and wise advice": the fourth Earl of Dorset and the English civil wars', *HJ* 34 (1991), which is a study of a moderate, constitutional royalist who sought accommodation. A helpful survey of the varying ideas and political groupings which emerged during this period is given in a series of essays by G.E. Aylmer entitled 'Collective mentalities in mid-seventeenth-century England' in *TRHS* 5th series: 'The puritan outlook', 36 (1986); 'Royalist attitudes', 37 (1987); 'Varieties of radicalism', 38 (1988); and 'Cross currents: neutrals, trimmers and others', 39 (1989).

As regards the active **involvement of ordinary people in the Civil War**, several theories of popular allegiance have been advanced. For illustrations of the 'deference' theory, see Peter Laslett, *The World We Have Lost*, (1965), Clive Holmes, *The Eastern Association in the English Civil War* (Cambridge, 1974) and Alan Everitt, *The Community of Kent and the Great Rebellion* (Leicester, 1966). For the 'neutralism' theory, see J.S. Morrill, *The Revolt of the Provinces* (1976), a masterly book on provincial reactions to the coming of war, which also considers the effects of the war on the country's institutions. For the 'class conflict' theory see two books by Brian Manning: *The English People and the English Revolution* (1976), which examines popular movements, the fear of papacy, the resistance of industrial districts, the importance of the 'godly people' and the legacy inherited by the Levellers; and, in an update of his ideas, *Aristocrats, Plebeians and Revolution in England, 1640–1660* (1996), which shows that popular movements had a decisive influence on the course of the war. In recent years, David Underdown has also advanced the 'ecological' theory, which is bound up with the cultural and religious differences which emerge in different agricultural regions. For his exposition of this see: 'The chalk and the cheese: contrasts among the English Clubmen', *PP* 85 (1979); 'The problem of popular allegiance in the English Civil War', *TRHS* 5th series (1981); and, especially, *Revel, Riot and Rebellion: Popular Politics and Culture in England, 1603–1660* (1985), with reference also to a critique of this by John Morrill, 'The ecology of allegiance in the English Revolution', *JBS* 26 (1987). David Underdown in addition offers a helpful synthesis of these various views of popular allegiance in an essay, 'Community and class', in Barbara Malament, ed., *After the Reformation* (Manchester, 1980).

The growing **conflicts between parliament and the army** after the ending of the Civil War are dealt with by a number of writers. The best starting point is Austin Woolrych, *Soldiers and Statesmen: The General Council of the Army and its Debates, 1647–1648* (Oxford, 1987), which discusses the relations between the Long Parliament, the king, the Levellers and the New Model Army, examining political activity within the army and offering a reinterpretation of the Putney Debates. These dealings are also well covered in Ian Gentles, *The New Model Army in England, Ireland and Scotland, 1645–1653* (Oxford, 1991), which, in giving a better balanced picture of radicalism within the army, modifies and extends the account provided in Mark Kishlansky, *The Rise of the New Model Army* (Cambridge, 1979). Two articles also discuss stages in the setting up of of the New Model Army: Mark Kishlansky, 'The case of the army truly stated: the creation of the New Model Army', *PP* 81 (1978); and A.N.B. Cotton, 'Cromwell and the Self-Denying Ordinance', *Hist.* 61 (1977). There are three useful articles which consider the Putney Debates: Richard Gleissner, 'The Levellers and natural law: the Putney Debates of 1647', *JBS* 20 (1980); Mark Kishlansky, 'Consensus politics and the structure of debate at Putney', *JBS* 20 (1981); and Mark Kishlansky, 'What happened at Ware?', *HJ* 25 (1982), which considers the significance of the suppression of the Leveller mutiny. On **the Leveller movement** itself, a helpful introduction is provided by Howard Shaw, *The Levellers* (1968), which deals with their rise and fall set against the social, economic and political background of the period. More perceptive and stimulating discussions are provided by G.E. Aylmer, *The Levellers in the English Revolution* (1985) and Joseph Frank, *The Levellers* (1944). These are supplemented by J.R. McMichael and Barbara Taft, eds, *The Writings of William Waldwyn* (Athens, Georgia, 1989), an invaluable source book for a study of the movement. The following articles are also relevant: J.C. Davis, 'The Levellers and democracy', *PP* 40 (1968); Roger Howell and David Brewster, 'Reconsidering the Levellers: the evidence of *The Moderate*', *PP* 46 (1970); Gerald Aylmer, 'Gentlemen Levellers', *PP* 49 (1970); and Ian Gentles, 'London Levellers in the English revolution: the Chidleys and their circle', *JEccH* 29 (1978). Finally, three publications make essential reading for **the crisis of 1648–49:** Brian Manning, *1649: The Crisis of the English Revolution* (1992), examines the part played by the Levellers, the radical soldiers, the women, the poor and the youth, emphasising the importance of class issues and the influence of the 'middling sort'; Ian Gentles, 'The struggle for London in the Second Civil War', *HJ* 26 (1983), which argues that London was deeply divided from early in 1646; and C.V. Wedgwood, *The Trial of Charles I* (1964), a vivid and gripping account of the trial and execution, which should be read alongside Patricia Crawford, ' Charles Stuart, that man of blood', *JBS* 16 (1977). As a supplement to the trial itself, A.L. Rowse, *The Regicides* (1994) provides an investigation of the identity of the regicides and their social background.

There are three good **general accounts of the years 1649–60.** Ronald Hutton, *The British Republic, 1649–1660* (1990) is a concise, readable study with fresh insights, particularly on the Major-Generals, which should be invaluable to first-time students. Austin Woolrych, *England Without a King, 1649–1660* (1983), in the Lancaster Pamphlets series, is a stimulating survey of the establishment of the Commonwealth and Protectorate, which challenges accepted views on the nature of the latter. Michael Lynch, *The Interregnum, 1649–1660* (1994) provides a helpful synthesis of recent reassessments of Cromwell, the Rump Parliament, the Protectorate Parliaments and the Restoration, together with a survey of the part played throughout by the lower orders in society. In addition, there are two good collections of essays on this period: G.E. Aylmer, ed., *The Interregnum: The Quest for Settlement, 1646–1660* (1972), which includes helpful pieces on the Levellers and the franchise, the Church in England, 1646–1660, social and economic policies, London's counter-revolution, Cromwell's ordinances and settlement in the counties; and John Morrill, ed., *Revolution and Restoration in England in the 1650s* (1992), which includes articles on foreign policy and the frustration of the godly.

There are three outstanding individual works on on **the politics of the 1650s,** which are essential reading for all those who wish to grapple successfully with this complex decade. David Underdown, *Pride's Purge: Politics in the Puritan Revolution* (Oxford, 1971) is a masterly survey of politics at both central and local levels, emphasising the deep division in parliament's ranks between the radical Puritans and the conservative gentry. Blair Worden, *The Rump Parliament* (Cambridge, 1974) is a brilliant portrayal of the Rump and its membership, policies, struggle for survival, quarrel with the army and dissolution. Austin Woolrych, *Commonwealth to Protectorate* (Oxford, 1982) gives a stimulating and fresh look at Barebone's Parliament with a valuable commentary on the political and constitutional developments during the years 1653–54. This should be read in conjunction with Tai Liu, 'The calling of Barebone's Parliament reconsidered', *JEccH* 22 (1971); Austin Woolrych, 'The calling of Barebone's Parliament', *EHR* 80 (1965); and Derek Hirst, 'The failure of godly rule in the English Republic', *PP* 132 (1991).

Articles on specific **aspects of the Protectorate** which might be of value in research include Austin Woolrych, 'The Cromwellian Protectorate: a military dictatorship?', *Hist.* 75 (1990); Peter Gaunt, 'The Single Person's confidants and dependents? Oliver Cromwell and his Protectoral councillors', *HJ* 32 (1989); Blair Worden, 'Providence and politics in Cromwellian England', *PP* 109 (1985); and G.D. Heath, 'The making of the Instrument of Government', *JBS* 6 (1967). The final breakdown of the Protectorate is covered partly in Derek Hirst, 'Concord and discord in Richard Cromwell's House of Commons', *EHR* 103 (1988), a reassessment of the traditional view of an alliance between republicans and crypto-cavaliers, and Austin Woolrych, 'The Good Old Cause and the fall of the Protectorate', *HJ* 13 (1957); but more fully in Ronald Hutton, *The Restoration: A Political and Religious History of England and Wales, 1658–1667* (Oxford, 1985), which gives an excellent account of the years 1658–60. The activities of the royalists during these years are considered in P.H. Hardacre, *The Royalists during the Puritan Revolution* (The Hague, 1956), which is particularly good on their suffering through sequestration and composition; David Underdown, *Royalist Conspiracy in England* (1960), which examines in a most convincing manner reasons for the failure of their plots; Austin Woolrych, 'Penruddock's Rising, 1655', *HAP* G29 (1955); and Ronald Hutton, *Charles II* (Oxford, 1989), which provides a lively study of the royalist court in exile.

The Restoration, 1660–1688

Two scholarly and long-established works by David Ogg, *England in the Reign of Charles II*, 2 vols, 2nd edn (Oxford, 1955) and *England in the Reigns of James II and William III* (Oxford, 1955) provide the classic reference books for the period of the later Stuarts. To these must now be added Geoffrey Holmes, *The Making of Great Britain: Late Stuart and Early Georgian Britain, 1660–1722* (1993), which studies Britain's transformation in commerce, financial organisation, foreign policy, intellectual life, social cohesion and national pride.

There are, in addition, three good concise publications which give a modern interpretation of events and personalities in the reigns of Charles II and James II: Paul Seaward, *The Restoration, 1660–1688* (1991), a clear introduction based on recent research, which examines just how safe the Restoration really was; Robert M. Bliss, *Restoration England: Politics and Government, 1660–1688* (1985), in the Lancaster Pamphlets series, which is both stimulating and readable; and John Miller: *Restoration England: The Reign of Charles II* (1985). John Miller has also produced two other pieces which consider a revision and reinterpretation of Restoration England. In 'The potential for absolutism in later Stuart England', *Hist.* 69 (1982) he considers whether the later Stuarts aimed to establish an absolute monarchy and what their chances were of doing so. This is expanded in John Miller, *An English Absolutism? The Later Stuart Monarchy, 1660–1688* (1993). On the Restoration itself, Ronald Hutton, *The Restoration: A Political and Religious History of England and Wales, 1658–1667* (Oxford, 1985) gives a scholarly and fascinating account based on a mass of documentary sources, thereby providing the best available narrative of these years and the fullest explanation of the policies involved. Paul Seaward, *The Cavalier Parliament and the Reconstruction of the Old Regime, 1661–1667* (Cambridge, 1989), a readable and enlightening book, examines in a most convincing manner what was restored at the Restoration; while Richard L. Greaves, *Deliver Us from Evil: The Radical Underground in Britain, 1660–1662* (New York, 1986) puts forward a clearly argued and well-documented case for the existence of a determined underground movement in the 1660s aimed at the overthrow of the restored monarchy. In a second volume, *Enemies under his Feet: Radicals and Nonconformists in Britain, 1664–1677* (Stanford, 1990), while failing to provide any real analysis of the nature and aims of the radical movement as a whole, he nevertheless gives a fascinating account of various conspiracies in the three kingdoms and the government's response to them. This theme of opposition is substantiated further in Tim Harris, 'The Bawdy House Riots of 1668', *HJ* 29 (1986), which illustrates the insecurities of the Restoration regime and popular attitudes towards the Stuarts. The government's counter-measures to all this subversion are well described in Alan Marshall, *Intelligence and Espionage in the Reign of Charles II, 1660–1685* (Cambridge, 1994). Three other articles are also relevant to the Restoration itself: N.H. Keeble, 'Rewriting the Restoration', *HJ* 35 (1992); J.R. Jones, 'Political groups and tactics in the Convention of 1660', *HJ* 6 (1963); and F.M.S. McDonald, 'The timing of General George Monck's march into

England, 1 January 1660', *EHR* 105 (1990), which considers in the light of new evidence reasons for the delay in Monck's advance.

The politics of the period and **the growth of political parties** are well covered in Tim Harris, *Politics Under the Later Stuarts: Party Conflict in a Divided Society, 1660–1715* (1993), a vividly written and invaluable study, which provides a synthesis of the latest scholarship and traces the origins of party organisation and party issues; Clyve Jones, ed., *Party and Management in Parliament* (Leicester, 1984), a series of essays which deal with varying aspects of party politics; K.D.H. Haley, *Politics in the Reign of Charles II* (Oxford, 1985), a detailed, well-structured and authoritative survey; D.T. Witcombe, *Charles II and the Cavalier House of Commons, 1663–74* (Manchester, 1966), which provides a concise description of the dealings between crown and parliament in each session; Maurice Lee, *The Cabal* (Urbana, 1965), a not altogether satisfactory survey of the responsibilities of the members of the Cabal between 1667 and 1674; John Miller, *Popery and Politics in England, 1660–88* (Cambridge, 1973), an excellent portrayal of the continuing importance of religion and the fear of popery in English political life after the Restoration; J.T. Cliffe, *The Puritan Gentry Besieged, 1650–1700* (1993), a study of what happened to the puritan gentry after their involvement in the Republic and whether their puritan commitment proved to be just a temporary pheno-menon; J.R. Jones, ed., *The Restored Monarchy, 1660* (1979) with articles on the political parties, the crown, the Church and foreign affairs; Tim Harris, Paul Seaward and Mark Goldie, eds, *The Politics of Religion in Restoration England* (Oxford, 1990), a collection of essays on the bishops and the Whigs, the Popish Plot, Danby and London radicals, which demonstrates that religion continued to be a major force in politics after the Restoration; K.D.H. Haley, *William of Orange and the English Opposition, 1672–4* (Oxford, 1953), which provides the background to the Third Anglo-Dutch War; J.R. Jones, 'Political groups and tactics in the Convention of 1660', *HJ* 6 (1963); John Miller, 'Political opinion in Charles II's England', *Hist.* 80 (1995); and David Allen, 'Political clubs in Restoration London', *HJ* 19 (1976).

On specific episodes before 1688, **the Exclusion Crisis** is particularly well covered in J.R. Jones, *The First Whigs: The Politics of the Exclusion Crisis, 1678–83* (1961), a survey of the origins of party conflict which is very different from that advocated in Jonathan Scott, *Algernon Sidney and the Restoration Crisis, 1677–1683* (Cambridge, 1991), though the latter is nevertheless excellent on Sidney's own involvement; and F.S. Ronalds, *The Attempted Whig Revolution of 1678–81* (Urbana, 1937), which deals effectively with the growth of pamphlet propaganda during the crisis. J.P. Kenyon, *The Popish Plot* (1972), a readable and persuasive account, remains the authority on this subject. A number of articles should also be consulted: J.D. Davies, 'The navy, parliament and political crisis in the reign of Charles II', *HJ* 36 (1993) examines the influence of the Duke of York over the navy and its response to the Popish Plot and Exclusion Crisis; Mark Knights, 'London's monster petition of 1680', *HJ* 36 (1993) assesses public opinion and the nature of the opposition during the Exclusion Crisis; Dan Beaver, 'Conscience and context: the Popish Plot and the politics of ritual, 1678–1682', *HJ* 34 (1991) deals with the impact of the plot on local society in Tewkesbury; D.J. Milne, 'Results of the Rye House Plot', *TRHS* 5th series 1 (1951); and Lois G. Schwoerer, 'William Lord Russell: the making of a martyr, 1683–1983', *JBS* 24 (1985) explains how this Whig conspirator became and remained the Whig martyr. The best accounts of **Monmouth's Rebellion** are Peter Earle, *Monmouth's Rebels* (1977), which contains a useful discussion on the nature and identity of the rebels; and Robin Clifton, *The Last Popular Rebellion: The Western Rising of 1685* (1984), which places the rebellion in its economic, social, political and religious setting.

The period leading up to **the Glorious Revolution** is well described in J.R. Western, *Monarchy and Revolution: The English State in the 1680s* (1972), which stresses the growth of royal power, whereas J.R. Jones, *The Revolution of 1688 in England* (1972) also traces out with clarity and precision the steps leading to James II's downfall. Michael Mullett, *James II and English Politics* (1994), in the Lancaster Pamphlets series, is a particularly valuable and concise reassessment of these critical years based on recent scholarship, emphasising the role of James II. An article by J.R.Jones, 'James II's Whig collaborators', *HJ* 3 (1960) should also be consulted in this connection. Maurice Ashley, *The Glorious Revolution of 1688* (1966) and S.E. Prall, *The Bloodless Revolution: England, 1688* (1972) both give good narrative accounts, while John Carswell, *The Descent on England* (1969) puts the Revolution into a European setting. George Hilton Jones, *Convergent Forces: Immediate Causes of the Revolution of 1688 in England* (Ames, Iowa, 1990), although weaker on analysis, provides a well-written and detailed narrative of events in England set against the background of the Dutch Republic. W.A. Speck, *Reluctant Revolutionaries: Englishmen and the Revolution of 1688* (Oxford, 1988), one of the best accounts yet published, combines a concise and lucidly written narrative with a clear analysis of the main problems based on new material. Lois G. Schwoerer, *The Declaration of Rights, 1689* (Baltimore, 1981) offers a new dimension to our understanding of the Glorious Revolution and its impact on the changing nature of English kingship.

The most helpful out of a number of useful collections of essays and lectures which were published to coincide with the tercentenary celebrations of the Revolution are: Jonathan Israel, ed., *The Anglo-Dutch Moment: Essays on the Glorious Revolution and its World Impact* (Cambridge, 1991), which deals with the role of the States General in supporting William's invasion, as well as the Revolution's impact on trade, alliances, economics and political thought; Eveline Cruickshanks, ed., *By Force or by Default? The Revolution of 1688–1689* (Edinburgh, 1989), which includes an examination of the role of the Tories in the Revolution, an assessment of James II's part and a study of the contribution of literature; Robert Beddard, ed., *The Revolutions of 1688* (Oxford, 1991), with particularly valuable contributions by Robert Beddard, 'The unexpected Whig revolution of 1688', and Mark Goldie, 'The political thought of the Anglican revolution'; and Lois G. Schwoerer, ed., *The Revolution of 1688–1689: Changing Perspectives* (Cambridge, 1992), including essays on foreign policy, John Locke and religious toleration. There are also several articles which are worth consideration: John Childs, '1688', *Hist.* 78 (1988), which sets out a re-examination of the nature of both the Restoration monarchy and the Revolution settlement; John Miller, 'The Glorious Revolution: *contract* and *abdication* reconsidered', *HJ* 25 (1982); Kathleen Wilson, 'Inventing revolution: 1688 and eighteenth-century popular politics', *JBS* 28 (1989), which challenges current accounts of the Revolution and its impact on popular political consciousness; W.L. Sachse, 'The mob in the Revolution of 1688', *JBS* 4 (1964); Lois G. Schwoerer, 'Press and parliament in the Revolution of 1688', *HJ* 20 (1977); Lois G. Schwoerer, 'Propaganda in the Revolution of 1688–9', *AHR* 82 (1977); D.H. Hosford, 'Bishop Compton and the Revolution of 1688', *JEccH* 23 (1972); Barbara Taft, 'Return of the regicide: Edmund Ludlow and the Glorious Revolution', *Hist.* 76 (1991), which examines reasons for Ludlow's return from exile and his desire to support William III; and Mark Goldie, 'John Locke's circle and James II', *HJ* 35 (1992). The continuity of political opinions in England from the 1640s to 1688 is a theme that is explored in both Lord Dacre, 'The continuity of the English Revolution', TRHS 6th series 1 (1991) and Jonathan Scott, 'Radicalism and restoration: the shape of the Stuart experience', *HJ* 31 (1988).

Later Stuart England, 1689–1714

The post-Revolution period has been enlivened by the furious debate which has taken place over **the nature of party politics.** This was sparked off by Robert Walcott, *English Politics in the Early Eighteenth Century* (Oxford, 1956), which contended that parties had little significance and that the structure of groupings was similar to the mid-eighteenth-century pattern noted by Namier. Battle was joined by numerous historians who argued in favour of the existence of parties, including Henry Horwitz, 'Parties, connections and parliamentary politics, 1698–1714: review and revisions', *JBS* 6 (1966). Other important contributions to this discussion of parties and politics in the period up to 1714 include Geoffrey S. Holmes, ed., *Britain after the Glorious Revolution* (1969), a series of simulating essays on the nature of political parties, as well as on the 1689 Settlement and the Church; J.H. Plumb, *The Growth of Political Stability in England, 1675–1725* (1967), a masterly and influential work, which stresses the gradual transition of the political arena from that dominated by party strife; Henry Horwitz, *Parliament, Policy and Politics in the Reign of William III* (Manchester, 1977), which, although somewhat off-putting in scale, offers a most detailed account and analysis of the politics of this reign; Geoffrey S. Holmes, *British Politics in the Age of Anne* (1987 edn), an outstanding study which argues that parties were still active and vital in political life and also offers a helpful introduction to this later edition, giving an update on current research; W.A. Speck, *Tory and Whig: The Struggle for the Constituencies, 1701–1715* (1970), which examines party organisation at elections; J.P. Kenyon, *Revolution Principles: The Politics of Party, 1689–1720* (1977); and B.W. Hill, *The Rise of Parliamentary Parties, 1689–1742* (1976), which provides a helpful guide to current thinking and a detailed narrative of party political activity throughout the whole period. By far the best guide for the student, however, is the book by Tim Harris which was featured in the previous section, *Party Politics Under the Later Stuarts: Party Conflict in a Divided Society, 1660–1715* (1993), which, as the first recent major study of party politics in this period, provides a synthesis of all the latest research in a most stimulating account. A collection of essays, edited by Clyve Jones, is also worth consulting: *Britain in the First Age of Party, 1680–1750* (1987), which is particularly valuable for its consideration of the instability of politics in an article by J.V. Beckett, 'Stability in politics and society, 1680–1750'.

On the subject of **Jacobitism**, the earlier standard work, G.H. Jones, *The Mainstream of Jacobitism* (Cambridge, Mass., 1954) has now been superseded by Paul Kleber Monod, *Jacobitism and the English People, 1688–1788* (Cambridge, 1989), which draws together the latest research and places the movement into its social context, stressing the importance of Jacobitism in English life, even though confined to a minority within the Tory party; Bruce Lenman, *The Jacobite Risings in Britain, 1687–1746* (1980), a readable book which shows that there was no general pattern to the several risings; and Daniel Szechi, *Jacobitism and Tory Politics, 1710–14* (Edinburgh, 1984), which offers fresh insights into Tory politics, confirming the small number of Jacobites within the parliamentary party and the fact that Jacobites in England were often out of step with the exiled court. Bruce Lenman and John S. Gibson have edited a useful collection of documents on Jacobitism – *The Jacobite Threat. Rebellion and Conspiracy, 1688–1759* (Edinburgh, 1991); while two collections of essays provide lively reassessments of the movement – Eveline Cruickshanks, ed., *Ideology and Conspiracy: Aspects of Jacobitism, 1689–1959* (Edinburgh, 1981) and Eveline Cruickshanks and Jeremy Black, eds, *The Jacobite Challenge* (Edinburgh, 1988). Three articles should also be consulted: Paul Monod, 'Jacobitism and country principles in the reign of William III', *HJ* 30 (1987), an examination of the influence of Jacobitism on politics during the reign; Edward Gregg, 'Was Queen Anne a Jacobite?', *Hist.* 57 (1972); and Daniel Szechi, 'The Jacobite revolution settlement, 1689–1696', *EHR* 108 (1993), a discussion of the religious tension that lay at the heart of the Jacobite cause.

Other worthwhile **books on specific topics** include J.O. Richards, *Party Propaganda Under Queen Anne* (1972), a consideration of propaganda pamphlets published at election time; J.A. Downie, *Robert Harley and the Press* (1979), which examines the breakdown of censorship and Harley's work in building up a highly effective government propaganda machine; and Geoffrey S. Holmes, *The Trial of Doctor Sacheverell* (1972), a vivid and detailed account of the trial and its consequences. One article should also be read in this connection: Geoffrey S. Holmes, 'The Sacheverell Riots: the crowd and the Church in early eighteenth-century London', *PP* 72 (1976). There are two useful articles on Robert Harley which are listed in the biography section, together with one by Geoffrey S. Holmes and W.S. Speck, 'The fall of Harley in 1708 reconsidered', *EHR* 80 (1965). Other articles relevant to the period are Henry Horwitz, 'The general election of 1690', *JBS* 11 (1971); P.W.J. Riley, 'The Union of 1707 as an episode in English politics', *EHR* 84 (1969); and Edward Gregg, 'Marlborough in exile, 1712–14', *HJ* 15 (1972).

4. Central and local government

One of the most concise and useful statements on the nature of government is Michael Hawkins, 'Government: its role and aims', in Conrad Russell, ed., *The Origins of the English Civil War* (1973). For a more detailed and general survey see M.A. Thomson, *A Constitutional History of England, 1642–1801* (1938) and Clayton Roberts, *The Growth of Responsible Government in Stuart England* (Cambridge, 1966).

The operation of parliament is well described in J.E. Neale, *The Elizabethan House of Commons* (1949), which should be studied alongside Sheila Lambert, 'Procedure in the House of Commons in the early

Stuart period', *EHR* 95 (1980) and G.A. Harrison, 'Innovation and precedent: a procedural reappraisal of the 1625 parliament', *EHR* 102 (1987), which examines the procedural changes made to expedite business in that year; Derek Hirst, *The Representative of the People?* (Cambridge, 1975), which deals most effectively with elections; and Elizabeth Read Foster, *The House of Lords, 1603–1649. Structure, Procedure and the Nature of its Business* (Chapel Hill, 1983), which is an invaluable guide to the workings of the Lords.

Two books by G.E. Aylmer, *The King's Servants: The Civil Service of Charles I, 1625–1642*, revised edn (1974) and *The State's Servants: The Civil Service of the English Republic, 1649–1660* (1973) between them provide a masterly and indispensable survey of the institutions of government and the **civil servants** who operated them. Office-holders are also dealt with by Kevin Sharp in a valuable essay, 'The court and household of Charles I, 1625–1642', in David Starkey, ed., *The English Court from the Wars of the Roses to the Civil War* (1987) and by Linda Levy Peck, 'Court patronage and government policy', in G.F. Lytle and Stephen Orgel, eds, *Patronage in the Renaissance* (Princeton, 1981). The development of a more professional civil service is crisply covered in Gerald Aylmer, 'From office-holding to civil service: the genesis of modern bureaucracy', *TRHS* 5th series 30 (1980). The work of **the Privy Council** is given detailed treatment in E.R. Turner, *The Privy Council of England in the Seventeenth and Eighteenth Centuries, 1603–1784*, 2 vols (Baltimore, 1927–28), while the business of one of the provincial councils is studied in Penry Williams, 'The activity of the council in the Marches under the early Stuarts', *WHR* 1 (2) (1961). The growth of cabinet government is the theme of two articles by Jennifer Carter, 'Cabinet records for the reign of William III', *EHR* 78 (1963) and J.H. Plumb, 'The organisation of the cabinet in the reign of Queen Anne', *TRHS* 5th series 7 (1957).

The authoritative account of **local government** is to be found in Anthony Fletcher, *Reform in the Provinces: The Government of Stuart England* (1986), a comprehensive and impressive volume, which provides a general synthesis of the considerable research undertaken recently in the localities. Alongside this, an article by G.C.F. Foster is also worth reading – 'Government in provincial England under the later Stuarts', *TRHS* 5th series 33 (1983). The importance of the work of the village constable in local government is first outlined by Joan Kent in an article, 'The English village constable, 1580–1642: the nature and dilemmas of the office', *JBS* 20 (1981) and then covered in greater detail in her book *The English Village Constable, 1580–1642: A Social and Administrative Study* (Oxford, 1986), which is based on parish records from 10 counties. The Books of Orders, which regulated the duties of the constable, are effectively dealt with in two articles – one by Paul Slack, 'Books of Orders: the making of English social policy, 1577–1631', *TRHS* 5th series 30 (1980) and the other by B.W. Quintrell, 'The making of Charles I's Book of Orders', *EHR* 95 (1980), which examines the Book of 1631.

A general introduction to **law enforcement** can be found in Jennifer Carter, 'Law, courts and constitution', in J.R. Jones, ed., *The Restored Monarchy, 1660–1688* (1979). The work of judges in the localities is considered in J.S. Cockburn, *History of English Assizes, 1558–1714* (Cambridge, 1972), but this has been superseded for the later period at least by J.M. Beattie, *Crime and Courts in England, 1660–1800* (Oxford, 1986), an impressive study of the administration of justice in the assize courts and quarter sessions. The appointment and functions of the local justices are discussed in Norma Landau, *The Justices of the Peace, 1679–1760* (Berkeley, 1984) and L.K.J. Glassey, *Politics and the Appointment of Justices of the Peace* (Oxford, 1979), while the political involvement of the judiciary is highlighted in W.J. Jones, *Politics and the Bench* (1971).

A useful introduction to the subject of **crown finance** is to be found in three articles – David Thomas, 'Financial and administrative developments', in Howard Tomlinson, ed., *Before the English Civil War: Essays on Early Stuart Politics and Government* (1983); Conrad Russell, 'Parliament and the king's finances', in Conrad Russell, ed., *The Origins of the English Civil War* (1973); and Howard Tomlinson, 'Financial and administrative developments in England, 1660–88', in J.R. Jones, ed., *The Restored Monarchy, 1660–1688* (1979). More detailed coverage is contained in M.J. Braddick, *Parliamentary Taxation in 17th-Century England: Local Administration and Response* (Woodbridge, 1994); F.C. Dietz, *English Public Finance, 1558– 1641* (1932); C.D. Chandaman, *The English Public Revenue, 1660–1688* (Oxford, 1975), which is now the definitive work on the period; and, for the later years, P.G.M. Dickson, *The Financial Revolution in England: A Study in the Development of Public Credit, 1688–1756* (1967), a first-class survey. For information on the Treasury see S.B. Baxter, *The Development of the Treasury, 1660–1702* (1957) and two books by Henry Roseveare – *The Treasury: The Evolution of a British Institution* (1969) and *The Treasury, 1660–1870* (1973). The crown's borrowing is the subject of Robert Ashton, *The Crown and the Money Market, 1603–1640* (Oxford, 1960), while Menna Prestwich, *Cranfield: Politics and Profits under the Early Stuarts* (Oxford, 1966) considers the efforts made to achieve economies. J.V. Beckett, 'Land tax or excise: the levying of taxation in seventeenth- and eighteenth-century England', *EHR* 100 (1985) provides a useful survey of the varying types of taxation in force, particularly during the 1690s. Other relevant articles include Robert Ashton, 'Deficit finance in the reign of James I', *EcHR* 2nd series 10 (1957–58); H.H. Leonard,

'Distraint of knighthood: the last phase, 1625–41', *Hist.* 63 (1978); Colin Brooks, 'Public finance and political stability: the administration of the land tax, 1688–1720', *HJ* 17 (1974); M.D. Gordon, 'The collection of ship money in the reign of Charles I', *TRHS* 3rd series 4 (1910); and E.A. Reitan, 'From revenue to civil list, 1689–1702: the Revolution settlement and the mixed and balanced constitution', *HJ* 13 (1970).

5. Foreign policy

Seventeenth-century foreign policy has not as yet been well served by historians. The best introductions to the subject are J.R. Jones, *Britain and Europe in the Seventeenth Century* (1966), which provides a clear, concise analysis of British foreign policy and the influences that helped to shape it; G.M.D. Haiti, *Stuart and Cromwellian Foreign Policy* (1974), a scholarly and chronological account; Timothy Venning, *Cromwellian Foreign Policy* (1995), a reassessment casting new light on Cromwell's problems and successes and restoring pragmatism above religious idealism as the determining factor; J.R. Jones, *Britain and the Wider World, 1649–1815* (1980); Keith Feiling, *British Foreign Policy, 1660–1672* (1930), which is less concise and somewhat outdated; and Jeremy Black, *A System of Ambition? British Foreign Policy, 1660–1793* (1992).

Jeremy Black has also edited a valuable collection of eight essays, *Knights Errant and True Englishmen: British Foreign Policy, 1660–1800* (Edinburgh, 1989), which includes items on French intervention in England, the influence of Dutch politics, 1677–88, and the economic consequences of William III's wars. Other useful essays include S.L. Adams, 'Spain or the Netherlands? The dilemmas of early Stuart foreign policy', in Howard Tomlinson, ed., *Before the English Civil War: Essays on Early Stuart Politics and Government* (1983); Roger Crabtree, 'The idea of a protestant foreign policy', in Ivan Roots, ed., *Cromwell: A Profile* (1973), which is one of the most perceptive surveys of Cromwellian foreign policy; J.R. Jones, 'English attitudes to Europe in the seventeenth century', in J.S. Bromley and E.H. Kossmann, eds, *Britain and the Netherlands in Europe and Asia* (1968); J.L. Price, 'Restoration England and Europe', in J.R. Jones, ed., *The Restored Monarchy, 1660–1688* (1979); G.C. Gibbs, 'The revolution in foreign policy', in Geoffrey Holmes, ed., *Britain after the Glorious Revolution, 1689–1714* (1969); M.A. Thomson, 'Parliament and foreign policy, 1689–1714' and other invaluable contributions on the later part of the period contained in R.M. Hatton and J.S. Bromley, eds., *William III and Louis XIV: Essays 1680–1720 by and for Mark A. Thomson* (Liverpool, 1968).

The Dutch Wars are well covered in Charles Wilson, *Profit and Power: A*

Study of England and the Anglo-Dutch Wars (1957); Simon Groenveld, 'The English civil wars as a cause of the First Anglo-Dutch war, 1640–1652', *HJ* 30 (1987); Simon Groenveld, 'The House of Orange and the House of Stuart, 1639–50: a revision', *HJ* 34 (1991); Steven Pinkus, 'Popery, trade and universal monarchy: the ideological context of the outbreak of the Second Anglo-Dutch war', *EHR* 107 (1992); and C.R. Boxer, 'Some second thoughts on the Third Anglo-Dutch war', *TRHS* 5th series 19 (1969). The subject of diplomacy is studied in P.S. Lachs, *The Diplomatic Corps under Charles II and James II* (New Brunswick, NJ, 1965); M.A. Thompson, *The Secretaries of State, 1681–1732* (Oxford, 1932); and A.D. Francis, *The Methuens and Portugal* (Cambridge, 1966).

Articles which are useful on **specific aspects of foreign policy** include Thomas Cogswell, 'Prelude to Ré: the Anglo-French struggle over La Rochelle, 1624–1627', *Hist.* 71 (1986), which re-examines the reasons behind the decision to launch the expedition to Ré in 1627; Thomas Cogswell, 'Foreign policy and parliament: the case of La Rochelle, 1625–1626', *EHR* 99 (1984); Ronald Hutton, 'The making of the Secret Treaty of Dover, 1668–1670', *HJ* 29 (1986); J.F. Bosher, 'The Franco-Catholic danger, 1660–1715', *Hist.* 79 (1994); R.A. Stradling, 'Spanish conspiracy in England, 1661–63', *EHR* 87 (1972); A.D. Francis, 'The Grand Alliance in 1698', *HJ* 10 (1967); B.W. Hill, 'Oxford, Bolingbroke and the Peace of Utrecht', *HJ* 16 (1973); and M. Sheehan, 'The development of British theory and practice of the balance of power before 1714', *Hist.* 73 (1988).

6. Military history

There is no shortage of good material on military affairs, particularly on the period from 1642. The best overall account of the Civil War is provided by Peter Young and Richard Holmes, *The English Civil War* (1974), which offers a concise and comprehensive guide to military strategy and activity during the war, based on original sources and personal knowledge of battlefield sites. Similar studies which are also worthy of consultation are John Kenyon, *The Civil Wars of England* (1988), a most readable narrative which combines the military, financial and the political aspects of the war; Maurice Ashley, *The English Civil War: A Concise History* (1974), which is well-illustrated and takes the story up to 1651; Richard Ollard, *This War without an Enemy: A History of the English Civil Wars* (1976), which is both well-written and beautifully illustrated; and John Adair, *By the Sword Divided: Eyewitnesses of the English Civil War* (1983), which provides eyewitness accounts of wartime experiences blended into a general narrative.

There are also several **helpful guides** for those wishing to explore specific aspects of military matters during this period. Peter Newman has published two such books – *Companion to the English Civil Wars* (Oxford, 1990), a useful reference book on the significant leaders, battles, ideas, events and terminology of the wars; and *Atlas of the English Civil War* (1985), a collection of maps (not always of the highest quality) with a clear commentary alongside. Peter Gaunt, *The Cromwellian Gazetteer* (Gloucester, 1987) is an illustrated guide to Cromwellian and Civil War sites throughout Britain and Ireland; whereas Wilfred Emberton, *The English Civil War Day by Day* (Stroud, 1995) provides a diary of daily developments in the war. Peter Harrington breaks new ground in his *Archaeology of the English Civil War* (1992), a valuable introduction to the exploration of Civil War sites through excavation. This helps, for instance, to confirm the work of W.G. Ross, *Military Engineering during the Great Civil War, 1642–9* (1887; reprinted), which examines the science of fortification and siege-craft during the Civil War, detailing plans of the defences in a number of key cities. Site plans also feature strongly in Martyn Bennett, *Traveller's Guide to the Battlefields of the English Civil War* (Exeter, 1990), which offers a lavishly illustrated reconstruction of the major battles together with a helpful narrative of the war at large.

Individual battles are given detailed coverage in A.H. Burne, *The Battlefields of England* (1951); Austin Woolrych, *Battles of the English Civil War* (1961), which highlights the encounters at Marston Moor, Naseby and Preston, at the same time setting them into a more general context; and H.C.B. Rogers, *Battles and Generals of the Civil Wars, 1642–1651* (1968), which uses contemporary accounts and battlefield sites as a basis for the study of the major battles. Perhaps the most vivid and best researched volumes, however, appear in a series which was largely inspired by Brigadier Peter Young, acknowledged at the time as the leading authority on Civil War military history: Peter Young, *Edgehill, 1642: The Campaign and the Battle* (Kineton, 1967); Peter Wenham, *The Great and Close Siege of York, 1644* (Kineton, 1970); Margaret Toynbee and Peter Young, *Cropredy Bridge, 1644* (Kineton, 1970); John Adair, *Cheriton, 1644: The Campaign and the Battle* (Kineton, 1973); Peter Young and Wilf Emberton, *Sieges of the Great Civil War* (Kineton, 1979); and Peter Young, *Naseby, 1645: The Campaign and the Battle* (1985).

Life and work within the parliamentary army are splendidly covered in three books: C.H. Firth, *Cromwell's Army*, 4th edn (1962), a highly readable classic which describes the military structure of the army, together with details on pay, commissariat, clothing, medical treatment, religion and politics; Mark Kishlansky, *Rise of the New Model Army* (Cambridge, 1979), which includes excellent chapters on its activity in Scotland and

Ireland; and Ian Gentles, *The New Model Army in England, Ireland and Scotland, 1645–1653* (Oxford, 1992), an impressive account of the army's campaigns, the tactics it employed and the motivations and aspirations of its soldiers. An article by James Scott Wheeler, 'The logistics of the Cromwellian conquest of Scotland, 1650–1651', *WS* 10 (1992) should be read in conjunction with the latter. **The royalist army** is given reasonable treatment in Joyce Lee Malcolm, *Caesar's Due: Loyalty and King Charles* (1983), which sets out useful material on the problem of royalist recruitment, propaganda and the trained bands; and Peter Young and Wilfred Emberton, *The Cavalier Army* (1974), which tackles the organisation and everyday life within the army, though in a somewhat slight and unsatisfactory manner. Far more substantial and worthwhile is Ronald Hutton, *The Royalist War Effort, 1642–1646* (1982), which pioneers new ground in providing a gripping account of the contribution made to the royalist cause by the community of Wales, the Welsh Marches and the West Midlands. Alongside this should be read the following articles, which have greatly added to our understanding of the royalist cause: P.R. Newman, 'The royalist officer corps', *HJ* 26 (1983); Ronald Hutton, 'The structure of the royalist party', *HJ* 24 (1981); and Ian Roy, 'The royalist council of war, 1642–1646', *BIHR* 35 (1962).

The impact of the Civil War on soldiers, civilians and local communities is the subject of a number of lively books and articles. One of the best is Charles Carlton, *Going to the Wars: The Experience of the British Civil Wars, 1638–1651* (1992), a detailed and vivid study of what it was like to be involved as either a soldier or a civilian. Stephen Porter, *Destruction in the English Civil Wars* (Stroud, 1994), on the other hand, looks at the damaging effects of the war on towns, villages and country houses. Ian Roy, 'England turned Germany? The aftermath of the Civil War in its European context', *TRHS* 5th series 28 (1978) considers the impact of the war on Gloucester, Worcester and Oxford, set against a general fear that the miseries of the German experience in the Thirty Years War would be repeated in England. To be read alongside this, Barbara Donagan, 'Codes and conduct in the English Civil War', *PP* 118 (1988) asks not only why England was able in fact to avoid that fate, but also how close it came to becoming another Germany. J.S. Morrill in 'Mutiny and discontent in English provincial armies, 1645–1647', *PP* 56 (1972) includes an examination of the economic effects of war through the systems of free quarter and billeting employed by the armies. Three other articles also deal with the impact of the war on ordinary people in local communities: Ian Roy, 'The English Civil War and English society' in Ian Roy and Brian Bond, eds, *War and Society: A Yearbook of Military History* (1975); David Pennington, 'The war and the people', in John

Morrill, ed., *Reactions to the English Civil War* (1982); and Charles Carlton, 'The impact of the fighting', in John Morrill, ed., *The Impact of the English Civil War* (1991), which also contains an essay by Ian Gentles on 'The impact of the New Model Army'. On a slightly different subject, Peter Gaunt, *A Nation Under Siege* (1991) gives a scholarly and enthusiastic account of the part played by Wales in the Civil Wars.

A spate of more recent books has gone a long way to correcting the paucity of material available on the **seventeenth-century navy**. K.R. Andrew, *Ships, Money and Politics: Seafaring and Naval Enterprise in the Reign of King Charles I* (Cambridge, 1991) gives a balanced picture of the effectiveness of the navy, including the fleet under the Earl of Warwick in the 1640s. This should be read alongside Bernard Capp, *Cromwell's Navy: The Fleet and the English Revolution, 1648–1660* (Oxford, 1989), which stresses the role of radicalism in the navy and the navy's contribution to the Restoration. Michael Baumber, *General-at-Sea: Robert Blake and the Seventeenth-Century Revolution in Naval Warfare* (1989) is a detailed book which combines an account of naval engagements and developments in naval warfare with a survey of Blake's own career. There are also two helpful articles: Michael Baumber, 'Cromwell's soldier admirals', *HT* (Oct. 1989) and Frank Fox, 'The English naval ship-building programme of 1664', *MM* 78 (1992). For the post-1660 period as a whole, the student should consult P.M. Kennedy, *The Rise and Fall of British Naval Mastery* (1976); Sari R. Hornstein, *The Restoration Navy and English Foreign Trade, 1674–88* (Aldershot, 1991), a study in the peacetime use of sea power; John Ehrman, *The Navy in the War of William III* (Cambridge, 1953); and J.H. Owen, *War at Sea under Queen Anne* (Cambridge, 1938).

The army in the period between 1660 and 1714 is dealt with effectively in Noel St John Williams, *Redcoats and Courtesans: The Birth of the British Army, 1660–1690* (1994), a fascinating account of the dramatic growth of a standing army and the problems of financing it, set against the political intrigue of the day; John Childs, *The Army of Charles II* (1976), a thorough account which examines popular anxieties about perceived growth in the size of the king's army; John Childs, *The Army, James II and the Glorious Revolution* (Manchester, 1980), a study of the army and James II's attempts to inculcate loyalty by divorcing it from civilian society; John Childs, *The British Army of William III, 1689–1702* (Manchester, 1987), a vivid and authoritative account of its development and the effectiveness of its organisation and administration in the large-scale campaigns in the Low Countries and Ireland; R.E. Scouller, *The Armies of Queen Anne* (Oxford, 1966), a scholarly description of the organisation and control of Marlborough's army; and John Childs, *The Nine Years' War and the*

British Army, 1688–1697 (Manchester, 1991), a clear analysis of reasons for the inconclusive nature of this war, in spite of vast outlay. There are, in addition, two books which between them cover the whole century and deal with the demands made by war on government and society, particularly in relation to the financial and administrative systems established: Mark C. Fissel, ed., *War and Government in Britain, 1598–1650* (Manchester, 1991) and John Brewer, *The Sinews of Power: War, Money and the English State, 1688–1783* (1989).

7. The localities

In recent years much of the most interesting research has been based on a study of the localities. This in turn has generated a controversy over **the relationship between the localities and the centre in political life.** The pioneer in this field was Alan Everitt, whose work (together with that of other historians) has portrayed the county community as a semi-autonomous unit, which provided the provincial gentry with an all-important focus for their activities. Many of them were therefore ill-informed about developments in the nation at large, thus creating a clear division between local and central politics. This situation inevitably led to widespread neutralism in the Civil War with only small numbers deeply committed to king or parliament, thus compelling military commanders to extract supplies by force from an apathetic local community. For a fuller understanding of Everitt's ideas, students should consult in particular Alan Everitt, *The Community of Kent and the Great Rebellion, 1640–60* (Leicester, 1966); Alan Everitt, 'The county community', in E.W. Ives, ed., *The English Revolution, 1600–1660* (1968); and Alan Everitt, *The Local Community and the Great Rebellion* (*HAP* 1969).

Other historians have adopted a similar line, although some of them have extended the argument by introducing a study of the ordinary people as well as the gentry. The most important of these are Anthony Fletcher, *A County Community in Peace and War: Sussex, 1600–1660* (1975); J.S. Morrill, *Cheshire, 1630–1660: County Government and Society during the 'English Revolution'* (Oxford, 1976); and J.S. Morrill, *The Revolt of the Provinces* (1976), which highlights the existence of neutralism as a major factor while, at the same time, stressing that the provincial response to the outbreak of war was conditioned by local events and local power structures.

These views on the nature of the county community have been challenged in particular by Clive Holmes and Ann Hughes, who argue that the county community was not in fact the only important arena for the activities of local gentry and that the very complexity of both central and local interests ensured that they were closely integrated. The key publications to consult concerning this interaction between local and national are Clive Holmes, *Seventeenth Century Lincolnshire* (Lincoln, 1980); Clive Holmes, *The Eastern Association in the English Civil War* (Cambridge, 1975); Clive Holmes, 'The county community in Stuart historiography', *JBS* 19 (1980); David Underdown, 'Community and class: theories of local politics in the English revolution', in Barbara Malament, ed., *After the Reformation* (Manchester, 1980); Ann Hughes, *Politics, Society and Civil War in Warwickshire* (Cambridge, 1987), which is based on the activities of 288 families and challenges the concept of a 'county community' as such; Ann Hughes, 'Warwickshire on the eve of the Civil War: a county community?', *MH* 7 (1982); Ann Hughes, 'The king, the parliament and the localities during the English Civil War', *JBS* 24 (1985), which argues for an intimate integration between the localities and the centre; and Ann Hughes, 'Militancy and localism: Warwickshire politics and Westminster politics, 1643–1647, *TRHS* 5th series 31 (1981).

Other articles which deal with this question of the inter-relationship between the centre and the locality include David Harris Sacks, 'The corporate town and the English state: Bristol's "little business", 1625–1641', *PP* 110 (1986); P. Lake, 'The collection of ship money in Cheshire during the sixteen-thirties: a case study of relations between central and local government', *NH* 17 (1981); Derek Hirst, 'The fracturing of the Cromwellian alliance: Leeds and Adam Baynes', *EHR* 108 (1993); John R. Kent, 'The centre and the localities: state formation and parish government in England, *c.*1640–1740', *HJ* 38 (1995); and P.J. Norrey, 'The Restoration regime in action: the relationship between central and local government – Dorset, Somerset and Wiltshire, 1660–1678', *HJ* 31 (1988).

A more balanced view has now emerged out of the controversy, as demonstrated in Anthony Fletcher, 'National and local awareness in the county communities', in Howard Tomlinson, ed., *Before the English Civil War* (1983); Kevin Sharpe, 'Crown, parliament and locality: government and communication in early Stuart England', *EHR* 101 (1986), which deals with the breakdown of communication with the localities, thus causing grievances to be referred directly to parliament; Richard Cust, 'News and politics in early seventeenth-century England', *PP* 112 (1986), which studies the impact of news within the localities; and Richard Cust and P.G. Lake, 'Sir Richard Grosvenor and the rhetoric of magistracy', *BIHR* 54 (1981), which is a study of an individual who was a mediator between the centre and the locality.

Of the many volumes published which deal with **the Civil War within a**

county or locality, one of the best is undoubtedly David Underdown, *Somerset in the Civil War and Interregnum* (Newton Abbot, 1973). Most of the following selection cover the political, religious and military aspects of the conflict, as well as the impact of the hostilities on ordinary people within the community: Eugene A. Andriette, *Devon and Exeter in the Civil War* (Newton Abbot, 1971); Malcolm Atkin, *The Civil War in Worcestershire* (Stroud, 1995); Malcolm Atkin and Wayne Laughlin, *Gloucester and the Civil War: A City under Siege* (Stroud, 1992); David Eddershaw, *The Civil War in Oxfordshire* (Stroud, 1995); Ross Lee, *Law and Local Society in the Time of Charles I: Bedfordshire and the Civil War* (Bedford, 1986); Roy Sherwood, *The Civil War in the Midlands, 1642–1651* (Stroud, revised edn 1992); Brian Stone, *Derbyshire in the Civil War* (Cromford, 1992); Mark Stoyle, *Loyalty and Locality: Popular Allegiance in Devon and Cornwall during the English Civil War* (Exeter, 1994); Mark Stoyle, *From Deliverance to Destruction: Rebellion and Civil War in an English City* (Exeter, 1996); Philip Tennant, *The Civil War in Stratford upon Avon: Conflict and Community in South Warwickshire, 1642–46* (Stroud, 1996); Philip Tennant, *Edgehill and Beyond: The People's War in the South Midlands, 1642–1645* (Stroud, 1992); Alfred C. Wood, *Nottinghamshire in the Civil War* (Oxford, 1937); and John Wroughton, *A Community at War: The Civil War in Bath and North Somerset, 1642–1650* (Bath, 1992).

Other county studies which largely fall outside the confines of the Civil War include Thomas G. Barnes, *Somerset, 1625–1640: A County's Government during the 'Personal Rule'* (1961), a trail-blazing book in the examination of local communities; Peter Clark, *English Provincial Society from the Reformation to the Revolution* (1977), which deals with the county of Kent; Andrew M. Coleby, *Central Government and the Localities: Hampshire, 1649–1689* (Cambridge, 1987), which usefully extends the controversy over the inter-relationship to the post-Civil War period; William Hunt, *The Puritan Movement: The Coming of Revolution in an English County* (1983), which investigates the background to the Stour Valley distur- bances of 1642; D.H. Hosford, *Nottingham, Nobles and the North* (Hamden, Conn., 1976), a study of the Revolution of 1688 in a locality; M.E. James, *Family, Lineage and Civil Society: A Study of the Society, Politics and Mentality in the Durham Region, 1500–1640* (1974); C.B. Phillips and J.I. Kermode, eds, *Seventeenth-Century Lancashire* (Gloucester, 1983), a collection of essays on aspects of Lancashire life and local government; S.K. Roberts, *Recovery and Restoration in an English County: Devon Local Administration, 1646–1670* (Exeter, 1985), which highlights the continuity of county administration throughout the period; J.A. Sharpe, *Crime in Seventeenth Century England: A County Study* (Cambridge, 1983), an impressive survey of crime in Essex between 1620 and 1680; Philip Styles, *Studies in*

Seventeenth-Century West Midlands History (Kineton, 1978), which includes an account of the City of Worcester during the Civil War; W.B. Willcox, *Gloucestershire: A Study in Local Government, 1590–1640* (New Haven, 1940); and David Underdown, *Revel, Riot and Rebellion: Popular Politics and Culture in England, 1603–1660* (Oxford, 1985), a study based on research in Somerset, Dorset and Wiltshire examining different local cultures brought about by different land usage.

The study of **urban history** has been greatly advanced in recent years by a number of important publications. For a general introduction to the subject and a review of the most recent debates concerning historians, students should refer to the introduction by Jonathan Barry to his book *The Tudor and Stuart Town: A Reader in English Urban History, 1530–1688* (1990), together with one of the articles contained in that volume: Penelope Corfield, 'Urban development in England and Wales in the sixteenth and seventeenth centuries'. The recent controversy concerning the extent of urban decline in the period to 1640 is examined in Alan Dyer, *Decline and Growth in English Towns, 1400–1640* (1991). For a broad overview, Peter Clark and Paul Slack, eds, *English Towns in Transition, 1500–1700* (1976) should also be consulted. One of the first and certainly one of the best individual works on seventeenth-century urban history is Roger Howell, *Newcastle-Upon-Tyne and the Puritan Revolution* (Oxford, 1967), which shows that local issues and local feuds were of vital importance in determining allegiance there. London is well served by five studies – Valery Pearl, *London and the Outbreak of the Puritan Revolution, 1625–1643* (1961); Valery Pearl, 'Change and stability in seventeenth-century London' in Jonathan Barry, ed., *The Tudor and Stuart Town: A Reader in English Urban History, 1530–1688* (1990); A.L. Beier and Roger Finlay, eds, *The Making of the Metropolis: London, 1500–1700* (1985); Tai Liu, *Puritan London: A Study of Religion and Society in the City Parishes* (1986), which is a scholarly survey of political, social and religious activity in 110 London parishes; Tim Harris, *London Crowds in the Reign of Charles II: Propaganda and Politics from the Restoration until the Exclusion Crisis* (Cambridge, 1897), a convincing account of the work of the London mob. There are two important and complementary works on Norwich – John T. Evans, *17th Century Norwich: Politics, Religion and Government, 1620–1690* (Oxford, 1979), which disputes the theory that mid-century conflict arose from personal feuds; and John Pound, *Tudor and Stuart Norwich* (Chichester, 1988). Other examples of urban studies include David Hey, *The Fiery Blades of Hallamshire: Sheffield and its Neighbourhood, 1660–1740* (Leicester, 1991), which includes an analysis of the life and work of the cutlers and the continuity provided by core families; Wallace T. MacCaffrey, *Exeter, 1540–1640: The Growth of an*

English County Town, 2nd edn (Cambridge, Mass., 1975); A.M. Johnson, 'Politics in Chester during the Civil Wars and Interregnum', in Peter Clark and Paul Slack, eds, *Crisis and Order in English Towns, 1500–1700* (1972); and Angus McInnes, 'The emergence of a leisure town: Shrewsbury, 1660–1760', *PP* 120 (1988). For a study of the impact of the Civil War on both town and country and the effects of this on their relationship see R.C. Richardson, ed., *Town and Countryside in the English Revolution* (Manchester, 1992).

Articles which are based on **specific local themes** include Richard Cust, 'Anti-Puritanism and urban politics: Charles I and Great Yarmouth', *HJ* 35 (1992); Richard Cust, 'Parliamentary elections in the 1620s: the case of Great Yarmouth', *PH* 11 (1992); Ronald Hutton, 'The Worcestershire Clubmen in the English Civil War', *MH* 5 (1979–80); Paul Gladwish, 'The Herefordshire Clubmen: a reassessment' *MH* 10 (1985); Simon Osborne, 'The war, the people and the absence of Clubmen in the Midlands, 1642–1646', *MH* 19 (1994); John K.G. Taylor, 'The civil government of Gloucester, 1640–46', *TBGAS* 67 (1949); R.N. Dore, 'The Civil War in Cheshire', *CH* 31 (1993); Peter Gaunt, 'The parliamentary war effort in Cheshire', *CH* 32 (1993); J. Binns, 'Scarborough and the Civil Wars, 1642–1651', *NH* 22 (1986); M.J. Stoyle, ' "Whole streets converted to ashes": property destruction in Exeter during the English Civil War', *SH* 16 (1994); B.G. Blackwood, 'Parties and issues in the Civil War in Lancashire and East Anglia', *NH* 29 (1993); Brian Lyndon, 'Essex and the king's cause in 1648', *HJ* 29 (1986); Brian Lyndon, 'The south and the start of the Second Civil War, 1648', *Hist.* 71 (1986); David F. Mosler, 'The other civil war: internecine politics in the Warwickshire county committees, 1642–1659', *MH* 6 (1981); John Miller, 'The crown and the borough charters in the reign of Charles II', *EHR* 100 (1985); C.G. Parsloe, 'The corporation of Bedford, 1647–1664', *TRHS* 4th series 29 (1947); Joan W. Kirby, 'Restoration Leeds and the aldermen of the corporation, 1661–1700', *NH* 22 (1986); M.A. Mullett, ' "Men of knowne loyalty": the politics of the Lancashire borough of Clitheroe, 1660–1689', *NH* 21 (1985); M.A. Mullett, 'Conflict, politics and elections in Lancaster, 1660–1688', *NH* 19 (1993); Colin Lee, ' "Fanatic magistrates": religion and political conflict in three Kent boroughs, 1680–1684', *HJ* 35 (1992); and B.G. Blackwood, 'Plebeian Catholics in later Stuart Lancashire', *NH* 25 (1989).

8. Economic history

The best introduction to the subject is D.C. Coleman, *The Economy of England, 1450–1750* (Oxford, 1977), which presents a concise and stimulating examination of each aspect of the country's economy both before and after 1650. Three other books should also be consulted for a general survey – B.A. Holderness, *Pre–Industrial England: Economy and Society, 1500–1750* (1977); C.G.A. Clay, *Economic Expansion and Social Change: England, 1500–1700*, 2 vols (Cambridge, 1984), which gives a more detailed coverage of people, land and towns in the first volume and industry, trade and government in the second; and Charles Wilson, *England's Apprenticeship, 1603–1763*, 2nd edn (1985), which highlights such topics as trade, manufacturing, public finance, agriculture and social welfare in a valuable account of the pre-Industrial Revolution economy.

Although somewhat formidable at first sight, two volumes edited by Joan Thirsk are particularly valuable for any study of **agriculture** during this century. These are *Agrarian History of England and Wales. Vol. IV: 1500–1640* (Cambridge, 1967) and *Agrarian History of England and Wales. Vol. V: 1640–1750* (Cambridge, 1984), which provide the standard source of reference for such topics as farming regions, prices, wages, rents, land ownership, estate management, agricultural policy and internal trade. Other useful books on the subject are Joan Thirsk, *England's Agricultural Regions and Agrarian History, 1500–1750* (1987); Ann Kussmaul, *A General View of the Rural Economy of England, 1538–1840* (Cambridge, 1990), which surveys the pattern of economic change based on a classification of parishes into arable, pastoral and industrial; Eric Kerridge, *The Agricultural Revolution* (1967), which argues that the revolution was chiefly a sixteenth- and seventeenth-century phenomenon; Margaret Spufford, *The Great Reclothing of Rural England: Petty Chapmen and their Wares in the Seventeenth Century* (1984), which provides an index to the growing prosperity of England through the rise of the chapmen; W.G. Hoskins, 'Harvest fluctuations and English economic history, 1620–1759' *AgHR* 16 (1968); E.L. Jones, ed., *Agriculture and Economic Growth in England, 1660–1815* (1967); and A.H. John, 'The course of agricultural change, 1660–1760', in L.S. Pressnell, ed., *Studies in the Industrial Revolution* (1960).

A valuable and concise introduction to the history of **manufacturing and mining** is provided in D.C. Coleman, *Industry in Tudor and Stuart England* (1975), a book which also challenges claims that an industrial revolution occurred at this time. To be read alongside this, therefore, is L.A. Clarkson, *Proto-industrialisation: The First Phase of Industrialisation?* (1985). Specific industries are well covered in John Hatcher, *The History of the British Coal Industry I: Before 1700* (Oxford, 1993); Marie Rowlands, *Masters and Men in the West Midland Metalware Trades before the Industrial Revolution* (Manchester, 1975); George Hammersley, 'The charcoal iron industry and its fuel', *EcHR* 26 (1973); Joan Thirsk, 'Industries in the countryside', in F.J. Fisher, ed., *Essays in the Economic and Social History of Tudor and Stuart England* (1961); Julia de L. Mann, *The Cloth Industry in the West of England from 1640 to 1880* (Oxford, 1971); Herbert Heaton, *Yorkshire Woollen and Worsted Industries from the Earliest Times up to the Industrial Revolution*, 2nd edn (Oxford, 1965); A.P. Wadsworth and J. de L. Mann, *The Cotton Trade and Industrial Lancashire, 1600–1780* (Manchester, 1931); and Eric Kerridge, *Textile Manufactures in Early Modern England* (Manchester, 1985), which is a clearly written survey of clothmaking in all its types and regions.

The topic of **trade** is concisely dealt with in Ralph Davis, *English Overseas Trade, 1500–1700* (1973), which examines the spread and structure of trade, its relation to the national economy and the methods used by traders. The same author in *A Commercial Revolution: English Overseas Trade in the Seventeenth and Eighteenth Centuries* (*HAP*, 1969) tackles the subject in the period after 1660. W.E. Minchinton, ed., *The Growth of English Overseas Trade in the Seventeenth and Eighteenth Centuries* (1969) is also worth consulting, as are Ralph Davis, *The Rise of the English Shipping Industry in the Seventeenth and Eighteenth Centuries* (1962) and Ralph Davis, 'English foreign trade, 1660–1700', *EcHR* 7 (1954). D.W. Jones, *War and Economy in the Age of William III and Marlborough* (Oxford, 1988) highlights the vital importance of England's textile exports to the funding of Marlborough's campaigns. Other relevant publications include J.A. Chartres, *Internal trade in England, 1500–1700* (1977); T.S. Willan, *River Navigation in England, 1600–1750* (1964); T.S. Willan, *The English Coasting Trade, 1600–1750* (Manchester, 1967); D.B. Quinn and A.N. Ryan, *England's Sea Empire, 1550–1642* (1983), which provides a fine introduction to colonisation; and Kenneth Andrews, *Trade, Plunder and Settlement: Maritime Enterprise and the Genesis of British Empire, 1480–1630* (Cambridge, 1984), a readable and stimulating book, which emphasises the weakness of England's performance in building empire.

Financial and money matters are investigated in Eric Kerridge, *Trade and Banking in Early Modern England* (Manchester, 1988), a valuable study of the origins of the banking system in England, the development of credit in domestic trade and the impact of the credit system on the growth of inflation. Material for the further exploration of this twin theme is provided in R.B. Outhwaite, *Inflation in Tudor and Early Stuart England*, 2nd edn (1982) and Julian Hoppitt, 'Attitudes to credit in Britain, 1680–1790', *HJ* 33 (1990). Demography is given excellent coverage in three books – R.A. Houston, *The Population History of Britain and Ireland, 1500–1750* (1992); J.D. Chambers, *Population, Economy and Society in Pre-Industrial England* (Oxford, 1982); and E.A. Wrigley and Roger Schofield, *Population History of England, 1541–1871: A Reconstruction* (1981).

Government economic policy is best studied in B.E. Supple, *Commercial Crisis and Change, 1600–1642* (Cambridge, 1970) and Joan Thirsk, *Economic Policy and Projects* (Oxford, 1978), although one article is also relevant – D.C. Coleman, 'Mercantilism revisited', *HJ* 23 (1980). Charles Wilson, *Mercantilism* (*HAP*, 1958) is a most useful introduction to the subject for first-time students.

9. Social history

An excellent starting point for an introduction to the social structure of seventeenth-century England is provided by two books – Keith Wrightson, *English Society, 1580–1660* (1982), which contains a brilliant synthesis of all the best recent research on the family, population, neighbourliness, crime, education and belief in magic; and J.A. Sharpe, *Early Modern England: A Social History, 1550–1760* (1987), a well-written and well-researched volume which gives to students a valuable portrait of life in England. Another worthwhile book in this category is Peter Laslett, *The World We Have Lost – Further Explored* (1983), which is an updating of his original book, taking account of recent research especially on population, literacy and working conditions. The question of social mobility and social change is the theme of two useful studies – Alan Everitt, *Change in the Provinces: The Seventeenth Century* (Leicester, 1969); and Lawrence Stone, 'Social mobility in England, 1500–1700', *PP* 35 (1966).

The fortunes of **the landowning classes** have been widely debated in the 'storm over the gentry' controversy, which dates back to 1941. The key publications in this saga are R.H. Tawney, 'The rise of the gentry, 1558–1640', *EcHR* 1st series 11 (1941); Lawrence Stone 'The anatomy of the Elizabethan aristocracy', *EcHR* 1st series 18 (1948); H.R. Trevor-Roper, 'The Elizabethan aristocracy: an anatomy anatomised', *EcHR* 2nd series 3 (1951); H.R. Trevor-Roper, 'The gentry, 1540–1640', *EcHR Supplement* (1953); J.H. Hexter, 'The storm over the gentry', in his *Reappraisals in History* (1961); and Lawrence Stone, *Social Change and Revolution in England, 1540–1640* (1965), which contains edited extracts from the works of historians who contributed to the gentry debate [see also Lawrence Stone, 'The bourgeois revolution of seventeenth-century England revisited', *PP* 109 (1985)]. In another work, *The Crisis of the Aristocracy, 1558–1641* (Oxford, 1965), the same author gives a brilliant survey of the social activities and lifestyle of the aristocracy, also putting forward a widely challenged argument that they were in a state of relative decline. A helpful synthesis of all the most recent work on the landed families has been provided in three articles by John Habakkuk, 'The rise and fall of the English landed families, 1600–1800', *TRHS* 5th series 29,

30, 31 (1979, 1980, 1981). A most valuable and more recent study of the behaviour and influence of the gentry is to be found in Felicity Heal and Clive Holmes, *The Gentry in England and Wales, 1500–1700* (1994).

There have been a number of recent studies of **the more humble folk** and their culture in seventeenth-century villages. The best of these are David Levine and Keith Wrightson, *Poverty and Piety in an English Village: Terling, 1525–1700* (1979), which highlights the effect of puritan preaching on a local society; David Levine and Keith Wrightson, *The Making of an Industrial Society: Whickham, 1560–1765* (Oxford, 1991), which sets out the problems arising in a northern parish when a community of copy-holders was transformed into an 'industrial society' of coal miners; David Hey, *An English Rural Community: Myddle under the Tudors and Stuarts* (1974); Robert von Friedeburg, 'Reformation of manners and the social composition of offenders in an East Anglian cloth village: Earls Colne, Essex, 1531–1642', *JBS* 29 (1990), which shows how religion added a cultural dimension to existing differences between rich and poor; Margaret Spufford, *Contrasting Communities: English Villagers in the Sixteenth and Seventeenth Centuries*, 2nd edn (1979); and David Underdown, *Fire from Heaven: Life in and English Town in the Seventeenth Century* (1992), a vivid and scholarly account of an attempt by puritan preachers to create a more godly and disciplined community in Dorchester following a major fire in 1613 and the beneficial social welfare reforms which resulted. On an allied theme, Ronald Hutton in *The Rise and Fall of Merry England: The Ritual Year, 1400–1700* (Oxford, 1994) describes in a most lucid and fascinating manner how early village festivals formed part of the church year, thus making them vulnerable to the growth of Puritanism in the seventeenth century. This reform of popular culture is also the subject of Martin Ingram, 'Ridings, rough music and the reform of popular culture in early modern England', *PP* 105 (1984). For a series of essays on popular culture, including religion, literature, protest, rough music, sex and marriage, see Barry Reay, ed., *Popular Culture in Seventeenth-Century England* (1985).

The 'middling sort' in town and country are given substantial treatment by various contributors in Jonathan Barry and Chris Brooks, eds, *The Middling Sort of People: Culture, Society and Politics in England, 1550–1800* (1994). For **social life in towns**, there are five books on London which are worthy of consultation – Peter Earle, *A City Full of People: Men and Women in London, 1650–1750* (1994), which gives a vivid description of the variety and colour of city existence, including work, education and home life; Peter Earle, *The Making of the English Middle Class: Business, Society and Family Life in London, 1660–1730* (1989), which gives a stimulating account of the business community and makes a valuable contribution to the history of social change; Richard Gassby, *The Business Community in Seventeenth-Century England* (Cambridge, 1995), which deals with the structure of business and the interaction between business and society; Robert Brenner, *Merchants and Revolution: Commercial Change, Political Conflict and London Overseas Trade, 1550–1653* (Cambridge, 1993), which includes an account of the social transformation of the prosperous mercantile community, who traded in a period of considerable change; and Jeremy Boulton, *Neighbourhood and Society: A London Suburb in the Seventeenth Century* (Cambridge, 1987), an exploration of the pattern of social relations in one London parish. Books which give a more wide-ranging view of urban life include Peter Borsay, *The English Urban Renaissance: Culture and Society in the Provincial Town, 1660–1770* (Oxford, 1989), a stimulating, well-written and scholarly account of the physical and cultural transformation of English provincial towns after the Restoration; Peter Clark, ed., *The Transformation of English Provincial Towns, 1600–1800* (1984), which includes essays on social structure, the links between town and country and the problem of migration; Phyllis Hembry, *The English Spa, 1560–1815* (1990), a well-researched study which is particularly good on the early Stuart spas; and Jonathan Barry, ed., *The Tudor and Stuart Town: A Reader in English Urban History, 1530–1688* (1990), a collection of essays based on recent research examining every aspect of town life.

The importance of the family as part of the ordered nature of society is well covered in Christopher Durston, *The Family in the English Revolution* (Oxford, 1989), an interesting discussion of the impact of war-time conditions and radical ideas on marriage and family relationships; Ralph Houlbrooke, *The English Family, 1450–1700* (1984), an excellent survey of recent research on marriage, the family and inheritance set against the economic and social background; Miriam Slater, *Family Life in the Seventeenth Century* (1984); and Susan Amussen, *An Ordered Society: Gender and Class in Early Modern England* (Oxford, 1988). The attempted regulation by the courts of sexual relations, set against the wider background of economic conditions, is brilliantly described in Martin Ingram, *Church Courts, Sex and Marriage in England, 1570–1640* (Cambridge, 1987), an outstanding contribution to social history based on a mass of documentary evidence; and, by the same author, in 'The reform of popular culture? Sex and marriage in early modern England', in Barry Reay, ed., *Popular Culture in Seventeenth-Century England* (1985). The theme of attempted regulation is taken up also by John Addy, *Sin and Society in the Seventeenth Century* (1989), which provides a discussion, based on research in the diocese of Chester, on the jurisdiction of church courts in the areas of sexual morality and matrimonial disputes; and by Christopher Durston,

'"Unhallowed wedlocks": The regulation of marriage during the English revolution', *HJ* 31 (1988). The nature of the marriage relationship and the position of children within it are explored by Lawrence Stone, *The Family, Sex and Marriage in England, 1500–1800* (1977). The same author also investigates the question of marriage breakdown and divorce in *Uncertain Unions: Marriage in England, 1660–1753* (Oxford, 1992); and in *Broken Lives: Separation and Divorce in England, 1660–1857* (Oxford, 1993). Another cause of family conflict, arising from the increase in the practice of making wills, is studied in John Addy, *Death, Money and the Vultures: Inheritance and Avarice, 1660–1750* (1992).

The role played by women in English society at the time is skilfully explored by Mary Prior, ed., *Women in English Society, 1500–1800* (1985), a well-presented collection of seven essays on various aspects of the life and work of women; Anne Laurence, *Women in England, 1500–1760: A Social History* (1994), a lucid and broad-ranging survey of the material world of women, their beliefs and their involvement in both popular culture and their local community; Lorna Weatherill, 'A possession of one's own: women and consumer behaviour in England, 1660–1740', *JBS* 25 (1986), an exploration of possible differences in cultural values between men and women; and Anne Laurence, 'Women's work and the English Civil War', *HT* (June 1992).

The growing **problem of poverty** in society is expounded in a number of more recent publications, including Paul Slack, *Poverty and Policy in Tudor and Stuart England* (1988), a stimulating account of the interaction of poverty and poor law legislation, drawing together the latest research and offering new insights on contemporary perceptions of poverty; A.L. Beier, *Masterless Men: The Vagrancy Problem in England, 1560–1640* (1985), which sheds fresh light on the alarm caused by vagrancy and the failure of Bridewells (or workhouses) to effect reform; Paul Slack, *The English Poor Law, 1531–1782* (1990), a concise introduction which is invaluable for students; Lotte Mulligan and Judith Richards, 'A radical problem: the poor and the English reformers in the mid-seventeenth century', *JBS* 29 (1990), an examination of attitudes to poverty and the new solutions to old problems; and Peter Rushton, 'The poor law, the parish and the community in north-east England, 1600–1800', *NH* 25 (1989).

Popular protest, public disorder and crime have received an increasing amount of attention from historians in recent years. Anthony Fletcher and John Stevenson, eds, *Order and Disorder in Early Modern England* (Cambridge, 1985) is a fine collection of essays on aspects of popular disorder and the symbols of order, including an important contribution from Margaret Spufford, 'Puritanism and social control?'. Buchanan Sharp, *In Contempt of all Authority: Rural Artisans and Riot in the*

West of England, 1586–1660 (1980) is based on massive research and examines in particular food riots and forest disorders. Roger B. Manning, *Village Revolts: Social Protest and Popular Disturbances in England, 1509–1640* (Oxford, 1988) gives a detailed account of rural protest and riot caused by enclosure and innovation; whereas John Brewer and John Styles, eds, *An Ungovernable People: The English and their Law in the Seventeenth and Eighteenth Centuries* (1980) offers a series of essays on popular protest and popular attitudes to the law, including an article by Keith Wrightson on the clash in early seventeenth-century villages between concepts of the magistrates and customary views of the people. Two works by Keith Lindley dealing with specific aspects of riot are *Fenland Riots and the English Revolution* (1982), which examines resistance to Fenland enclosures and drainage schemes, and 'Riot prevention and control in early Stuart London', *TRHS* 5th series 33 (1983). The standard text now on the subject of seventeenth-century crime is J.A. Sharp, *Crime in Early Modern England, 1550–1750* (1984), a well-written book which surveys the latest work on the subject as well as his own research on Cheshire and Essex. The same author's article, 'Last dying speeches: religion, ideology and public execution in seventeenth-century England', *PP* 107 (1985) places execution into a broader social and cultural context, while Cynthia B. Herrup, 'Law and morality in seventeenth-century England', *PP* 106 (1985) discusses the moral underpinning of the law.

Illness is a topic which is tackled by Paul Slack in *The Impact of Plague in Tudor and Stuart England* (Oxford, 1990), a vivid and detailed account of the deadly effects of bubonic plague on English towns and its dramatic disappearance after 1665; by Roy Porter, *Disease, Medicine and Society in England, 1550–1860* (1987); and by Michael Macdonald, *Mystical Bedlam: Madness, Anxiety and Healing in Seventeenth-Century England* (1981).

The development of **education** is surveyed in M.V.C. Alexander, *The Growth of English Education 1348–1646: A Social and Political History* (University Park and London, 1990); in Rosemary O'Day, *Education and Society, 1500–1800* (1982); and in two articles by Lawrence Stone – 'The educational revolution in England, 1560–1640', *PP* 28 (1964) and 'Literacy and education in England, 1640–1900', *PP* 42 (1969). Literacy and numeracy are examined in David Cressy, *Literacy and the Social Order: Reading and Writing in Tudor and Stuart England* (Cambridge, 1980), which studies literacy levels by areas and social classes; Margaret Spufford, *Small Books and Pleasant Histories: Popular Fiction and its Readership in Seventeenth-Century England* (1981), which explores the extent of literacy and the range of chapbook distribution; and Keith Thomas, 'Numeracy in early modern England', *TRHS* 5th series 37 (1987).

10. Religion

For a general introduction to the Church in England during the first half of the century, the following books provide a good starting point – H.G. Alexander, *Religion in England, 1558–1662* (1968), which provides a useful analysis of the problems; Susan Doran and Christopher Durston, *Princes, Pastors and People: The Church and Religion in England, 1529–1689* (1991), which gives an excellent overall survey; Claire Cross, *Church and People, 1450–1660: The Triumph of the Laity in the English Church* (Glasgow, 1976); and Christopher Hill, *Economic Problems of the Church from Archbishop Whitgift to the Long Parliament* (1956), which examines both the need for reform within the Church and reasons why reform was not accomplished.

On **the Jacobean Church**, two of the most outstanding books are undoubtedly by Patrick Collinson – *The Religion of Protestants: The Church in English Society, 1559–1625* (Oxford, 1992) and *Godly People: Essays on English Protestantism and Puritanism* (1983), which together advocate his view that Puritanism was nothing but authentic Protestantism and not a long-term cause of the Civil War. Nicholas Tyacke's stimulating work on Arminianism is to be found in 'Puritanism, Arminianism and counter-revolution', in Conrad Russell, ed., *The Origins of the English Civil War* (1973); and *Anti-Calvinists: The Rise of English Arminianism, c.1590–1640* (1987), which puts forward the view that the dominant doctrine in the Church by the early seventeenth century was predestination, but that it was overthrown by an Arminian revolution led by Archbishop Laud. His views have been challenged by, among others, Peter White, 'The rise of Arminianism reconsidered', *PP* 101 (1983) and *Predestination, Policy and Polemic: Conflict and Consensus in the English Church from the Reformation to the Civil War* (Cambridge, 1992). In the latter, he questions the traditional idea of a clash within the Church of England between the court's Arminianism and the majority's Calvinism by pointing to a broad band of moderate opinion. This controversy over the nature of the Jacobean Church has been continued by Nicholas Tyacke and Peter White, 'The Rise of Arminianism reconsidered', *PP* 115 (1987); an article by G.W. Bernard, 'The Church of England, c.1529–c.1642', *Hist.* 75 (1990), which examines all the issues at stake; and a stimulating book edited by Kenneth Fincham, *The Early Stuart Church, 1603–42* (1993), which attempts a synthesis. A fascinating survey of parochial clergy in the diocese of Bath and Wells and their compliance with national religious policy, including that of Archbishop Laud, is given in Margaret Stieg, *Laud's Laboratory: The Diocese of Bath and Wells in the Early Seventeenth Century* (1983). Julian Davies, *The Caroline Captivity of the Church: Charles I* *and the Remoulding of Anglicanism, 1625–1641* (Oxford, 1992) provides a valuable contribution to the debate over ecclesiastical policy with a helpful analysis of local impact.

There are several important books concerning the doctrinal beliefs of various religious groups at the beginning of the seventeenth century. English Calvinism and predestination are well treated in R.T. Kendall, *Calvin and English Calvinism to 1649* (Oxford, 1979), Dewey Wallace, *Puritans and Predestination* (Chapel Hill, 1982) and William Haller, *The Rise of Puritanism* (New York, 1938); while the best account of millenarianism is to be found in W.M. Lamont, *Godly Rule, 1603–1660* (1969), which highlights the shared beliefs on the millennium held by both the Puritans and their opponents. Catholicism is the subject of an outstanding book by John Bossy, *The English Catholic Community, 1570–1850* (1975), although students should also read Alan Dures, *English Catholicism, 1558–1642* (1983); Christopher Haigh, 'From monopoly to minority: Catholicism in early modern England', *TRHS* 5th series 31 (1981); and Caroline Hibbard, 'Early Stuart Catholicism', *JMH* 52 (1980). The history of religious dissent in general is helpfully outlined in M.R. Watts, *The Dissenters from the Reformation to the French Revolution* (1978).

The ecclesiastical policy of James I has been closely considered by a number of historians. Roland Green Usher, *The Reconstruction of the English Church*, 2 vols (1910), though daunting at first sight, contains valuable material on the work of Archbishop Bancroft and the Hampton Court Conference. On the latter, students should also read Frederick Shriver, 'Hampton Court re-visited: James I and the Puritans', *JEccH* 33 (1982) and Mark H. Curtis, 'The Hampton Court Conference and its aftermath', *Hist.* 46 (1961). The subsequent pressure placed on Puritans by the episcopate is covered in B.W. Quintrell, 'The royal hunt and the Puritans, 1604–1605', *JEccH* 31 (1980) and S.B. Babbage, *Puritanism and Richard Bancroft* (1962). The episcopate is stoutly defended in an impressive volume by Kenneth Fincham, *Prelate as Pastor: The Episcopate of James I* (Oxford, 1990), in which he reassesses its reputation and that of Archbishop Abbot, highlighting at the same time two groups of bishops – 'preaching pastors' and the custodians of order. Susan Holland, 'Archbishop Abbot and the problem of "Puritanism" ', *HJ* 37 (1994), in a study of Abbot's attitude to puritan nonconformity, refutes accusations of laxity on his part, while John J. LaRocca, ' "Who can't pray with me, can't love me": toleration and the early Jacobean recusancy policy', *JBS* 23 (1984) studies James I's attempts to introduce religious toleration. A helpful survey of the king's policy is given in an article by Kenneth Fincham and Peter Lake, 'The ecclesiastical policy of James I', *JBS* 24 (1985).

The best introductions to **the Church during the period of the Civil War and Interregnum** are provided by John Morrill, 'The church in England, 1642–9', in John Morrill, ed., *Reactions to the English Civil War* (1982) and Claire Cross, 'The Church in England, 1646–60', in G.E. Aylmer, ed., *The Interregnum: The Quest for Settlement, 1646–60* (1972). For reference purposes, W.A. Shaw, *A History of the English Church during the Civil Wars and under the Commonwealth*, 2 vols (1900) is invaluable. On specific aspects of the struggle over religion, the following articles are all worthy of consultation – John Morrill, 'The attack on the Church of England in the Long Parliament', in Derek Beales and Geoffrey Best, eds, *History, Society and the Churches* (Cambridge, 1985); John Morrill, 'The religious context of the English Civil War', *TRHS* 5th series 34 (1984); John Morrill, 'Sir William Brereton and England's "wars of religion" ', *JBS* 24 (1985); I.M. Green, 'The persecution of scandalous and malignant parish clergy during the English Civil War', *EHR* 94 (1979); and J.C. Davis, 'Religion and the struggle for freedom in the English Revolution', *HJ* 35 (1992). There are, in addition, two important books – Robert S. Paul, *The Assembly of the Lord: Politics and Religion in the Westminster Assembly and the 'Grand Debate'* (Edinburgh, 1985), which provides a detailed description of the debates in the Assembly over the introduction of a presbyterian system for England; and Anne Laurence, *Parliamentary Army Chaplains, 1642–1651* (Woodbridge, 1990), a detailed study which attacks the traditional view that radical preachers in the army were responsible for stirring up the soldiers' demands for a move to democracy and toleration.

For a study of **the radical sects**, there are three books in particular which provide valuable introductions – J.F. McGregor and Barry Reay, eds, *Radical Religion in the English Revolution* (Oxford, 1984), which includes useful essays on the Baptists, Seekers, Ranters, Quakers, Fifth Monarchists and Diggers; R.J. Acheson, *Radical Puritans in England, 1550–1660* (1990), which is a study of the growth and changing fortunes of religious separatism; and Christopher Hill, *The World Turned Upside Down* (1972), an outstanding account of the development of radical ideas during the Revolution with particular emphasis on the Levellers, Seekers, Ranters and Quakers. On particular sects, an excellent introduction to the Quakers is provided by Barry Reay, *The Quakers and the English Revolution* (1985), a concise and lively survey of the impact of the movement in the 1650s. The following articles also deal with the subject and take it beyond the period of the Revolution – Barry Reay, 'Quaker opposition to the tithes, 1652–1660', *PP* 86 (1980); Stephen Roberts, 'The Quakers in Evesham, 1655–1660: a study in religion, politics and culture', *MH* 16 (1991); Michael Mullett, 'George Fox and the origins of

Quakerism', *HT* (May, 1991); and Richard Greaves, 'Shattered expectations? George Fox, the Quakers and the Restoration state, 1660–85', *Alb.* 24 (1992). The Ranters are effectively put into perspective by J.C. Davis, *Fear, Myth and History: The Ranters and Historians* (1986), which argues that they did not exist as a coherent movement, but are really a myth created by contemporary writers and recent historians. Students should also read two articles which further this debate – G.E. Aylmer, 'Did the Ranters exist?', *PP* 117 (1987); and J.C. Davis, 'Fear, myth and furore: reappraising the Ranters', *PP* 129 (1990). The beliefs and activities of the Congregationalists are explored in Geoffrey Nuttall, *Visible Saints* (Oxford, 1957); the Independents in Murray Tolmie, *The Triumph of the Saints* (Cambridge, 1977); the Fifth Monarchists in P.G. Rogers, *The Fifth Monarchy Men* (1966); the Baptists in B.R. White, *The English Baptists of the Seventeenth Century* (1983); the Levellers in G.E. Aylmer, ed., *The Levellers and the English Revolution* (1975) and J.C. Davis, 'The Levellers and Christianity', in B.S. Manning, ed., *Politics, Religion and the English Civil War* (Manchester, 1973); and the Muggletonians in Christopher Hill, Barry Reay and William Lamont, *The World of the Muggletonians* (1983) and in a debate by Christopher Hill and William Lamont, 'The Muggletonians', *PP* 104 (1984). Finally, William Lamont, *Puritanism and Historical Controversy* (1996) discusses the rise of Puritanism and its influence on ideas in society.

The subject of **witchcraft** is brilliantly described by Keith Thomas in an original and thought-provoking book, *Religion and the Decline of Magic* (1971). He not only analyses popular belief and magical traditions in England, but also examines the growth of witchcraft as a consequence of the protestant Reformation, which 'attempted to take the magic out of religion'. Alongside this, students should also consult Stuart Clark, 'Inversion, misrule and the meaning of witchcraft', *PP* 87 (1980) and Peter Rushton, 'Women, witchcraft and slander in early modern England: cases from the church courts of Durham, 1560–1675', *NH* 18 (1982), which examines different aspects and definitions of witchcraft.

There are three books which between them provide an excellent survey of **the Church between 1660 and 1714**: John Spurr, *The Restoration Church of England, 1646–1689* (1991), which, in giving a brilliant synthesis of earlier research and the best survey to date of church politics, shows that a distinct form of Anglicanism was created during these years; O.P. Grell, J.I. Israel and Nicholas Tyacke, eds, *From Persecution to Toleration: The Glorious Revolution and Religion in England* (Oxford, 1991), which includes essays on William III and toleration, freedom of conscience, the Jews in England, the twilight of Puritanism, English Catholics after 1688 and the reception of the Huguenots; and Norman Sykes, *From*

Sheldon to Secker: Aspects of English Church History, 1660–1768 (Cambridge, 1959). On a more specific aspect, the revival of the Church of England at the Restoration is discussed in I.M. Green, *The Re-establishment of the Church of England, 1660–63* (1978); Anne Whiteman, 'The re-establishment of the Church of England, 1660–63', *TRHS* 5th series 5 (1955); John Spurr, '"Latitudinarianism" and the Restoration church', *HJ* 31 (1988), which reassesses the forces of moderation and toleration; J.A. Champion, 'Religion after the Restoration', *HJ* 36 (1993); R.A. Beddard, 'Sheldon and anglican recovery', *HJ* 19 (1976); and R.S. Bosher, *The Making of the Restoration Settlement: The Influence of the Laudians, 1649–1662* (1951), which also highlights the work of Sheldon. The plight of nonconformists is the subject of Richard L. Greaves, *Enemies under his Feet: Radicals and Non-Conformists in England, 1664–1677* (Stanford, 1990); and G.R. Cragg, *Puritanism in the Period of the Great Persecution, 1660–1688* (Cambridge, 1957).

For the period from the Glorious Revolution onwards, the following are useful – E.G. Rupp, *Religion in England, 1688–1791* (Oxford, 1986); David L. Wykes, 'James II's religious indulgence of 1687 and the early organisation of dissent: the building of the first nonconformist meeting-house in Birmingham', *MH* 16 (1991); George Every, *The High Church Party, 1688–1718* (1956); John Spurr, 'The Church of England, comprehension and the Toleration Act of 1689', *EHR* 104 (1989); G.M. Straka, *Anglican Reaction to the Revolution of 1688* (Madison, 1962); G.V. Bennet, 'King William and the episcopate', in G.V. Bennet and J.D. Walsh, eds, *Essays in Modern English Church History* (1966); and Craig Rose, 'Providence, protestant union and godly reformation', *TRHS* 6th series 3 (1993).

11. Science and the arts

Out of the many publications covering this field, it has only been possible here to highlight a small selection of those that will be most valuable to students. There could be no better introduction than Boris Ford, ed., *17th Century Britain: The Cambridge Cultural History* (Cambridge, 1989), which is a well-illustrated and comprehensive survey of the arts in seventeenth-century Britain set against the social and political background. Also worthwhile as a starting point are T.G.S. Cain and Ken Robinson, eds, *Into another Mould: Change and Continuity in English Culture, 1625–1700* (1992), a collection of helpful essays on such topics as religious thought, the visual arts, architecture and politics; and Charles Webster, ed., *The Intellectual Revolution of the Seventeenth Century* (1974), which emphasises the links between religion and science.

The cultural life at court is well covered in Linda Peck, ed., *The Mental World of the Jacobean Court* (Cambridge, 1991), a collection of essays on intellectual activities at court, including theology, literature, art and political thought; Roy Sherwood, *The Court of Oliver Cromwell* (1977); Erica Veevers, *Images of Love and Religion: Queen Henrietta Maria and Court Entertainments* (Cambridge, 1989), which reassesses the Queen's religious and intellectual activities; R.M. Smuts, *Court Culture and the Origins of a Royalist Tradition in Early Stuart England* (Philadelphia, Penn. 1987), a stimulating book which reassesses the cost, nature and legacy of court culture, dismissing the view that it was totally isolated from a hostile country; and Jerzy Limon, *Dangerous Matter: English Drama and Politics, 1623–24* (Cambridge, 1986), a consideration of the topical implications of the plays and masques which were produced in 1623 after Buckingham's return from Spain.

The development of English **newspapers, propaganda pamphlets and broadside ballads** during the seventeenth century is described in Joseph Frank, *The Beginnings of the English Newspaper, 1620–1660* (Cambridge, Mass., 1961); James Sutherland, *The Restoration Newspaper and its Development* (Cambridge, 1986), which traces the story from 1660 to the early eighteenth century with particular emphasis on the years 1679–82, which saw a severe outbreak on unlicensed printing; F.S. Siebert, *Freedom of the Press in England, 1476–1776* (Urbana, Ill., 1965); F.J. Levy, 'How information spread among the gentry, 1550–1640', *JBS* 21 (1982), which deals with education, the printing of books, news pamphlets, letters and corantos (weekly journals); Tessa Watt, *Cheap Print and Popular Piety, 1550–1640* (Cambridge, 1991), a study of cheap printed material (including broadside ballads, pictures and chapbooks) and its impact on the spread of Protestantism; James Holstun, ed., *Pamphlet Wars: Prose in the English Revolution* (1992); Joseph Frank, *Cromwell's Press Agent: A Critical Biography of Marchmont Nedham, 1620–78* (1980); Lois Potter, *Secret Rites and Secret Writing: Royalist Literature, 1641–1660* (Cambridge, 1989), which is particularly good on the underground printers of the revolutionary period; Joad Raymond, ed., *Making the News: An Anthology of the Newsbooks of Revolutionary England, 1641–60* (1993), which provides helpful comment and commentary on a selection of newsbooks, classified into sections dealing with crime, persecution, religious dissidence, etc.; and J.A. Downie, *Robert Harley and the Press: Propaganda and Public Opinion in the Age of Swift and Defoe* (Cambridge, 1979).

The revolution which took place during the seventeenth century in **science** is described in D.C. Lindberg and R.S. Westman, eds, *Reappraising the Scientific Revolution* (1990), which is the most sensible starting point for students; A. Rupert Hall, *The Revolution in Science,*

1500–1750 (1983), which provides an examination of a wide range of sciences, including life sciences; R.S. Westfall, *The Construction of Modern Science* (Cambridge, 1977); P.M. Harman, *The Scientific Revolution* (1983); A.G.R. Smith, *Science and Society in 16th and 17th Century England* (1972); R. Briggs, *The Scientific Revolution of the Seventeenth Century* (1969); and Michael Hunter, *Science and Society in Restoration England* (1981). On particular aspects of science, the following all offer useful introductions – Roger Finch and Andrew Wear, eds, *The Medical Revolution of the Seventeenth Century* (Cambridge, 1989), a set of stimulating essays on medicine, science and philosophy; John Thomas Kelly, *Practical Astronomy during the Seventeenth Century: A Study of Almanac-Makers in America and England* (1991); and Mordecai Feingold, *The Mathematicians' Apprenticeship* (Cambridge, 1984).

Good general introductions to the world of **literature** are to be found in Douglas Bush, *English Literature in the Earlier Seventeenth Century* (Oxford, 1962); Graham Parry, *The Seventeenth Century: The Intellectual and Cultural Context of English Literature, 1603–1700* (1989); C.A. Patrides and Raymond B. Waddington, eds, *The Age of Milton: Background to Seventeenth Century Literature* (Manchester, 1980); Michael McKeon, *The Origins of the English Novel, 1600–1740* (Baltimore, 1987); Gerald Hammond, *Fleeting Things: English Poets and Poems, 1616–1660* (Cambridge, Mass., 1990); Robert Shafer, *The English Ode to 1660* (Princeton, 1918); and Thomas Healy and Johnathan Sawday, eds, *Literature and the English Civil War* (Cambridge, 1990). Books which give a useful background to the period, as well as a detailed examination of the work of a particular author include James Anderson Winn, *John Dryden and His World* (1987), a comprehensive survey of Dryden's writings and the political events in which they are set; Warren L. Chernaik, *The Poet's time: Politics and Religion in the Work of Andrew Marvell* (Cambridge, 1983), which investigates the link between poetry and religion, providing a historical setting for Marvell's writings (Cambridge, 1983); Bernard Capp, *The World of John Taylor the Water-Poet, 1578–1653* (Oxford, 1994), which examines the world and social background of a London waterman who became a celebrity both in literary circles and at court; and C.A. Patrides and R.B. Waddington, eds, *The Age of Milton* (Manchester, 1980), which is an excellent introduction to the cultural world in which he operated. Annabee Patterson, *Censorship and Interpretation: The Conditions of Writing and Reading in Early Modern England* (Madison, 1984) explores the effect of censorship on Elizabethan and Stuart writers. Several authors investigate the relationship between literature and politics, including Jonathan Goldberg, *James I and the Politics of Literature: Jonson, Shakespeare, Donne and their Contemporaries* (1983); Kevin Sharpe, *Criticism and Complaint: The*

Politics of Literature in the England of Charles I (1987), a masterly study of the importance of popular culture to the understanding of politics, especially in relation to the masque; Kevin Sharpe and Peter Lake, eds, *Culture and Politics in Early Stuart England* (1994), a collection of essays designed to show how the study of culture can help us to reconstruct the languages through which contemporaries interpreted their politics; David Norbrook, *Poetry and Politics in the English Renaissance* (1984); and C.V. Wedgwood, *Poetry and Politics under the Stuarts* (Cambridge, 1960), which traces the development of political verse against the background of political turmoil.

Books which represent **other aspects of cultural and intellectual life include** Oliver Millar, *The Age of Charles I: Painting in England, 1620–1649* (1972), a lavishly illustrated volume which traces the development of portraiture; Percy A. Scholes, *The Puritans and Music in England and New England* (Oxford, 1934), a well-researched account of the Puritans' involvement with music, including opera, church music, organs and psalms; Howard Clovin, *A Biographical Dictionary of British Architects, 1600–1840* (1978); Colin Platt, *The Great Rebuildings of Tudor and Stuart England* (1994), which provides a succinct introduction to the major themes in English domestic architecture; Timothy Mowl and Brian Earnshaw, *Architecture without Kings: the Rise of Puritan Classicism under Cromwell* (Manchester, 1995), which gives a total reappraisal of the career of Inigo Jones and the architectural creativity of the period; Richard Kroll, Richard Ashcroft and Perez Zagorin, eds, *Philosophy, Science and Religion in England, 1640–1700* (Cambridge, 1992); and Perez Zagorin, *History of Political Thought in the English Revolution* (1954).

12. Scotland, Ireland and Wales

Scotland

There are three well-established and valuable introductions to the history of seventeenth-century Scotland – Gordon Donaldson, *Scotland: James V to James VII* (Edinburgh, 1965), which provides an excellent narrative; William Ferguson, *Scotland: 1689 to the Present* (Edinburgh, 1968), which is strong on social and economic history; and T.C. Smout, *A History of the Scottish People, 1560–1830* (1969), which concentrates on the role of ordinary people. To these have now been added Keith M. Brown, *Kingdom or Province? Scotland and the Regnal Union, 1603–1715* (1992), which is a first-class starting point for new students; Jenny Wormald, ed., *Scotland Revisited* (1991), a collection of essays on Scotland's links with Europe, the nobility, kirk and crown, municipal enterprise and Restoration politics; and Bruce Lenman, 'Reinterpreting Scotland's last two centuries of independence', *HJ* 25 (1982), which gives a concise survey of changing views in the light of ongoing research.

The first part of the century is well dealt with in Maurice Lee, *Government by Pen: Scotland under James VI and I* (Urbana, Ill., 1980); Maurice Lee, *Great Britain's Solomon. James VI and I in his Three Kingdoms* (Urban, Ill., 1990); J.M. Brown, 'Scottish politics, 1567–1625', in A.G.R. Smith, ed., *The Reign of James VI and I* (1973); and Jenny Wormald, 'James VI and I: two kingdoms or one?', *Hist.* 68 (1983). The best narrative for the reign of Charles I is Maurice Lee, *The Road to Revolution: Scotland under Charles I, 1625–37* (Urbana, Ill., 1985).

The critical period **1637–1651 and the making of the Covenant** have received good coverage in recent years. Peter Donald, *An Uncounselled King: Charles I and the Scottish Troubles, 1637–1641* (Cambridge, 1990) contains a lucid narrative and a clear explanation of the 'Incident' of 1641. Mark Charles Fissel, *The Bishops' Wars: Charles I's Campaigns against Scotland, 1638–1640* (Cambridge, 1994) analyses the logistics of the war and shows why the king could not reduce Scotland by force. Alan I. Macinnes, *Charles I and the Making of the Covenanter Movement, 1625–1641* (Edinburgh, 1991), a scholarly work, particularly stresses the importance of Caroline finance, economic nationalism and the Revocation Scheme. The essays contained in John Morrill, ed., *The Scottish National Covenant in its British Context, 1638–51* (Edinburgh, 1990), including a most perceptive introduction by the editor, deal with the making of the Covenant and other aspects of the Scottish revolt against Charles I. Maurice Lee, *The Road to Revolution: Scotland under Charles I, 1625–37* (Urbana, Ill., 1985) is also well worth reading, as are two slightly older books by David Stevenson – *The Scottish Revolution, 1637–1644* (Newton Abbot, 1973) and *Revolution and Counter-Revolution in Scotland, 1644–1651* (1977), both of which offer first-class narrative with analysis. Of his later work, *The Covenanters: The National Covenant and Scotland* (Edinburgh, 1988) is a pocket-guide to covenanting in the seventeenth century; while his collection of edited essays, *The Government of Scotland under the Covenanters, 1637–51* (Edinburgh, 1982), provides an informative introduction to the evolution and structure of the covenanting system of goverment. Walter Makey, *The Church of the Covenant, 1637–1651: Revolution and Social Change in Scotland* (Edinburgh, 1979) gives a thorough account of the nature and course of the Covenanter movement and the support provided by churches. E.G. Cowan, *Montrose: For Covenant and King* (1977) sets out a sound and readable narrative of the conflict involving Montrose, whereas I.B. Cowan, *The Scottish Covenanters, 1660–1688* (1976) deals with the later activities of the Presbyterians in the light of government policy.

The best book on Scotland in the middle of the century is F.D. Dow, *Cromwellian Scotland* (Edinburgh, 1979), although an essay by David Stevenson, 'Cromwell, Scotland and Ireland', in John Morrill, ed., *Oliver Cromwell and the English Revolution* (1990) provides a more concise introduction for new students. For **the Restoration period**, good general accounts are to be found in Ronald Hutton, *Charles II: King of England, Scotland and Ireland* (Oxford, 1989) and John Miller, *James II: A Study in Kingship* (1978). More particular aspects are treated in Julia Buckroyd, *Church and State in Scotland, 1660–1681* (Edinburgh, 1980); and A.I. Macinnes, 'Repression and conciliation: the highland dimension, 1660–1688', *SHR*, 66 (1986). For the **period from 1688** students should consult I.B. Cowan, 'The reluctant revolutionaries: Scotland in 1688', in Eveline Cruikshanks, ed., *By Force or Default? The Revolution of 1688–89* (Edinburgh, 1989); P.W.J. Riley, *King William and the Scottish Politicians* (Edinburgh, 1979); and Paul Hopkins, *Glencoe and the End of the Highland War* (Edinburgh, 1986).

The development of **the idea of union** between the two kingdoms is convincingly dealt with in Bruce Galloway, *The Union of England and Scotland, 1603–1608* (Edinburgh, 1986); G.S. Pryde, *The Treaty of Union of Scotland and England, 1707* (1950); T.I. Rae, ed., *The Union of 1707: Its Impact on Scotland* (Glasgow, 1974); P.W.J. Riley, *The Union of Scotland and England* (Manchester, 1978); Brian P. Levack, *The Formation of the British State: England, Scotland and the Union, 1603–1707* (Oxford, 1987), which clearly outlines the ideas and fears expressed by both Englishmen and Scotsmen during the century over the matter of union; and Christopher Whatley, 'Economic causes and consequences of the Union of 1707: a survey', *SHR* 83 (1989), which stresses the importance of economic factors in persuading Scottish parliamentarians to support the Union.

There are three excellent books on **the Scottish economy** dealing with the situation at the beginning and end of the century – S.G.E. Lythe, *The Economy of Scotland in the European Setting, 1550–1625* (1960), which is broad-ranging in its coverage of agriculture, industry and trade; T.C. Smout, *Scottish Trade on the Eve of Union, 1660–1707* (1963), which concentrates on the changing fortunes of trade within the period; and T.M. Devine, *The Transformation of Rural Scotland: Social Change and the Agrarian Economy, 1660–1815* (Edinburgh, 1994). Michael Lynch, ed., *The Early Modern Town in Scotland* (1987) gives a good description of the urban élite. Studies which tackle aspects of social history are K.M. Brown, 'The nobility of Jacobean Scotland, 1567–1625', in J.M. Wormald, ed., *Scotland Revisited* (1991) and J.M. Wormald, 'Bloodfeud, kindred and government in early modern Scotland', *PP* 87 (1980), both of which deal with the Scottish aristocracy; W. Hamish Fraser, *Conflict and Class: Scottish*

Workers, 1700–1835 (Edinburgh, 1988); Rosalind Mitchison and Leah Leneman, *Sexuality and Social Control: Scotland, 1660–1780* (Oxford, 1989), which deals not only with sexual attitudes and behaviour, but also with the characteristics of pre-industrial society in Scotland; and Rosalind Mitchison, *Lordship to Patronage: Scotland, 1603–1745* (1983), a survey of social, political, economic and religious history.

Useful works on **religion in Scotland** include W.R. Foster, *The Church before the Covenants: The Church of Scotland, 1596–1638* (Edinburgh, 1975), which provides a fascinating survey of the mixed episcopal and presbyterian system; Gordon Donaldson, *The Making of the Scottish Prayer Book* (Edinburgh, 1954); A.L. Drummond and James Bulloch, *The Scottish Church, 1688–1843* (Edinburgh, 1973); L.K. Glassey, 'William III and the settlement of religion in Scotland, 1688–1690', *RSCHS* 23 (1989); James Kirk, *Archbishop Spottiswoode and the See of Glasgow* (Glasgow, 1988); J.A. Lamb, 'Archbishop Alexander Burnet: 1614–1684', *RSCHS,* 11 (1951–53); and Julia Buckroyd, *The Life of James Sharp, Archbishop of St Andrews, 1618–1679: A Political Biography* (Edinburgh, 1987), which reassesses his career and motives.

There is comprehensive coverage of the Scottish literature of the period in R.D.S. Jack, ed., *The History of Scottish Literature. Vol. 1: Origins to 1660* (Aberdeen, 1987); and Andrew Hook, ed., *The History of Scottish Literature. Vol. 2: 1660–1880* (Aberdeen, 1987).

Ireland

For an introduction to Irish history in the seventeenth century, T.W. Moody, F.X. Martin and F.J. Byrne, eds, *A New History of Ireland*. Vol. 3: *Early Modern Ireland, 1534–1691* (Oxford, 1976) provides an outstanding survey; R.F. Foster, *Modern Ireland, 1600–1972* (1988) offers an impressive commentary on the course of Irish history; Margaret MacCurtain, *Tudor and Stuart Ireland* (1972) deals concisely with the colonisation of the island; J.C. Beckett, *The Making of Modern Ireland* (1966) is particularly helpful on economic and social matters; Brendan Fitzpatrick, *Seventeenth-Century Ireland: The War of Religions* (Dublin, 1988) sets out a mainly political review of the century; Ciaran Brady and Raymond Gillespie, eds, *Natives and Newcomers: Essays on the Making of Irish Colonial Society, 1534–1641* (Dublin, 1986) covers the latest research on the development of Irish towns, Gaelic economy and society, Stuart Munster, the Reformation, the causes of the 1641 rising and the problem of govern- ment; and J.C. Beckett, *Confrontations* (1972) consists of a collection of valuable essays on various aspects of Irish affairs during this period. Richard Bagwell, *Ireland Under the Stuarts*, 3 vols (1963 reprint) is still valuable for reference.

The history of colonisation in Ireland is the theme tackled by Philip S. Robinson, *The Plantation of Ulster: British Settlement in an Irish Landscape, 1600–1670* (Dublin, 1984), which describes Ulster before the plantation and the aims, methods and achievements of plantation policy; Raymond Gillespie, *Colonial Ulster: The Settlement of East Ulster, 1600–1641* (Cork, 1985), which gives a scholarly and lucid account of a much neglected subject; Aidan Clarke, *The Old English in Ireland, 1625–1642* (1966), which outlines the declining dominance of the earlier settlers; T.W. Moody, *The Londonderry Plantation: The City of London and the Plantation in Ulster* (Belfast, 1939); and K.S. Bottigheimer, *English Money and Irish Land* (Oxford, 1971), which examines the efforts of the land speculators in the 1640s and the Irish policies of the government during the Interregnum. One of Charles I's most controversial policies is clearly examined in Aidan Clark, *The Graces, 1625–1641* (Dublin, 1968).

The policies and achievements of **the Earl of Strafford's regime** are reappraised in H.F. Kearney, *Strafford in Ireland, 1633–1641* (Manchester, 1959), while the Irish Revolt of 1641 is admirably analysed by A. Clarke, 'The genesis of the Ulster rising', in Peter Roebuck, ed., *Plantation to Partition* (Belfast, 1981); C.P. Meehan, *The Confederation of Kilkenny* (Dublin, 1905); and Brian MacCurta, ed., *Ulster, 1641: Aspects of the Rising* (Belfast, 1993). The best coverage of the policies of English governments during **the Commonwealth and Protectorate** is given in T.C. Barnard, *Cromwellian Ireland: English Government and Reform in Ireland, 1649–1660* (Oxford, 1975) and St J.D. Seymour, *The Puritans in Ireland, 1647–1661* (Oxford, 1969 reprint), while D.M.R. Esson, *The Curse of Cromwell* (1971) describes Cromwell's conquest of Ireland, 1649–1653, and parliament's policy of integration. Cromwell's conduct at Drogheda in 1649 is the subject of one of the lucidly written essays on important aspects of Irish History in J.G. Simms, *War and Politics in Ireland, 1649–1730*, edited by D.W. Hayton and Gerard O'Brien (1987). An article by James Burke, 'The New Model Army and the problem of siege warfare, 1648–51', *IHS* 27 (1990) stresses the effectiveness of the army and the political importance of mastering siege warfare in Ireland. David Stevenson, *Scottish Covenanters and Irish Confederates* (Belfast, 1981) provides a useful survey of Scottish-Irish relations in the mid-seventeenth century.

The period after 1660 is well served by S.J. Connolly, *Religion, Law and Power: The Making of Protestant Ireland, 1660–1760* (Oxford, 1992), a stimulating, detailed and readable account of religion, politics and society during a period when the protestant landed class consolidated their power; David Dickson, *New Foundations: Ireland, 1660–1800* (Dublin,

1987); and Kevin McKenny, 'Charles II's Irish cavaliers: the 1649 officers and the Restoration land settlement', *IHS* 28 (1993), which studies the fortunes of protestant cavalier officers. The years following the Glorious Revolution are successfully covered by J.G. Simms, *Jacobite Ireland, 1685–1691* (1969), which deals with both military and political events; J.G. Simms, *The Jacobite Parliament of 1689* (Dublin, 1966); P.B. Ellis, *The Boyne Water* (1976), which narrates the 1690 campaign; Raymond Gillespie, 'The Irish Protestants and James II, 1688–90', *IHS* 28 (1992), which stresses the division of the Irish protestant community along religious, factional, social and ideological grounds; W.A. Maguire, ed., *Kings in Conflict: The Revolutionary War in Ireland and its Aftermath, 1689–1750* (Belfast, 1990), which includes a useful survey of the years 1685–1707 and the consequences of the protestant victory; Wouter Troost, *William III and the Treaty of Limerick, 1691–1697: A Study of his Irish Policy* (Leiden, 1983); J.G. Simms, *The Treaty of Limerick* (Dublin, 1965 reprint); D. Hayton, 'The Williamite revolution in Ireland, 1688–91', in J.I. Israel, ed., *The Anglo-Dutch Moment: Essays on the Glorious Revolution and its World Impact* (1991); and J.G. Simms, *The Williamite Confiscation in Ireland, 1690–1703* (1956), which considers the extent of the forfeitures.

There are two particularly valuable **biographies** – J.C. Beckett, *Cavalier Duke: A Life of James Butler, First Duke of Ormond, 1610–1688* (Belfast, 1990), a helpful study of this dominant Irish figure and the background of intrigue in which he lived; and K.M. Lynch, *Roger Boyle, First Earl of Orrery* (1965), a well-researched account of his work both before and after the Restoration.

Economic, social and religious aspects of Irish history are dealt with in L.M. Cullen, *An Economic History of Ireland since 1660* (1973); Edward MacLysaght, *Irish Life in the Seventeenth Century: After Cromwell* (Shannon, 1969 reprint); Patrick O'Flanagan, ed., *Rural Ireland: Modernisation and Change, 1600–1900* (Cork, 1987), which includes essays on changes in rural housing, the rise in population, the role of religion and the position of women; L.M. Cullen, *The Emergence of Modern Ireland, 1600–1900* (1981), another collection of essays which tackles cultural and sectarian tensions and the evolution of living standards; T.M. Devine and David Dickson, eds, *Ireland and Scotland, 1600–1850: Parallels and Contrasts in Economic and Social Development* (Edinburgh, 1983); J.C. Beckett, *Protestant Dissent in Ireland, 1687–1780* (1948); Isabel Grubb, *Quakers in Ireland, 1654–1900* (1927); and Patrick J. Corish, *The Catholic Community in the Seventeenth and Eighteenth Centuries* (Dublin, 1981), which studies how the mass of the Irish people managed to remain Catholic, in spite of the conquest of Ireland by Protestant England. Finally, there is a useful source book – R.W. Dudley Edwards and Mary O'Dowd, *Sources for*

Early Irish History, 1534–1641 (Cambridge, 1985), which covers administrative records, contemporary accounts, maps, drawings and repositories for source material; and an excellent chronology – J.E. Doherty and D.J. Hickey, *A Chronology of Irish History since 1500* (Dublin, 1989).

Wales

Wales in the seventeenth century has not been particularly well served by historians. There are three basic textbooks, which will give the student a reasonable introduction – Hugh Thomas, *A History of Wales, 1485–1660* (1971); Gareth Elwyn Jones, *Modern Wales: A Concise History*, 2nd edn (Cambridge, 1994) and E.D. Thomas, *A History of Wales, 1660–1815* (1976). More detail is provided by G. Dyfnallt Owen, *Wales in the Reign of James I* (Woodbridge, 1988), a scholarly and readable account which concentrates on the work of the Council of Wales, the gentry and the Catholics; and by A.H. Dodd, *Studies in Stuart Wales* (Cardiff, 1952), which consists of a series of essays on specific themes. The Civil War is given specific coverage in a well-illustrated book by Peter Gaunt, *A Nation under Siege: The Civil War in Wales, 1642–48* (1991), which also considers pre-war economic conditions, reasons for allegiance and the impact of the war.

Useful **histories of particular counties** include G. Williams, ed., *Glamorgan County History. Vol. 4: 1536–c.1770* (1974); A.H. Dodd, *History of Caernarvonshire* (1968); Norman Tucker, *North Wales in the Civil War* (n.d.); and H. A. Lloyd, *The Gentry of South-West Wales, 1540–1640* (1978), which considers the insularity and apathy of the backward gentry from these parts. Michael Price, ed., *The Account Book of the Borough of Swansea, Wales, 1640–1660* (Lewiston, 1990) provides a valuable study in local administration during the Civil War and Interregnum.

Religion is covered, not altogether satisfactorily, in two books by Thomas Richards – *History of the Puritan Movement in Wales, 1639–1653* (1920) and *Religious Developments in Wales, 1654–1662* (1923). A far more perceptive and readable account is provided by Geraint H. Jenkins, *Protestant Dissenters in Wales, 1639–1689* (Cardiff, 1992); and Philip Jenkins, ' "The old leaven": the Welsh roundheads after 1660', *HJ* 24 (1981), which deals with the survival of militant Puritanism into the 1680s. Cultural life, including religion, is reassessed in a stimulating book by Geraint H. Jenkins, *Literature, Religion and Society in Wales, 1660–1730* (1978).

13. Documents

This is just a small selection of the most useful collections available for this period. Of paramount importance is J.P. Kenyon, *The Stuart Constitution, 1603–88*, 2nd edn (Cambridge, 1986), a collection of well-edited constitutional, political and religious documents with a revised commentary which takes account of new interpretations and recent research. For reference alongside this are the modern editions of *Stuart Royal Proclamations*, edited by J.F. Larkin and P.L. Hughes (Oxford, 1973) and J.F. Larkin (Oxford, 1982). The period of the revolution is well covered by S.R. Gardiner, *Constitutional Documents of the Puritan Revolution, 1625–1660*, 3rd edn (1906); Stuart E. Prall, ed., *The Puritan Revolution: A Documentary History* (1968), which offers a wide selection of documents covering most aspects of the Revolution; Ivan Roots, ed., *Speeches of Oliver Cromwell* (1989), which contains all Cromwell's major speeches with an incisive introduction by the editor; and A.S.P. Woodhouse, ed., *Puritanism and Liberty, being the Army Debates, 1647–9*, 3rd edn (1986 – with a revised preface 1992). For the later period W.C. Costin and J.S. Watson, *The Law and Working of the Constitution. Vol. 1: 1660–1783*, 2nd edn (1961) is an indispensable guide, particularly on the constitutional aspects; and Andrew Browning, ed., *English Historical Documents. VIII: 1660–1714* (1953) covers a wide range of topics each with perceptive editorial comments.

SECTION SEVEN

Table and maps

1. Genealogical table: the house of Stuart and the succession to the English throne

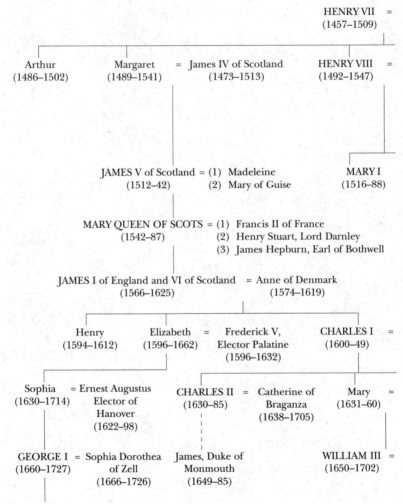

HENRY VII =
(1457–1509)

Arthur   Margaret = James IV of Scotland   HENRY VIII =
(1486–1502)   (1489–1541)   (1473–1513)   (1492–1547)

JAMES V of Scotland = (1) Madeleine   MARY I
(1512–42)   (2) Mary of Guise   (1516–88)

MARY QUEEN OF SCOTS = (1) Francis II of France
(1542–87)   (2) Henry Stuart, Lord Darnley
                      (3) James Hepburn, Earl of Bothwell

JAMES I of England and VI of Scotland   = Anne of Denmark
(1566–1625)   (1574–1619)

Henry   Elizabeth = Frederick V,   CHARLES I =
(1594–1612)   (1596–1662)   Elector Palatine (1600–49)
                              (1596–1632)

Sophia   = Ernest Augustus   CHARLES II = Catherine of   Mary =
(1630–1714) Elector of   (1630–85)   Braganza   (1631–60)
             Hanover   (1638–1705)
             (1622–98)

GEORGE I = Sophia Dorothea   James, Duke of   WILLIAM III =
(1660–1727) of Zell   Monmouth   (1650–1702)
             (1666–1726)   (1649–85)

(issue)

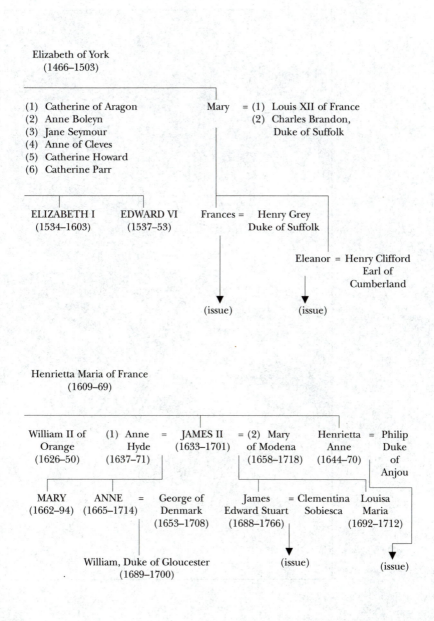

Elizabeth of York
    (1466–1503)

(1) Catherine of Aragon   Mary = (1) Louis XII of France
(2) Anne Boleyn   (2) Charles Brandon,
(3) Jane Seymour   Duke of Suffolk
(4) Anne of Cleves
(5) Catherine Howard
(6) Catherine Parr

ELIZABETH I   EDWARD VI   Frances =   Henry Grey
(1534–1603)   (1537–53)   Duke of Suffolk

                                        Eleanor = Henry Clifford
                                                     Earl of
                                                     Cumberland

         (issue)   (issue)

Henrietta Maria of France
    (1609–69)

William II of   (1) Anne   =   JAMES II   = (2) Mary   Henrietta = Philip
  Orange   Hyde   (1633–1701)   of Modena   Anne   Duke
(1626–50)   (1637–71)   (1658–1718)   (1644–70)   of
                                                                       Anjou

   MARY   ANNE   =   George of   James   = Clementina Louisa
(1662–94)   (1665–1714)   Denmark   Edward Stuart Sobiesca   Maria
                           (1653–1708)   (1688–1766)   (1692–1712)

           William, Duke of Gloucester   (issue)   (issue)
                  (1689–1700)

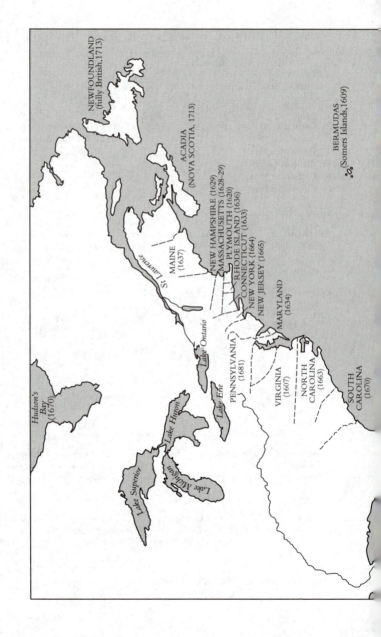

NEWFOUNDLAND
(fully British, 1713)

ACADIA
(NOVA SCOTIA, 1713)

BERMUDAS
(Somers Islands, 1609)

ST LAWRENCE

MAINE
(1637)

NEW HAMPSHIRE (1629)
MASSACHUSETTS (1628-29)
PLYMOUTH (1620)
RHODE ISLAND (1636)
CONNECTICUT (1633)
NEW YORK (1664)
NEW JERSEY (1665)

MARYLAND
(1634)

Lake Ontario

Lake Erie

PENNSYLVANIA
(1681)

VIRGINIA
(1607)

NORTH
CAROLINA
(1663)

SOUTH
CAROLINA
(1670)

Hudson's
Bay
(1670)

Lake Huron

Lake Superior

Lake Michigan

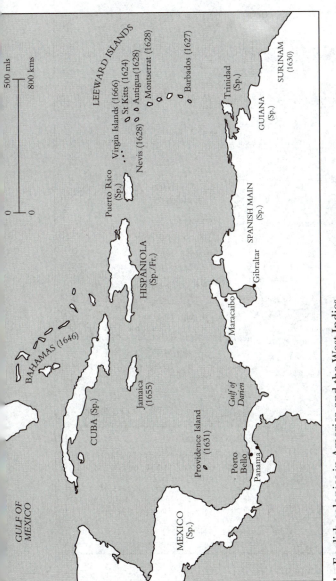

1. English colonies in America and the West Indies
(To be used in conjunction with the Chronology of Trade and Colonies)
Dates refer to the first settlement or gain of the territory through treaty or capture

0   50 mls

0   80 kms

Newcastle

Carlisle

Marston Moor
(1644) ✗

York

Leeds

Preston
✗ (1648) ✗
Adwalton Moor
(1643)

Hull

Gainsborough
✗ (1643)

Liverpool

Chester
Rowton Heath ✗
(1645)

Nantwich
✗ (1644)

Lincoln

Winceby
(1643) ✗

Newark

Uttoxeter (1648) ✗

Nottingham

Shrewsbury

Hopton
Heath
(1643)

Leicester

(1650) ✗

Naseby (1645)

Worcester ✗

Edgehill (1642)

Powick Bridge (1643) ✗

Cropredy Bridge (1644)

Colchester

Pembroke

Gloucester

Oxford

Chalgrove Field (1643)

Bristol
Roundway
Down
Lansdown (1643) ✗ ✗ (1643)

Reading

LONDON

Dover

Newbury (1643,1644)

Langport (1645) ✗

Taunton

Sherborne

Maidstone ✗
Cheriton (1644)   (1648)

Stratton (1643) ✗

Lyme

Exeter

Poole

Portsmouth

Braddock Down
(1643)

Weymouth

Lostwithiel ✗
(1644)

Plymouth

Civil War Sieges

Bristol: 1643, 1645   Newark: 1643, 1644, 1646
Chester: 1644, 1645   Oxford: 1645-46
Colchester: 1648   Pembroke: 1648
Gloucester: 1643   Plymouth: 1643, 1644
Hull: 1643   Sherborne: 1642, 1645
Leicester: 1645   Taunton: 1645
Lyme: 1644   York: 1644
Nantwich: 1644

2. The Civil Wars in England
(To be used in conjunction with the Chronology of Military Events in England)

3. Scotland in the seventeenth century

(To be used in conjunction with Scotland: chronology of events)

4. Ireland in the seventeenth century

(To be used in conjunction with the Ireland: chronology of events)

Index

The reader will find that the glossary and biographies sections are listed alphabetically. Entries in those sections are also highlighted in this index by the use of bold type. The main subheadings used in the lists of major officers of state and in the bibliography section are given in the table of contents. In the interests of economy of space, however, these sections have been excluded from this index.